The Correspondence
of Mother Jones

SEP 1 4 2001	DATE DUE		
SEP 2 5 2001			
OCT 2 3 2001			
APR 1 6 2003			

PITTSBURGH SERIES IN LABOR HISTORY

THE CORRESPONDENCE OF MOTHER JONES

The Correspondence of

MOTHER JONES

Edward M. Steel, Editor

University of
Pittsburgh
Press

Published by the University of Pittsburgh Press, Pittsburgh, Pa., 15260
Copyright © 1985, University of Pittsburgh Press
All rights reserved
Feffer and Simons, Inc., London
Manufactured in the United States of America

Library of Congress Cataloging in Publication Data

Main entry under title:

The Correspondence of Mother Jones.

  (Pittsburgh series in labor history)
  Includes index.
  1. Jones, Mother, 1843?–1930. 2. Trade-unions—United States—History. 3. Labor
and laboring classes—United States—History. 4. Working class women—United
States—Correspondence. I. Jones, Mother, 1843?–1930.
II. Series.
HD8073.J6A4   1985   331.88′092′4   84-29788
ISBN 0-8229-3514-7

The title page illustration is taken from a photograph in the Archives and Manuscripts Section, West Virginia Collection, West Virginia University Library.

This volume was supported by research and publication grants from the National Historical and Records Commission.

To Barbara

Contents

Acknowledgments xxi

Introduction xxiii

Editorial Practices xlvii

To John Mitchell   30 November 1900   3
From John Mitchell   3 December [1900]   4
From Eugene V. Debs   28 January 1901   6
From John Mitchell   1 April 1901   8
To John Mitchell   5 April 1901   9
From Elizabeth C. Morris   6 April 1901   9
To John Mitchell   13 April 1901   10
To John Mitchell   31 July 1901   10
From John Mitchell   3 August [1901]   11
From William Warner   8 August 1901   12
From William Warner   13 August 1901   13
From William Warner   18 August 1901   14
To John Mitchell   20 October 1901   15
To William Bauchop Wilson   15 November [1901]   16
To John Mitchell   2 December 1901   17
From Thomas Haggerty   9 December 1901   18
From John Mitchell   11 December [1901]   18
To John Mitchell   7 February 1902   20
To William B. Wilson   19 February 1902   21
To John Mitchell   27 February 1902   22
From John Mitchell   6 March 1902   24
To John Mitchell   14 March 1902   25
From John Mitchell   15 March 1902   27
To John Mitchell   2 April 1902   27
To William B. Wilson   5 April 1902   28
To John Mitchell   6 May 1902   29
From John Mitchell   10 May 1902   31
From John Mitchell   13 June 1902   32
To John Mitchell   23 June 1902   33
From John Mitchell   25 June 1902   34
To Leon Greenbaum   28 June 1902   35
To John Mitchell   25 July 1902   36
To William B. Wilson   [August 1902]   36
To William B. Wilson   8 September 1902   37
From John Mitchell   15 September 1902   38

Contents

To John Mitchell   [September 1902?]   39
Fragment from Mitchell papers   [September 1902?]   40
To John Mitchell   8 November 1902   40
From John Mitchell   3 March 1903   42
From William Mailly   15 April 1903   43
To Henry Demarest Lloyd   19 April 1903   44
To Theodore Roosevelt   [15 July 1903]   45
To Theodore Roosevelt   30 July [1903]   46
From B. F. Barnes   1 August 1903   48
To William B. Wilson   29 October 1903   48
To Colorado State Fed. of Labor   11 January 1904   50
From J.C. Sullivan and H.B. Waters   11 January 1904   50
To John Mitchell   16 April 1904   50
To John H. Walker   4 January 1904[05]   52
To William B. Wilson   9 May 1905   53
To Western Federation of Miners   29 May 1905   54
To William B. Wilson   4 October 1905   54
From William B. Wilson   6 October 1905   55
To William Johnson   15 December 1905   56
To Terence V. Powderly   9 May 1906   58
To the Socialists of Massachusetts   [18 August 1906]   60
To Mrs. Potter Palmer   12 January 1907   61
To Terence V. Powderly   24 May 1907   63
To Phillip Henry Callery   21 December 1908   65
To Thomas J. Morgan   30 December 1908   65
To the Socialists and Trade Unionists of America
    20 February 1909   67
To Gottlieb Hoehn   17 June 1909   69
To Gottlieb Hoehn   27 June 1909   70
From J. Mahlon Barnes   17 July 1909   71
To Thomas J. Morgan   20 July 1909   71
From Ricardo Flores Magón, Antonio I. Villarreal, and
    Librado Rivera   31 November 1909   72
To William Howard Taft   [2 December 1909]   73
Statement of Mother Jones   12 May 1910   75
To Thomas J. Morgan   1 August 1910   77
From William Parker   1 September 1910   79
To Thomas J. Morgan   9 September 1910   80
To Thomas J. Morgan   14 October 1910   81
To Thomas J. Morgan   16 December 1910   82
To Thomas J. Morgan   25 December 1910   83
From Joseph D. Cannon   7 January 1911   85
Affidavit of Mother Jones   31 January 1911   87

Affidavit of Mother Jones   January or February 1911   89
To Catherine M. Conroy   5 February 1911   90
To Thomas J. Morgan   11 February 1911   91
To Thomas J. Morgan   12 March 1911   92
To [Thomas J. Morgan?]   16 March 1911   93
From Charly [Mahoney?]   24 March 1911   93
To Thomas J. Morgan   27 March 1911   94
To William B. Wilson   15 April 1911   95
To James Beauchamp Clark   7 August 1911   95
To Thomas J. Morgan   8 August 1911   96
To Manuel Calero   25 October 1911   97
To Ricardo Flores Magón   4 November 1911   100
To Thomas J. Morgan   [1911?]   101
To Thomas J. Morgan   [1911?]   102
To [Thomas J. Morgan?]   [1911?]   102
To [Thomas J. Morgan?]   [1911?]   103
To Thomas J. Morgan   [1911?]   103
To [Thomas J. Morgan?]   [1911?]   103
To Thomas J. Morgan   [1911?]   104
To Peter Joseph Conroy   [1911?]   105
To Caroline Lloyd   27 November 1912   106
To William B. Wilson   [February 1913]   107
To William E. Borah   [ca. 20 February 1913]   107
To Terence V. Powderly   3 March 1913   108
To Caroline Lloyd   17 March 1913   109
To Caroline Lloyd   [4 April 1913]   109
To William B. Wilson   5 April 1913   110
To Caroline Lloyd   27 April 1913   111
To Maude Walker   27 April 1913   112
To Terence V. Powderly   1 May 1913   113
To John Worth Kern   4 May 1913   114
To Caroline Lloyd   7 May 1913   115
To Members of the *Appeal* Army   21 May 1913   116
To Eugene V. Debs   5 July 1913   117
To William B. Wilson   30 July 1913   118
From William B. Wilson   4 August 1913   118
To William E. Borah and James E. Martine
    9 September 1913   118
To Terence V. Powderly   20 September 1913   119
From Frank J. Hayes   28 November 1913   120
To Terence V. Powderly   22 March 1914   122
To the Public   31 March 1914   125
To the *Appeal* Army   9 May 1914   126

Contents

To John D. Rockefeller, Jr.   [12 May 1914]   127
To Caroline Lloyd   5 June 1914   128
To the Editor of *The Appeal to Reason*   [11 July 1914]   128
To Caroline Lloyd   21 July 1914   129
To *The Appeal to Reason*   [8 August 1914]   130
To The Editor, *Miners' Magazine*   13 August 1914   130
From James Lord   9 October 1914   131
To James Lord   23 December 1914   132
To John D. Rockefeller, Jr.   15 March 1915   134
To Walter Watson Stokes   17 March 1915   134
To James Lord   23 March 1915   136
From John D. Rockefeller, Jr.   [March 1915]   138
From James Lord   3 April 1915   139
To Mary Field Parton   10 June 1915   140
From John P. White   8 October 1915   141
From William B. Wilson   19 October 1915   142
From Tom Mooney   15 December 1915   142
From John H. Walker   29 May 1916   146
To G. W. P. Hunt   12 June 1916   147
To G. W. P. Hunt   12 June 1916   148
From G. W. P. Hunt   14 June 1916   149
To Edward Crough   30 June 1916   149
To John H. Walker   30 June 1916   151
From John H. Walker   1 July 1916   153
To Ed Nockles   7 July 1916   154
To Ed Nockles   20 July 1916   155
From John H. Walker   9 August 1916   156
From Marguerite Prevey   26 October 1916   157
From Katherine L. Schmidt   29 October 1916   157
To Marguerite Prevey   31 October 1916   161
From Tom Mooney   25 November 1916   162
From Charles Batley   28 November 1916   164
From Henry Hagelstein   1 December 1916   166
To J. Clancy   2 December 1916   167
To Edward M. House   9 December 1916   167
From John P. White   9 December 1916   169
To Joseph P. Tumulty   13 December 1916   169
To Tom Mooney   15 December 1916   169
From Emma T. Martin   27 December 1916   171
From Tom Mooney   28 December 1916   171
To Mr. & Mrs. John D. Rockefeller, Jr.   1 January 1917   173
From Samuel Graham   2 January 1917   173
From John D. Rockefeller, Jr.   6 January 1917   174

Contents

To the Editor, New York *Call*   [January 1917]   174
From John H. Walker   12 July 1917   176
From John H. Walker   19 July 1917   177
To John H. Walker   [1917]   178
To John H. Walker   25 August 1918   181
From John H. Walker   29 August 1918   181
To Miners and Other Working Men of Colorado
   31 August 1918   182
To Walter Wayland   15 November 1918   184
To Sara J. Dorr   16 December 1918   185
To John H. Walker   18 December 1918   186
To John H. Walker   28 December 1918   187
From John H. Walker   8 January 1919   189
To Ed Nockles   14 January 1919   190
To John H. Walker   5 February 1919   190
From John H. Walker   7 February 1919   191
From John H. Walker   11 February 1919   192
To Terence V. Powderly   19 June 1919   192
From A. Mitchell Palmer   11 July 1919   194
To Ryan Walker   12 December 1919   194
To Otto Branstetter   26 January 1920   196
To John H. Walker   9 March 1920   196
From John H. Walker   16 March 1920   198
To Otto Branstetter   21 April 1920   200
To John H. Walker   27 April 1920   200
From John H. Walker   4 May 1920   201
From Terence V. Powderly   15 June 1920   202
To John H. Walker   18 June 1920   203
From John H. Walker   25 June 1920   205
To John H. Walker   21 July 1920   206
From John H. Walker   4 August 1920   207
From John H. Walker   13 August 1920   209
To John H. Walker   17 August 1920   210
To Theodore Debs   18 August 1920   211
From John H. Walker   18 August 1920   211
To Ryan Walker   21 September 1920   212
To Terence V. Powderly   14 December 1920   213
To Woodrow Wilson   16 December 1920   213
From Terence V. Powderly   28 December 1920   214
To John H. Walker   28 December 1920   216
From John H. Walker   31 December 1920   217
From G. W. P. Hunt   15 February 1921   220
To John H. Walker   22 March 1921   221

Contents

From John H. Walker	24 March 1921	222
To Terence V. Powderly	5 April 1921	223
To John H. Walker	5 April 1921	223
To Terence V. Powderly	6 April 1921	224
From Terence V. Powderly	9 April 1921	224
From Roberto Haberman	[April 1921]	225
To John Fitzpatrick and Ed Nockles	16 May 1921	226
To John H. Walker	27 May 1921	228
From John H. Walker	6 June 1921	230
From John H. Walker	6 June 1921	231
To John H. Walker	21 June 1921	232
From John H. Walker	20 July 1921	233
To Ephraim F. Morgan	29 August 1921	233
From Ephraim F. Morgan	29 August 1921	234
To John Fitzpatrick	10 September 1921	234
To Terence V. Powderly	23 November 1921	235
To William Green	27 December 1921	236
To Ephraim F. Morgan	27 December 1921	238
To [John H. Walker?]	[1921]	240
To William Green	4 March 1922	241
To Ephraim F. Morgan	4 March 1922	242
From William Green	8 March 1922	243
From John H. Walker	18 March 1922	244
To John H. Walker	20 March 1922	244
From John H. Walker	23 March 1922	245
To John H. Walker	29 March 1922	246
From John H. Walker	6 April 1922	247
To John H. Walker	22 April 1922	248
From John H. Walker	27 April 1922	248
To John H. Walker	26 June 1922	249
From John H. Walker	29 June 1922	251
To John H. Walker	27 July 1922	252
From John H. Walker	1 August 1922	253
From John H. Walker	8 August 1922	254
From Katherine [Schmidt?]	4 September 1922	255
From Federated Shopcrafts and Brotherhoods of Texas 6 September 1922		255
From Ephraim F. Morgan	6 September [1922]	255
From Dan W. Stevens	7 September 1922	256
To William Green	2 October 1922	256
To John H. Walker	4 October 1922	257
From John H. Walker	9 October 1922	257
From William Green	13 October 1922	259

From Ephraim F. Morgan   20 October 1922   260
From John H. Walker   22 October 1922   260
To John H. Walker   [October 1922]   261
From John H. Walker   7 November 1922   261
To John Fitzpatrick   5 December 1922   262
From John H. Walker   12 December 1922   263
To John H. Walker   20 December 1922   264
To William Green   24 December 1922   265
From John H. Walker   26 December 1922   266
From William Green   29 December 1922   267
From Thomas Francis Cairns   2 January 1923   268
From John H. Walker   3 January 1923   269
From John H. Walker   9 January 1923   270
To Emma Powderly   23 February 1923   271
To Terence V. Powderly   1 March 1923   271
To William Green   29 March [1923]   272
From William Green   30 March 1923   273
To William Green   4 April 1923   273
From John H. Walker   4 April 1923   274
From Ephraim F. Morgan   10 April 1923   274
To Ephraim F. Morgan   16 April 1923   275
To Ephraim F. Morgan   17 April 1923   276
From Ephraim F. Morgan   19 April 1923   277
To Robert Watchorn   April 1923   277
To Terence V. Powderly   3 May 1923   279
To William Green   18 May 1923   280
From William Green   21 May 1923   281
To William Green   24 May 1923   282
To Ephraim F. Morgan   9 June 1923   283
To Emma Powderly   11 June 1923   284
From Ephraim F. Morgan   19 June 1923   284
To Ephraim F. Morgan   12 July 1923   285
To William Green   23 July 1923   286
From William Green   25 July 1923   287
To Terence V. and Emma Powderly   10 November 1923   288
To William Green   23 November 1923   289
From William Green   4 December 1923   291
From John H. Walker   8 December 1923   291
To Ephraim F. Morgan   9 December 1923   292
From Ephraim F. Morgan   11 December 1923   292
From John H. Walker   13 December 1923   293
To John H. Walker   14 December 1923   294
From John H. Walker   17 December 1923   295

Contents

To John H. Walker	18 December 1923	296
To John Fitzpatrick	20 December 1923	297
To John H. Walker	25 December 1923	298
From John H. Walker	27 December 1923	298
From Mrs. Peter Benner	27 December 1923	299
From John H. Walker	29 December 1923	300
To John H. Walker	31 December 1923	301
To Ephraim F. Morgan	[1923?]	302
To John H. Walker	11 January 1924	303
To William Green	14 January 1924	304
From John H. Walker	16 January 1924	304
From William Green	19 January 1924	305
To Ephraim F. Morgan	31 January 1924	306
From Ephraim F. Morgan	1 February 1924	307
To John H. Walker	11 February 1924	308
From John H. Walker	14 February 1924	308
To John Fitzpatrick	29 February 1924	309
To Emma Powderly	31 March 1924	310
To Emma Powderly	8 April 1924	311
To William Green	30 June 1924	311
To John H. Walker	2 July 1924	313
From John H. Walker	7 July 1924	314
From William Green	18 July 1924	315
To John Fitzpatrick	31 July 1924	316
From Claude Erwin	16 August 1924	317
To John H. Walker	[January 1925]	318
From John H. Walker	7 February 1925	319
Assignment of Bond	31 March 1925	320
To John H. Walker	30 July 1925	320
To John H. Walker	15 February 1926	321
From John H. Walker	22 February 1926	323
To John H. Walker	10 June 1926	325
From John H. Walker	14 June 1926	326
From Katherine [Schmidt]	25 June [1926]	326
From John H. Walker	25 August 1926	327
To John H. Walker	28 September 1926	327
From John H. Walker	3 October 1926	328
To John H. Walker	13 November 1926	329
From John H. Walker	20 November 1926	330
To John H. Walker	16 December 1926	330
From John H. Walker	21 December 1926	331
From Susana DeWolfe	24 March 1927	332
To John H. Walker	15 April 1927	333

From John H. Walker   30 April 1927   333
From Susana DeWolfe   9 September [1927?]   333
To John Fitzpatrick and Ed Nockles   14 November 1927   335
From John H. Walker   17 November 1927   335
From Katherine [Schmidt?]   18 November 1927   336
From Catherine Yarnell   24 November 1927   337
To John Fitzpatrick   14 December 1927   337
From Cora Meyer   9 January 1928   338
To John Fitzpatrick   11 January 1928   338
From John H. Walker   29 August 1928   339
To John H. Walker   13 September 1928   340
From John H. Walker   18 September 1928   340
From Roger Baldwin   5 March 1929   342
From the Chicago Federation of Labor   30 April 1929   342
To Tom Mooney   [21 March 1930]   344
Last Will and Testament   28 April 1930   344
From John H. Walker   29 April 1930   345
From John D. Rockefeller, Jr.   2 May 1930   346
To John D. Rockefeller, Jr.   3 May 1930   346
To John Fitzpatrick   20 June 1930   346
To William H. Amerland   25 June 1930   347
From John H. Walker   18 October 1930   347
To Finley Peter Dunne   [Undated]   349
To John Fitzpatrick   [Undated]   349
To Adolph Germer   [Undated]   349
To Emma Powderly   [Undated]   349
To Unknown   [Undated]   350
From Catherine Yarnell   [Undated]   351

Index   353

Acknowledgments

Any collection such as this rests on the labors of so many people that to acknowledge all of them would require excessive space. Scholars and staff at many institutions went far beyond the requirements of courtesy to supply information and engage in sometime fruitless searches. I wish to acknowledge my debt to them, specifically at the following institutions: the AFL-CIO Library; Archivo General de la Nación, Mexico City; Arizona State University; Catholic University of America; the Chicago Historical Society; Duke University; the Historical Society of Pennsylvania; Indiana University; Indiana State University; the Library of Congress; the Minnesota Historical Society; the National Archives; the Ohio Historical Society; the Pennsylvania State University; Pittsburg State University; Princeton University; the Rockefeller Archive Center; the State Historical Society of Wisconsin; the Tamiment Institute at New York University; the University of California; the University of Chicago; the University of Illinois; and West Virginia University.

My special thanks go to Nancy Grossman, the principal editorial assistant, and to Irmgard Keiderling, for endless typing and retyping. John Morgan searched for references and read proof, and Penny Pugh assisted in procuring needed materials. Lois McLean shared her files and her profound knowledge of Mother Jones, and Fred Thompson his wide acquaintance with labor and radical movements in this century.

I am grateful also to the National Historical Publications and Records Commission for the grant which made possible the final stages of this work. Mary Giunta and others on the staff at the National Archives led me through the mazes of official records, pointed out new areas to search, and explored possible sources for me.

Finally, my greatest debt is to my wife, Barbara, whose aid and support never faltered.

Introduction:
Mary Harris Jones
and Her Correspondence

On 1 May 1930 Mary Harris Jones, known to most people only as Mother Jones, attended a hundredth birthday party at the home of Walter and Lillie May Burgess near Hyattsville, Maryland, where she had been living for the past two years. Wearing a new dress for the occasion, but rejecting a bouquet of flowers as uncharacteristic, she came down from her room on the second floor to greet relays of union leaders who traveled out from Washington to honor her, to open congratulatory letters and telegrams, and to share the cake donated by the bakers' union. Reporters from Washington exchanged repartee with her and newsreel cameramen recorded the event. The county authorities had even resurfaced the road leading to the house in anticipation of heavy traffic. It was a genuine celebration, but it was also a media event.[1]

It is almost certain that Mother Jones was not born in 1830, and it is unlikely that 1 May was her birthday. However, she had been using those dates for many years, and since she herself was the source of virtually all information about the first sixty years of her life, no one questioned them. The little documentary evidence that exists confirms her general statements about her life, but not specific dates; whole decades lack any support other than her assertions.[2]

She was born in Cork, Ireland, probably in 1836, the daughter of Richard and Mary Harris, and spent her first six years there. Her father emigrated to the United States and took out naturalization papers. When his family joined him, however, it was in Toronto, where his work on the railroad had led him. Mary attended school in Toronto and went on to the recently founded normal school. In 1859 she became a lay teacher in the school established in Monroe, Michigan, by the Sisters, Servants of the Immaculate Heart of Mary. After one year at Monroe, she went to Chicago, but the following year she

1. Lillie May Burgess MSS; Washington *Herald, Star,* and *Daily News,* 1 May 1930; unidentified news clippings, Mother Jones Papers. Lillie May Burgess left behind reminiscences of Mother Jones's residence with her.

2. For details of Mother Jones's life, her *Autobiography* (Chicago: Charles H. Kerr Company, 1925) is essential in spite of its anecdotal nature, vagueness, and inaccuracies. Dale Fetherling, *Mother Jones: The Miners' Angel* (Carbondale: Southern Illinois University Press, 1974), has the best full-length account. Except as otherwise noted, this sketch follows them. Reporters who interviewed Mother Jones placed her birth date variously from 1830 to 1844. Lois McLean of Beckley, West Virginia, who is working on a study of her, has found an appropriate baptismal notice in the Cork parish records dated 1836.

was in Memphis, Tennessee, where she may have again taught in a parochial school.

In Memphis she met and married George Jones, an official in the moulders' union, and over the next several years they had four children. They lived in Memphis during the Civil War and after until 1867, when a yellow fever epidemic ravaged the city. To that disease, her husband and children succumbed. When the epidemic had run its course she moved to Chicago and opened a dressmaking shop.

The great fire of 1871 left Mary Harris Jones homeless and destitute again, and in the difficult times following the fire she first became interested in a rising labor organization, the Knights of Labor. According to her own account, she became an organizer for the union. Whatever her official status, she showed a remarkable talent for being on hand when violent incidents occurred in connection with labor protests. She was in Pittsburgh for the 1877 railroad strike and spent some time in California when Dennis Kearney led the anti-Chinese immigration movement there. In the eighties she was working in Chicago with Thomas J. Morgan's socialist group to elect candidates for local office, and she was involved in the eight-hour-day movement that formed the background for the tragic Haymarket incident in 1886. She was back in Pittsburgh in 1892 to witness the battles between Pinkerton detectives and striking steelworkers at the Homestead works. In 1893 she helped feed a column of Coxey's Army as it passed through Chicago, and in 1894 she addressed striking miners and railroad men in the American Railway Union strike in Birmingham, Alabama, while the main events were being played out in Pullman, Illinois. In 1896 she attended the Populist party convention in St. Louis as a member of the group which Henry Demarest Lloyd led from Chicago to try to procure the presidential nomination for Eugene V. Debs.

For many of these early activities, only her own reminiscences or the writings of reporters who interviewed her supply information, but as the last decade of the century passed her name began to crop up in newspapers in connection with strikes or with socialist affairs. She joined the Socialist Labor party in Kansas City in 1895, and she was a member of the Social Democracy organized by Eugene V. Debs in 1897 and a successor organization, the Social Democratic party. She moved naturally into the Socialist Party of America when a 1901 convention united most of the socialist factions into a single organization.[3]

The newspapers devoted more attention to Mother Jones's colorful

3. Mother Jones's own account of her Socialist affiliations appears in affidavits of February 1911, Thomas J. Morgan Papers; see also Howard Quint, *The Forging of American Socialism: Origins of the Modern Movement* (Columbia: University of South Carolina Press, 1953), pp. 293, 320.

organizing forays among the miners than to her Socialist activities. In Arnot, Pennsylvania, in 1899, she turned what had seemed to be a losing strike into a success with her rousing speeches to the men and her dramatic parades of women and children. When she left to carry the fight to the hold-out Blossburg Coal Company in the Toby valley, the citizens of Arnot gave her a farewell party at the opera house. Use of similar techniques brought the Blossburg Company to terms. From Pennsylvania she moved across the border into Maryland for the coal miners' strike there in 1900.[4]

By 1900, when she became an official organizer for the United Mine Workers of America, Mother Jones had already established the persona which she was to maintain for the rest of her life: the mild-looking motherly figure who was metamorphosed into a Joan of Arc when she mounted the platform and converted an uncertain crowd into a purposeful group of unionists, or who worked among the women and children, comforting them in their hardships and organizing them in protest parades. For the next four years she injected herself into the continuing struggle to attract or hold firm the members of the union, moving from Pennsylvania and Maryland into West Virginia, where she was in charge of a special organizing team in the Kanawha Valley in 1901–1902. Later in 1902 she moved to the northern West Virginia field, with frequent trips back to the anthracite district in Pennsylvania as the strike in that area moved toward a national crisis. Simultaneously, she continued to speak for socialism, campaigning with candidate Eugene V. Debs in Philadelphia, for the Massachusetts state ticket in Haverhill, and in the Chicago municipal elections.[5]

Her activities in the Fairmont field of northern West Virginia led to her first jail term. The Consolidation Coal Company, which dominated coal production in the area, had successfully kept out union organizers for the past ten years, but the UMWA made it a special target in 1902. When Mother Jones joined the team in that area in the spring, the demonstrations and clashes between strikers and guards mounted. After Tom Haggerty, the organizer in charge, was jailed for violating an injunction, she carried on his work. At a rally in Clarksburg, she and most of the remaining organizers were arrested for violating another injunction by federal judge John J. Jackson and transported to

4. For news coverage in the Pennsylvania strikes, see Harry Donald Fox, Jr., "Thomas T. Haggerty and the Formative Years of the United Mine Workers of America" (Ph.D. diss., West Virginia University, 1975); for the Maryland strike, Katherine A. Harvey, *The Best-Dressed Miners: Life and Labor in the Maryland Coal Region, 1835–1910* (Ithaca: Cornell University Press, 1969), is most complete.

5. Philadelphia *North American,* 26 October 1900; Haverhill *Evening News,* 6, 21 October 1902; Chicago *Socialist,* 28 February, 14 March 1903.

the jail in Parkersburg to await disposition of the case. Judge Jackson sentenced the other leaders to varying terms for contempt, but dismissed Mother Jones with a scolding. She departed to make speeches in the anthracite strike and in Massachusetts before returning to southern West Virginia to face more injunctions.[6]

The activity that attracted the most national attention during this period, however, was her work with the striking textile workers in Philadelphia. During the summer of 1903 she led an "army" of child textile workers on a march from Philadelphia to Oyster Bay, Long Island, to ask President Theodore Roosevelt to support child labor legislation. Although her army melted to only a handful of children, its progress across New Jersey attracted nationwide attention. Roosevelt managed to avoid a confrontation.[7]

In the latter part of 1903, Mother Jones was back with the miners, this time in the Colorado coal fields, where the UMWA had instituted a major organizing drive in the Trinidad area. The simultaneous Cripple Creek strike of the metalliferous miners had already brought about a declaration of martial law by the governor, and there were frequent violent clashes between miners and militia. Mother Jones was especially successful in her organizing efforts in the southern Colorado field, and when the UMWA leadership recommended that the miners in the northern field accept a settlement she actively opposed John Mitchell and the executive board. Although this eventually led to her resignation as an organizer for the miners' union, she continued to work with the southern Colorado miners through the winter and spring, with an interruption caused by serious illness.[8]

During the years from 1904 to 1911, Mother Jones formed her most radical associations. She became an official lecturer for the Socialist party, helped to found the Industrial Workers of the World, and took up the cause of Mexican revolutionists in the United States, especially the Partido Liberal led by the anarchist Ricardo Flores Magón. This apparent turn to the left represented no ideological conversion, for her public utterances and private correspondence reveal no new directions. Her Socialist activities differed from previous ones mainly in the amount of time she devoted to party affairs. Her role with the IWW was confined to founding mother, and she kept up no connection with

6. Edward M. Steel, "Mother Jones in the Fairmont Field, 1902," *Journal of American History* 57 (September 1970), 290–307.

7. Helen Collier Camp, "Mother Jones and the Children's Crusade," (M.A. thesis, Columbia University, 1970).

8. Emma Langdon, *The Cripple Creek Strike* (Denver: Great Western Publishing Company, 1905), and Barron B. Beshoar, *Out of the Depths* (Denver: Golden Bell Press, 1958), both quote from Mother Jones's speeches at this time.

the Wobblies after the first six months. The Mexican connection began accidentally and led to extensive tours to raise money for the legal expenses of imprisoned Mexicans and to pleas to President William Howard Taft for their pardon. She lobbied in Washington for an investigation of their treatment and testified before the congressional committee that was set up for that purpose.

The strain of her organizing efforts in southern Colorado in the fall of 1903 took a heavy toll, and Mother Jones fell ill to the point of requiring a stay in the hospital. Her Socialist friends rallied around, and Bertha Howell Mailly, wife of the national secretary of the party, went to Trinidad to help care for her. The latter part of January 1904 was spent convalescing at the Mailly home in Omaha. After a rapid recovery, the old organizer rejoined the battle in Colorado, where her defiance of the militia soon led to her deportation at bayonet point in March. She then went to Helper, Utah, only to be quarantined because of alleged contact with a sufferer from smallpox. In June she returned to Denver as the guest of the Western Federation of Miners and addressed their convention.[9]

Later in 1904 she went back to Chicago, where in January 1905 she became a paid lecturer for the Socialist party of Illinois, meeting a heavy schedule of speaking engagements in small towns across the state. Later the same year she went on the payroll of the national party as a lecturer, assigned first to Montana as one of a team of four, and later to the "southwest," which included Indian Territory, Missouri, Arkansas, and Texas. For the next four years she stumped the southwest for the Socialist party, taking time out to throw herself into particular strike efforts, such as that of the copper miners in Arizona in 1907, the telegraphers in Chicago in the same year, the textile workers in Avondale, Alabama, in 1908, and the garment workers in New York and Philadelphia in 1909.[10]

In early 1910 Mother Jones traveled to Milwaukee at the invitation of the brewery workers' union to organize the women in the industry. She began her campaign by interviewing owners and operators and attempting to secure permission to visit the work places where women were employed to wash returned bottles. She held meetings with

9. Chicago *Socialist,* 23 January 1904; William Mailly to William B. Wilson, 26 January 1904, William B. Wilson Papers; *Miners Magazine,* 28 April, 2 June, 9 June 1904; *The Appeal to Reason,* 6 February, 14 May 1904; Langdon, *Cripple Creek Strike,* p. 267.

10. St. Louis *Labor,* 11 March 1905, 4 May 1907, 11 April, 2 May, 19 September 1908; Chicago *Socialist,* 28 January, 11 February, 18 March, 27 May, 17 June, 12 August 1905; *The Appeal to Reason,* 9 March, 23 March, 20 April, 11 May, 23 November, 7 December 1907, 13 June 1908, 27 March, 31 July, 28 August, 4 September, 23 September, 30 October 1909; New York *Call,* 20 December, 30 December 1909.

workers and then published a series of muckraking articles on wages and working conditions in the breweries. In March she journeyed to Cincinnati, where she appealed to a special convention of the UMWA to strengthen her hand by passing a resolution of support for the brewery women. The threat of a boycott of Milwaukee beer by miners, she asserted, would bring the brewers' association to terms. If it did not, she planned to seek a law in the Wisconsin legislature prohibiting the employment of women in breweries. Within months, the Pabst and Schlitz companies had capitulated and recognized the newly formed women's local, and at the next round of contract talks, the bottle washers gained substantial wage increases. It was one of Mother Jones's most successful organizing campaigns.[11]

The cause nearest to her heart in these years came to be that of the Mexican revolutionaries who were fighting the Diaz regime in Mexico from the United States. Her initial involvement seems to have been accidental, when she saw the kidnapping of a Mexican, Manuel Sarabia, on the streets of Douglas, Arizona, when she was organizing the copper miners of the area. She immediately led local protests that brought about the return of Sarabia to American authorities. Subsequently she became the champion of members of the Partido Liberal who were imprisoned on various charges. In their behalf she addressed meetings all over the country, and she was credited with having raised four thousand dollars for their defense. Unsuccessful in her attempts to have the Socialist party take up their cause officially, she lobbied extensively in Washington on her own and eventually testified before a congressional committee appointed to make an investigation of the treatment of Mexican refugees in the United States. In 1909 her friend Terence V. Powderly secured for her an interview with President William Howard Taft, in which she plead for pardons for some of the Mexicans who had been sentenced to prison in the United States.[12]

Simultaneously with her battles for the Mexican exiles, Mother Jones became involved in an internecine struggle within the Socialist party. Although a member successively of the Socialist Labor party, the Social Democratic party, and the Socialist party, she was no ideologue. Her letters contain very few references to socialism, except that she frequently began them with the salutation "Dear Comrade" and

11. UMWA *Proceedings,* 1910, pp. 60–63; Milwaukee *Daily News,* 19 January 1910; *The Appeal to Reason,* 5 February, 19 April 1910; *Miners Magazine,* 14 April 1910; Thomas C. Cochran, *The Pabst Brewing Company* (New York: New York University Press, 1948), p. 300.

12. W. Dirk Raat, *Revoltosos: Mexico's Rebels in the United States, 1903–1923* (Texas A&M University Press, 1981), puts Mother Jones's relationship to the Mexicans in perspective.

concluded them with "Yours for the Cause." At various times she campaigned for Socialist candidates for office, but her usual stance showed a millennialist leaning; she saw herself as an educator of the workers who would eventually see their true interest and seize power at the ballot box in some unspecified future. Although inconsistent in her public pronouncements, she constantly recurred to some basic ideas: the inevitability of the class struggle, the desirability of government ownership of the means of production, and above all the need for solidarity among workers. Her understanding of the class struggle was passionate rather than logical, and she scorned theoreticians. As a grass roots lecturer and organizer, she had all the traditional contempt of the line officer for the staff.

For Eugene V. Debs she had friendship and admiration, but she had little use for the other leaders of the party, particularly those who held offices in the period 1907–1911. Her enmity focused on J. Mahlon Barnes, the national secretary. Working with Thomas J. Morgan, a party stalwart from Chicago, she compiled charges against Barnes for dereliction of duty and for dishonesty in not repaying money that she had lent him when the move of the party headquarters to Chicago had created financial difficulties for him. Her charges, along with others, eventually provoked an official investigation that resulted in Barnes's resignation as secretary; however, a committee exonerated Barnes of the charges she had made, and she herself was expelled from the party in 1911. She did not even attend the hearings, since she was already embarked on a new phase of her career, touring the coal fields of Pennsylvania once again as an organizer for the UMWA.[13]

It was during the years from 1911 to 1916 that Mother Jones made her greatest impact as a labor leader, largely through personalizing the conditions of labor in the coal mining industry. In the tide of progressivism that was mounting nationally, organized labor was gaining a greater voice in public affairs. The Department of Labor was established under the leadership of William B. Wilson, her old friend and strike companion from the Pennsylvania coal fields. The Clayton Act of 1914 recognized the new position of labor in the economy, and in the Commission on Industrial Relations labor leaders gained a national investigative body to explore conditions of work in many different fields. Through her own experiences as an organizer, Mother Jones was able to dramatize the difficulties which unions faced in the mining industry. Over the course of eighteen months, she was instrumental in

13. *Miners Magazine,* February, March, April, 1911. Nearly all the correspondence in this collection between Mother Jones and Thomas J. Morgan deals with the battle against Barnes, 1907–1911.

initiating special congressional investigations in three different mining areas, Michigan, West Virginia, and Colorado. In the latter two states her imprisonment by military authorities gained nationwide attention. In Colorado she was able to play the role of a victim of the oppression of John D. Rockefeller, Jr., the embodiment of the capitalist control of the coal mines of that state.

During 1911 Mother Jones divided her time between Pennsylvania and Colorado, in both of which states long and bitter strikes continued. Her organizing activities were interrupted by a trip to Mexico to confer with President Francisco Madero and other officials of the new government. She served as their emissary to Ricardo Flores Magón in Los Angeles, but she failed to convince him to abandon his independent course and return to Mexico.[14] From Los Angeles she went back to the strike area in Colorado, but in June 1912 she transferred her activities to the critical Paint Creek strike in West Virginia, which was to be scene of her endeavors for the next year.

Within the West Virginia strike area, Mother Jones ranged up and down the Kanawha Valley, organizing nonunion mines and sustaining the spirits of the unionized strikers. In a series of fiery speeches in Charleston, she urged the miners to buy guns to defend themselves against the brutalities of the mine guards. She also held mass meetings in Cincinnati, Cleveland, New York, and Washington to invoke outside support for the striking miners. In February 1913, just after she had returned from a speaking engagement in the East, she was arrested on the streets of Charleston and transported to the martial law zone, where she spent the next three months in prison. A military court sentenced her to a term in the penitentiary, but since only a few records of the court have survived, the precise charges and sentence are uncertain. In later speeches she said she was sentenced to five years for stealing a cannon and blowing up railroad tracks. Unlike most of those condemned by the military court she was never transferred to the penitentiary, but was kept isolated under guard in a private house in Pratt, West Virginia. However, her captors allowed her to receive and send mail, and her pleas for assistance, some of them smuggled out surreptitiously, reached a wide public.

Mother Jones imprisoned may have been more powerful than Mother Jones at liberty. Since the military authorities merely monitored her mail, she was able to seek help from friends, who responded with a flood of petitions to various officeholders in Washington. One telegram,

14. See Mother Jones to Manuel Calero, 25 October 1911, and Mother Jones to Ricardo Flores Magón, 4 November 1911, Ramo Revolución Politica, Correspondencias Varios, 1910–1919.

an appeal to John W. Kern, the Democratic majority leader of the Senate, contributed a dramatic note to the debate on a resolution to investigate conditions in the coal fields of West Virginia. Within days Governor Henry D. Hatfield of West Virginia had arranged for her release, and she had the satisfaction of listening from the Senate gallery to the conclusion of the debate and the adoption of the resolution.[15] After testifying before the committee and holding another mass meeting in Washington, she departed in August 1913 for a whirlwind campaign in the copper mining area of Michigan. There, too, the state militia and the miners were embattled, and she pointed out the value of federal intervention in the form of a congressional investigation.

During the remainder of 1913 and 1914, Colorado became the scene of her endeavors. The parallels between West Virginia and Colorado conditions were striking. In both states, coal operators maintained almost complete economic and political control in the mining areas and were adamantly opposed to dealing with the union. In the Colorado conflict, many of the mine guards were Baldwin-Felts agents who were veterans of the West Virginia struggle; they even used the same machine guns and armored vehicles. As the two sides confronted one another, violence between strikers and guards became endemic, and in each case the governor of the state sent militia into selected areas to preserve order. In both states the initial success of the state troops deteriorated and greater violence erupted.

There were great contrasts, also. The wider valleys and horizons of Colorado presented logistical difficulties for both sides. The Colorado climate was harsher, and the sufferings of the strikers in their tent colonies were probably more severe. The miners of West Virginia were predominantly native born and long-time residents of the area, while in Colorado the contingents of Greek, Italian, and Mexican workers were numerous. In West Virginia the mines were operated by many individual companies, none dominant, joined in an association. While they generally agreed in opposing the union demands, there were enough differences among them for the new governor, Henry D. Hatfield, himself closely allied with the coal mining interests, to work out a settlement that brought an uneasy peace to the disputing parties. In Colorado, on the other hand, the principal companies, Victor-American and Colorado Fuel and Iron, were parts of the Rockefeller financial empire in close communication with their headquarters. They maintained their position and had the unswerving support of smaller

---

15. The most detailed scholarly account of the Paint Creek strike is to be found in Judith Elaine Mikeal, "Mother Mary Jones: The Labor Movement's Impious Joan of Arc" (M.A. thesis, University of North Carolina, 1965).

operators, and Governor Elias Ammons contributed no leadership toward a solution. In the end, he was forced to ask President Woodrow Wilson to send federal troops to keep order, and it was a federal proposal that brought about another uneasy truce.[16]

In both states, Mother Jones followed her usual pattern, making speeches to encourage the strikers, organizing demonstrations, and visiting the bleak tent colonies to hearten the residents. A month after the southern Colorado miners struck in September 1913, Governor Ammons sent the state militia into the southern fields to preserve order. Mother Jones went to Washington to lobby for an investigation by Congress, but returned to Trinidad, only to be deported by the militia. She slipped into Denver secretly in December to address the State Federation of Labor and to lead the delegates in a protest march to the capitol. Governor Ammons rejected their demand for the withdrawal of the militia, but suggested that they set up a committee to substantiate charges of misconduct by militia officers and men, and especially the induction of imported mine guards into the ranks of the militia.

Early in January, Mother Jones returned to Trinidad and was immediately arrested on order of General John Chase. Deported to Denver, she threatened to go back into Trinidad as soon as she was freed. With the cooperation of railroad workers, she evaded militia surveillance and arrived in Trinidad on January 14. General Chase ordered her arrest and removal to Mt. San Rafael Hospital, where she was kept under close confinement, with no visitors and no mail. Once again her imprisonment set off a wave of sympathy nationwide, and in February 1914 the House of Representatives authorized an investigation of conditions in the mining fields of Michigan and Colorado.

Repeated attempts by the union to free Mother Jones by use of the writ of habeas corpus finally bore fruit in that she was taken to Denver and released on the day before the state supreme court was scheduled to pronounce on her case. She made speeches in Denver vowing to return to the strike area, and on 22 March she boarded a train for Trinidad, but military authorities removed her from the car early the next morning in Walsenburg and imprisoned her in the Huerfano County jail. There she spent the next twenty-six days under close guard, without legal indictment or recourse. On her release she went to Washington, where the Committee on Mines and Mining had resumed its hearings. One of their witnesses was John D. Rockefeller, Jr., who defended the antiunion policies of the companies in Colorado

16. George Stanley McGovern and Leonard F. Guttridge, *The Great Coalfield War* (Boston: Houghton Mifflin, 1972), is the best account.

in which he held an interest. Mother Jones followed him to the stand and presented a striking contrast of views.

In Colorado, the situation remained tense, even though all but two companies of the militia had been withdrawn. The two that remained, composed for the most part of guards and other employees loyal to the mine owners, pursued a course of violence that led directly to the tragic Ludlow Massacre, when women and children were burned to death in the firing of a tent colony. In the face of the armed violence and arson that followed throughout the state, Governor Ammons asked President Wilson to send federal troops, and the first detachments arrived on 29 April 1914. Mother Jones returned to Denver to address a large protest meeting before departing on a national speaking tour to generate support for the strikers.

Over the course of the summer, a proposal for a three-year truce was worked out. In September, the miners of District 15 approved it at a convention in which Mother Jones called for its endorsement. The mine operators refused to accept the proposal, and Mother Jones and other union leaders in an October interview with President Wilson urged him to seize the mines and impose a settlement. He would not go so far, but he did appoint the committee of arbitration that the proposal suggested, and in December the UMWA called off their strike. It had cost the union treasury four million dollars for the five-year battle, and they had gained none of the specific objectives for which they fought, but the drama of the confrontation had drawn attention to conditions and had generated a number of governmental reports that were favorable to the union. The repercussions of the Colorado strike continued into 1915 and 1916. John D. Rockefeller, Jr., testified before the Commission on Industrial Relations in January 1915, and after his testimony introduced himself to Mother Jones and invited her to a conference next day in his office. He later followed her advice to go in person to see conditions in Colorado, and with the assistance of William Lyon Mackenzie King designed a new policy that gave Colorado miners a voice through company unions. The working out of more peaceful conditions in Colorado continued to be a major concern of Mother Jones in these years, but she also participated in garment workers' strikes in Chicago in 1915 and in New York in 1916, and another strike by transit workers in New York the same year.

During the years from 1916 to 1920 the earlier tide of progressivism ebbed, and the coming of the First World War changed the conditions under which Mother Jones worked. In the election of 1916 the Democrats emphasized that their candidate Woodrow Wilson had "kept us out of war," but they gave equal emphasis to his plans for preparedness if war should come. On July 22, a bomb exploded during a Preparedness Day parade in San Francisco, killing ten people and injuring others. The subsequent murder conviction of the radical labor leader Tom Mooney gave Mother Jones a cause that was to occupy her attention to the last months of her life, for she raised money for his defense and the long fight for pardon and carried petitions in person to the successive governors of California. Her main occupation continued to be free-lance agitation for the UMWA, with Charleston, West Virginia, as her base. She was determined to establish the UMWA in the militantly nonunion Pocohontas field and the increasingly important unorganized mines of McDowell, Mingo, and Logan counties. When the United States entered the war, her task was made easier by the wartime labor policies adopted by the Wilson administration. Working with a swaggering, one-legged organizer, Lawrence Dwyer, she mounted an attack on the Pocohontas field that at times ignored the no-strike clause of the Fuel Administration policy. Although the work of organizing did not have to be carried on secretly as in former days, it had to be accomplished in the face of the hostility of mine guards and operators. She counted it a great triumph when in August 1920 she was able to hold a large union meeting in Princeton, West Virginia, almost on the doorstep of the Baldwin-Felts Detective Agency which supplied mine guards to operators.

In the middle of her campaign in southern West Virginia, she spent the better part of the year 1919 in efforts to unionize the steelworkers of the country. The chairman of the organizing committee was John Fitzpatrick of Chicago, an old friend, but the field commander was William Z. Foster, with his headquarters in Pittsburgh. One of his major problems was to break the almost complete social control that steel companies exercised in the company towns. To gain a voice in these towns he created a Flying Squadron of speakers who were willing to be arrested when they went into company towns and violated ordinances or spoke without permits. The group included Mother Jones and Philip Murray from the UMWA, Jay Brown of Seattle, James Maurer of the Pennsylvania Federation of Labor, Foster himself, and others. They were repeatedly arrested, but they made their voices heard. By injecting the issue of freedom of speech into the fight, they attracted wide notice. Mother Jones also spoke on behalf of the steelworkers outside the Pittsburgh area, delivering addresses to large crowds in Buffalo, Gary, and Chicago.[17]

17. See David Brody, *Labor in Crisis* (Philadelphia: J. B. Lippincott Company, 1965), passim, and the accounts of active participants: William Z. Foster, *Pages from a Worker's Life* (New York: International Publishers, 1939); *The Great Steel Strike and Its Lessons* (New York: B. W. Huebsch, 1920); and Mary Heaton Vorse, *Men and Steel* (New York: Boni & Liveright, 1920).

Another new element during these years was close government surveillance, of which Mother Jones was very much aware. Military intelligence agents monitored speeches and meetings in San Francisco, in Chicago, Gary, Peoria, East St. Louis, and Rockford, Illinois, and in Eskdale and Charleston, West Virginia. In the Department of Justice, a young clerk named J. Edgar Hoover began to compile a dossier on her, largely because of the complaints of Governor John J. Cornwell of West Virginia, who looked on her organizing efforts in his state as subversive. The UMWA at the same time was filing complaints with the Justice Department about the denial of their right of free speech in Cornwell's West Virginia.[18]

The year 1921 was crucial in Mother Jones's career, for she achieved her greatest recognition as a labor leader in Mexico City, and she suffered her greatest defeat in the West Virginia coalfields.

The Pan American Federation of Labor scheduled its convention to meet in Mexico City in January 1921, and Mother Jones was invited to speak to the assembled delegates. Some time in 1920 she also received an invitation from the Mexican government to be the nation's guest during her stay in that country. One of the men whose cause she had championed in the days before Diaz was overthrown, Antonio Villarreal, was now minister of agriculture, and she knew other governmental leaders from the days of the revolution. Her visit would therefore give her a chance to renew old acquaintances as well as address the convention.

As the special train carrying her neared Mexico City, workers stopped it and overwhelmed her with flowers. She was escorted to her hotel, where servants, a car, and a chauffeur were put at her disposal. Her speech to the delegates was received enthusiastically, but Samuel Gompers, who had prudently turned the gavel over to teamster Daniel Tobin before her address, must have shuddered at her statement that organized labor shared the same spirit of unrest as the Bolsheviks. She and her companion Fred Mooney, secretary of District 17, made excursions in her government car to points around Mexico City and attended receptions given by President Obregon and Ambassador Dwight Morrow.[19]

The welcome of the Mexican officials was so warm that Mother Jones returned to Mexico in April, when a villa and servants were once more put at her disposal by the government. She made speeches in the

18. RG 65 Z0632S, 32351, 72761, 364074; RG 165 10110/70, 670, 988, 1241, 1627, 6–4; RG 174/280, 170/891; RG 174, 16/514A, 33/390, National Archives.

19. Pan American Federation of Labor, *Proceedings 1921* (Washington, D.C., 1921); J. William Hess, ed., *Struggle in the Coal Fields: The Autobiography of Fred Mooney* (Morgantown: West Virginia University Library, 1967), pp. 79–85.

industrial city of Orizaba and in Yucatan, apparently undeterred by the language barrier. She was rumored to be considering a permanent residence in Mexico, but her letters contain no such hint and refer more frequently to her uncertain health which she blamed partly on the altitude.

When Mother Jones reached West Virginia in the summer of 1921, she plunged immediately into a situation where violence had reached unprecedented proportions.[20] During her absence in Mexico the UMWA had increased its efforts to organize the nonunion mines in Mingo and Logan counties. The numerous murders and armed clashes of the last two years had provoked repeated declarations of martial law by Governors John J. Cornwell and Ephraim F. Morgan, along with requests for federal troops, which had been denied. Currently, another congressional investigation of conditions in West Virginia was in progress. But the union miners were unwilling to wait for the results and began arming themselves and gathering in large numbers for a march into Logan County. Fresh from her triumphant months in Mexico, Mother Jones at first encouraged the belligerent miners, but when the march threatened to get under way, involving at least five thousand armed miners and thousands of defenders on the other side, she reversed her stand. She addressed the miners gathered at Marmet, telling them that she had a telegram from President Warren G. Harding in which he promised to intervene to end the armed guard system in West Virginia. When doubts were expressed about the authenticity of the telegram, she appealed to President Keeney and Secretary Mooney of District 17 for support, but refused to allow them to see the telegram. The union officials then telegraphed to Washington and received a reply from President Harding's secretary that the president had sent no such telegram to Mother Jones, and they so informed a committee of the miners' army. The exposure of her deception badly damaged her influence with the miners. Although the urgings of other union leaders temporarily halted the march on Logan, it was resumed after a week. It culminated in the four-day battle of Blair Mountain, involving thousands of men on both sides; the toll of killed and wounded has never been precisely ascertained. Order was restored on September 4 only after federal troops and a detachment of the Army Air Corps had been sent to West Virginia.

Stunned at her betrayal by the district leaders, Mother Jones retreated to her room at the Powderly home in Washington and then

20. The postwar crisis in the West Virginia coal fields is most clearly narrated in Daniel P. Jordan, "The Mingo War: Labor Violence in the Southern West Virginia Coal Fields, 1919–1922," in Gary M. Fink and Merl E. Reed, eds., *Essays in Southern Labor History* (Westport, Conn.: Greenwood Press, 1977).

visited the John H. Walkers in Springfield, Illinois. Falling ill, she recovered partially and returned to Washington. In June she journeyed to Denver, but a recurrence of her illness sent her back to the capital. There her health worsened, and her life was despaired of. For two weeks in August 1922 she required around the clock nursing, but by 20 September she was declared out of danger, though still very weak. While offers of sympathy and financial assistance came in from unions across the country, she began a slow recovery.

During the last nine years of her life, illness and infirmity curtailed her activities, but she continued to maintain a travel schedule remarkable for a person of her age. Rheumatism made it increasingly difficult for her to walk, and many of her travels were made in search of weather conditions that would alleviate the periodic attacks. Two serious illnesses led to hospitalization and lengthening periods of recuperation. Nevertheless, she participated in strikes from time to time, continued to answer invitations to speak, wrote her autobiography, sat for a portrait bust by Jo Davidson, and used her influence with federal and state officials on behalf of imprisoned workers and old friends. After 1921 her official ties with the miners' union were severed. In a UMWA dominated by the dictatorial John L. Lewis, there was no place for an independent organizer like Mother Jones; when he was in firm control, he did not renew her appointment as organizer, and bad health prevented her attending the conventions even as a guest. Almost the only man at headquarters in whom she still had confidence was William Green, the secretary-treasurer, and to him she poured out her concern over the direction the union was taking and her fears about labor generally. She directed disparaging remarks at the character of current labor leaders, and she also deplored the increasing centralization and bureaucratization that saw national officers enjoying power and perquisites at the same time that the rank and file members, especially in mining, were losing jobs and the power to bargain.

By early 1923 Mother Jones's health had improved to the point that she was able to travel to Illinois to embark on a new project, the writing of her autobiography. After a visit with the Walkers in Springfield, she took up residence with Ed Nockles, secretary of the Chicago Federation of Labor, and began the task of putting words to paper. She continued to feel a major concern over the situation in West Virginia and in April felt well enough to go to Charleston to make a special plea to Governor Ephraim F. Morgan for miners who had been imprisoned for their part in the violence of recent years. She returned to Chicago to complete the autobiography during the summer.

In September she went to California to mount a three-month campaign to free Mathew Schmidt, convicted of complicity in the Los

Angeles *Times* bombing of 1910, from San Quentin prison. She returned to Washington in time to spend Christmas at the home of T. V. Powderly and began a similar lobbying effort with Governor Gifford Pinchot to secure the release of a prisoner from the Pennsylvania penitentiary. Another bout of pneumonia and constant pain from rheumatism led her to plan another trip to California, where she hoped her health would improve and she could renew her campaign to free Schmidt. At the end of March 1924 she traveled to Los Angeles by way of Charleston, West Virginia, and Chicago. Four months in the California sunshine brought about improvement in her health, and she accepted an invitation to address a Labor Day rally at Johnson City, Illinois, in September. The death of her old friend Terence V. Powderly while she was in California was a severe emotional blow.

The same pattern continued for the next two years, with the winter months spent in California and the spring and early summer with Emma Powderly in Washington. The semiannual trips gave her a chance to see old friends in Chicago. While the climate in California might be better, in Washington she was able on good days to visit the Department of Labor or AFL headquarters where she could get the latest news and occasionally preempt the services of a typist to help with her correspondence. In September 1926 she made her last public speech when she was the guest of honor at a Labor Day rally in Alliance, Ohio.

The winter in California was not so pleasant in 1927, for she fell ill again, but by May she had recovered enought to visit Bisbee, Arizona, where she had organized copper miners for the Western Federation of Miners two decades earlier. She planned to spend the next winter in Washington. On the train trip in November she fell ill and had to pass up her planned stop in Chicago. Just after her arrival in Washington, a crisis in her illness sent her to Garfield Hospital for a month's stay. Recovery at Emma Powderly's home proceeded slowly.

Among the frequent visitors there were Walter and Lillie May Burgess, who sometimes took her to their rural home near Hyattsville, Maryland, for a day's outing or an overnight stay. These visits turned into a permanent arrangement, and she spent the last two years of her life there as a guest, lovingly tended by Mrs. Burgess. She still enjoyed automobile trips into Hyattsville, and she even returned at last to the church which she had so often excoriated during her earlier career. She was looking forward to her "hundredth" birthday, 1 May 1930. For years she had planned a celebration in Chicago, but the state of her health made a trip out of the question; the Burgess home would have to be the place, and the Washington press and labor leaders would help to make it a grand occasion. Her deteriorating health imperiled the plans, but the day before the party she rallied. On the first of May she once more played the public role of agitator with touches of her old fire, but it was clear that the sands were running out. Through the summer her health was precarious, and in the fall it worsened. She began to have only intermittent periods of lucidity, and she died 30 November 1930. After a requiem mass at St. Gabriel's Church in Washington, her body was transported to the miners' cemetery in Mt. Olive, Illinois, for burial.[21]

So ended a long and restless life, conducted with single-minded purpose. The significance of the career of Mother Jones in twentieth-century America is difficult to assess because so much rested on the unrecorded spoken word. To her contemporaries, she was an agitator without peer, and if she did not bear within her the seeds of violence she showed a distinct affinity for it. She left no institutional monument, even though she brought many members to the UMWA and embodied a spirit that they cherished. As a strike leader she scored a few triumphs such as the organizing of the women in the breweries, but she was more frequently associated with lost or uncertain causes where the successes, if any, were limited. She may have had some impact on John D. Rockefeller, Jr., when, with the advice of William Lyon Mackenzie King and Ivy Lee, he created his company union policy after the Colorado strikes. Probably her most important contribution was her very personal role in bringing about congressional investigations of conditions in the mining areas of West Virginia, Michigan, and Colorado, another step toward the time when the federal government would be a countervailing force between big business and big labor. On the humanitarian side, many a man owed to her personal influence his release from imprisonment. Her speeches moved thousands of people to action or inspired them with a vision of the future, and the memory of her indomitable spirit has made her into a minor folk herione.

Since so little is known of her early life, a biographer can do no more than speculate about early influences. In general, her immigrant background and Catholic upbringing echo through her life. The only member of her family that she ever mentioned was her father, whom she extolled as a fighter for Irish nationalism. There is one religious figure who may have impressed the youthful Mary Harris. When in 1859 she accepted a position as a lay teacher in Monroe, Michigan, the convent that had established the school was going through a crisis. The founder of the order, Mother Theresa Maxis, found herself in dis-

---

21. Lillie May Burgess MSS; New York *Times,* 1, 4, 8, 9 December 1930; unidentified newspaper clippings, Mother Jones Papers.

agreement with the bishop of Detroit about the governance and direction of her order, and the differences were exacerbated by a jurisdictional dispute between the bishops of Detroit and Philadelphia. Mother Theresa was displaced and in effect exiled for nearly thirty years from the order that she had founded. The example of this dedicated and determined daughter of the church can hardly have failed to impress the young lay teacher, who left the convent school at the height of the crisis.[22] For all her later anticlericalism and profanity, Mother Jones saw herself as a sort of secular nun, her whole life consecrated to a holy cause, the gospel of socialistic trade unionism.

The letters in this volume are parts of what must have been a much larger correspondence, most of which has disappeared. Of the many letters sent to Mother Jones while she was imprisoned at Pratt, West Virginia, or the greetings to her at the time of her birthday celebration, only a handful remain. The disappearance of the bulk of her correspondence reflects in part her life and personality. Since she had no fixed home and believed in traveling light, she kept few letters permanently. Most were addressed to her at some union headquarters, and several references indicate that she would come into a union office, commandeer the services of a typist, and dispose of accumulated mail by dictating answers before destroying the mail that she did not wish to keep. The letters that have been saved are for the most part found in the private papers of some man whose institutional or political prominence has led archivists to preserve them.

The spoken, not the written, word was Mother Jones's forte. Generally, her letters were forceful and direct, but full of errors which can often be attributed to haste or carelessness. Her punctuation and capitalization were erratic. Her handwriting was distinctive and legible, even in her later years, but poorly formed letters and omissions occasionally puzzle the reader. For stationery, she used whatever was at hand, and the bulk of her letters appear on the letterhead of some union headquarters or on hotel stationery. She disliked the act of writing and whenever opportunity permitted she took advantage of secretarial assistance. The persistence of very obvious errors, such as three different spellings of the name Ryan in one letter, indicate that she did not reread letters once they were written. Her few interlined corrections usually dealt with the meaning of a passage rather than matters of form or grammar. Events of the moment, people, and their motives were her subjects, along with her own reactions; only occa-

22. For the career of Mother Theresa Maxis, see Sister M. Rosalita, *No Greater Service: The History of the Sisters, Servants of the Immaculate Heart of Mary* (Detroit, 1948), esp. pp. 130–238.

sionally did abstractions or subtleties concern her. She wrote with fluency and verve, but preferred to talk to people face to face. For all their gaps and deficiencies, her letters carry the reader headlong into protest rallies, confrontations in the streets, the inner circles of national labor unions, and the tent colonies where strikers fought their battles for recognition. Hers was an authentic voice from the barricades, giving a commentary on twentieth-century America that is rarely heard.

The starting point for any collector of Mother Jones's letters is the Mother Jones Collection at the Catholic University of America. It contains more newspaper clippings than letters, but the letters in this collection seem to have been preserved largely for their sentimental value. Therefore, though not numerous, they are useful in helping the reader to capture some of the emotional dimensions of their subject.

The Terence Vincent Powderly Collection, also at Catholic University, contains letters between Mother Jones and both Powderly and his wife Emma. For much of the period after 1900, the relationship with the Powderlys was the most stable in her life. She sometimes addressed him as "My dear son," and a room was kept permanently available for her at the Powderly home in Washington. Although she may have known him as early as the 1870s, no early correspondence has come to light. After 1900, Powderly's position as an official of the Immigration Bureau insured that he had a stenographer to make and file carbon copies of his letters, so that in some instances both sides of their correspondence is available. It might be thought that Powderly, whose Knights of Labor had generally eschewed strikes, and Mother Jones, who spent most of her life encouraging strikers, would not be compatible. But he was no longer active in the labor movement, even though he kept in touch with developments as an elder stateman. He and Mother Jones shared memories of men and incidents reaching back to the 1870s, and they seem to have accommodated themselves to living with their differences. He was quick to defend her when she attracted unfavorable comment, and he put his knowledge of the Washington bureaucracy at her disposal. She customarily referred to his house as "home," and even after his death in 1924 she depended on the kind offices of Emma Powderly as her health and vigor declined.

A third collection at Catholic University, the John Mitchell Papers, presents a different view of Mother Jones. As president of the UMWA, Mitchell appointed her as an official organizer for the union in 1900. Since his letters to her, as well as her frequent reports to him, have been preserved, the nature of their relationship is clearly revealed. She was a faithful lieutenant, complying with her superior's orders, and she seems to have seen herself as a kind of inspector general for him, evaluating conditions, men, and morale in the field. Their differences over policy in the Colorado strike of 1903 led to her resignation, but they enjoyed a good working relationship in their earlier association. However, she was never fully at ease with him personally, as she was with Powderly.

In the William B. Wilson Papers at the Historical Society of Pennsylvania and in the files of the Department of Labor, a closer personal relationship appears. She was quite capable of issuing a peremptory order to Wilson when he was secretary of labor to come from Washington to Chicago or to Calumet, Michigan, to intervene in strikes, and he was diplomatic enough to reject such importunities without impairing her regard. Like Powderly, he paved the way for visits with the president, and he gave her letters of introduction to influential political figures. Their mutual regard continued after he retired from public office, but their correspondence is most frequent when he was secretary-treasurer of the UMWA and in the earlier years of his tenure as secretary of labor.

During the years from 1904 to 1911, when Mother Jones's interest focused on socialism and the Mexican political exiles, the extant correspondence is thin. The papers of Thomas J. Morgan, preserved at the University of Chicago and at the University of Illinois, contain the largest number of her letters. They were old friends from the local political battles in Chicago in the 1880s, and Morgan was both a Socialist and a practicing attorney who helped her prepare her attack on J. Mahlon Barnes. Nearly all of the letters are concerned with the party dispute, and Morgan died shortly after her expulsion.

Mother Jones's activities frequently brought her into contact with state governors, either in confrontation where she represented striking workers or as a petitioner for the release of imprisoned men. Her two favorite governors were George W. P. Hunt of Arizona, a progressive Democrat for whom she campaigned in 1916, and Ephraim F. Morgan, a conservative Republican of West Virginia. Their treatment of her personally, rather than any political factors, seems to have determined her attitude toward them. Unfortunately, only a few of her exchanges with Hunt have been preserved, but both sides of her correspondence with Morgan over several years throw light on several obscure aspects of her career. She credited Morgan with warning her in time to try to persuade the armed miners in West Virginia to abandon their march against antiunion forces. He, in turn, felt that had she not been undermined by the district officials, she might have succeeded in diverting the men from their purpose. The conservative governor and the agitator seem to have been on excellent personal terms, and she frequently visited him in the governor's mansion in Charleston.

The papers of John Fitzpatrick, president of the Chicago Federation of Labor, have been preserved at the Chicago Historical Society. They contain a series of exchanges beginning in 1921 and continuing to the end of Mother Jones's life. Her letters to Fitzpatrick are sometimes addressed jointly to him and to Edward A. Nockles, secretary of the federation, in whose home she stayed while she was writing her autobiography, and the two men acted as executors of her will. Her earliest known association with Fitzpatrick was in 1919, when he headed the steel organizing committee, but she probably had been acquainted with both men earlier in their careers.

Her correspondence with William Green, for many years president of the American Federation of Labor, covers the years 1922–1924, when he was secretary-treasurer of the UMWA and before his elevation to the presidency of the federation. Green was the last of the old-timers still holding national office in the UMWA of John L. Lewis, and the letters are filled with her complaints about the current leadership in the labor movement.

The largest single collection of letters to and from Mother Jones is to be found in the John H. Walker Papers at the University of Illinois. If Terence V. Powderly was her "dear son," Walker might be considered her favorite grandson. They first became acquainted when the young organizer from Illinois came to West Virginia in 1901 to assist in the drive that she was directing to unionize the southern coal fields. She took to him immediately, and the warm feelings established then continued to the end of her life. Most of the letters belong to the period after 1916, and they sometimes reach weekly regularity in the 1920s. When his lobbying activities as president of the Illinois Federation of Labor made a permanent move to Springfield advisable, she advanced him money to help purchase a house, and her financial assistance also aided in the education of his daughter Esther. Mother Jones visited the Walkers for weeks at a time, particularly when she felt the need to recuperate after one of her strenuous speaking campaigns.

The other letters in this collection are drawn from many sources, often single items with no context. However, widely divergent sources sometimes complement one another. A number of letters have been resurrected from journalistic sources, since no originals have been found. Some of them, such as the open letter to Mrs. Potter Palmer of 12 January 1907, may have been mere bids for publicity, but they have been included as evidence of her concerns at a particular time, if not as genuine communications.

Since so many of Mother Jones's correspondents were officials of the UMWA, and she herself was employed by the union over a period of two decades, some knowledge of the structure of the organization at that time can give additional meaning to the letters that appear here.

Introduction

When the UMWA first employed her in 1900, the organization was ten years old and had the largest membership of any union, an "international" that included members in Canada as well as in the United States. It was divided into some twenty districts, whose boundaries frequently coincided with those of a state, so that District 12 was synonymous with Illinois. However, there were also districts based on the type of coal being mined, such as the anthracite district of eastern Pennsylvania. The districts were divided into geographical subdistricts. Each of these entities had its own set of officers. Bargaining between the union and associations of employers usually took place at the district level, but the Central Competitive Field, which included western Pennsylvania, Ohio, Indiana, and Illinois, was the most important in terms of production and union membership. Other district agreements were often tied to those worked out in the central field.

Yearly, later biennially, the members named delegates to an international convention which reviewed the state of the industry, set policies, and instructed the international officers who had previously been elected by the membership at large. During much of the time that Mother Jones was associated with the union, the central staff was small. The president and vice-president spent much time in travel, and the secretary-treasurer supervised the small headquarters staff in Indianapolis, as well as the UMWA *Journal.* The most important office post was statistician, the position from which John L. Lewis stepped into the vice-presidency. The miners maintained no permanent legal staff, although they added a publicity director and a professional economist on a consulting basis after 1912. Between conventions, policy decisions lay in the hands of the International Executive Board, consisting of one representative from each district. They met periodically and at the call of the president. Political maneuvering within the union was therefore focused on the control of the districts and the naming of the representatives to the executive board, with a separate system of election of the president, vice-president, and secretary-treasurer. The power of the president was limited, but by the strength of personality or the manipulation of the machinery of the union he might exert a dominating force. The president had the power to appoint international organizers, each of whom was nominally attached to a district, but who might be sent singly or in teams to carry out special organizing efforts. In addition, the president might appoint special organizers or representatives, and he might assign to special tasks organizers appointed by the districts. Presidents varied in their management of the international organizers. John Mitchell kept in close touch with their day to day activities. John P. White, on the other hand, left the assignment and supervision to his vice-president, Frank Hayes. John L. Lewis made effective use of the appointment of organizers and special representatives in his drive to dominate the UMWA.

John Mitchell appointed Mother Jones as an organizer for the UMWA in 1900, and she held the position until 1904. She had no official appointment during the presidency of T. L. Lewis, although she did attend conventions and sometimes addressed them. When John P. White took over the presidency in 1911, he again employed her as an international organizer, but there is no evidence that he gave her orders. She went where and when she chose, and drew her salary and expenses from the miners' organization. Frank Hayes, who succeeded White during the First World War, apparently followed the same lenient policy toward her. When John L. Lewis took over from Hayes, there is no record that he assigned her to any specific duties, but he did ask her to help in the work of the steel organizing committee of 1919 as part of the UMWA contribution to that effort. When Lewis was firmly in the saddle as president, he did not reappoint her as an organizer.

The majority of the correspondents in this collection were or had been officers of the UMWA, but Mother Jones stood on almost equal terms with the leaders of other unions. Most of these men were immigrants or the sons of immigrants, with obvious talents but frequently limited education, who moved quickly up through the ranks of their organizations and in many instances held regional or national office for thirty years. They were practical men, dedicated to the advancement of their crafts, and within the bounds of their institutions they wielded power and managed large groups of people skillfully. Their success depended on their ability to articulate the desires of their constituents, and many of them became powerful speakers, but few wrote with ease or grace. With such men Mother Jones was at home; she, too, had been an immigrant girl, was dedicated to the cause of organized labor, and lived by her tongue.

Editorial Practices

The purpose of the editor has been to present an accurate text of the correspondence of Mary Harris Jones. In general, the letters have been literally transcribed, with all their errors of spelling, grammar, and punctuation, but there are a few departures from this practice. In typed material, strikeovers and obvious reversals of letters, such as *ot* for *to,* have been corrected without notice. The addition of a hyphen or dash after a colon in salutations has been eliminated. Where handwriting presented uncertainties—for example, whether a capital or a small letter was intended—modern correct usage has been adopted. Unmistakable errors, however, have been left as they stand. The erratic punctuation and capitalization may sometimes demand a second reading, but the meaning is usually clear, and such passages present no more problems to a reader than the writings of e e cummings or don marquis.

The greatest liberties have been taken with the spacial arrangements of the documents, since there is no way to translate accurately the variations of different sizes of paper, of handwriting, or of typing. All letters have been put into the same general form, even when such uniformity entailed breaking a long line in two or moving a return address from the end of a letter to the beginning. In all these cases, however, the spelling and punctuation of the original have been preserved. Where superscript letters have been used, the word has been converted into an abbreviation by bringing the superscripts down to the normal line and adding a period; thus, *Sup'* becomes *Supt.* Spacing within lines has been indicated, but with no attempt at precise reproduction.

With the exceptions noted, all editorial intervention has been indicated by brackets. Mother Jones was a careless writer and frequently omitted words. The assumption has been made that the reader can supply these omissions as he would in any familiar correspondence, but the editor has not hesitated to introduce suggested readings in brackets when a failure to do so might make the passage incoherent. If a question mark follows words in brackets, the wording in the original is uncertain. If the handwriting is totally illegible, the number of unreadable words, if known, is included in the bracketed notation. Interlineations have been inserted in brackets at the point indicated in the original by carets, lines, or slashes, or at the choice of the editor if no location was marked. Marginal additions or comments have been treated in the same manner, if brief. Extensive marginalia have been transferred to the end of the letter, following the signature, as additional paragraphs identified by brackets and notes. In letters that presented special problems, departures from these general practices have been specified in footnotes.

The source of each letter follows the text; a list of the collections and their locations is given below.

Abbreviations

ALS	Autograph Letter Signed
TLS	Typed Letter Signed
TLC	Typed Letter Copy
D	Draft

AFL	American Federation of Labor
CIO	Congress of Industrial Organizations
IWW	Industrial Workers of the World
UMWA	United Mine Workers of America

Locations of Manuscript Collections

AFL Papers, Mining Department	State Historical Society of Wisconsin
William H. Amerland Papers	Minnesota Historical Society
Lillie May Burgess MSS	West Virginia University
Ida and Phil Callery Papers	Pittsburg State University
Eugene V. Debs Collection	Indiana State University
Finley Peter Dunne Papers	Library of Congress
John Fitzpatrick Papers	Chicago Historical Society
Adolph Germer Papers	State Historical Society of Wisconsin
William Green Papers	Ohio Historical Society
Haldeman MSS II	Indiana University
George W. P. Hunt Papers	Arizona State University
Mother Jones Papers	Catholic University of America
Justice Department Records	National Archives, Washington, D.C.
Labor Department Records	National Archives, Washington, D.C.
Henry Demarest Lloyd Papers	State Historical Society of Wisconsin
John Mitchell Papers	Catholic University of America
Thomas J. Mooney Papers	University of California

Ephraim F. Morgan Papers	West Virginia University
Thomas J. Morgan Papers	The Joseph Regenstein Library, University of Chicago
Thomas J. Morgan Papers	University of Illinois, Urbana
Terence V. Powderly Papers	Catholic University of America
Probate Records, Cook County	Chicago, Illinois
Ramos de Revolución Politica Interior, Correspondencias Varios	Archivo General de la Nación, Mexico City
Historical Collections and Labor Archives, Pattee Library	Pennsylvania State University Libraries, University Park, Pa.
Rockefeller Papers	Rockefeller Archive Center, Pocantico Hills, N.Y.
Socialist Party Papers	Duke University
State Department Records	National Archives, Washington, D.C.
Mrs. Philip Taft, Collector	New York University
Walker MSS	Indiana University
John H. Walker Papers	University of Illinois
West Virginia Collection	West Virginia University
William B. Wilson Papers	Pennsylvania Historical Society
Woodrow Wilson Papers	Library of Congress

THE CORRESPONDENCE OF MOTHER JONES

1900

To John Mitchell[1]

Prest. J Mitchell
Indianapolis Ind
Comrade Mitchell

I hasten to reply to your inquries. first B. James[2] told the blackest lie without one Shadow of foundation unless it was that which he found in his narrow brain. I consider James a dangerous man when he will Stoop to anything so base as to lie about his Brother to his Superior Officers. Duffy[3] is an honest Sober Straight forward fellow not a Stero-typed orator but the kind of a Soul that we need in these dark days. James Said to me that Duffy might go to H—— he be d—— if he would take any orders from him—— he Said he proposed to use every effort to down Duffy and he has I replied I regretted to see what Spirit I thought we had come to the time when we Should put aside petty bickering and work for the good of all I believe the organization is bigger than you or Duffy take your fight to the Street then come in and like men Shake hands his answer was that he would down Duffy with the organization.

He said he had the nomination for V. P. for De to the A. F. of L for Board Member for Prest of the District and an offer to be general rostabout but he can get Ninety-five dollars a month more than the U. M. W. gives him I told him he ought to take it I will Sum up the whole thing in these words—I consider James a very dangerous man in an organization there is no man whose Character he will not Stoop to blacken if he Stands in his way the Sooner he is moved the better for all concerned

I have been up to Carbondale to Vandling had a fine meeting—everything looks bright

You know you need news

Send any request to me. I am ever ready to help our poor helpless people Just Say the word and I am off Suffering Humanity needs our best efforts and we Should not Spare ourselves particularly the Slaves of the Caves need to be Saved.

Markle's[4] clerk went to Hungarian the other day ask the H to Sign a paper the H replied John Mitchell look after my bis he bring me paper me sign you me no sign you Markle man for bis he no good for me me

3

get John Mitchell look for me *good* no you—Will leave for Virginia Sunday or Monday   With best wishes for your health and happiness I am fraternally yours

Mother

The best interest of the organization must be looked at first last and always   I have watched Slosson[5] closely find him a hard honest worker   his people are true to him

A Pointer

James and Louis[6] left Indianapolis togather   from some things he droped keep your Eyes open at the Convention

I will forward Some matters to you to night but after reading return to Prest. Duffy in McAdoo if you think best.

Mother

ALS (John Mitchell Papers)

1. John Mitchell (1870–1919), president of the UMWA, 1898–1908, appointed Mother Jones to the position of international organizer in 1900, and she reported directly to him on her activities.

2. Benjamin James of Jeansville, Pennsylvania, was a member of the executive board of the UMWA.

3. Thomas Duffy of McAdoo, Pennsylvania, was president of District 7 of the UMWA.

4. Probably John Markle, mine operator for the George B. Markle Company.

5. Possibly Anthony Schlosser, an international organizer.

6. Possibly T. L. Lewis, vice-president of the UMWA.

From John Mitchell

December 3rd, [1900]

Mrs. Mary Jones,
Hazleton, Pa.
Dear Mother:

I am in receipt of your two letters of recent date, which I have read with interest and apprehension.

I cannot imagine how a man who has been trusted as much as James can find it in his heart to be either ungrateful to his friends or untrue to the movement. Every upward step he has taken since he left the times has been by the assistance of myself and other friends. I have received information from other sources which connects and corresponds with what you say; and in consideration of all these circumstances I think it better for you to remain in the Hazleton field for some time, although I counted very much upon you services in West Virginia; and I shall be glad if you will keep me informed of the exact status of affairs, because you know there are very few people whom it is absolutely safe to take into one's confidence.

I shall set a movement on foot to get information which will probably prove of great value to us should anything occur of a serious nature.

Wishing you every success, I am,

Yours truly,
[John Mitchell]
President U. M. W. of A.

TLC (John Mitchell Papers)

From Eugene V. Debs[1]

Terre Haute, Ind.
Jan. 28th 1901

Dear Mother Jones:

I am very sorry I could not be with you this afternoon, particularly on your own account. But it could not be otherwise and so I yield without regret. In a day or two I leave to fulfill my Wisconsin appointments. When you get through at Indianapolis I wish you would drop me a line here and advise me of your address so I can write you about a little business matter in which we can be of mutual service besides helping the cause. I am trying to build up a little book business out of which to make a living so that I shall not have to accept anything from any source for any service I may render the cause. I feel confident you can help me a little and at the same time help yourself as well as the movement.

I have been reading the papers and as usual find myself the victim of calumny. I have no complaint to make, but it does seem as if there should be a limit to such cruel outrages. The press dispatches spread the report broadcast that the statement was made on the floor of the convention that a Pennsylvania delegate collected money from starving miners for me and that I accepted it all. Of course the presumption is that a vast sum was paid me and that it was gouged from the lives of the famishing Miners. I can scarcely belive that such a villainous false-hood was uttered, and yet the effect with the general public is the same and I am once more freshly nailed to the cross. But I can stand it without a trace of resentment and if I can ever give a hand to the Miners in any struggle, if that hand is not feely extended as it has always been in the past, it will be because it is paralyzed.

You know without my telling you that I did not accept one dollar for my service from anyone and that with the exception of a trifling part of my railroad fare, I paid all my own expenses besides. If any statement to the contrary is made it is maliciously false and in that case I desire you to ask the author of the statement how much money he gave me and if he names the amount, then challenge him to produce the receipt for it. If the press statement is correct the author of the statement is a self confessed criminal. He stands condemned out of his own lying mouth. What right had he to collect money from starving miners? and if he did so, is he not infamous to an extent that his word has no value? Next, is it likely that starving miners have any money?

Then again, on whom was he drawing for his own living expenses? Perhaps the operators might answer this latter question.

You have known me many years and you know if I would in any extremity take money from a striking starving miner. I would first destroy myself. I must correct you on a point touching the statement made by you as reported by the press in regard to the charges that were circulated about certain Labor Leaders receiving large sums of money for alleged services to striking miners in '97. Those reports originated at the Nashville Convention of the A. F. of L. held that year. The matter was discussed and charges and insinuations were made on the floor of that convention and they were exaggerated and telegraphed over the country. The files of the Nashville papers which were sent me at the time report the matter fully. Mailly, who was there at the time, will doubtless remember all about it. My name was included with the rest and not one was there to rescue it from the slander. I have had a number of personal apologies since in regard to it. The statements were made not at the Columbus convention of Miners but at the National Convention of the A. F. of L. I am writing this simply for your information and not because I desire any defense or vindication. That will come to me in good time. That I am on all occasions made the target for calumny is simple evidence of the fact that the capitalist press is aware that I cannot be bribed or bullied and that therefore I must be undermined my slander; and that delegates to Labor Conventions are the active instrumentalities in coining and circulating such calumnies simply shows that the capitalist class and their corrupt political bosses have their miserable tools in the councils of Labor to keep the enslaved workers securely manacled and to prevent any ray of emancipating light from pentrating their dismal dungeons.

Ah, but Socialism cannot be kept out a Labor organization any more than the rays of the rising sun can be prevented from dispelling the mists of darkness. Hail to Socialism, in which the miner can lift his bowed form from the earth and stand erect, a new being throbbing with immortal life.

I thank you from a grateful heart for your kindness Mrs. Debs joins me. Our only complaint is that you are too generous by far. Give Mitchell, Wilson, Scott and all the boys my cordial greetings and best wishes, and believe me ever

Yours sincerely
Eugene V. Debs

ALS (William B. Wilson Papers)
1. Eugene Victor Debs (1855–1926), five times Socialist candidate for president of the United States.

From John Mitchell

St. Charles Hotel, Scranton, Pa.,
April 1st, 1901

Mrs. Mary Jones,
Corning, O.

Dear Mother:

District No. 1 will hold a convention at Archbald on Monday, April 8th: the people of Archbald will have a celebration on that date, and are very anxious for you to attend. I promised them that I would write you requesting you to be there, and I hope that you will arrange your affairs so as to reach Archbald on time.

There will be some important matters come up in the convention regarding the antagonistic and unfriendly attitude of the Scrantonian. You, of course, know that they have been making vacious attacks on me; and I have instituted legal proceedings against Mr. Little, charging him with criminal libel, and hope to be able to send him to prison. I know that many people think that I should pay no attention to such unscrupulous attacks; but I feel that I cannot permit anyone to question my honor, even if it costs me all of the savings of my life time. While all who know him look upon him with distrust and suspicion, yet there are always those among the workers who are always ready to believe any false statements that are made against the officials of labor organizations. If your views are in accord with my own I think it would be advisable for you to attend meetings in District No. 1, and particularly in the vicinity of Scranton, and show this fellow up in his true light. While I have never asked anything from my craftsmen more than they agree to pay me, yet I do believe that I deserve to be respected by the anthracite miners.

Trusting that you will reach this region in time for the convention Monday, I am, with kind regards,

Yours truly,
[John Mitchell]
President U. M. W. of A.

TLC (John Mitchell Papers)

To John Mitchell

St. Charles Hotel, Scranton, Pa.,
Apr. 5 1901

To Prest. John Mitchell
Scranton, Pa.
Dear Comrade

Just got your letter this morning. There was a fine meeting here Haskins was here poor boy he has his hands full—I gave them a few words about the movement you proposed to our many comrades in Lattermer I tourned the audiance my way regret I could not go to other places that they wanted but I promised with your permission to come the 4th of July.

You have done just what you should have done. Now you will find out who has been the Traitor in the miners camp. They will be brought to the front by this trial while the traitors were laying traps to ruin the character of their officials they were not shrewed enough to cover up their tracks Now they should be showen up to the miners You owe this to your children.

Let me say so long as you are the John Mitchell you are I'll be with you. I will be in Scranton in a day or two. I leave here to day but will stop in Pittsburg a day or so

Take care of your health

fraternally yours
Mother

ALS (John Mitchell Papers)

From Elizabeth C. Morris

April 6, 1901.

Mother Mary Jones,
Scranton, Pa.
My Dear Mother Jones:

Your letter of recent date written from Ohio to President Mitchell is received and will be brought to Mr. Mitchell's attention upon his return to the office in a day or two.

Hoping you are well, I am with best wishes,

Yours very truly,
[Elizabeth C. Morris]
Secretary to the President

TLC (John Mitchell Papers)

9

To John Mitchell

Scranton, Pa.,
Apr the 13th 1901

Comrade Mitchell

The boys from St Louis have asked me to speak there on the 16th of June the anniversary of the murder of our boys last summer   I consented provided you did. Then at the same time I can go to Ohio— Now let me say that you can make your own arrangements for me without consulting me   I am always ready   You will not have to write for my consent.

The convention was o. k. The corporation tools were there   I went for them and laid them out in good style. I want to say they took back water had little to say after that morning   When brother Demsey[1] sees you he will tell how quickly they shut up   Prest Nichol[2] was called home his boy was not expected to live   I have not heard from him since   I have not had a minute to spare since I got back there is so much to do one hardly knows where to begin   Let me know if I can go to St Louis   then I will inform the boys   Keep up courage   Never mind what the tools of capitalism do   the time will come when right will prevail—take care of your health

fraternally yours
Mother

ALS (John Mitchell Papers)
    1. Probably John T. Dempsey, secretary of District 1, UMWA.
    2. Thomas D. Nichols, president of District 1, UMWA.

To John Mitchell

Sewell W. Virginia
July the 31st 1901

My dear Comrade Mitchell

For some reason which I cannot account for I have neglected writing you   you asked why I did not get to Lassalle   one reason I found when I got to St Louis I could not make connections and return to Bellville. They had made their time long in May I did feel that it would be dealing fair with them not to keep my word   Then the Clay Miners at the Brick yards were on a strike. They came in to St Louis and beged me to go out and help them. They had music and flags and a big parade of men women and children they [one word illegible] in a few days after that and I knew that you would rather see those poor wretches turn out than have me at Lassalle

I regreted not having seen you when at Indianapolis but I presume

Mr. Wilson told you the object of my visit. I regreted to find the conditions of the Local in York as I did those boys promised me that they would abide by the desicion of the National they only wanted to be right but they feel they have been unfairly dealt with   I think so the fact that three Locals from Macdoo made up the call for that convention to annal their charter looks to me rather suspicious and let me give you my honest judgment of the move   the Company are behind the Prest and has worked on Pres Duffys religious superstition   I told Pes. Duffy thing looked suspicious and had to be handled with care   The women are taking a hand in it. If could have remained with them I think I could have healed up the breach   There is no question in my mind but what it is a shrewd move of the Co. if that Local is broke up in a row it will spread   it has reached to Silver Brook the boys there came to me about it. I wish I could see you before the Board meet   I am familiar with some things that has not been explained to you

I enclose a letter from our mutual friend which will explain itself. I know him to the hearts core believe him to be a true friend of yours   if he was not I would use my best efforts to make him one   I intended sending this long ago you will over look my neglience

We were up the mountain at S Caperton last night and came down the goat path after 12 o'clock   I had to slide down most of it. My bones are all sore today   Boscowell is sick after his trip and Ed Cahill[1] says if they never come into the union I wont go up there again. One *Gen Manager* did not go with us he went to Charleston. The Ill boys are good hard workers but they are beginning to realize this is not the smoothest field in the country to work in   I hope your little is better   take good care of your own health

> Believe me always faithfully fraternally yours
> Mother

ALS (John Mitchell Papers)
   1. Samuel Boskill and Edward Cahill were both international organizers.

From John Mitchell

August 3, [1901]

Mother Mary Jones,
Sewell, W. Va.
Dear Mother:

Your communication of July 31st, with enclosure from 'Gene Debs, is received. I have read both of the letters with keen interest.

I note the reason which kept you away from LaSalle; and desire to say that in my judgment you acted wisely.

I think, Mother, that you should be careful in climbing those hills in West Virginia, as you certainly are not physically able to take risks when the men who are there are not able to stand it. Can you not hire a horse or a buggy or something to take you up and down those hills?

I am well aware that the work in West Virginia is discouraging; but we shall either be compelled to organize West Virginia this year or face a reduction in wages in our next Inter-State convention. I have a plan outlined for West Virginia which I think will work all right; I shall submit it to the Executive Board at their meeting next Monday; and if it is approved I shall then acquaint all organizers in that state with the plan of procedure.

Referring to the letter from Brother Debs, I note that he says that he has faith in me, but expresses the wish that I were strong enough to point out and expose the rotten sub-leadership in the miners' organization. I am free to confess that I do not understand what 'Gene [*second page of letter is missing*]. not cause me any concern, as I was not looking for personal credit, and if the interests of our craftsmen were safeguarded I should not have cared who received the credit for it.

Wishing you every success, I am, with love and respect,

Yours truly,
[John Mitchell]
President U. M. W. of A.

TLC (John Mitchell Papers)

From William Warner[1]

Clarksburg, W. Va.
Aug 8, 1901.

Dear Mother Jones,

I am informed of a statement Mother, that you told Secy. Wilson that I had advised Albert Manka[2] to accept money from the coal companies of this region, which resulted in President Mitchell instructing Geo Purcell to inquire into the facts. I have not been informed officially anything about this, nor of the results of any inquiry. I am not given to believing everything I hear, because many things I have left go by unnoticed.

I hope it is not true, if you did not say it, it is wrong that any such statement should be attributed to you.

If it is true, then I have been vitally wronged, inasmuch as I was not informed of it being against me. I wish to hear the truth from you. I remember of you and I talking of such a statement being made to you by Manka himself. You did not indicate to me, that you believed any truth in it, of any wrong on my part, or that you would tell anything to the National Office, that would result in such of an affair. I remember of speaking to you of many other wrongs Your actions and expressions, indicated plainly to me, that your influence would be used to wipe out wrong, and not to add too, wrong. I have always been loyal and true to you, and will beleive nothing until I hear from you. I hope you will realize that I am doing right by writeng you. To work successfully for labors cause, the leaders should do no wrong to each other. I have a few dollars of money of yours, and if this reaches you and you tell me where to send it too, I will do so.

I have written you several letters and have received no reply.

Yours Truly,
Wm. Warner.

ALS (William B. Wilson Papers)

1. William Warner, a UMWA organizer, had led the strike of the Maryland miners in 1900, when Mother Jones was an associate in the field. Later in life he became a mine superintendent.

2. Albert Manka, like Warner an international organizer, had worked in West Virginia the preceding year, when Warner was still involved in the Maryland strike.

From William Warner

Clarksburg W. Va.
Aug 13. 1901.

My dear Mother Jones.

I received your letter, and glad to hear from you, and carefully considered its contents. I agree, with all the sentiments you expressed. I deem it unnecessary, to state that my experience, in the labor movement my principle of loyalty, and sense of justice enables me, as well as any person, to recognize what is right and what is wrong.

I need not take a back seat from any person living, when it comes to recognizing what is right and the interest of our people. Of course you should keep no secret from Secy Wilson. I find no fault in you telling him every word Manka told you, are anything else you thought of interest. My letter to you, registered no objection on that score. But if the impression was left on Secy Wilsons mind that I advised any one to accept a bribe, and if the same impression was transfered to Pres Mitchell, which resulted in an inquiry, then undoubtly it was an infamous wrong to me.

I sincerely appreciate your statement that you did not beleive such a statement as Manka made. The information I received, gave me no understanding of what any persons belief was, but simply that an inquiry was made, without my knowledge, of an infamous statement that

I was supposed to have made, which makes by blood boil. If no wrong exists in such a transaction, then Almighty God, has given me a wrong power of conception. I dont beleive God would do that.

I have received a letter from Secy Wilson regarding it. Your statement that you did not beleive Manka, or beleive me guilty of this wrong I appreciate, but it gives me no assurance of what Mitchell or Wilson beleives. I trust they dont beleive it. And sincerely hope that this misconception of fellow man, will cease.

It is not true, that I pay to much attention to little things. This is not a little thing but it is to me as serious as life itself.

I can cite to you many greivious things which I have left pass almost unnoticed. I have too often been attacked, for nothing and by persons, who are themselves guilty of sufficient wrong to sink them into perdition. I also can, recognize my shortcomings and while recognizing the shortcomings of others, I never mailcously attacked others for their mistakes, when I myself could have done no better. No *Mother* I know if all my associates treat me, with justice I can and will always return justice. I have not been treated with justice by many, with whom I have dealt with with a most honest heart, some I would have given my life for them. I would give my life to-day to accomplish the principle, I hold.

No Mother, I am not a victim of any imagination, nor am I given to notice little things. But I have seriously experienced the deceit and treachery of my fellow man. It is that, I have come to recognize as labors enemy, and not Capitalism. Capital is only labors creature. In conclusion, I assure you, that this affair henceforth will not burden me, it will only be an additional lesson to my lifes experience. I am glad to hear of your progress. We have thoroughly unionized Clarksburg. Will tell Tom of all your request.

Hoping this will reach you.

I am most sincerely

Yours
Wm. Warner

ALS (William B. Wilson Papers)

From William Warner

Clarksburg, W. Wa.,
Aug. 18. 1901

Dear Mother Jones.

It seems that the statement, that I advised Manka to accept bribes, has had effect. Pres Mitchell has notified me, that my employed will end with this month.

It leaves me in bad shape without any chance to find employment and I am in debt as a result of my efforts to avoid going to prison last January. I have always worked honestly to do my duty, and God is witness, that I am guilty of any wrong, except mistakes of any ordinary man. I am given no chance to establish the truth, or to face those who have been the cause of createing, wrong and untruthful impressions about me.

The position I find myself in now, after nine years of earnest work for the Miners always trying to do right is enough to drive me mad and to suicide   If I only had one months time to find work, it would not be so bad.

Mother, if you beleive, that I am honest, will you favor me by writing to Pres Mitchell or Secy Wilson and use your influence, to get me a chance to find work. I did would have thought that any body would beleive, that I would advise any would to accept bribes. And especially, why should such a man as Manka be allowed to cause such a wrong against me   Surely I have been more faithful and of more good than he has been.

If you will do this for me, you know I will appreciate it.

Yours truly,
Wm. Warner

ALS (William B. Wilson Papers)

To John Mitchell

Sewell West Virginia
Oct. the 20th/01

My dear Comrade Mitchell

Have to let you know what I did yesterday. I told you what Lang[1] did on the night of the 7th   The miners themselves arranged a meeting for me at Redash Mine for Sunday the 20th   John L. told I could not speak. I sent L word I was going there to speak and he could bring Sheriff Judge and Jury   I told lang there was not enough men in West Virginia to stop me   At the apointed time I was there   So was my audiance   they came from all over the mountains for ten miles   John L did not show up   Needless to state he won't interfere again. I had the crowed at fever heat they cheared for the U. M. W. and for myself all arouse and I read the obligation to them   They paid their dues. Sect. Wilson has the money for their Charters. As many as ten camps came and asked me to come up and organize them   I have a good Budie in Walker[2] he is a fine fellow workes hard and faithful   I wished I had four more men like him in here   You can rest content that J L got thrown down not by the hands of the miners but by the toung of a woman. The fellow feels so shamed he holds his head down. The whole country is laughing at him

Good look to the cause of the oppressed.

fraternally yours
Mother

I am just going to start to beury for a meeting

I had to walk 6 miles up the track   After hiking long my poor feet are so sore

ALS (John Mitchell Papers)

1. John Laing (1865–1943), superintendent of the Rush Run Mine and later owner and operator of several mines. He served as head of the West Virginia Department of Mines, 1908–1913.

2. John Hunter Walker (1872–1955), a national organizer from Illinois, later became president of the Illinois Federation of Labor.

To William Bauchop Wilson[1]

Sewell West Virginia
Nov the 15th [1901]

My dear Comrade Wilson

I note all you say about making war on the forces   I realize it is not not [sic] the best policy but if you could see what I see you would not blame me. You know I pour my whole soul out to you

John Walker and myself are getting this New River organized   The whole place is stired up for organization   It is creating a jealosy in the minds of some who have made a failure of their own district   Now they are laying their plans to get a hold of this place and do as they did on Kanawha   Tear down what had been done here   I want to tell you that if Chris Evans[2] send Burk[3] in here that I will leave the field   I have a good deal to tell you when I see you and I think Walker will return to Ill. You nor the Prest do not know all. I will fight for right even if those traitors stab me to the heart.

Well I went to a meeting alone Wensday night and organized the whole camp   Take the $15.00 out of my salary. I did not get done untill after Eleven OClock   Then I walked up the track one mile and a quarter   Frank freeman had promised to meet me but the General Manager would not let him come, and Boskill had gone up Thurman Mountain   I had to divide up so as to get what work we could on this side of the River before the Convention   This is not a safe place for the men to go alone not to talk of me but its alright I did work they failed to do for the poor slaves I have come to the final conclusion that those fellows dont want a woman in the field   I will have a talk with

you both when at Huntington in another month   All of New River
will be organized Provided we are left to work together I mean Walker
and I and freeman   Write me when you can   it is the only comfort I
have to hear from you and that noble soul Geon [sic] D— It will all
come right some day

fraternally yours
Mother

ALS (William B. Wilson Papers)

   1. William Bauchop Wilson (1862–1934), secretary of the UMWA; later congressman
and first U.S. secretary of labor (1913–1921).
   2. Chris Evans, a longtime union official, was currently serving as statistician for the
UMWA.
   3. Thomas Burke, executive board member of the UMWA.

To John Mitchell

Sewell West Virginia
Monday 12/2/01

My dear Mr Mitchell

   I have hesitated to add to your already heavy burden let me tell you
I am not surprised West Virginia has not been organized.

   I have well grounded suspicions that Boskill is in the hands of our
enemies. It would be to the best interest of the organization to move
him at once.   for several months I have watched him without anyone
knowing that I had any suspicions nor do anyone know it now   I
cannot go over the field here in this letter to you. I thought that good
motherly council might keep him on the right track but some *natures
are rotton* to the core   here is one

   We had a fine meeting yesterday   John went to Arbuckle this
morning   he is one of Gods noble boys

   I leave for Norton tomorrow with some regrets as the work here
needs me for another month then I could go way and stay. Keep up
courage   everything will be alright and Virginia will be with us   the
boys are responding noblely

Sincerely fraternally yours in the Cause
Mother

ALS (John Mitchell Papers)

1901

From Thomas Haggerty[1]

Reynoldsville Pa
Dec the 9 1901

Der Mother Jones

I write to inform you that I had hoped by this tim you would have been able to have made your way to Reynoldsville according to both telegrams and letters I made arrangements for you to speak and you would have had a rousing meeting but unfortenly you was Debared from coming now Mother Jones you will not be able to do much until after the Holladays and I hope you will see your way clear to com here about Christmas time if so let me know I don think I will return to W Va til after new years Com if you can as these People is anishius for you aspishely the textile workers

Hoping to here from you within the next few days I am yours verry trouly

Thomas Haggerty

Write soon

ALS (William B. Wilson Papers)

1. Thomas Haggerty (1865–1946), member of the executive board of the UMWA from Pennsylvania.

From John Mitchell

St. Charles Hotel, Scranton, Pa.,
December 11, [1901]

Mother Mary Jones
Coeburn, Va.

My dear Mother:

Your letter reaches me at Scranton, where I am attending the convention of the American Federation of Labor. As I am very busy I shall not attempt to reply at great length.

I received a letter from John telling me about Boskill. I wired Chris telling him to change Boskill from the District in which he was employed and place some one else there to help John while you are absent. I thank you very much for keeping me informed of the true condition of affairs and of the actions of those who are remiss in their duty. Just as soon as I can get at it I shall displace Boskill altogether; to say the least he is a very unsatisfactory field worker.

Trusting that your mission in the Norton District will prove helpful in terminating the strike now on there, I am, with best wishes,

Yours truly,
[John Mitchell]
President U. M. W. of A.

P. S. I met our friend Mailley[1] here and had a brief but pleasant conversation with him.

TLC (John Mitchell Papers)
1. William Mailly (1871–1912), a prominent Socialist, later party secretary.

To John Mitchell

Montgomary West Virginia
2. 7. 1902

My dear Comrade

Owing to the frightful weather we have had I have very little of importance I have not been doing much for the last few days only getting nervous. There are so many calls from all quarters [I] cannot reach them owing to the waters being up My boys are doing good work. We meet every Monday morning and hold a council—outline our work for the week so that each worker will know where to go and all know where the others are The first fellow who goes into a Saloon will be court marsheled and put in Irons for a week. We have no drinking every move must be strictly business. All are in Harmony and there is Some pleasure in doing the work every night if we are near each other we gather in the General Managers Room (Thats me) and [discuss?] things in general Change the program if we think best We have a big Mass Meeting billed for next Sunday at Brooklin I expect to have a clash with John Lang. Rest assured it will be the last one We are going to organize that camp next Sunday. I have my crowed There are some noble fellows in here

Comrade Mitchell, I am very surprised at the statement the Ill. boys made as to the amount of money it would take If Ill gives you $50000 and leave you pick the men I will give you this State organized inside of a year They had wheels in their heads—That to say the least of it is poor policy. We give the enemy his weapon to strike us with The operators say in the statement of their own men they have in field.

Then some Board Member said during the National Convention that the output of coal was *umlimated* So was the *Ignorance of the West Virginia Miners* That is an outrages statement for any man to make whom those miners are paying We are sent out to raise our craftsmen in the public mind and not lower them. If the author of that expression would look at home to my knowledge he would find as much Ignorance at his door as in West Virginia Kiss the babies for me when you go home.

Mother

ALS (John Mitchell Papers)

To William B. Wilson

Sewell West Virginia
2nd 19th 1902

Dear Comrade Wilson

Here I am in this God Cursed Monopolistic State. With all its dismal forbodings I feel that there is a ray of sunshine breaking for those so long in bondage.

Yesterday there were 300 miners young and old at Thurmond when the train pulled in they heard I was on they jumped on all rushed to get my hand and the cry of Mother you are going to stay with us went up from young and old   The meeting was pathetotic   black and white alike rushed to grasp my hand   the conductor wept he said it was the most touching seen he had ever witnessed   they had brought the body of a comrade who got killed by a fall of slate. They were shipping the body home. They had their U M W buttons on and were not afraid or ashamed to wear it   When I look back at six short months ago and compare then and now   These men were afraid to look at me or Comrade Walker but today they are realizing they are men and have some rights on this earth. Some day they will let their masters know that. Money is not all man lives for

For all my weary tramps in the dead of night counting the rails on the R R track at walking many miles after a meeting with those slaves of the dismal caves that meeting has compensated for all I would not exchange that meeting for all the palaces or millions earth has   The affection that came from their weary hearts beamed out of their eyes dimed by the darkness of earth caverns meant volumes for the future generation as William Morris says. in days to come how Bishop Hoben[1] and Ireland[2] will stop a while and ponder on their Hypocry in those bitter days of old when they drank wine and worshiped at the God cursed gold. If Arch Bishop Ireland-Potter could witness that meeting of young men with the old grey headed dispised labor agatater they would tell Morgan give all you have to the poor and from henceforth walk in Christs foot paths.

everything looks good here   Arnbucle boys are most all lined up they told me they had over three hundred members   I promised them to go up next meeting night   I have not been on the Kanawha yet for I find work to do here untill the weather settles.

hope Agness[3] got there safe

I had a long talk with Max   Spoke for the boys in Erie and believe they will win out there   The Long Shore Men Shore Men [sic] are getting sore at D. Keefe   their getting on to him you can't fool them all the time.

1902

My poor people in Arnot were at war again Well I need not tell you I gave lincoln all he looked for it is a God blessing he is gone.

I ran up to N. York. Just the day they were going to hold that Indignation Meeting I got our people to have nothing to do with it. They agreed not there were no speakers that amounted to anything. While there was a good house it died out for the lac of speakers the thing was got up by [soareheads?] The papers have been giving it to our friend Tillet poor jovial good hearted fellow I heard from some of our boys he was mixed up in some women scandel I did not [ask?] for information its the old old story of the race

I had a long talk with Bishop Hoben he had been up dedicating a church that Schwab[4] gave to the Catholics Sure the Bishop and Schwab dined together he gave me a synopsis of their diner talk they had wined and dined on the backs of the robbed of Homested all in the name of *Christ the Parasites*

They talked of labor leaders Schwab said he did not have any confidence in Shaffer some others "but he said for that man Mitchell I have the highest regard he is the soul of honor true to the people he represent he will fight for the last inch that is theirs concede to his oponent only what he believes to be his" The Bishop said he was glad to hear him say what he did he told the Bishop he did not oppose organization it was the combination

I told the B—— that Schwab lied Why did he send his lap-dog to watch the 70 men who started to organize when he found those men organized he blacklisted them I told the Bishop they all become filled up humanities interest when they were filling their stomach at our expense (*Dam* that kind of Reliegion)

Mother

ALS (William B. Wilson Papers)
1. Michael John Hoban (1853–1926), bishop of Scranton.
2. John Ireland (1838–1918), archbishop of St. Paul.
3. Agnes Hart Wilson served as her father's secretary.
4. Charles Michael Schwab (1862–1939), president of the U.S. Steel Corporation.

To John Mitchell

Montgomary WV
2n 27th 1902

Comrade Mitchell

I am at the old post with plenty of hard work ahed

Last night Brother Carrell[1] and myself made inroads on the Kanawha Meet with good success lined up old Morris Creek There are

some fine boys there   I think that we will give you this River organized by the 1st of May.

I spoke at Mount Hope last Sunday   had a tremendous Mass
Meeting   Spoke at Glen Jean Sat night the result of which brought 64
members to the U—that practically takes in every miner in Squire
Collins[2] mines

Monday and Tues at Armbucle have most all of the miners in the
Local   The Boys are full of enthusiasm ready to fight when you say
so. Last night at Morris Creek   Tonight Montgomary   Tomorrow at
Union. it has been frightful weather   Mud up to my knees   hard
Tromping but it has been done with good grace   Who would not
Tramp for the young boys and break their chains   My heart goes out
to these boys   We are doing good work   don't want a general
Manager   get along just as well without   The organization can save
that money   This man Carrell is doing good work   I have not much
confidence in this fellow Davis   I do not know where he got his Training but he is a clear cut *T L. Man*[3] and is leaving not stone unturned to
make others the same   I am watching this fellow with all my eyes

Rend[4] is importing men in here   Serving the U boys mean gives
them no cars while he gives to others all the cars. I have requested the
boys to send in their Tax to National

Rend discharged the President of the local   While I am not in favor
of taking those fellows up and carring them in our arms but I do think
this fellow can do good work   he is honest inteligent and while Carrell
and I are out he is one of the men we can trust   There are so many
places over there that have to be looked after every meeting night and
I feel he would do good work besides taking care of his local. There
are over 250 men in the Local they seem to have so much confidence
in him I fear if he would leave it might go back.

Rend imported some men in here   Some one I wont say who but
you can guess sugested to a few fellows to organize a Mulligan Brigade. Which they did. one night they served notice on the imported
fellows to get out of the Camp by three oclock in the morning all were
gone and the fellow who brought them in *Scadadled* with   They have
not showed up since nor do I think they will   Say it was fun to hear
the young bloods tell how they did it   They have adopted the same in
other camps

I am not very well today   I had a frightful walk last night in mud
and rained like fury   So I say good bye with God bless and spare you
to those who sadly need your guidance   Believe me always fraternally
yours

Mother

ALS (John Mitchell Papers)

    1. Probably J. W. Carroll, a national organizer for the UMWA.

    2. Justus Collins, a Cincinnati coal operator with extensive West Virginia interests.

    3. Refers to T. L. Lewis, vice-president of the UMWA, rival of John Mitchell and his successor as president.

    4. W.P. Rend, operator of several mines on land leased from W. R. Thurmond.

From John Mitchell

Hotel Fey, Peoria, Ill.,
March 6, 1902.

Mother Mary Jones,
Montgomery, W. Va.
My dear Mother:

Your favor dated February 27th has just been forwarded to me at Peoria, where I am attending the Illinois joint convention.

I have read with much interest the result of your meetings on the Kanawha, and I am glad to note the success which has crowned your efforts. I sincerely hope that the miners of West Virginia will be governed by the advice you give them.

I am very much worried at the outlook in Illinois; the joint convention has been in session for nearly two weeks, and the prospects of a settlement appear remote. I fear very much that we shall have a strike of considerable magnitude upon our hands unless one side or the other gives way. Our own delegates are unreasonably obstinate in some things, and the operators the same in others. I am compelled to leave here Saturday to attend the Iowa convention, which is also in a tangle. From there I shall go to Shamokin to take part in the movement to secure recognition for the anthracite field.

I have noted carefully all you say concerning the discharge of the President of the Local Union at Rend's mines. I do not know if he is the man with whom I have been in correspondence; the man I have in mind is named Duncombe. Please let me know if he is the one to whom you refer. In any event we cannot at this time place him in the field. I might say, Mother, that nearly every mail brings from one to six applications for positions as organizer from West Virginia miners, and I fear the fact that we have employed some men who were discharged has resulted in more harm than good because it has impressed others with the idea that our organization is financially able to place on salary every one of them who happens to be so unfortunate as to lose his job; and while personally I should be happy to take care of those men, I am forced to the conclusion that the best interests of the West Virginia miners will be conserved by teaching them that they must, to some extent, depend upon themselves. However, just as soon as I can dispose of many matters which are pressing at this time and causing us so much worry, I shall again take up the matter of the employment of local men to help our organizers who are stationed there.

I presume that by the time you receive this letter John Walker will have joined you, and possibly another man from Illinois, named Wilson.

I quite agree with you, Mother, that things will move along in the Kanawha and New River districts better without a general manager; and if anyone is sent there to have charge of the District I shall see that it is someone who is up to date.

I hope that you will try to take care of your health and not expose yourself unnecessarily or overexert your energies.

With love and best wishes, I am,

Yours truly,
[John Mitchell]
President U. M. W. of A.

P. S. I shall take care of that man Davis.

TLC (John Mitchell Papers)

To John Mitchell

Montgomary West Virginia
3—14—1902

My dear Comrade Mitchell

Been over the mountains for the last few days with Boys found your letter when I got back. I am having glorious Meetings   The Boys are responding to the bugle call last night we had a fine meeting here and took in a large no to the local

Sunday we have a large Mass Meeting here in the Opera House   The owner gives me the use of it just for the cleaning up   I am going to heave a band of music out   last Sunday I had a mass meeting at Brooklin had a band march up the track got the Boys all in with us   John Lang never showed up he said I was a good old woman   he was not going to bother me any more   The boys say he is completely whiped that a woman to do it. No matter who did it So its done   I agree with you that it was a mistake to undertake to provide for those men who get out of work for any cause   They think that the National Tres is a mint

I spoke of this man Duncomb for the reason that he was Pres of the Local and good inteligent fellow. The Local is a large one and for a while have to be cared for besides there is a great deal of local work he could do   I learned that Carrell asked for Tincher[1] to be put on   I told Carrell I did not considered it for the best interest of the or-ganization   The Boy is a good boy without any experience a regular

25

talking machine   Would do more harm than good   We have found him work in three mines   let him go and work. This fellow is young but he has got the office bug running around in his head

A Pointer for you

This man is a good honest fellow faithful worker   I mean Carrell   be a little slow in taking stock in his Judgement I find him rather deficient. A noble fellow Some what of an *Egotist*   I regret the Ill. miners do not realize the time is not ripe yet for us to defy our Masters. I know how unreasonable our people can be how unyeilding they are at times   The other Side is just the Same because they can be.

I feel sometimes the burden is more than you can bear   I only wish I could assume part of it. All I can do is to keep this old heart true to you in my humble way help you all I can

This fellow Davis is doing some very good work among the young men   I have him with me you can depend I'l switch him on the side of right   he was in the wrong company for a while   the boy is young wants to be right and will be when he understands things

When I came in here I found a Slate for the offices. I held council with the boys bursted up the Slate   I do not like the Complextion of things in the fairmont field   I fear those fellow are fooling Tom   I see Flyn has swoped places with Springer[2] there is some deal   I do not take much stock in Flyn he is an office seeker   We dont want any Squires at the head of the miners   They are tricky. I hope you or Comrade W—— will be able to come to the Convention

honest John Walker is here   It did me good to see him   I think this Boy Wilson[3] will make a fine worker   I am going to make him read up

You will laugh   I think I won Murreys watch   I am going to tell you if so they wont get it back   I have no use for that gang of Traitors

God bless and guide you for those who need you most

fraternally yours

Mother

ALS (John Mitchell Papers)

1. Probably Thomas Tincher of Local 195, District 17, UMWA, in Sun, West Virginia.

2. J. A. Springer had been president of District 17, UMWA.

3. Probably Peter Wilson, another member of the organizing team that was working with Mother Jones.

From John Mitchell

Morgan Hotel, Des Moines, Ia.,
March 15, 1902.

Mother Mary Jones,
Montgomery, W. Va.
Dear Mother:

Acknowledging your favor of the 7th instant, which has just reached me at Des Moines, I desire to express my gratification at the progress you are making, and my approval of the methods which you and the other organizers in that field are pursuing.

By the way, both you and I are being urged to attend the first of April celebration at Streator, Illinois. I wish you would arrange to go there, and if it is possible for me to complete our business in the anthracite field I shall be there also; however, the chances of my attending are problematical. There will be an immense meeting, and much good will result therefrom. Please write me at the office acknowledging the receipt of this letter and letting me know if you can comply with this request.

Trusting that you will excuse this brief reply, as I am leaving to-night for the anthracite field, I am, with best wishes,

Yours truly,
[John Mitchell]
President U. M. W. of A.

TLC (John Mitchell Papers)

To John Mitchell

Montgomary West Virginia
4—2—02

My dear Comrade Mitchell

I have received both your letters. Will comply with your instructions.

There are three mass meetings billed for next Sunday at all of which I have to speak   It will be a hard day for the reason that I have to go to Bufflo on Saturday night and on Sunday morning have to count the rails for five miles in order to get the Train for those meetings   If the meeting at Streeter was on Tues. I would have to miss one of the others. I think there are good officers at the head for the next year. There had to be some good engineering to get them there

This fellow Duncomb of Rend has got work in another place. I agree with you that it was a mistake at first to undertake to look after any of them   It takes away from their manhood and opens the avenue for imposition   To me the quicker that is shut off the better for all. I have them every day. I tell them where they can get work   They dont bother me any more

I may stop off on Tues at office and give you a little information that you ought to have. I hope the anthacite will come out all right alright   So that you can have a little peace for a while

Prest. Vanhorn[1] sent for me to go before the Scole Com. of Ind.   I gave them a good straight talk and think it will have its effects   I went down from Huntington to Terre Haute to talk to the Street Car Men held three big mass meetings on the same day and left for here   The next morning went over to Rend on the same night that I got here untangled some difficulty they had. Got everything straightened out, and left them all happy   This Local is between 4–500 strong   Now that quite move of the Mulligan Brigade stoped P. R from Importing any more Black Legs   *it worked well*

I hope to have a few minutes talk with you while in Streeter

Always yours
Mother

ALS (John Mitchell Papers)

1. W. D. Van Horn of Terre Haute was president, and later executive board member of the UMWA from District 11 (Indiana).

To William B. Wilson

Montgomary W Virginia
4–5–1902

Comrade Wilson

Good news. The Board of Education gave orders that all School Houses shall be thrown open to the miners and if the Trustees refuse they shall be called on to resign their office. Thats what going after what belongs to you brings   That speech I made in the Court House in Huntington last fall though I was misquoted by the Assoicated Press has had its effect on the Public Officials.

I had three fine meeting in Terre Haute Sat—I talked 2 hours at the Armery in the afternoon had two overflow meetings at night at which I talked for two hours   When I went to the Hotel at twelve oclock, I was worn out   I did not have you or Comrade Debs to get me any *Medicine*   he was out of town did not get home untill midnight. I lost all my tired feeling when I saw him   he spoke so kindly of you and Mr Mitchell   holds you both in high esteem.   its well the world has such men they are the lights of the Race I found things tangled up a little when I got back. I had to go to Armbucle on Monday and get things straightened out there   I put things in running order. They are four hundred strong there and are good men. Their Prest. was drawing on their Tres. for a Sal every week   I put a stop to it then and there   Made the fellow go to work. I appealed to the fellows manhood how degrading it was to live off his fellow he trembled went and got work the next morning. I do not believe it is a wise policy to put any of those fellows on the force before the State is organized it creates a jealouscy among them   I think if they want to get on and build up they organization   Make district offices and Sub. district and Pay them out of their own funds. They would burst ten national banks. I have not got rested yet my flesh seems so sore. I have so much to tell you that you both should know   I will stop off at Indianapolis on my way to Streeter

Good bye
Mother

ALS (William B. Wilson Papers)

To John Mitchell

Montgomary   West Virginia
5—6 1902

My dear Comrade Mitchell

Pardon me for failling to carrie out your instructions requesting me to write every week   There has not been a single night since I saw you in Indianapolis that I have not had a meeting. After I walk 8 or 10 miles and talk for 2 or 3 hours which I always do I am a little nervous and have to rest up next day so as to be ready for my work at night   Then I know that some of the others write you all the time.

Well the cause is moving on. our people are responding like braves. I made a raid on Kellys Creek one morning. Captured it   They had a couple of Thugs watching me   I outwitted the pirates and got in took Clark Johnson[1] and Ben Davis.[2] These fellows were never in any move like this before and they hardly knew what was going to drop   They are both good honest boys their heart in the work. After three weeks of hard work I feel Kelley Creek is ours There has been more money spent last Summer to get this place and Ceder Grove organized without any response   They are both in line now. After I capture three or four Strong holds I can move to the Norfolk & Western   This place will Soon be in line

Dont pay any attention to such letters as [Lewis?] sends   Not that he does not mean alright but it is a trick of the Operators   Some of them are shaking and they don know how to play their game   poor inocent Wright[3] from Indiana he is too tenderhearted for these Crooks   he got wore out   I told him to rest for a day

This fellow Tinchure is no Gods Earth good and when they tell you that he could not get work it is false I got the fellow work in three places he would not take it. everything belonging to him blackeleged I do not trust him any fellow would scheme as he did to saddle himself on to his fellow man for support is not Safe he is an indiscreet talker has no knowledge of the movement he went to Mount Hope Local the other night, called the men a narrow minded lot You told him to go to Lens Creek he never went Richard[4] told him go to Paint Creek he never went—he went to fayette last week Called a meeting The men Turned out he never showed up nor told any one else to go there The men came after me and told me how they were treated The sooner this fellow is got rid of the safer for all concerned More so for the movement he is an office Hunter. from the time he left the National Convention where he remained longer then he Should untill the State Convention he did not work a day but going round the Locals getting himself nominated for Vice President he got defeated the men showing him that he had [more?] gaul than principle I understand the statement was made that his father lost his job because he harbored the ["National" interlined] organizers that is not true No organizer stoped at his fathers house They did not have to because there were boarding Houses and Hotels around there None of us ever stops at a miners House We Steer Cleer for we know they will have themselves discharged the next day thinking the organization will [make?] them. These people in here must be made to know this [is] their fight and that we have no nursing bottle for them The miners are finding falt with a black legs son being carried when honest men have to suffer and fight The Co bought his father to blackleg for a Suit of Clothes and the women went in the mines pulled him out I wont trust him I told Pres Richards not to let him come on this river I wont work with anything I am suspicious of their honesty this is a cruzial hour for this State Those fellow working for their rotten Selves at the expense of the Human race, will do things we cannot undo *I am of the candid opinion this fellow is not* safe

I have writen a longer letter than I thought I would when I began We have no meeting to night The Red Men are here So that is why I have time to right

I find this boy Davis an honest earnest worker quite Inteligent in time he will make a factor in the movement

I hope the anthracite Trouble will be settled without a strike I know you must be worn out. I often wish I could bear part of your heavy burden. I can only do my part here When the Sun of Amancipation begins to shine for these poor wretches we can take our long looked for rest.

I have the R R boys with me here They give me some good pointers one sent me a note Saturday about how the operators were going to head me that night Their trick did not work The boys came to the meeting and we took 22 new members last Sunday I had a mass meeting billed for Smothers Creek The bosses went round all day telling men not to come out. It was the largest meeting ever held there That just how much they feared him I roasted the fellow before I closed.

Jack Roahen[5] holds a meeting after mine I go back and hold another tear his argument all to pices I showe him for bringing out such pauper Idies he has quit. he gave up the job in disgust. I sent a Com down to ask [*one word illegible*] who went to shoot P. W. to come to my meeting he said he did not have time I organized the men that Sunday at Green Wood he sent a niger to watch me I took care of the N. while Ben read the obligation Take care of yourself

Good bye
Mother

ALS (John Mitchell Papers)
1. Clark Johnson was the secretary, District 17, UMWA.
2. Benjamin Davis was the executive board member of the UMWA from District 17.
3. Harry Wright, of Carbon, Indiana, was secretary, District 8, UMWA.
4. J. A. Richards was president of District 17, UMWA.
5. John M. Roan, general manager of the Hocking Valley Coal Company and later commissioner of the Central Ohio Coal Operators' Association in Columbus, Ohio.

From John Mitchell

St. Charles Hotel, Scranton, Pa.,
May 10, 1902.

Mother Mary Jones,
Montgomery, W. Va.
Dear Mother:

Your favor dated May 6th is received at Scranton.

I have read very carefully what you say of the situation there, and the action of Organizer Tincher. Replying will say that I am writing him to-day, notifying him that his services will not be continued after the 15th of this month. When I met him in Indianapolis I was impressed with his apparent ability, and he was strongly recommended by Board Member Carroll and President Richards, and in the belief that he had been victimized because of his activity in the organization I thought he might make a good local organizer.

I am glad to note the progress that is being made, and I wish things were so that you could leave that field and give the boys a hand either in the Fairmont or on the Norfolk & Western. I think the Fairmont would be the place in which you could do the most good, as the coal companies up there have evidently scared our boys, and of course, with good reason, as they have brutally beaten some of them. I dislike to ask you always to take the dangerous fields, but I know that you are willing to go wherever you can perform the best service; however, remain where you are for the time being.

You have, no doubt, learned from the daily papers of the situation in the anthracite field. A temporary suspension has been ordered, to take effect Monday; and a convention of the three districts will be held at Hazleton on Wednesday, at which time I have every reason to believe that the strike will be made general and permanent. I am of the opinion that this will be the fiercest struggle in which we have yet engaged. It will be a fight to the end, and our organization will either achieve a great triumph or it will be completely annihilated. Personally I am not quite satisfied with the outlook, as the movement for a strike is strongly antagonized by the officers of the lower District, and of course the success of the strike depends entirely upon all working in harmony and unison.

I think, Mother, that it would be advisable for you not to exert yourself as much as you are doing, and you should take a rest now and then, so as to recuperate your strength. We cannot expect to do all the work ourselves, or see it done even in our lives, and I hope that you will not destroy your health and usefulness in the labor movement by over exertion.

With love and best wishes, I am,

Yours truly,
[John Mitchell]
President U. M. W. of A.

TLC (John Mitchell Papers)

From John Mitchell

Hotel Hart, Wilkes Barre, Pa.,
June 13, 02

Personal.
Mother Mary Jones,
Clarksburg, W. Va.
Dear Mother:

Your letter dated June 11th received and read carefully.

Replying will say that I am overjoyed at the success of the strike

movement in West Virginia. It is a splendid endorsement of the judgment of the majority who attended the Huntington conference; and a
severe rebuke to the gentleman from Ohio[1] who so vigorously antagonized the inauguration of a strike, and who has refused to go to the
Fairmont District to take part in the struggle, remaining at home,
quibbling over technicalities as to what his power would be and what
instructions he should have.

I earnestly hope that the strike will be prosecuted to a successful
issue, and regret that my duties here prevent my being with you to
take an active part in the fight.

I trust that you will take as good care of yourself as is possible under
the circumstances.

Hire bands, or anything that is necessary.

May God bless all those who do their duty in this supreme crisis.
With love and best wishes, I am,

Yours truly,
[John Mitchell]

TLC (John Mitchell Papers)
1. T. L. Lewis.

To John Mitchell

Parkersburg W Virginia
6-23-'02

My dear Comrade Mitchell

Just before I go back jail which I expect to have to do after the old
zar[1] of West Virginia gets through with me on Tuesday I will write you
things as they are. You heard of the poor Italian getting beat up by the
corporation thugs. Of all the cowards that Barney and blakely are the
worst   They ran away left the poor Italian by himself to be beat up by
the Corporation blood hounds   They ran away and left me   If you
hunted the U. S. you could not get a gang of bigger cowards than you
have got in here   every time those dogs gets after them they wont
show a bit of fight   They have made up their mind they have us all
coward   I would not give Tom H——[2] for the whole shooting
match   There are some of them whould like that this thing would a
failure for when ever anything happens that gives us a little back set
the silent glances exchange with a smile of derision

Dont trust this fellow Blakely   he wont do to bet on.   he is a T.
L[. Lewis] man dont be fooled in him.

This came over the Telephone Sat.   I was in the jail office, heard all. T L called Morgan up asked what he could do   Said he would like to come over here. Where are you said M—in Bridgeport. doing anything.   No.   Ill see said M then he went up talked to Barney. B said tell him come on at once he is to be here today. I gave Barney H—— for tying your hands.   he is no man for this place to deal with these tricksters   between you and I the whole shooting match outsid of Tom ought to have a Nursing Bottle   keep up   dont worry   I think the others will all go free   I will take my medicine gracefully perhaps after it will better for the cause I feel it will   Take care of yourself the cause would miss you   God bless

Mother

ALS (John Mitchell Papers)

    1. Judge John J. Jackson of the federal district court in Parkersburg, West Virginia. On 20 June 1902, Mother Jones, along with international organizers William Blakeley and Bernard Rice, was arrested for violating an injunction issued by Judge Jackson. For an extended account of the episode, see the *Autobiography*, chap. 6.

    2. Probably Tom Haggerty, who had been arrested earlier for violating an injunction by a West Virginia judge.

From John Mitchell

Hotel Hart, Wilkes Barre, Pa.,
June 25, 1902.

Mother Mary Jones,
Parkersburg, W. Va.

Dear Mother:

Your letter dated June 23rd is just received and read carefully.

Replying, it is a source of much regret to learn of the actions of some of those who should give the cause for which we are struggling their very best effort, and be willing to make any sacrifice in the interest of our cause. However, the time will come when those who take pleasure in our reverses will be called upon to give an accounting of their actions.

I regret, more than it is possible for me to express, that I cannot be with you in West Virginia. My own time, from early morning until late at night, is consumed with my duties here; and it is absolutely impossible to absent myself even for one day. I trust that you and other organizers will be acquitted by Judge Jackson, although we can expect little justice and no mercy from him; at least, he has the reputation of being bitterly opposed to the organizations of labor. If you are convicted I shall carry the matter to President Roosevelt and ask him to issue pardons.

I am, with love and best wishes,

Yours truly,
[John Mitchell]
President U. M. W. of A.

TLC (John Mitchell Papers)

To Leon Greenbaum[1]

Parkersburg Jail, W. Va.,
June 28, 1902.

My dear Comrade Greenbaum:

Knowing you are anxious to hear from me I drop the comrades a line. All human liberty is dead in America. Tell the boys not to go out and mock the silent dead on the inglorious fourth of July. On Thursday night I was served with a federal injunction, warned not to hold a meeting in sight of that most sacred of things in America the Coal Company property. The meeting was billed several days before. The ground belonged to the United Mine Workers. The striking miners assembled there, so did many farmers and other citizens. I was the only speaker. I told the miners to beg their craftsmen to join us. When I got through I was placed under arrest by the U. S. Marshal along with eleven others who had not said a word, put on the train, brought from Clarksburg to Parkersburg at 12 at night, lodged in jail with murderers and thieves, but who to me were much more civilized than the coal barons. Poor things, they told sad tales of the causes that led to their crime. They said they hoped we would stay with them. We ordered breakfast in and divided with these unfortunates. You should see them enjoy it. There was not one of these criminals that could not be made good citizens with proper economic conditions. Yet men vote for their own enslavement. We go to trial before the czar of West Virginia. I look for him to give me six months because I have been giving the injunction H–ll. Tell the comrades I will be ready for the fight when I come out.

Fraternally,
Mother Jones.

Printed letter (*The Chicago Socialist,* 12 July 1902)
1. Leon Greenbaum was national secretary of the Socialist Party of America.

1902

To John Mitchell

Parkersburg, W. Va.
Noon friday 7–25–1902

Dear Comrade

Will write you Tomorrow have just been down to the Jail to see the boys. took them some *Med* The Jailor and the Marshal are both on my string and they let me take anything I want to the boys I leave to night for Clarksburg where I shall do my full duty until you call me out

I think they have abandoned the Idea of bringing Sec Wilson [here this month?] The gang of pirates reconsidered the matter thought it was best not to bother any more

Take care of yourself for the cause needs you now more than ever. I hope you feel better than when you were in the West

Good bye God bless
Mother

The boys were laughing Send you lots of love

I got the best of the Coal barrens

I got a Confidential Tip from a post newspaper man The Corporation and som influential politians were making a deal with T. L. [Lewis] to have me removed from Will [write] you more Tomorrow
Mother

ALS (John Mitchell Papers)

To William B. Wilson

[August 1902]

My dear Comrade Wilson

I just want to drop you a line about things here. I have had meetings every day. They are good brave people and if they were not this Strike would be lost long ago. of all the insulting tyrants that have ever had athourty this fellow Purcell beats them. We had a meeting of the field workers last Monday it was disgraceful he abused coursed every one he was the whole thing I have had nothing from anyone but complaints from [the] hour I landed to this. he has been putting in his licks about you I do not know where he heard it unless Pres M—— mentioned it that you are a canidate for Congress last Sunday I was told of Some of his Sayings he went to See St. Clair last friday and gave it away that our *funds* were getting *low* but we were not *whiped yet* St. Clair Tumbled refused any further Concession he boast[s] of getting a friendly invatation from the operators I have not time to write you all for I am going on this Train

36

I Saw a Telegram from McGuffin to one of the operators last Sunday I went into the office to See one of the Telegraphers who is a warm friend of mine. McCail is willing to Settle and I think [we] had better take it

give harry the money to Settle with his field hands he is worth a car load of P—— he is a beast

I wish I had time to write you this fellow is drunk half his time

Good bye
fondly
Mother

[*In top margin of first page*] Send me Some Money

ALS (William B. Wilson Papers)

To William B. Wilson

Montgomary, W. Va.
Sep the 8th 1902

My dear Comrade Wilson

I drop a line to tell you that gradully the Operators are coming our way. McCail sent for me last Sat I made an apointment for next Tuesday Will take with me Board Member Wright and the Sub. dis. Pr.

Saturday, This place was all excitement Yesterday we called a meeting and cleared it all up. There were rumors flying thick and fast, that they were being sold out for $8000 They came to me like helpless children pleading for protection. I showed them yesterday what fools Operators would be to give one cent for no one but the miners themselves could settle this strike for there would have to be a convention called and let them decide They are as sollid as rocks this morning I must say that I love those people They seem to have such abiding faith in me. I had over 3000 people at yesterdays meeting I got the whole crowed in the best of spirits everyone spoke of what a stroke of diplomacey it was and they went their way rejoicing They came for miles.

Now I must give you the [facts] leading up to all this trouble. P[urcell?] had a quarrel with Squire Montgomary[1] who is an Operator and Mayor of this place I have always held his respect and could get him to do anything I want The Mayor came and told me he was the dirtiest man he ever saw told me how he attacked him in his own office. The Mayor is a viscious man when aroused I have no doubt but was instrumental in the story P has placed himsel in a position to be suspicioned inocent thou he may be he told St Clair[2] in conference that he had 20 bills on his desk that he could not meet the funds were

37

giving out at the National and they would have to quit   St Clair went to Rends and made that statement in a speech. I saw Mr Mitchell and gave him a History of the whole   I went directly from Ohio to the anthracite and gave him a history of the whole thing. This fight is won now.   he is another Warner but he has not got have the sense Warner had. I think the Pres will move him and send in Vasey   The thing no doubt will be closed up here soon   O my he has made so many Blunders frightful   If I could only see you to tell you the fool things this fellow has done he is soaked with whiskey all the time

I sent after money but I never got it. Tell Miss May to mark all my letters just Mother Jones other wise they get opened   I have had so many of my letters opened

Just as soon as I can I will make out my expence   I dont have a moment   There is so much to do and I am on the go all the time. After the strike is over I will take a rest, but you [know] there will be no time for rest   There are some good boys in here and they are fighting for dear life.

My love to all at home—Were going to win here

fondly
Mother

I am clean out of money   I had to borrow money from Mr Mitchell

ALS (William B. Wilson Papers)
1. Samuel B. Montgomery (1876–1923), a state senator and commissioner of labor, acted at various times as attorney for the UMWA.
2. James William St. Clair (b. 1853) was a prominent lawyer and politician of Fayetteville, West Virginia.

From John Mitchell

Hotel Hart, Wilkes-Barre, Pa.,
September 15, 1902.

Personal.
Mother Mary Jones,
Montgomery, W. Va.
Dear Mother:

I presume you received my letter notifying you that arrangements had been made for your meetings in Iowa, and that you have communicated with Reese[1] letting him know when you will reach there.

Bye the way, I sent for George.[2] When he came here he reported to me that a rumor had been circulated in West Virginia that you had stated that you would have him removed from there. He was very indignant, and evidently believed that you had made such a statement to some one. You can readily appreciate the embarrassing position in which it placed me, and that I could not premptorily remove him while he was under the impression that you had made the statements attributed to you. I have therefore sent him back for a short period; just as soon as I can make arrangements to relieve him I shall do so. Regard this information as confidential, as no doubt some one is carrying things to him, and this person may be posing as friendly to you. I, of course, do not believe that you ever made the statement that has been conveyed to him, but he, nevertheless, believes you did. We are therefore forced to move along lines that will create the very least friction.

> With love and best wishes, I am,
> Yours truly,
> [John Mitchell]

TLC (John Mitchell Papers)

1. Probably John P. Reese, president of District 14, UMWA.
2. Probably George Purcell, a UMWA international organizer from District 11, who joined Mother Jones in the Kanawha field.

To John Mitchell

> Montgomary West Virginia
> [September 1902?]

Dear Comrade Mitchell

I have just been informed that the Caperton Local have sent out letters to other Locals asking them to assess themselves so much a month So as to put a Local organizer in field here

This is a diplomatic move of the Companies They will name the man and the poor devils pay him In that way they will have their work well covered removed from all shadows of suspicion I have not said a word to stop it as I feared by so doing they might suspicion we were on to the trick.

My sugestion would be that you reserve the right to appoint the organizers for this field.

This in my oppinion is a very schrewed move of the Companies and of those who would sell their children for a mess of Potage You know we are going to have many Judases. I have meetings galore for the next two weeks I am making good use of this Phonograph [*line missing*] George droped to St Clair that the funds would be cut off then he said were not whiped by any means St Clair used that and would not concede another thing. I am onto the whole secret I droped into a rail road office The agent and I are good friends I saw a Telagram on the agents desk from the operator McGuffin to another operator telling him they were going to keep quite for a few days Something was going to develope O if I could see you and tell you all I know it would Parilize you I will run up and see you just as soon as I leave Ohio. perhaps you had better wait a Phil untill I come

fondly
Mother

Send me Mr. Masons address

ALS (John Mitchell Papers)

[Fragment from Mitchell Papers, September 1902?]

Things are in disorder here. I hate to add more trouble to that which you already have but there is no use keeping you in the dark. Yesterday there was a meeting of the field workers it was war for three hours—abuse curses was the order of the hour a shame to our cause George Purcel is something of the Savage yet. This field could have been settled before now if he would keep his mouth shut. McCail will settle on this basis

A check way man

A two weeks pay. Checque off at office and employ nothing but Union men If this will agree with you wire me to accept by yes or no dont wait to write Gere has droped something

AL fragment (John Mitchell Papers)

To John Mitchell

Montgomery, W. Va.
Nov the 8th 1902

My dear Comrade Mitchell

The papers I mailed you last night I learned that coppy of it was served on C. D. Wright and that on the 14th they are going before the Commission it is the work of the A. P. A. it was their Constitutional La[w]yer who handed this to the party from whom I took it There is some underhand work being done so watch

Mail that back to me for I promised to return it when I read it if I could

[*One line or more missing*] remained in Washington a few days I could perhaps get on to the move that old woman from Chicago was not far off She heard something for when I linked her tale with something I heard in Washington I am lead to think that they [are] doing some dirt.

Good bye
God bless you
Mother

ALS (John Mitchell Papers)

From John Mitchell

St. Nicholas Hotel, Springfield, Ill.,
March 3, 1903

Mother Mary Jones,
Montgomery, W. Va.
Dear Mother:

Your esteemed favor of February 26th has been forwarded to me at Springfield, where I am attending the joint convention of Illinois miners and operators.

I notice that in your letter you say you will go to *Linton* for April 1st. I presume there must have been an error in my letter, as Clinton, Indiana, is the place to which you have been invited.

I note what you say concerning Richards. Just as soon as the West Virginia convention is over we shall dispense with his services. After my conversation with you in Wilkes-Barre I felt that we were under obligations to keep him in the field until the convention has adjourned, when his regular term would have expired.

I am sorry not to have met you on your visit to Indianapolis, as I should have liked to talk over with you the situation in that field.

I deeply appreciate what you say, Mother, concerning the future. I have always felt that I could count upon your friendship. I know, only too well, what has come in the past to those who have been applauded by the public. You may rest assured that the demonstrations which have been made have in no wise turned my head. They cannot shut out the picture of what I know to be the fate of those prominent in the labor movement, and they will not deter me from doing my level best for our people so long as I have opportunity.

I am, with love,
Yours truly
[John Mitchell]

TLC (John Mitchell Papers)

From William Mailly

Omaha, Nebr.
April 15, 1903.

Mother Jones,
Clarksburg, W. Va.,
My dear Mother Jones:

I have your favor of the 12th written from Montgomery and I am going to answer it right away and make you an official offer to become a lecturer for the Socialist party. I can see by your letter that you are tired of your present work and I should like to free you from it and put you out for the Socialist party. I know of nothing that would arouse more genuine enthusiasm among our members than for the announcement to go out from this office that you had become a National lecturer for the Socialist party, and that your entire arrangements for meetings would be in the hands of the National Secretary. If you will decide to come with us I shall arrange a tour for you through the states where I think you are most needed and can do the best work, and I shall pay you from the time you start, $3.00 a day and your hotel and traveling expenses. This would mean every day in the week although I would not ask you to speak every day. You would be simply a lecturer and I would arrange interstate tours for you through the state secretaries with the locals and charge them a certain amount for your tours. We would not wish to make any money off of you, but we would only try to clear your expenses. We might charge $15.00 or $20.00 a lecture and give you four or five dates a week so that the income would cover your entire expense. If you would wish any more than this, please let me know, but this is the same price we are paying Chase,[1] Slayton[2] and the other speakers traveling under the direction of this office. I am sure that it will be easy for me to arrange tours for you, but it would not be necessary for you to start out for a month or two. First, because I know you should have a rest, and second, because it would require some time for me to make the dates for you. Please let me hear from you at once what you think of this and if you accept my proposition I shall let the anouncement go out at once. It would be a big thing for the party and for me if I could get you. If there is any other information you want, do not hesitate to ask.

It would not be necessary for you to have anything at all to do with the party work. We have organizers who will attend to that. All you would have to do is to speak and you need not become tangled up in any of the party affairs if you did not wish too. This would relieve your mind a great deal and as you are a favorite with all the comrades you would have none of the worries that beset you now.

1903

Dear Mother, I know that this is the year that we must do our best work and that is why I am striving hard to get things going so that the best speakers can go on the road. If we get out educating and organizing done now we will be in splendid shape for the campaign next year. From a personal standpoint I believe you would be better off and you would not be over-worked as you are now. There are other reasons also which I would prefer to talk over with you. The party is now in a position where it can guarantee its speakers fair remuneration for their work. The revenue is increasing here every day and I have issued a call for a special organizing fund, which I am certain will bring a generous response.

I enclose my last weekly press bulletin, which will give you the results of the elections. As you spoke in Pullman, it will be gratifying for you to learn of Johnson being elected on the board of Aldermen in Chicago.[3]

I wish I could see you and have a talk with you. If you can arrange to come here within the near future I shall be happy to see you.

Mother is not keeping much better, but I shall not touch on personal matters in this letter, but leave that for a private note.

Now Mother answer me right away and let me know what you think of my proposition and please keep it to yourself until we have arrived at a definite agreement.

With my love, as ever, I am,

Your Comrade,
[William Mailly]
National Secretary.

TLC (Socialist Party Papers)

1. John Chase had been elected mayor of Haverhill, Mass., in 1898 and was active in Socialist affairs.

2. Probably J. W. Slayton, a lecturer on the Socialist lyceum circuit.

3. William Johnson, a Socialist who worked in the Pullman Car Shops, won the election for alderman in Chicago's Thirty-third Ward.

To Henry Demarest Lloyd[1]

Montgomery West Virginia
4—19—1903

Mr. H. D. Lloyed
Chicago, Ill

My dear Mr. Lloyed

I send you by request of Mr. Mitchell some clippings. The thank you Judge is not correct. I did not thank him. he told me not to violate his Injunction I told him I would not violate the *Law* I was going out to continue the work for which I was arrested. If that violated his Injunction I feared it would be violated. he Said I ought to join some Charity Organization I told him If I had my way I would tear down every Charity Institution in the country to day build on their ruins the Temple of Justice My plea was for Justice not Charity.[2]

After two years of hard work the Miners have won a victory The Operators of the Combine have met the miners in Joint Convention little by little we are getting the poor slaves awakened

fraternally
Mother Jones

I am putting Literature into their hand and making them read and think for themselves

ALS (Henry Demarest Lloyd Papers)

1. Henry Demarest Lloyd (1847–1903), author of *Wealth versus Commonwealth* and other muckraking books, had been associated with Mother Jones in reform politics in Chicago in the 1890s.

2. Probably refers to her appearance before Judge John J. Jackson in Parkersburg, West Virginia, the preceding summer.

To Theodore Roosevelt[1]

[July 15, 1903]

To Theodore Roosevelt
President of the United States
Dear Sir:

Being citizens of the United States of America, we, members of the textile industry, take the liberty of addressing this appeal to you. As Chief Executive of the United States, you are, in a sense, our father and leader, and as such we look to you for advice and guidance. Perhaps the crime of child slavery has never been forcibly brought to your notice.

Yet, as father of us all, surely the smallest detail must be of interest to you. In Philadelphia, Pa., there are ninety thousand (90,000) textile workers who are on strike, asking for a reduction from sixty to fifty-five hours a week. With machinery, Mr. President, we believe that forty-eight hours is sufficient.

If the United States Senate had passed the eight-hour bill, this strike might not have occurred. We also ask that the children be taken from the industrial prisons of this nation, and given their right of attending schools, so that in years to come better citizens will be given to this republic.

These little children, raked by cruel toil beneath the iron wheels of greed, are starving in this country which you have declared is in the height of prosperity—slaughtered, ten hours a day, every day in the week, every week in the month, every month in the year, that our manufacturing aristocracy may live to exploit more slaves as the years roll by.

We ask you, Mr. President, if our commercial greatness has not cost us too much by being built upon the quivering hearts of helpless children? We who know of these sufferings have taken up their cause and are now marching toward you in the hope that your tender heart will counsel with us to abolish this crime.

The manufacturers have threatened to starve these children, and we seek to show that no child shall die of hunger at the will of any manufacturer in this fair land. The clergy, whose work this really is, are silent on the crime of ages, and so we appeal to you.

It is in the hope that the words of Christ will be more clearly interpreted by you when he said "Suffer little children to come unto me." Our destination is New York City, and after that Oyster Bay. As your children, may we hope to have the pleasure of an audience? We only ask that you advise us as to the best course.

In Philadelphia alone thousands of persons will wait upon your answer, while throughout the land, wherever there is organized labor, the people will anxiously await an expression of your sentiments toward suffering childhood.

On behalf of these people, we beg that you will reply and let us know whether we may expect an audience.

The reply should be addressed to "Mother" Jones's Crusaders, en route according to the daily papers.

We are very respectfully yours,
"Mother" Jones, Chairman

Printed letter (Newark *Evening News,* 16 July 1903)
1. Theodore Roosevelt (1858–1919), president of the United States, 1901–1909, refused to see Mother Jones and an "army" of child employees of textile mills that she led in a march from Philadelphia to Oyster Bay.

To Theodore Roosevelt

New York,
July 30. [1903]

The Hon. Theodore Roosevelt
President of the United States
Oyster Bay, Long Island
Your Excellency—

Twice before have I written to you requesting an audience, that I might lay my mission before you and have your advice in a matter which bears upon the welfare of the whole nation.

I speak of the emancipation from the mills and factories of the hundreds of thousands of young children who are yielding up their lives for the commercial supremacy of the nation.

Failing to receive a reply to either of the letters, I went yesterday to Oyster Bay, taking with me three of these children that they might plead to you personally. Secretary Barnes informed us that before we might hope for an interview with you we must first lay the whole matter before you in a letter. He assured me of its delivery to you personally, and also that it would receive your attention.

I have espoused the cause of the laboring class in general, and of suffering childhood in particular. It was for them that our march of principle was begun. We sought to draw the attention of the public to these little ones, so that sentiment would be aroused and ultimately the children freed from the workshop and sent to schools. I know of no question of to-day that demands from those who have at heart the perpetuity of this republic more attention.

The child of to-day is the man or woman of to-morrow, the one the citizen and the other the mother of still future citizens. I ask, Mr. President, what kind of citizen will be the child who toils twelve hours a day in an unsanitary atmosphere, stunted mentally and physically, and surrounded with often immoral influences. Denied education, he cannot assume the duties of true citizenship, and enfeebled physically he falls a ready victim to the perverting influences which our present economic conditions have created.

I grant you, Mr. President, that there are State laws which should regulate these matters, but results have proved that they are inadequate. In my little band are three boys, the eldest 11 years of age, who have worked in the mills a year or more, without interference from the authorities. All efforts to bring about reform have failed.

I have been moved to this, Mr. President, because of actual experience in the mills. I have seen little children without the first rudiments of education and no prospect of acquiring any. I have seen little children with hands, fingers and other parts of their bodies mutilated because of their childish ignorance of machinery.

I feel that no nation can be truly great while such conditions exist without attempted remedy.

It is to be hoped that our crusade on behalf of enslaved childhood will stir up a general sentiment and secure the enforcement of the present laws.

But that is not sufficient as this is not alone a question of separate States, but of the whole nation. We come to you as the chief representative of that nation. I believe Federal laws should be passed and enforced governing this evil and including a penalty for violation.

If this is practicable, and I believe you will agree that it is, surely you can advise me of the necessary steps to pursue.

I have with me three children who have walked one hundred miles, serving as living proof of the truth of what I say.

If you decide to see these children, I will bring them before you at any time you may set.

Secretary Barnes has assured me on an early reply, and this should be sent care of the Ashland House, New York City.

Very respectfully yours,
Mother Jones

Printed letter (Newark *Daily Advertiser,* 31 July 1903)

From B. F. Barnes

Oyster Ba, N. Y.,
August 1, 1903.

Mother Jones,
Ashland House,
New York, N. Y.
Dear Madam—

I beg to acknowledge the receipt of your letter of the 30th ult., and state that it has been brought to the President's attention.

The President, as was shown by his action while Governor of New York, has the heartiest sympathy with every effort to prevent child labor in factories, and on this matter no argument need be addressed to him, as his position has been announced again and again.

Under the constitution it is not at present seen how Congress has power to act in such a matter. It would seem that the States alone at present have the power to deal with the subject.

Very truly yours,
B. F. Barnes
Acting Secretary to the President

Printed letter (Newark *Daily Advertiser,* 5 August 1903)

To William B. Wilson

Trinidad, Colorado,
10–29–1903

My dear Comrade Wilson

I am here with the Boys on my way out I stoped between trains   Saw the boys of the Western federation. There will be no more attacks on Pres. M. in their paper   I have got them strongly in the notion of going into the Federation   They strongly and honestly agreed with me that there should be no lines dividing labor   We are to meet some time in the future and outline Plans for the amalga[mation]   These are fine fellows, and if I bring no other result my visit here will not have been lost.

The Labor Commissioner said he had no information of my coming to Colo. and that he would come to Trinidad to find out which he did   he arrived here the next morning.   asked me to go lunch with him   I declined.   but treated him kindly and with a great deal of diplomacy. I got considerable news out of him which will serve me in the future. I will play my cards as slick as he.

There is one thing must be impressed on the officers here that they must keep the affairs of the national office quiet. They rush in to the news papers with to much of the affairs of the organization   I have learned that men are as big mouthed as women and are just as empty brained. The Cripple Creek miners have asked me to come down and speak for them   their national officers and the boys themselves have sent me a request. I promised them to let them know in a few days. What had I better do

A word more   ask Mr. M not send old Haddow[1] in here   it is no field for him and it is a waste of money   I wish I could be as open with Mr. M. as am with you it would be of benefit all around   there is no use I cannot   Will write you again soon

Love to all   Save for yourself a fair share

fraternally yours
Mother

ALS (William B. Wilson Papers)
  1. Probably John Haddow, national organizer for the UMWA.

To Colorado State Federation of Labor

Trinidad, Colorado
11 January 1904

To the Delegates of the State Federation of Labor, Greeting. Let your deliberations be tempered with a high sense of justice for all mankind—malice toward none, for you are the bulwark of the nation. The day dawneth when you shall get your own.

Fraternally in the cause of labor

Mother Jones

Telegram (*Miners Magazine,* 21 January 1904)

From J. C. Sullivan and H. B. Waters

Denver
11 January 1904

Mother Jones
Trinidad, Colorado

The greatest labor convention ever held in the state sends you greeting and wishes you health and God-speed.

J. C. Sullivan, President
H. B. Waters, Secretary

Telegram (*Miners Magazine,* 21 January 1904)

To John Mitchell

Helper Utah
Apr the 16th 1904

My dear Comrade Mitchell

I have been on the go ever since I was driven out of Trinidad[1] the history which you know. The next thing the Colorado Canobol will do will be to kill me   Thats all they have left undone.

I find things here in a bad shape   This man price is down with Small Pox. Then from what I learn other things are not all smooth

They tell me that he never gets out of here to look the field over and he drinks

It seems that there are about 180 members? in the Camp here   When the delagate was going to the Convention in Trinidad he told him to say that there were 280   It looks as if there was something wrong   I got this from a lot of Italians but they all tell the same thing.

Something else you ought to know, our organizers have not observed the S. L. P. are making strong inroads in the organized camps   Meet with no opposition from the Co.   You know what that means in the future for the organization   We have a sample of their work in the Pitts. Dist.   The men who are in the field are not familiar with their Tactics so have taken no steps to stop their work   It has all been done since the strike.

I will never forget the expression on Bro Fairleys[2] face that night when Peabodys henchmen were chasing me out with the the Bayonets? I will allways remember with fond affection his kind and respectful treatment to me while I worked with him   he was all that a brother could be to me   I could always go to him and always got a respectful hearing   There was no move but I could consul with him.   it was a mistake that he did not have charge of that strike at first   I hope you will take care of yourself   dont go to Trinidad   Those Vilians are afot to do something with you.

Mother

P.S. if it is Possible for you to send some one in here to take charge of this strike and investigat things I think it most essential for the good of the organization

Mother

ALS (John Mitchell Papers)
1. Governor James H. Peabody ordered the state militia to deport Mother Jones from Trinidad, Colorado, where she had been active in a coal miners' strike. She went to Helper, Utah, where another strike was in progress, and local authorities imprisoned her in an isolated shack, allegedly under quarantine for contact with smallpox.
2. William Fairley, UMWA executive board member from Alabama.

1905

To John H. Walker

Canton, Ill.,
1–4–04[05]

My dear John—for such you are to me:

Your very kind letter reached me this morning. No one could write that letter but a true comrade and no one could appreciate it as I do but a true and tried comrade.

John, I opposed a ring of fools that had charge of that strike in Colorado. I felt it my duty to do so. I know that Mitchell would have to bear the brunt; they could retire and not be heard of again, but he would have to suffer the result. I *want to say right here,* I may never see him again, but one thing one thing [*sic*] certain, I will fight to death for him against any false assertion. I know the labor movement; I know the philosophy of the *monster capitalism.* Sometimes a man or women are to be carried away by the glitter of the tinsel. I *for one shall be his defender.*

I resigned[1] because I fought; some of the dirty ignoramuses that represented the national office were against me. I do not want to put John in a position where he would have to oppose them; his fight is hard enough. John Mitchell does not know everything those fellows did out there. I will fight the cause of the miners anyway, whether I am directly in their service or not. John Mitchell can always depend on me. I know whatever mistakes he has made, he is right at heart.

So far as Debs is concerned, I think he will take my word as quickly as anyone else in the United States. We have been close comrades on the battle ground for 14 long years. We can trust our lives in the *hands of each other.* I went up from Paris to see him; he had got up from a sick bed; I did not approach him upon anything but his health and the future of the workers' cause. Some of these curs were telling him what they were going to do at that convention. The D—— traitors did not *chirip.* It is impossible for me to break away from my engagements. You know the Socialist party has never in its history given me five cents. I am going out for the cause to wake the people up, and I can be more independent as I am. There is no man in the world that I will I will [*sic*] approach for a job. If John wants me he can send for me. I expect to go to N. Y. in April. I will call on him then, making only a friendly visit. I am not afraid of suffering. The boys of the W. F. of Miners will see that I am not hungry, if the time ever comes; and what if it does?

52

John, I have been offered many good positions; indeed, I could be in Europe now if I wanted to. Let me tell you, John, you will always find me on the firing line with you.

I will write Debs to keep quiet until I have a chance to see him, and talk things over with him. We cannot afford to serve that dam Pittsburg gang so well.

Yes, John, I know that poor Sam would would [sic] give me the last cent he had. He is a man with a soul; every inch a man.

Tell Tom that I love him just as I always did; that I often wish that I could be with him over there. Poor Tom and [I] were in many battles together. Regard to poor Noon and that clean, honest soul, Flaherty; get him elected than I will have another friend on the Board. If I could see John and tell him about that old coward Ream and Bousfield, the only fellow the national had was Fairley. He came too late.

Good bye, John, I am always

Loyally,
Mother.

Write me at 43 Walton Place, Chicago, Ill.

TLC (John Mitchell Papers)

1. Mother Jones resigned her position as organizer for the UMWA because of policy differences with the executive board regarding the Colorado strikes the preceding year; she returned to the employ of the UMWA six years later when John P. White became president. Shortly after the writing of this letter she participated in the launching of the IWW, though her close association with that organization lasted only a few months.

To William B. Wilson

Stevensville, Montana
5–9–1905

My dear Comrade Wilson

Here I am out in the mountains not on a plesure but on duty waking up the Shumburg Joint. I spoke in Butte last night under the auspices of the Smeltermen Union. I had house packed stage and all the boys did not know what to do for me. They gave me one hundred dollars and my fare to and from Chicago. They want to remain out here all summer and go to the Springs for a rest they would pay the bill. I could not do that poor boys they earn their nickles to hard. if you could see them when they come home from those smelters in the evening you would feel they needed the Springs worse than anyone else. Who on earth did Sam marry his stenographer. I wished he had not for those old people needed him at home however that is something we cannot govern   They will do as they want to.

I am glad Mrs. W—— and the children are well   I will be in the State of N. Y. for three months this fall   I will make an effort to go and see them while East   I want to see Joe before I die. Take care of him.

I speake in Helena on Miners day the 13th of this month Back to Butte for two more meetings then I go to Coaldale for the Coal Miners then I go East. I have so much to tell you when I see you. The time seems so long. I am going to go before I am due   So that I just gaze on that face a reflex of the heart that has been true to the people. In looking over the field it looks as if you were going to have trouble next year.   in fact it looks to me as if many crafts were on the thresold of Industrial War.   let it come we only can do what we can for them. We are permeating them with clear conception of their class interest trying to put the Spirit Solidarity in them   let me warn you against that Board Member Jones of Wyo.[1]   he is no Gods earth good for God or man. What cur will stoop to like the feet of those in poor for a job   I am going to see you soon   Love to Miss May a Agnes your own good self

fondly
Mother

ALS (William B. Wilson Papers)
    1. W. E. Jones of Dietz, Wyoming, was executive board member from District 22, UMWA.

To Western Federation of Miners

Dietz, Wyoming,
May 29, 1905

Convention Hall, Salt Lake

To the brave officers and miners in convention, greeting. May your deliberations awaken the slumbering giant from his long dream of ages.

Mother Jones

Telegram (*Miners Magazine,* 8 June 1905)

To William B. Wilson

New York,
Oct. the 4th 1905

My dear Comrade

I know you have not much time to read letters much less answer them   I regretted I did not see Agnes while in Indianapolis but I lost the address. I spent Labor day at Montgomary. The Boys would not let me go before I spoke. Things are not right in there but it's none of my affair now No wonder some of them wanted to get rid of me There's a rotten Cur that Iseman of Terre Haute. I often wonder if we will ever be able to resque the poor wretches from the clutches of those Tratiors in there own rank They only care for that job that they hold as organizers.

Well I have tremendous meeting in N Y. Night after night I have I speak to thousands of people. Some day they will overthrow the whole rotton machine

Now I want to ask you to do me a favor. Will you get that Phonograph packed up and sent to Chicago out of your way and all those pictures I have several invatations to go over to Europe from the comrades in France and England I am going South this winter to do some work in the factories A gentleman in Europe will put up the money. My love to Sam Life after all is worth living when we meet such loyal souls we feel there are some grand souls yet left out of the struggle when comes the true and tried No matter the filthy minds may say whose own mothers were rotton to the core I know that you and Sam believe me still a woman *pure and true.*[1] Come what will, you will both find me true to you They have not injured me with people last night two thousand people wanted to carry me on their shoulders! even if Mr Mitchell did have my Picture torn down from the stand in Wilksbarre where the Capitalist Henchman Rosefelt was going to speak I give Rosefelt H—— about that Commission. Well so long as you and Sam and my own dear Debs [stand by me?] I dont care for all the world

fondly loyally
Mother

ALS (William B. Wilson Papers)

1. Refers to the publication in *Polly Pry,* a Denver weekly, 2 January 1904, of charges that Mother Jones had been a madam in brothels in Denver, Omaha, Kansas City, Chicago, and San Francisco in the 1880s and 1890s.

From William B. Wilson

Oct. 6, [190]5

My dear Mother Jones;

I have your letter of the 4th inst. and in accordance with your request have shipped by express to 163 Randolph St., Room 27, Chicago, Ill., graphophone and records, together with photographs we had in office here. I trust they will arrive in good condition.

I would not worry about that incident at Wilkes-Barre. While I have not seen Mr. Mitchell since that time, I do not believe that he had anything to do with the taking down of your picture from the stand. If it was taken from there at all, I am satisfied that it was entirely due to political influence because President Roosevelt was going to speak there, and not because of any desire to that effect on Mr. Mitchell's part. I know that Mr. Mitchell has a high appreciation of the work you have done for the United Mine Workers of American and knowing that, I do not believe that he can in any manner be connected with or responsible for the removal of your picture after it had been placed upon the stand. I regret very much that the incident occurred. If your picture had not been placed there at all, nothing would have been thought of it, but to place it there and then have it removed, was very embarrassing to you and your friends.

I have worked with you in the trade union movement in the past and I know something of the sacrifices you have made for the cause of humanity, and while you and I may not always agree on the best policy to pursue to reach the end we are both striving for, you can rest assured that no amount of slander will ever reduce my high opinion of your goodness.

With sincere love I am, as ever,

Your friend,
[William B. Wilson]

TLC (William B. Wilson Papers)

To William Johnson

New York,
December 15, 1905.

William Johnson,
Supt. Vivian Coal and Mining Co.,
Jacksonville, Ind.
Dear Sir:

I have a letter from you under date of December 15th, asking for terms for furnishing men to coal mines. Allow me to say that the terms depend entirely upon how many men you want and what you want them for. We have a great number of able bodied men here who are more than willing to go anywhere and men who are not afraid of the police, militia, court injunctions, or government interference in any form. In fact each and every one of them can and will be vouched for by "Mother Jones" whose guarantee should satisfy any coal company in Indiana or elsewhere. If you will state how many you want and just when you want them, also whether they are destined for the bull pens or coal mines, we will be pleased to give your needs our prompt attention. In fact we will be willing to work overtime.

Truly yours,

Secretary Society for the Prevention
of Cruelty to Superintendents.

P. S. Fortunately, "Mother Jones" has just come into the office and she gives me her personal word that if you want her to head the procession she will gladly come. She would like to know whether the men are to come with arms or armless.

Printed letter (*Miners Magazine,* 4 January 1906)

To Terence V. Powderly

Chicago, Ill.
May 9—1906

T. V. Powderly
502 Quincy St., N. W.
Washington, D. C.
My own Dear Comrade:

You no doubt wonder why you have not had a reply to your letter before this time. When I left you I went to Indianapolis spent a day or two there and proceeded to Danville, Ill., and was laid up for a month in the home of a Physicain friend and he patched me up for the work again.

Strange that I should have been thinking of you, and the work you did in the past, the day before and that day that I reached Chicago and found your letter awaiting me. Some how I felt that you would rebuke Gooding[1] and their method. When I read your letter and read the clipping from the News Paper it brought tears to my eyes, and I thought of the days when we were together in battle, how they had accused you and maligned you, and how patiently you bore it all for the cause so dear to you.

I saw Darrow yesterday, he tells me he thinks it will be a long drawn out trial, and it will need a great deal of finance to carry it on, and we must have it.[2] He had a letter from Bolton Hall,[3] he gave him much incourasement and every guarantee of assistance. I wanted to go to Denver to have a long talk with the boys at the head of the Federation, but Darrow advised me not to go, for possibly there would be some charge trumped up against me and I would be put behind the bars out there, so I took his advice and will stay away, believing that I can do more good out of Jail than in it.

I must tell you something. Robert Hunter,[4] the man who wrote "Poverty" went to Washington to see the "Big Stick" and the "Big Stick" said, "so you are the man who wrote "Poverty" are you?" Hunter said yes, and of course Teddy did not like that because he had been swinging the circle in a Special Car telling all about the wonderful prosperity. He pased up and down the Cabinet Room, and said "every one of the Western Federation of Miners ought to be hung, they are nothing but a gang of criminals" and then he said the "Beef Trust ought to be hung also." If I had been there I would have told him to go down to the Senate of the United States, and take a rope with him, and hang some of those commercial pirots.

I regretted to learn from your letter that you were not feeling well. Courage, Comrade, the day is dawning, as you say, and out of the darkness will come the light. The world needs more like you. Do not let any incident of the past distress you, you are the same honest T. V. Powderly of years ago, when the present Labor Lords were not heard of. You broke up the clay, and sewed the seed, and they are now reaping some of the harvest, and whatever comes or goes, whatever the dark day may be I shall always see you in the shadows of the past when you worked so faithfully, and patiently in labors cause. Some day the unwritten history will be given to the children yet unborn, and it is possible that they will make pilgramages to your grave and plant flowers there on. We live not for to day, but for the ages yet to come, and the children yet unborn.

I expect some time soon to get to Washington and write up that book I promised you would be written.

Poor Douglas Wilson,[5] go to see him some time, it will cheer him up. I have always had a warm spot in my heart for him, he has been true to the cause. It is a sad sight for me to go to Washington and look upon that once magnificent frame, what a total wreck it is.

I expect to go to Oklahoma in a few weeks to do some work down there, and I would like to hear from you and above all keep cheerful and the future will be ours.

I have no words to express my appreciation for your rebuke to Gooding.

I am as ever yours faithfully and loyally for the Social Revilution.

[*Remainder of letter is holograph.*] Take care of yourself   write a line   let me know how Douglass feels   Send me that book we talked about if you can   cheer up

Mother Jones

TLS (Terence V. Powderly Papers)

1. Probably Frank R. Gooding, governor of Idaho, where the trial was to be held.

2. Clarence Darrow (1857–1938) played a prominent role in a number of labor cases. He currently headed the defense for the Western Federation of Miners leaders, Haywood, Moyer, and Pettibone, on trial for murder. Darrow and Mother Jones had known one another since the mid-1890s.

3. Bolton Hall (1854–1938), an official of the longshoremen's union and also a successful businessman, wrote *Three Acres and Liberty* (1907).

4. Robert Hunter (1874–1942), Socialist lecturer and writer, was the author of *Poverty* (1904).

5. D. Douglas Wilson (d. 1915) for twenty years edited the *Machinists' Monthly Journal,* regarded by some as the best labor journal of its day.

To the Socialists of Massachusetts

[18 August 1906]

Through the columns of the *Appeal* I desire to give expression of my deep appreciation of the thoughtful and kind consideration of the Massachusetts comrades during my recent illness. Your letter to Comrade Hogan,[1] instructing him to spare no expense and that you would foot the bills, bears within itself a deep sense of comradeship which is worth much to us in the movement. I have never yet had to call on the comrades, having always felt that the Socialist movement had no right to pay my bills. My life work is consecrated to the oppressed and suffering ones of the human race; nevertheless, I feel a deep sense of gratitude to our Massachusetts comrades who so promptly and generously offered such substantial assistance.

While life remains I shall always be with you in the conflict.

Mother Jones.

Printed letter (*The Appeal to Reason,* 18 August 1906)

1. During her illness, Mother Jones had been cared for in the home of Daniel Hogan, a Socialist lawyer in Huntington, Arkansas; Hogan's daughter Freda later married the Socialist journalist Oscar Ameringer.

1907

To Mrs. Potter Palmer[1]

43 Welton Place, Chicago, Ill.,
January 12, 1907.

Mrs. Potter Palmer,
100 Lake Shore Drive,
Chicago, Ill.

Dear Madam:

By the announcement of the daily press I learn that you are to entertain a number of persons who are to be present as representatives of two recognized classes of American citizens—the working class and the capitalist class, and that the purpose of this gathering is to choose a common ground on which the conflicting interests of these two classes may be harmonized and the present strife between the organized forces of these two classes may be brought to a peaceful and satisfactory end.

I credit you with perfect sincerity in this matter, but being fully aware that your environment and whole life has prevented you from seeing and understanding the true relationship of these two classes in this republic and the nature of the conflict which you think can be ended by such means as you are so prominently associated with, and with a desire that you may see and understand it in all its grim reality, I respectfully submit these few personal experiences for your kind consideration.

I am a workman's daughter, by occupation a dress-maker and school teacher, and during this last twenty-five years an active worker in the organized labor movement. During the past seventy years of my life I have been subject to the authority of the capitalist class and for the last thirty-five years I have been conscious of this fact. With the years' personal experience—the roughest kind best of all teachers—I have learned that there is an irrepressible conflict that will never end between the working-class and the capitalist-class, until these two classes disappear and the worker alone remains the producer and owner of the capital produced.

In this fight I wept at the grave of nineteen workers shot on the highways of Latterman, Pennsylvania in 1897. In the same place I marched with 5,000 women eighteen miles in the night seeking bread for their children, and halted with the bayonets of the Coal and Iron police who had orders to shoot to kill.

I was at Stanford Mountain, W. Va., in 1903 where seven of my brother workers were shot dead while asleep in their little shanties by the same forces.

I was in Colorado at the bull pens in which men, women and children were enclosed by the same forces, directed by that instrument of the capitalist class recently promoted by President Roosevelt, General Bell, who achieved some fame for his declaration that "in place of Habeas Corpus" he would give them "Post Mortems."

The same forces put me, an inoffensive old woman, in jail in West Virginia in 1902. They dragged me out of bed in Colorado in March, 1904, and marched me at the point of fixed bayonets to the border line of Kansas in the night-time. The same force took me from the streets of Price, Utah, in 1904, and put me in jail. They did this to me in my old age, though I have never violated the law of the land, never been tried by a court on any charge but once, and that was for speaking to my fellow workers, and then I was discharged by the federal court whose injunction I was charged with violating.

The capitalist class, whose representatives you will entertain, did this to me, and these other lawless acts have and are being committed every hour by this same class all over this land, and this they will continue to do till the working-class send their representatives into the legislative halls of this nation and by law take away the power of this capitalist class to rob and oppress the workers.

The workers are coming to understand this and the intelligent part of that class while respecting you, understand the uselessness of such conferences as will assemble in your mansion.

Permit me to quote from Goldsmith's "Deserted Village," where he says:

> "Ill fares the land, to hast'ning ills a prey,
> Where wealth accumulates and men decay."

Quite appropriate to this fair land to-day.

Sincerely yours, for justice,
Mother Jones

Printed letter (*Miners Magazine,* 24 January 1907)
1. Bertha Honoré Palmer (1849–1918), Chicago socialite and mild reformer, first gained public recognition for her management of the Woman's Building at the Columbian Exposition of 1893.

To Terence V. Powderly[1]

Bisbee, Arizona,
May 24, 1907.

Mr. T. V. Powderly,
Washington, D. C.
My dear Friend and Comrade:

For a long time I felt that I wanted to drop you a few lines and let you know that I am still alive, and fighting the common enemy as best I know how. I was in Washington last Fall and went there principally to se you, and spend a week or ten days getting notes on the old time fights, but after I arrived I found out that you had gone to Europe, a trip I considered you badly needed, after the long years of kicks and abuse you got from those you had faithfully served; and though all the world may abuse you there will still be one, who will defend you. I know of the many dark battles you had to fight. You were rocking the cradle of the movement, you made it possible for others to march on. No doubt, with many of us you made blunders, but I know and feel that you did the best you knew how under the conditions with which you had to deal. It was the early stages of the training school for the future conflict. Last month I happened to be within a few miles of Bruceville; as the train was passing through there in the early morning, I stopped off and went out to see the pillow of clay on which the head of poor Martin Irons[2] rested. He sleepeth well, Jay Gould cannot awaken him now. His grave was marked by a piece of iron, it is his only tombstone. It marked the spot where that brave warrior of labors battles rested. No tender hand seemed to care for it, but the wild flowers did not forget to plant their perfume around his grave. One thing struck me in the early morning, and that was that the birds had not forgotten that he was resting there, they had awakened from their slumbers, and were calling their mates to enjoy God's sunshine. They were not responding to the call of a trust whistle, only to the call of nature.

While waiting for the train I called upon Dr. Harris, to my regret he was not home. I met his charming daughter, and left a message of deep appreciation from both you and me for the doctor for his kindness to Martin in his last hour.

I enclose you a few leaves from his grave, Knowing how deeply you will appreciate them, and how poor Martin would feel if he saw you press your lips to them.

Now Comrade let me congratulate you on the manly and fearless steps you have taken in defense of our brave boys in Idaho. It is needless for me to say to you, that capitalism has no soul, nor no love for humanity or its sufferings, and those who take up the battle for the oppressed, must bear the penalty. How the spectacular performer in Washington has put his foot in it. The word "undesirable citizen" will go down in history.[3] He and his crew of pirates would no doubt give a great deal to undo that.

I hope you go out to see douglas Wilson. He needs your consoling words in his lonely condition, and his faithful wife needs some words of encouragement, I have always loved Douglas. He is a true brave fellow and the labor movement misses him from the field of battle. Tell him from me that I am going to write him a long letter some day in the near future, I would have done it before But I lost his adress.

The enclosed circular, will tell you the same old story of the robber and the robbed.

Will you be home next Winter? There are some things of the past, over which I want to talk with you. I want to spend a week or ten days in Washington,

Beleive me every faithfully Yours in the cause of suffering humanity,

Mother Jones

[*Holograph note*] If you can get me a copy of the government report of the Colo War do so   I am told it is out of print.[4]

TLS (Terence V. Powderly Papers)

1. Terence Vincent Powderly (1849–1924), Grand Master Workman of the Knights of Labor, 1879–1893, and an official in the Bureau of Immigration, 1907–1921, kept a room in his house in Washington prepared for Mother Jones whenever her travels brought her there.

2. Martin Irons (1833–1900), a Knights of Labor official, was blamed by his associates for the failure of a strike against the Missouri Pacific Railroad in 1886; blacklisted by employers, he died in poverty.

3. Theodore Roosevelt, in a letter released to the press in April 1907, used the words in reference to Debs, Moyer, and Haywood. Labor leaders were incensed, especially because of the approaching legal proceedings against Moyer and Haywood.

4. Probably *Labor Disturbances in Colorado*, Senate Document No. 122, 58th Congress, third session (Washington, D.C.: GPO, 1905).

1908

To Phillip Henry Callery

Springfield, Ill.,
12–21–1908

Dear Comrade Callery[1]

I have been slow in answering your letter that does not mean that I have forgotten you. I never will forget you Phil you are one of my true Comrad. I do not hear a word from Comrade Debs. he seems to have forgotten me. but I will not forget him. poor fellow. he was worn out

I am working in this part of the State raising money for the Mexicans who are held in Jail in Los Angeles and Arizona   I am going to Save their lives if money will do it: how I would like to be with you Chrixmass but I cannot Phil   See this article   read it over   Send it back to me   I want to write you a long letter but have to go to a meeting in a few minutes. Phil is this damnable   this is the way the poor Comrades are Swindled

Loyally yours
Mother

ALS (Ida and Phil Callery Papers)
1. Phillip Henry Callery (1880–1954), attorney for District 14, UMWA, in Pittsburg, Kansas.

To Thomas J. Morgan[1]

E. St. Louis,
December 30th, 1908.

My dear Comrade Morgan:

I received your letter a day or so ago forwarded to me from Springfield. I appreciate very much the correction you made, only I thought it might have been well to have left the wife question out. I did not catch what you said about the Daily. The letter you sent me, that is the personal letter you sent me, I think it got in the fire with some other mail that I was destroying before I fully read it. I am afraid that Daily is going to involve us all in some trouble before we get thro' with it. Hoehn[2] thinks I had better not put that letter in the press owing to the criticism the enemies of the movement would make and the capital they might make out of it against the cause, but he says for me to send it to every national committeeman and every state secretary and all members of the executive board, also to the national office for the Bulletin. Let me have your opinion about it before I start out. I expect the bunch will move that I be thrown out of the party of course for exposing this graft, but then I'll stand that, I'll still be a socialist. Now, I wrote to that King[3] of ours about that $200 he owes me and I have received no reply. I am inclined to think that he wants some trouble, and if he does, I'll give him all he wants of it.

I am yours for the cause,
Mother Jones

TLS (Thomas J. Morgan Papers, Urbana)

1. Thomas John Morgan (1847–1912), machinist union officer, lawyer, and leader of the socialist movement in Chicago. He and Mother Jones were associated in socialist and labor affairs in Chicago in the 1880s, and perhaps earlier.

2. Probably Gottlieb A. Hoehn (b. 1865), shoemaker turned Socialist journalist, editor of *Labor,* a St. Louis journal.

3. John Mahlon Barnes (1866–1934), once an official in the cigar makers' union, became secretary of the Socialist party in 1905 and served until 1911.

1909

To the Socialists and Trade Unionists of America

20 February 1909

From out the bastiles of capitalism in California and Arizona comes the appeal of our Mexican comrades and brothers, Magon, Villareal, Rivera and Sarabia, our Mexican Comrades, who have been bravely fighting for liberty in Mexico, are behind dungeon bars, the victims of the persecution of the Mexican dictator, aided and abetted by the hirelings of capitalism in the United States.

These valiant defenders of the people's rights are charged with having violated the neutrality laws of this country, a flimsy excuse for their incarceration. The real reason is that they espoused the cause of their enslaved people and could not be bribed or intimidated to betray them.

Being driven from their own country by the hounds of the dictator, they went to St. Louis, where they organized the junta of the Mexican liberal party and there began the publication of a paper exposing the whole diabolical conspiracy of the two governments to establish a system of mutual co-operation in the interests of the capitalist class by keeping the Mexican workers in a state of industrial peonage.

The Standard Oil company, the Southern Pacific Railway company, the Philip Dodge Copper company and others heavily interested in the exploitation of Mexico all feared they would lose their grip if the liberal party should be allowed to rise in that country.

Let it be understood that Mexico is today an absolute despotism. Diaz rules with an iron hand, concealed in a glove of velvet. The heartless old hypocrite smiles his approval of James Creelman's characterization of him as a benevolent and fatherly old ruler. He is fatherly to his subjects in the same sense that Nicholas is the "Little Father" of the wretches whose life blood the vampire is sucking.

Diaz is surrounded by an army of spies who do his bidding without question. Criticism of his tyranny is treason, followed by imprisonment or death. Never was there a greater sham than the so-called "Republic" of Mexico. The "Republic" is merely an empty shell, a deception, a fraud, "a whited sepulchre filled with dead men's bones."

It is against this blood-stained despotism that our Mexican heroes, who have been lying in our jails these past fifteen months, have made their fight, and they have had to make it under circumstances which

67

would have appalled and disheartened less resolute and unconquerable spirits.

There is not a doubt that Rockefeller, Morgan, Harriman and other Wall Street pirates are backing up the persecution of these Mexican patriots. They are the holders of Mexican bonds and the owners and exploiters of Mexican interests and they, of course, lend a ready hand to Diaz in keeping his hordes of peons in slavish subjection. Any uprising of the slaves would be a menace to the interests of our American capitalists and that is why the capitalist press is either silent while these outrages are being perpetrated or gives its influence to Diaz in crushing out the spirit of liberty among his subjects.

This crew of commercial pirates dictates to presidents, cabinets and congresses. The house of lords, known as the senate, consists of its special representatives. The courts are its private possession. Governors, legislators and other public officials are all under its domination. Alabama is a recent case in point where the governor proved himself the pliant tool of the plutocracy in crushing the famishing coal miners.

Morgan, the moving spirit among the capitalists and Taft the political instrument of that class, soon to be inaugurated president, were both the special guests of the monster who sits on the Russian throne at Petersburg and doubtless exchanged hearty congratulations upon the outlook.

Elihu Root, as secretary of state, was the special guest of Diaz, and it is easy to understand the mission of this foxy lawyer who got his start in the service of Boss Tweed, the notorious New York crook and boodler.

"Colonel" Green has sold out his mines in Mexico to the Standard Oil company. An English and Canadian syndicate owns all the street car lines. The Philip Dodge copper syndicate of New York owns vast mining interests. The Southern Pacific has large railroad concessions and so have other companies of American capitalists, and *this is the milk in the cocoanut.* These capitalists would crush out the last vestige of Mexican liberty to keep in the graces of Diaz and protect their brigand interests which are rooted in a peonage as cruel and heartless as history records in the middle ages.

When it is understood that the wages of these peons, hundreds of thousands of them, is from 15 to 25 cents a day for making gigantic fortunes for American, English and Mexican capitalists, it can be readily understood why the rising spirit of revolt is to be crushed and why Magon and his compatriots are to be shot to death or buried alive in some hellish dungeon.

This is but a small part of the gruesome and revolting story of our

Mexican comrades. They are fighting as brave a battle as men have ever engaged in at any time in history. They are the people's champions and have risked their lives over and again to serve the masses who look to them trustingly to lead their almost forlorn hope.

Can we be indifferent to the duty we owe these brave comrades of ours who are fighting for the same cause we are under far greater difficulties?

Comrades and fellow workers, let us all unite in a determined effort to rescue these patriots from their impending fate. There is no case against them. They are innocent of crime. They have violated no neutrality laws. All they have done is to rise in revolt against the despotism of Diaz and this it was not only their right but their duty to do and for this they ought to be honored by every liberty-loving citizen of the American republic and especially by the organized workers who themselves know what it is to be persecuted for the sake of serving the masses in servitude.

You have saved Moyer and Haywood, you have saved Rudowitz, and now you have got to save our heroic Mexican comrades!

Mother Jones

Printed letter (*The Appeal to Reason,* 20 February 1909)

To Gottlieb Hoehn

Washington, D. C.,
June 17, 1909.

Editor Hoehn,
St. Louis, Mo.
Dear Comrade:

I have been hard at work for a week, working for the release of the Mexican Political Refugees. Yesterday the President gave me an audience. I presented a sworn statement from Guera, who has been sentenced to the Federal penitentiary at Leavenworth, Kansas. Warden McCloughery was extremely courteous and sympathetic in every way.

T. V. Powderly, one of the early fighters for Labors' rights in the stormy days of the past, arranged a meeting with the attorney of the Board of Pardons; he gave me a very respectful hearing, and promised to send the papers to the President as soon as possible.

When the President and I met, his salutation was: "Mother Jones, it seems to me that you are always working in behalf of the friendless?" I replied: "Well Mr. President, those who got many friends do not need my assistance." I explained my mission to him; he said: "I am afraid that if the pardoning power was invested in you, there would be no need of jails and penitentiaries." "Well, Mr. President, I remarked, if we would direct half of our money in making people good, that we are in making criminals, we would be better off!" The President said: "There is some truth in that, Mother!" I showed up the case to the President, and that these men were not getting a square deal in the West. The President promised to take the matter up as soon as possible, and he would let me know the results.

I have every reason to believe from the President's expression on the matter that the man Silva from El Paso will receive his pardon; he has been hounded by the tyrannical Diaz and his dogs of war for twenty years. He is now perishing in the federal penitentiary.

The case of Guera I showed the President that Joseph Priest, the secret service man in San Antonio, was the man most responsible for this poor fellow's conviction, he misrepresented the statement of his own lawyer and told him to plead guilty, much against his own convictions he did so. I think the President will take action in the matter.

I must state that the President seems to be on entirely different type of an American than his predecessor. I don't think when he retires from office, he will go out to kill monkeys way off in the jungles of Africa.

I hope that justice will be done to these poor refugees, and I believe that President Taft will see that justice is done.

However, we must keep up the agitation in behalf of justice, keep the matter everlastingly before the public.

Yours truly,
Mother Jones.

Printed letter (St. Louis *Labor*, 26 June 1909)

To Gottlieb Hoehn

Pittsburg, Pa.,
June 27, 1909.

Editor
St. Louis Labor
Dear Comrade:

Have been quite busy of late. This is the first opportunity I have to write you a few lines. Am here in Pittsburg now and must take next train to New Castle. I went down to Baltimore where I met your mother and sister. Your mother looks as if she were only forty years old; is a fine and strong woman. Came down from Washington and spent afternoon with her. I guess you received my last week's Washington letter?

Yours truly,
Mother Jones.

Printed letter (St. Louis *Labor,* 3 July 1909)

From J. Mahlon Barnes

Chicago, Ill.,
July 17, 1909

Mother Jones,
c/o Miners' Magazine,
605 Railroad Bldg.,
Denver, Colo.

In consideration of your letter of June 24th and the fact that I have word from your attorney that the suggested financial arrangements are satisfactory, I deem it proper to advise you that the National Executive Committee of the Socialist Party will hold a session at National Headquarters on the 23rd inst.,

Respectfully yours,
J. Mahlon Barnes.

TLS (Thomas J. Morgan Papers, Urbana)

To Thomas J. Morgan

Denver, Colorado,
July 20, 1909.

Thos. J. Morgan,
Attorney-at-Law,
Unity Bldg. Chicago, Ill.
Dear Comrade Morgan—

I received your letter yesterday and glad you brought the thing to time. Strange that the fellow didn't have honor enough as a representative of a great cause to respond to my request like a man instead of acting like a contemptible sneak. He forced me to take the action I did, and I am glad that you advised me as you did. I more than appreciate your action.

Enclosed in this letter you will find a note from him also to me. I discussed the matter of the Daily Socialist with a few loyal comrades in Kansas City. They were at a quandary as to what to do. I told them to write to you for information. I think the trouble with our movement today is that the rank and file do not understand things as they are, but I am doing my part to wake them up whether it offends the national committee or the national secretary. I intend that the Comrades shall be made familiar with things as they are, and I am perfectly willing to face the music. Mills[1] forced himself on the Comrades in Kansas City. They took him down to a little town—He charged $15.00 for his lecture and $1.00 for his expenses, and the poor fellows had to dig down in their pockets and put up the cash. If this thing isn't stopped, there is going to be a terrific upheaval in the movement.

Now, I want to call your attention to the enclosed note and to the tone of it. I ask you—would an honorable man write such a note after holding that money for four years without ever opening his mouth about it? Is a man of that small caliber fit to hold the position he does in the Party? He has never before advised me when the National Executive Committee was going to meet, nor do I even get a ballot to vote on, but if he wanted me to do any dirty work for him I would soon get all the ballots I could use and all the notifications I could.

Retain the check until I see you. If you wish to communicate with me you can write to Snider Hotel, Troost Ave and Twelfth St. Kansas City Mo.

Accept my appreciation for the work you have done. I know that you were the last person he wanted to get ahold of those documents. I am

Loyally yours for the Cause,
Mother Jones.

TLS (Thomas J. Morgan Papers, Urbana)
1. Walter Thomas Mills (1857–1942), an economist and educator of Berkeley, California, wrote and lectured for the Socialist party.

From Ricardo Flores Magón, Antonio I. Villarreal, and Librado Rivera[1]

Territorial Prison,
Florence Arizona, Nov 31, 1909.

Beloved Mother Jones:

You will find enclosed a long statement in regard to the Mexican cases. Read it carefully, and kindly do everything in your power to fulfill those of our recommendations you consider practicable and well founded.

Despite all restrictions calculated to keep us from reading Socialist papers, we have succeeded in obtaining information about your splendid work. You are setting a noble example and teaching a lesson humanity should not forget. You, an old woman, are fighting with indomitable courage; you, an American, are devoting your life to free Mexican slaves.

And they will be freed in the near future, and they will learn to call you Mother.

You are conforming the beautiful thought of Lamartine: "There always is a woman at the foundation of every great movement." You are the woman at the foundation of this tremendous struggle for the emancipation of our country and you will live forever in the hearts of all liberty loving Mexicans.

> With best wishes, we are,
> Yours for the Revolution,
> R. F. Magón,
> Antonio I. Villarreal,
> Librado Rivera.

TL (Terence V. Powderly Papers)

1. Ricardo Flores Magón (1873–1922) was the leader of the refugee revolutionary Partido Liberal and the editor of its organ, *Regeneracion*. He died in the federal prison at Leavenworth, Kansas, while serving a sentence for violating the neutrality laws of the United States. His brothers Enrique (1887–1954) and Jesus (1872–1930) were associated with him in the formation of the Partido Liberal junta, but broke with him in 1910–1911 to assist in setting up the government of Francisco I. Madero. Antonio I. Villarreal (1879–1944), was the secretary of the Partido Liberal, but broke with Flores Magón to serve as a brigadier general and consul general to Spain for Madero. In 1920–1921 he was the secretary of agriculture under Adolfo de la Huerta and Alvaro Obregon. Librado Rivera, writer and teacher, was associated with the original Partido Liberal manifesto.

From 1906 to 1911 Mother Jones spoke at meetings across the United States to arouse sympathy and raise money for the defense of the Mexican revolutionaries.

To William Howard Taft[1]

[2 December 1909]

Dear Mr. President:

You may remember that I called upon you last April and June and had a personal interview, in which I presented the case of Guerra and his two companions, the Mexican revolutionists who are now lying in the government prison at Leavenworth, Kansas, having been convicted of conspiracy against a friendly power.

I also spoke of the case of the three others who are incarcerated in the government penitentiary at Florence, Arizona, under the same charge. These six men, in my estimation, were moved by exactly the same motives which were felt by Washington, Jefferson, Adams, Patrick Henry and the fathers of our own American Revolution. They are merely striving to institute in Mexico, a sister republic the same free institutions which we presumably enjoy in this country, and it shows how far we have receded from our original ideas of freedom when, instead of giving these men seats of honor in this country, we put them in our jails, and it also shows to what extent the power of international capital has grown when it is oppressing freedom of speech and press in all countries of the world.

However, I am not going into any lengthy defense of their action; you know the facts of the case and if you do not see fit to pardon them I have nothing more to say, but I would remind you when I had my conversation with you that what I dwelt upon was the particular inhumanity of keeping Guerra in prison, for he is shortly to die of consumption. When I left him last April he was in the hospital without any practical hope of recovery.

After leaving you I called upon the attorney for the Board of Pardons and he said that an application for Guerra's pardon was not on file, but on my insistence that it was he looked into it and apologized for his mistake, and said he would give it immediate attention and he thought it was a case that certainly merited action of some sort. I have been waiting patiently for a long while to see what would be done, and certainly thought after my interview with you and with the attorney for the Pardon Board I would at least hear what was the final decision, but so far I have heard nothing.

I make this appeal to you again in behalf of a dying patriot, who some day will be mentioned as one of the martyrs who gave up his life to institute a real democracy in Mexico. I am convinced that we never can sustain our reputation of being a truly Christian nation if we continue in the path of inhumanity marked by our action toward Guerra.

I do not want to bother you with further letters or personal calls, but if you would intimate that you will receive me again so that I can give you further light upon the entire Mexican situation, I am at your command.

Very respectfully yours,
Mother Jones.

Printed letter (New York *Call*, 2 December 1909)

1. William Howard Taft (1857–1930), the twenty-seventh president of the United States, had granted Mother Jones an interview on June 16 at which she pleaded the cases of the Mexican revolutionists. This open letter may never have been mailed; it does not appear in the index to the Taft Papers.

1910

Statement of Mother Jones

Peoria, Ill.
May 12, 1910.

In April or May 1905, National Secretary Barnes came to me and said he was in some trouble. He wanted to bring his wife to Chicago, but a woman lived in the House with him, who had a mortgage on a lot that he owned in Philadelphia, and she would not let them move out of the House and take their furniture until such time as he paid the $200.00 due on the mortage. He said I have been to see Tommy Morgan about it, but he has not been able to give me any assistance. I am afraid I will lose the lot. I said, Barnes, it would be too bad for you to lose that lot. Perhaps, I can help you out. I will send to a friend of mine, and maybe I can get the money from him. You ought to have your wife here by all means.

I immediately wrote and got $200.00 from a friend of mine. As I was going away and the money had not yet reached me, I told Secretary Barnes that the letter would probably reach the office in a few days and that he could open the letter and if he found a check for me, he could cash it and bring his wife to Chicago, which he did. He forwarded the letter to me, stating that he had taken out contents. A year or so afterwards he came and asked me if I would go out under the auspices of the National Executive Committee. I declined to do so, stating that I had made up my mind never again to be under the dictates of any master, if I could avoid it. He asked me if I would go out for the National Office, as they were pressed for some debts they owed, when National Secretary Maily retired. I said, in that case, I will go out and do what I can. I said you can bill me right away. He made the statement that he was only drawing $25.00 a month from the office. I said, "Why, Barnes, You can't live on that in Chicago, believing he was telling me the truth, which I afterwards found out was a lie. I sent him down $50.00 by Mrs. Flaherty the morning I was going away. I took no receipt for it. He had never acknowledged the receipt of it. I raised $500.00 and sent it into the office without its costing the National Office a single penny. I then stopped when the $500.00 was collected as the debt and was eased up. I was sick in Huntington and received the care and hospitality of Attorney Dan Hogan and his family. I probably never would have gotten well if I had not been in such kind hands. Years passed on and I did not ask

Mr. Barnes for the money. In the National Office I observed some things that I did not think was right in the National Office of the Socialist Party. I met him on the street one day, and he reached out his hand to shake his hands with me. *I declined to shake his hand, stating that I considered him a traitor and would not contaminate my hand by putting it into his.* On account of the Unpleasantness that existed between he and I, and the campaign year coming on I did not allude to the money in any way that he has in his possession belonging to me. Immediately after the campaign was over I took up the Mexican Refugee Case and wrote to him stating that I needed the money to defend my comrades who were in the bastile in Los Angeles. I received no reply for several week. I then wrote again another letter, reminding him of the time he borrowed the money and for which purpose. Again I received no reply. I wrote the third time, went to the post-office and registered the letter and took a receipt for it. The following Saturday night he sent me $50.00 by Miss Flaherty, stating to her that that made the second time he had paid that $50.00. He told Comrade Slick[1] that he had borrowed that money in Philadelphia from me, which was a diabolical falsehood. I remained quiet for a while and made no demand on the $200.00 he owed me. When in New York in June, I concluded that it was time that he was taking some steps to pay the other $200.00. I wrote him a letter, the contents of which is in the hands of Attorney Morgan. I gave him until the 15th of July to settle. He wrote an evasive answer and said he would tend to me the 15th. I was going away through the country, working on the Mexican Refugee case and no time to fool any further with him. I went over to Attorney Morgan, turned the whole matter over to him and told him to do as he pleased with it.

In conclusion, Comrade Slick told me, he is dead and in his grave now, I would not tell a falsehood on him, and he said: Mother, Barnes did not borrow that money to pay any debt with, but a woman in Philadelphia told him that if he did not send her $200.00, she would come to Chicago and expose him. I have not hesitated to repeat this to faithful comrades, for the party who keeps a man of that make-up at the helm is in danger, and the party and its principles is far dear and near to me than all the Barnes on the soil of America.

Comrades every word of this is true. I ask my God to witness this statement—every word of which is true.

Mother Jones

DS (Thomas J. Morgan Papers, Urbana)

1. Slick was the bookkeeper and Miss Flaherty a clerk and stenographer at the headquarters of the Socialist party of America.

To Thomas J. Morgan

Hazleton, Pa
Aug 1st 1910

Thomas H. Morgan
79 Dearborn St.
Chicago, Ill.
My Dear Comrade:

Your letter of July 16th at hand. Glad to hear from you and to find out that you and Frankel[1] were in the lead in Chicago. I am glad that Brower[2] was elected to the National Committee. I hope he will take no back water, and that he will fight that corrupt gang to a finish. Yes, Comrade we have nothing to loose but everything to gain for the slaves and our cause. I had a long talk with Stokes[3] and Walling.[4] Lemont[5] I went to the Call office to see him but he had just left. I know him very well from Kansas City. He is a good fellow. Comrade Morgan I have known you for almost thirty years in the fight I have never known you to flinch, although the bunch have tryed to blacken you everywhere through the country. If this movement is going to move onward for the benefit of the workers we must take our stand boldly and fearlessly with the working class. Not with the gang of self and notoriety seekers. Think of a movement called a working class movement that would not allow that Mexican question to come up in the Congress, and the questions involved, the right of asylum, the right of free speech and free press. But we forced the U. S. Congress to take the matter up and not the so called Socialist Congress that spend three days discussing the Immigration question, the so called sex question that is not a class question. I believe that it was the dam rottenness of that Congress that made me sick in Cincinnatti

I am going to send you a copy of the hearing before the Committee of Congress in Washington so that you will get a grasp of the work I have been doing for the last two years. Comrade Morgan I brought that question up before Congress all alone. No Socialist gave me aid. You see the dirty whelp must be guilty or he never would have made the slimy attack on me he did. I am laying low for that fellow, and when I open up on him he will wish he had never known me.

The very fact that he made that attack on a woman of seventy-six years who spend the best part of her days in the cause of humanity should condemn him in the estimation of every honest man and woman. I never drew a dollar from the movement. I have put money into it. The money I collected I can account for every dollar of it and when I get through with him he will wish he had never known me.

77

Comrade the more I get through the country the more rottenness I discover. And that bunch in the National Office that can be owned by Hilquitt,[6] Berger,[7] Spargo[8] must be cleaned out of it, or the National office will be busted. And the Socialist movement will go by the board. If a Labor Party is ever started in this country, I am feeling the pulse as I go along and I want to tell you the sentiment of the people. Comrade Morgan you will agree with me that a party is rotten to the core that send a junketting part composed of eight members, not any of them of the working class to Copenhagen to represent working mans movement. We have five hundred of our brave comrades in the bastiles of Capitalism in Argentine, pleading with us to do something for them. Instead of giving that money wrung from the blood of the working class back again to the commercial class, would it not have been better for us to have sent it to our comrades to fight them with. Do you wonder that the old warriors in the movement are getting discouraged and giving up the battle in despair. It seems a horrible indictment against our movement. I feel sometimes as if something will happen to tear us to pieces. You could not have conveyed any better news to me than the fact that you and Frankel stood at the front of the helm in the vote. If we could only tour the State of Ill and turn it upside down we might be able to change Cook county.

I did not see you before I left Chicago. But I through it into Bental strong before I left there. If a change does not come and we don't put in class conscious men on office we are doomed. However I have confidence in the rank and file if we can awaken them. Send the Provoker[9] to Charles P. Gildea, 23 W. Tamarack St. Hazelton Pa. He is one of our brave fighters and loyal to the end. He will help you in the fight and you can trust him. And also Alex Dwyer,[10] 8th & Alter Hazleton, Pa. I am holding big meetings here for the miners. I have not quite got over my attack in Cincinnatti. Write me again as soon as you can and beleive me always me as one of those who wants to be on the forefront of the battle for right even though I stand alone. Boland[11] in Washington is a fine fellow. Clean to the core. Well we will see what will come out of the junketting tour. The boys will send you subscription for the Provoker. And get you as many more subscriptions in the right place as they can.

I am Always your in the fight,

Mother Jones

TL (Thomas J. Morgan Papers, Urbana)

1. Probably G. T. Fraenckel, secretary of the Cook County, Ill., Central Committee of the Socialist party.

2. Probably George D. Brewer, who for many years was associated with the Socialist *Appeal to Reason*.

3. James Graham Phelps Stokes (1872–1960) was a wealthy, nonpracticing physician who devoted himself to settlement work and other liberal causes. He was a member of the Socialist party, 1906–1917, and a member of the executive committee, 1908.

4. William English Walling (1877–1936), a writer and journalist of independent means, devoted himself to Socialist and labor causes and was one of the founders of the National Women's Trade Union League. He sided with Mother Jones and the radical wing of the party in the internecine Socialist quarrels of 1909–1912.

5. Probably Robert Rives LaMonte, a Socialist party lecturer.

6. Morris Hilquitt (1869–1933), a Russian-born Socialist lawyer, author, and lecturer, was a member of the national executive committee.

7. Victor Berger (1860–1929) became a Socialist editor in Milwaukee and the first Socialist to be elected to Congress, in 1910. Denied a seat after his reelection in 1918, he was convicted of antiwar activities, but won a long struggle for a reversal and served three consecutive terms in Congress in the 1920s.

8. John Spargo (1876–1966) came to the United States from England in 1901, entered actively into Socialist affairs, and wrote books on social problems. In 1917 he resigned from the party.

9. A weekly socialist paper published by Morgan.

10. Charles P. Gildea and Alex Dwyer were organizers for the UMWA.

11. Possibly John Peter Boland, a young labor priest from Buffalo who served on the New York and U.S. labor relations boards in the 1930s and 1940s.

From William Parker

Sept–1–10

My Dear Comrade Jones

Your letter of the 30th rec and I am Sorrow that things have turned up that is making you feel a little sore on us comrades here in Du Bois. Now Comrade you say "the whole bunch of us have much to learn about the Socialist Revolution." Now as for myself I plead *Guilty* So that is just the reasons that I want to have you come to DuBois. I know that there is something rotten with our National Secy also the N. E. C. and I for one worked hard, to have them defeated. I want a workingmen N. E. C. and there is others who is very prominent in our movement who's life is like a closed book to me and most of the comrades here, and that is another reason [*line illegible*]. No one will deny that she is a grand talker but she is one who's life is like a closed book to me, and I want to tell you my dear old Comrade, that you will not need to stand alone in the fight to keep our movement clean, for I for one will stand by you. You be the general in this cleaning up of our movement Just give me one of your soldiers the orders and we to-gether that is all the revolutionists will clean it up, but how do you expect us to know what to do when even our publications are in control of the Fakers in our movement, where can we get the information if you and the true Revolutions dont come and tell us, that again is a good reason why you should come to Du Bois [*three lines illegible*] saying what train and date that I can expect you in Du Bois and you will find me at the depot ready to meet you

Your's for the *Revolution* with or without any way by God the Capitalists want it.

William Parker

ALS (Thomas J. Morgan Papers, Urbana)

To Thomas J. Morgan

Hazleton. Pa.
Sept. 9th 1910

Mr. Thomas Morgan
Chicago, Ill.
Dear Comrade Morgan:

I have been apparently a little indifferent lately in not writing. That is no indication that I have not been just as deeply interested   I have been doing some work along the line, talking about conditions. In going through the fileds from some of the Socialists I have concluded that there is a concerted movement on the quiet to blacken you or to kill any influence that the Provoker may have. Whenever some of them are asked Do you read the Provoker? edited by Tommy Morgan? the first reply that comes—"God Dam Tommy Morgan. "He wants to Morganize the movement". If you ask them, Do you know Tommy Morgan? the reply will come "No I don't, but he wants to Morganize the movement."

If you tell them "that is strange" Morgan has been in the Socialist movement over twenty five years; he has never attempted to Morganize it; He has tryed to keep the movement under the control of the rank and file; Ask him Do you know that you have not sent a working person to Europe to represent the American movement; they will tell you No? they don't know that". And the fact of the matter is they don't know who went to Europe outside of Victor Berger and Luella Twining, and Haywood.[1] However I am picking out good comrades to have the Provoker sent too. Charley Gildea and I, have been talking it over among our selves as to how we can organize throughout the country and get the Paper enlarged and sent out.

Is it true that Simmons[2] has gone to Girard. I don't see any notice of it in the Appeal. I hope that Wayland and Warren[3] wont be trapped into establishing another paper there. How very strange it is the selection of delegates to Copenhagen should come entirely from those who are bleeding the movement and forcing there notoriety upon the comrades. I see now they are calling for funds to defray that junketting tour. to Europe. They have five hundred of our brothers in Argentine locked up. It seems to me if we understood Socialism instead of sending eight delegates to Europe we would send one and use the balance of the money to get our comrades in Argentine out of the clutches of the money power. That bunch of pleasure seekers who attended the Socialist Congress in Chicago didn't consider it worth while to take up the Mexican question when it was the right of free speech, the right of free press the right of Asylum that was involved. The United States Congress was forced to see the importance of it. The question was forced before the public which prevented the poor Mexican refugees from being rearrested. I want to say that is as cold blooded a gang at the head of the Socialist movement as any gang of capitalist combination you can find. I want you to write to Charley Gildea 23 W. Tamarack St. He is one of us and he understands what is going on. I notice you have had Germer[4] from Illinois at a picnic in Chicago. He has been trained by Hunter and the gang. The enclosed clipping is taken from the Hazleton Pa Standard. You will note what I am doing.

Yours for the fight,
Mother

The enclosed letter you keep until I see you in Chicago.

TL (Thomas J. Morgan Papers, Urbana)

1. Luella Twining was a member of the National Women's Committee of the Socialist party. William Dudley Haywood (1869–1928) served as secretary-treasurer of both the Western Federation of Miners and the IWW. Arrested for sedition in 1918, he jumped bail in 1921, fled to Russia, and spent the rest of his life there.

2. Algie Martin Simons (1870–1950), writer and economist, edited the *International Socialist Review,* the Chicago *Daily Socialist,* and other Socialist organs. He was married to May Wood Simons, economist.

3. Julius Augustus Wayland (1854–1912) edited the most successful Socialist journal of the day, *The Appeal to Reason,* in Girard, Kansas. Fred D. Warren (1872–1959), served as associate editor of the *Appeal.*

4. Adolph F. Germer (1881–1966), a longtime member and official of the UMWA, served as national secretary of the Socialist party, 1916–1919. He later became a major figure in the CIO.

To Thomas J. Morgan

Akron, O.,
Oct. 14, 1910.
Write 160 this place

Thomas J. Morgan
Attorney-at-law,
Chicago, Ill.
Dear Comrade Morgan:

I have been trying to reach you with a letter for some weeks, but you know how hard it is for me to write and paticuliarly to get some one to do the writing for me. Well, I see that the Committee has covered up the mess in the National Office, but not for all time   what a bunch of trimers we have at the helm of our movement   I wish you could write and get some information from a comrade by the name of Slusser in Cleveland, O., he could give you some information about Mrs. Barnes and Lewis. He has gone West now and if there was any way that you could reach him, but I don't know how to put you on. I will inclose his card in this letter and he will tell you something that will startle the King. Keep on with the Provoker   you can't imagine how it has disturbed the boyes in New York and what a force it is lining up for a house-cleaning. I took a trip up to Cleveland for the express purpose of feeling the pulse of the Comrades   I am doing work here now on that line. I am going to Canton, Sunday and will do my part down there to awaken comrades down there, if those fellows think we are not going to clean house they are very much mistaken and they don't know who they are dealing with   I for one won't let up nor neither will anyone who understands the philosophy of the movement. We are not building a movement for free-lovers and job hunters. Just think of that bunch composing that N. E. C. establishing themselves as judge and jury and telling us they are the movement. You are going to get a number of subscribers from this place   Mrs. Prevey[1] will gather them up here and forward them to you   When you see Frankell give him my regards. What is Brower doing? Drop me a line to this place as soon as you can.

I am,

> Yours to the end in the cause that
> needs us all,
> Mother Jones

TLS (Thomas J. Morgan Papers, Urbana)
1. Mrs. Marguerite Prevey, an optometrist, was a prominent Akron socialist with whom Mother Jones sometimes stayed in her travels.

To Thomas J. Morgan

> Greensburg, Pa.
> December 16, 1910

Dear Comrade Morgan

I have been up to my ears in a strike of the miners here I have not had a moment to spare   20 thousand men and women are here to be looked after   I have not had a moment to spare for the last six weeks. I just got back after ten miles going and coming in a blizzard to a house away from Civilization   I find the father down with Typhoid fever the mother and six children shivering with cold no clothing not a thing to eat. Our junketing crew [*six words illegible*] these wretches have been on a strike since last March living in tents. The little ones ailing with cold. Our wise nice Ex. Bd. feel their pains They know or care nothing for their suffering. I have not seen a Socialist paper for weeks nor do I hear anything from the seat of war—it would not surprise me if you did not hear of Congress from Milwaukee banquetting with Civic Federation next.

I have not been able to do anything for the Provoker here in this strike the people are not here. I am only stiring them up on the class war. It is a horrid picture of Capitalist Brutality

The movement has turned into a woman suffrage [,Temperance?,] Negro, salary grabing movement the class struggle is lost sight of entirely. I never had any use for Beelym his face to me does not indicate neither strength of character nor a depth of sincerity.

I see by the Bulleton that Goebel[1] wants to throw you and the provoker out I will be thrown out to he did not dare go that far Let them play their game they will have to get down and out Now whatever you say is the best course for me to pursue I will follow your advice.

[*Two lines illegible*] know not the struggles of the working class.

I am quitely informed by parties in the Government Service that the Gov in Washing is gathering up notes about Wilshires[2] money scheme If the prove them fradulent he will go up. There has been some notes taken from the *provoker*. Send me the last 4 or 5 provokers I guess they turned the world up side down when they met in N. Y.

Loyally
Mother

ALS (Thomas J. Morgan Papers, Urbana)

1. George H. Goebel (b. 1876), a carpenter from New Jersey, helped to found the Socialist Party of America and remained an active leader in the organization for more than two decades.

2. Henry Gaylord Wilshire (1861–1927), author and editor of *Wilshire's Magazine*, was frequently a Socialist candidate for office, running for Congress in California and New York, and for seats in the British and Canadian parliaments.

To Thomas J. Morgan

Greensburg, Pa.
Dec. 25, 1910

Dear Comrade Morgan

Just came in from the camp of a lot of strikers. Some of them in tents. it is the Class War in its reality The poor little ones look as if the old world is hopeless for them   The day is cold and I am cold with it   The Scabs gave a dance last night   There was a Keg of Powder somewhere round   it went off and 25 of the wretches are in Hospital as a result of an explosion. These industrial wars are fierce but as long as the profit system lasts lives will be cheap.

[*One line illegible*] N. E. C. meeting—I do not see where any justice to us will come from that Board. Hilquit put him in there   Lewis and Goebel [got] their job from him   Spargo said they were not a debt collecting agency   That I was a frivolous old woman. They read the letter I sent him. They could learn from that he never replied untill I threatened to expose him   They had Miss Flahertys evidence bowers and they said we were liers. It seems to me I should ignore them   I remarked [*two lines illegible*] before them after 8 months they call on me. I [have] no time to go nor money to spend   I will not take the money of the party. I am here in an industrial battle against the powers that oppress my class I have neither time nor strength to waste with that bunch of midle class dictators.

Yes I know what Chase have done   I guess the fellow in Haverhill is not the only victim he has exploited that ex Mayor of Haverhill to a finish   They will lick the feet of the fellow who will give them an easy [*one line illegible*] but come what may I will stand with you for a clean movement   Don't think that I will flinch   They can put me out of the party but out of the movement never   Count on me.

They have been doing their dirty work   Their henchmen have been Daming Thommy Morgan   Dam the Provoker   To Hell with old Mother Jones   Shes getting old   We will make her shut up   She must go off and die   The capitalist don't think I am getting old   They wish I was   Well Merry Xm   it is a little lonely for me

> Always yours untill I rest
> in the [*illegible*] Earth
> Mother

ALS (Thomas J. Morgan Papers, Urbana)

From Joseph D. Cannon[1]

Box 2178, Bisbee, Ariz.,
Jan. 7, 1911.

Dear Mother Jones:

Your kind letter of the 28th ult. to hand, and of course I am always glad to hear from you. I had heard that you were in the Greensburg District, and I know of the kind of conditions with which you have to deal there, and I also know of the almost hopeless situation which must be there at this time, but the fact that those men will hold out the way they have done, in such a backward district as that has been is good reason for hope for the future.

It is too bad, that the election of officers in the organization should receive the entire attention of those whose first duty should be to concentrate the attention of organized labor of the entire country on the Greensburg district until this battle is won, but so far, this seems to be the usual conduct of most union officials.

Yes there seems to be something doing about our conduct here in making the fight for the right of the Socialist Party to have the privilege of making its political fight in Arizona. Those who would silently stand by while we were being surely outlawed as a party seem to be very anxious to put us out of the party and have a nice little mutual admiration club of their own, but it is very probable that we will give them all the fight that we can, and just possible that that will be as much as they want. I do not know just what the status of the matter is yet, I had one letter from Barnes, which is not specific enough, and have written to him again for a full explanation. If they have taken action to expell the Arizona locals which made the fight here for political freedom, I propose to have the rank and file of the party in the country take the matter up, and decide whether or not any one, or any locals can be expelled from the party without notice that action is to be taken, and if the referendum vote of a state is to be overturned without the state being notified that such action is contemplated.

Morrison, at Benson seems to be the one who is pushing the matter just what his soreness is I am not sure, but I think that he feels hurt because he was not the union attorney here, as well as attorney for the Mexicans when that trial was on.

When I hear from Barnes, if the action taken, means that the Arizona locals which made this fight are to be expelled, I will let you know at once, and we must get busy and put a stop to these "star chamber proceedings". It seems to be much like the DeLeon methods of expelling any local which does not do just as the ones on top want done.

However, I believe that the National Office was misinformed, that Morrison has deliberately lied to the N. E. C., and that committee in its superior wisdom has decided that there could be nothing on which it could be misinformed.

We got the constitution for the new state in pretty good shape. Of course it is not a socialist constitution, but it is the best state constitution in any of the states and provides for complete direct legislation, and amendment to the constitution by the people on 15% petition as well as many other advanced measures among which is one forever prohibiting fees in the primary laws.

The constitution may be rejected in Washington. There is a big fight being made there for that purpose. The recall seems to be more than the corporations want to stand for, and every influence that they can use is being used to kill the constitution there. If they succeed in their efforts the old territorial laws will be in force, primary, with the rest, and in that case these who have objected so much to the work we done will have a chance to show their good faith by paying the primary laws, when the time for another election comes around.

If they succeed in expelling us, we will not be supposed to interfere with the primary elections, although we can vote the ticket when it is put up, but the putting of it up will be the duty of the regular party members.

Martins, in Phoenix, are now running a rooming house. They have rented their home, and giving all their attention to the former. You would not be able to do much writing there, as it is too noisy, but when you are ready to undertake the work, let me know and I will try to see what can be done in finding a place where you can do the work at the best advantage.

Martins is getting old, and it seems to me childish. He has room in his head but for one idea at a time and that must be completely worked over before he discards it to take up another.

Yes it is true that the Mexicans are always wanting more money, and if there were not so many other places where it was just as necessary to send it, it would not matter. It seems that every one that gets any help consider that they are entitled to hang on forever.

When we paint their virtues to the public, for the purpose of advancing their cause, they believe everything we tell of them, and look for assistance accordingly.

Well good bye Mother for the present,

As ever your Comrade,
Jos. D. Cannon.

TLS (Thomas J. Morgan Papers, Urbana)

1. Joseph D. Cannon (1871–1952), an organizer and officer of the Western Federation of Miners; later a CIO official. He was a Socialist candidate for various offices in Arizona and New York.

Affidavit of Mother Jones, 31 January 1911

State of Illinois)
) SS
County of Cook)

Mary (Mother) Jones, being first duly sworn on oath deposes and says; that she is 77 years of age; that she entered the Labor movement during the strikes of 1877; that she became a member of the Knights of Labor, and in 1895 she became a member of the Kansas City Local of the Socialist Labor Party and is now a member at large of the socialist Party, that since 1894 she has been an active speaker and participant in the strikes of the miners, and since 1900 has been officially engaged by the miners union in the work of organization and strike service; she says further that she has no permanent residence, that for years her home has been in the tents, huts, and "homes" of striking men, women and children; that she is now on her way to Colorado under the instruction of the Western Miners Union to address a mass meeting February 2, 1911 in Denver and from there to speak at other places in that state in public protest against the usurpation of power by the Courts, by which sixteen members of the Union have been deprived of their liberty; that because of this duty she is unable to be present at the meeting of the investigating committee February 4, 1911 at the National Headquarters of the Socialist Party.

Affiant further says, the charges filed by her dated May 12, 1911 [sic] against National Secretary J. Mahlon Barnes are true and that she herewith suplements said charges by this affidavit.

Affiant says, she became acquainted with the said Barnes during a strike in Hazelton, Penna. in 1900, when he visited her in Company with Mrs. A. M. Simons, then engaged on the Philadelphia Inquirer, a Capitalist paper; that affiant met the said Barnes again during the Textile Strike in Philadelphia in 1903, together with comrads Slick and Rihl; that after his election in 1904 to the office of National Secretary she met him in Chicago; that the said Barnes came to her at [that time?] and said he was financially unable to bring his family to Chicago because of debt of $200, due on a lot held by some woman; that he had sought the advice of Tommy Morgan and now came to her; Affiant says she loaned him $200, that soon after he came to her again, stating he could only draw $25 a month for his office, and secured another loan of $50; that she then collected at meetings held in various places, from comrades a sum approximating $500 and paid by her into the National office to relieve the financial stringency asserted by the said Barnes, and which she believes was entered in the accounts of the National Office by Comrade Rihl book-keeper. Affiant further says that this contribution was obtained by her without the cost of one cent to the National office: Affiant further says that with this cooperative acquaintance with the National Secretary and his office, she visited the headquarters then located in Dearborn Street, Chicago, during her occasional passages through this city until her discoveries compelled her to discontinue.

Affiant says that while in the National office one afternoon, and in the absence of Barnes, Lena Marrow [*sic*] Lewis[1] opened the mail at Barnes' desk, being surprised, affiant says she asked comrade Slick about it and he said yes, it was the general thing, and there were more things she, affiant, ought to know.

Affiant further says that on another occasion she was in the National office from 1 p. m. to 5 p. m., that the said Barnes did not appear till 4:30 p.m., when Lena Marrow Lewis came into the outer room with him, she remained there while he came into the stenographer's [*word omitted*] near affiant, threw letters down and demanded copies. Affiant observed his appearance and manner and saw he was partly intoxicated. Affiant further says, she spoke to Comrade Slick about this appearance of Mrs. Lewis and Barnes and evidence of drinking and said the office needed a cleaning up.

Affiant further says that on another occasion while in the National office she saw Lena Marrow Lewis, go to the files and extract papers therefrom and leave the office.

Affiant says she spoke to comrades Slick, Flaberly [Flaherty] and Rihl, and was told Mrs. Lewis frequently used the files that way. Affiant further says that these discoveries destroyed her confidence and respect in National Secretary Barnes, and in the security and confidential preservation of the official correspondence in which comrades and friends of the movement placed themselves at the risk of public disclosure of their private political action and contributions to the party and by which they might lose position or be subject to annoyance and perhaps blackmail.

Affiant further says that while so impressed with this use of the correspondence and disregard of the National Secretary of the official confidence and trust reposed in him by comrades she was invited by Barnes to have lunch with him. This invitation she refused, and meeting him again the next day affiant says she responded to his salutation by denouncing him as a trator to the party.

Affiant further says that when her demand was made upon Barnes for a return of the $50 loaned him, he paid it with the declaration that he had paid that sum back twice, implying that he had paid affiant $100 for the loan of $50, this charge affiant declares to be false.

Affiant further says she was living in tents with the women and children of the miners on strike in the hills of Pennsylvania. The said Barnes declared in the National Bulletin that the affiant was a briber of Editors and officials of the Socialist Party, and a recipient of a large revenue from her activities in the Labor and Socialist movements.

Affiant declares these charges are false and asks that the said Barnes be required to produce whatever facts he has on which he has built his accusation. Affiant further says she regrets her duty to the imprisoned miners in Colorado is so imperative as to preclude her appearance before the investigating committee and affiant declares that at present she could add nothing to or take anything from her charges previously filed, or from those contained in this affidavit.

D (Thomas J. Morgan Papers, Urbana)
1. Lena Morrow Lewis (1862–1950), Socialist activist and journalist, was a member of the national executive committee of the Socialist party, 1900–1911.

Affidavit of Mother Jones

[January or February 1911]

State of Illinois)
) SS
County of Cook)

Mary (Mother) Jones being first duly sworn on oath declares the following statement to be true in substance and in fact:

Statement

That she is the Mother Jones whose charges of dishonesty against National Secretary J. Mahlon Barnes was filed with the N. E. C. May 12 1910 and in which I declared he was a traitor to the party.

That the publication in the National Buletin by the N. E. C. that these charges were made by Thomas J. Morgan and were Frivolous was a misrepresentation and an attempted fraud on the party.

That the statement of Barnes published in the Bulletin and thereby indorsed by the N. E. C. that I bribed party officials and Editors in support of which not a single name has been given, is both on its face and in fact a malicious falshood.

That his assertion in the same statement that as a free lance in the party I had made a large revenue and had slandered all the officials of the party is a double falshood.

That his denial that I collected and paid into him the sum of $500.00 to aid him when he was first elected, is a falshood.

That his assertion that he had been subjected for yers to my subterraenean attacks and threats is false.

That his charge that I Black-mailed him to the amount of $250.00 or any other amount is an infamous Lie. A lie proved over his own Signiture over which on July 12 1909 he confesses he is indebted to me in the sum of $200.00 and latter paid it without a word of question or denial of the amount due or reason for with-holding that sum for over four years.

That this charge of blackmail is further exposed as a lie in the denial under Oath of one on whom he named as a witness.

That his still more infamous charge that I have led an immoral life is a more infamouse lie. I am now 77 years old, have been a Widdow 43 years, During the last 30 years I have been active in the labor movement particularly in the organization and strikes of labor unions. In this servis I have been required to travel all over the United States and live with and under the observation of thousands of Fathers, Mothers, and Husbands and Wives, and but once has my honor as a woman been questioned prior to the attack of Barnes supported by the N. E. C. and that was by the Mine-Owners, Citizens Allicence, and Pinkerton Detective Agency in Denver Colorado, the combination which Kidnapped Haywood, Moyer and Pettibone and tried to hang them, and marched me out of the State at the point of the bayonet. This is the charge resurrected by Barnes and given new life by official support of the N. E. C. which makes the charge there own.[1]

D (Thomas J. Morgan Papers, Urbana)

1. This draft affidavit is unsigned, and the last paragraph is bracketed with a holograph notation, "She cut this out."

To Catherine M. Conroy[1]

Denver, Colo.,
Feb. 5, 1911.

My Dear Mrs. Conroy:

I arrived here on Wednesday night and was nearly worn out. I witnessed a big parade which was a protest against the courts. The gathering which followed was four miles long as they marched to the Capitol. I attended the meeting and addressed fully 12,000 people. It was a great day in the history of the labor movement in Colorado. I am very lonesome after my room and all of you—parturally after little Joe. I hope the strike will go on successfully in the Irwin field and I know that I shall be anxious about its' success. Tell John for me that I want him to quit reading novels and study a very important question—that is—the economic questions that confront the day. I wish that you would do up all my things and send them to 802 Buckingham Place, Chicago, Ill., I hope some day to come back and see you all and I will always remember what a kind, nice home I had with you—I miss my room very much and I don't know when I will get another like it. Tell Mr. Conroy to take good care of his health and don't you overwork yourself.

I am, believe me always yours for

A Grander Civilization
Mother Jones

Drop me a line to 605 Railroad Building, Denver, Colo.

TLS (Historical Collections and Labor Archives, Pattee Library)
1. During the 1910–1911 strike, Mother Jones rented a room from Peter Joseph Conroy (1869–1951) and Catherine M. Conroy (1874–1959) near Greensburg, Pa. Their son Joe (1902–1978) served as a messenger boy for her, carrying bail money to the sheriff to obtain the release of jailed miners. Later in life, young Joe helped to organize the Federation of Telephone Workers of Pennsylvania.

To Thomas J. Morgan

Denver, Colorado,
February 11, 1911

Mr. Thos. J. Morgan,
79 Dearborn St., Chicago.
My dear comrade Morgan:
I received your letter this morning and have no words to express my appreciation of your efforts. I have just mailed your letter to Solomon[1] and expect a return answer from him. I shall attend to the other letters to be forwarded to you at Chicago from this point. He took his attack from a statement that the Mine Owners made on me when I was here seven years ago and they put me out of the State by bayonet. He has to be shown up, and his colleagues with him, at any cost. You must have had a time at the investigation. His own statements would condemn him before any court in the country. Why did he undertake to pay you that money without a protest. Don't you know that no man would do such a thing, give up money that he did not own without protesting and furnishing some proof that he had paid it before.

I shall be in Chicago on the 22nd of this month. I had a telegram from Comrade Millard, of Cincinnati, telling me that all expenses would be paid. I concluded from his telegram that he is a pretty fair minded fellow. We had just as well fight this thing out now and clean up the rotteness in the movement. Let us take no back water, but go boldly to the front and either have a clean-cut movement or let us pull out from them. I have no fear of the result if we stand together and I believe we can and we will clean up the National Executive Committee and put them on record forever. Now, I am not in a mood to write you a long letter just after reading yours. But you will pleas locate John P. Hopkins for me. I want to write him a letter for he has known me for thirty-eight years. I will close by saying,

Victory to our Cause,
Mother Jones

TLS (Thomas J. Morgan Papers, Urbana)
  1. Secretary of the New York Socialist party.

To Thomas J. Morgan

Denver Colo
March the 12th 1911

Dear Comrade Morgan

Enclosed you will find a letter from Goebel It speaks for itself I had to leave Chicago Sunday night I had meetings billed in the mining camps

I realized the entire program was fixed before we went to the Hall I found out that fellow McFeeley was a part of the gang. I was the fellow who was sent on the Red Special I wanted to feel his pulse which I did. The whole combination is rotten to the core. There will have to be a house cleaning Those who eat at the Pie Counter will stand for any corruption for their [illegible word(s)]. Burger [Victor Berger] says "This is so bad it will hurt the party it will go all over the country" You should have tended to this last May Burger If the party can't stand the Search light, let that party down and out So far as I am concerned There's going to be something doing soon I wish I could get a list of the locals We want to send out a statement to them. The Miners Magazine is going to clean them up in a few days When he gets through with Germer there won't be so much left of [him.] I won't let up on that gang If they put me out of the party I am [going] to keep up this fight So far as these slurs at me it don't go I have put many years in the Movement bleeding it to death. I expect to put the rest of my life doing as I have been doing Send me back No of the Provokers for the last few weeks O Neil[1] will fix things They won't hang things up in the young peoples Hall Germer will not be very big when they get their doses

Well I have to close   I must go to a meeting of the striking coal miners

I am always yours in the Cause of truth

Mother

ALS (Thomas J. Morgan Papers, Chicago, box 1, folder 7)
1. John N. O'Neill was editor of the *Miners Magazine,* the official organ of the Western Federation of Miners.

To [Thomas J. Morgan?]

Denver Colo
March the 16th 1911

Here is a Sub[scription] for the Provoker   This fellow went to Copenhagen attended the Congress.   he does not give a very flattering report of the American junketting gang. The great Spargo speakes here tonight   The State will be revolutionized. Sure Jack the next No of the Miners Magazine will be a hot one   I will send you a doz

Keep quite about it   don't let up the fight   They will get cleaned up yet

Yours for a clean Movemt
Mother

ALS (Thomas J. Morgan Papers, Chicago, box 1, folder 7)

From Charly [Mahoney?][1]

Butte Mont.
Mar. 24, 11

Dear Mother:

Just a few lines to let you know I am well. Hope this will find you better than ever. I received the Provokers from Tommy. I am sending you a few to give to those boys out at Erie. I am giving the truth to the boys here. Barnes must be defeated, and I have decided to stay in until the next election and help show him up throughout the country. If I see it is impossible for to defeat him and his gang then I am going to throw them overboard. Well Mother if he thinks he injured you any he is much mistaken. I meet many of your old friends up here and they will show Barnes where to get off. They expelled Ida Crouch Hazlett[2] from the Party here in Montana, and then she joined in Chicago. These people here insists that Barnes publishes her expulsion in the Bulletin. He refuses. Now the State Committee has decided, that unless the National Committee makes known to the membership her expulsion from the party here in Montana, they are not going to pay any dues to the Party. Oh things are moving.

I have had a great time here with the I.W.W. bunch. I think I cleaned them up fairly well. President Sullivan[3] of the Union stated that if I had kept out of here, the Charter would be defeated. But now he states it will carry 3 to 1. I had a meeting in Anaconda. It will carry there by 8 to 1. Moyer will be here to-morrow or the next day. How are you getting along. Have you heard from Goebel? Well Mother I am waiting to hear from you. So with fondest love I remain as ever

Yours
Charly

Unless you soon write, I will think you are not well.

ALS (Thomas J. Morgan Papers, Chicago, box 1, folder 7)
1. Charles Mahoney was vice-president of the Western Federation of Miners.
2. Ida Crouch Hazlett, writer and lecturer, had worked with Mother Jones at organizing Socialist party units in Montana in 1905.
3. J. C. Sullivan was president of the Colorado Federation of Labor.

To Thomas J. Morgan

Denver Colo
March the 27th 1911

Dear Comrade Morgan

Let me have all the Provokers since the 25th I want them for ONeil. he wants to look them over—get some statements out of them. Germer is beginning to Squeel he read last weeks Magazine I guess—he is getting a little bit afraid Wait untill ONeil gets done with the Gang They will hold a [caucus?] there will be hell to Pay— Let her go.

Spargo was here handling the gang—that fellow [Flattery?] is as rotten as they make them I [have] a lot to tell you about that fellow more of the crew

Tell Car[1] not to take any back water The thing has got to be cleaned up. We cannot for the sake of the cause permit a gang to dominate & turn the revolutionary Spirit of the workers from what I can learn there is going to be something doing in the party. within the next three months.

Let me have all the news

Yours for Justice
Mother

don't you think that fellow Gobel is a double dealer.

94

ALS (Thomas J. Morgan Papers, Chicago, box 1, folder 7)
1. The Rev. Ellis E. Carr, editor of the *Christian Socialist,* was helping Morgan prepare Mother Jones's case against J. Mahlon Barnes.

To William B. Wilson

Denver, Colorado,
April 15, 1911.

Hon. W. B. Wilson,
Washington, D. C.
My dear Mr. Wilson:

Permit me the pleasure of introducing to you one of New York's foremost citizens, Mr. Jos. T. Keiley,[1] and a very esteemed friend of mine. He has taken quite an interest in the persecution of the poor Mexicans. Any service that you can render him, I shall more than appreciate and it will also be well rendered for the benefit of humanity. I am

Always yours,
Mother Jones

TLS (William B. Wilson Papers)
1. Joseph T. Keiley was a New York attorney.

To James Beauchamp Clark[1]

Denver Colo
Aug 7–11

Hon Champ Clark,
Speaker House of Reps
Washn DC

Jose Maria Rangel leader Mexican Liberal Party forces Prisciliano E and Reuben Silva and others handed over without trial to Mexican Federal forces by El Paso authorities. I ask you in the name of Justice and humanity to prevent this cold blooded murder as undoubtedly they will be shot unless some action is taken.

Mother Jones

Telegram (State Department Records, RG59 812.00/2269, National Archives)
1. James Beauchamp Clark (1850–1921), long-time congressman from Missouri, served as speaker of the House during the administration of Woodrow Wilson.

To Thomas J. Morgan

Denver, Colorado.,
August 8, 1911.

Mr. Thos. J. Morgan
79 Dearborn Street, Unity Bldg., Chicago, Ill.
My dear Comrade Morgan:

I received a copy of the latest developments in the National Office. They are horrible to think of. It seems to me that the honest men in Chicago ought to go up there and clean out the whole machine. No wonder Dan White[1] got up and lied at the 7th Ward Branch to protect the leper so that he would get a chance to eat at the "pie-counter" and get his $125.00 a month from the sweat and blood of the dupes who pay the dues in to support those leeches. They will have to clean out Work,[2] Chase, White and that whole bunch of blood-sucking grafters. Ever Socialist in the Nation today should blush with shame for allowing such moral lepers to get at the head of the party. No wonder that Simons and others were going over to beat the head of you for daring to expose the machine.

Well, things are developing much faster than I thought they would and the whole affair is horrible to think of. I don't know what we are going to do about it. The machine is in power and if they turn him down he will expose them, and so there you have it. There is going to be a terrible struggle within the party ranks, between the real Socialist and the Capitalistic Socialist. Strange that we have stood this thing as long as we have. Here is the National Executive Committee acting as officers, employing themselves, electing themselves to go to Europe, bleeding the poor unfortunate wretches for their fare and expenses, blind-folding them every way they can.

I think the Socialist of this Country owe me a debt of gratitude for the exposures. They jumped all over me, but now they see that I was right, and perhaps they will wake up and perhaps they won't. You send a copy of that stuff to Theodore Debbs,[3] Terre Haute, Indiana, and one to Mrs. Prevey, 162 So. Main Street, Akron, Ohio, one to Mrs. George A. Bates, 217 E. Myrtle Ave & Hoesley Street, Youngstown, Ohio.

Strange that he did not tell us something in the bulletin about this stuff. He was so anxious to attack other people in the bulletin why don't he show himself up. There should be a committee organized at once, to go over and take possession of the books in the office, because they will be all changed if the thing is not watched at once. I may go through Chicago inside of a couple of weeks on my way to Pennsylvania. I shall stop off for a day or two with you, and I want to meet all of you. Carr is a bigger man now than he has been before he was expelled and he will be a far bigger man and more important to the movement, when the comrades wake up to the injustices that has been done to him. But that is the fate of all brave warriors who take the bit in their teeth and fight for a principle. The brave die only once, the cowards have many queer deaths, and that contemptible leech will die many deaths.

Well get at it and clean it up even if you have to take the police force in with you. Write me a few lines and let me know what that railroad scheme was that they were going through with in Milwaukee. How many more villainous schemes will they put up in order to rob and impoverish the already plundered class. Carrie Lowe[4] and Dan White, and Harry Orchard ought again go to the 7th Ward, and defend their Nero.

Well, I am up to my ears in work here and have not a moment to spare for anything only the Industrial battle. I am yours for exposing D——rascals. All honor to you Morgan, Long may you live.

Mother Jones

TLS (Thomas J. Morgan Papers, Chicago, box 1, folder 7)

1. Dan A. White received a salary from the Socialist party as a national lecturer.
2. John McClelland Work (1869–1961) succeeded J. Mahlon Barnes as secretary of the Socialist party, 1911–1913.
3. Theodore Debs (1864–1945) acted as secretary for his brother Eugene.
4. Caroline A. Lowe came to Chicago from Kansas City in September 1910 to work in party headquarters as correspondent for the Women's National Committee.

To Manuel Calero[1]

Denver, Colo.,
Oct. 25, '11.

To The Honorable Mr. Calero,
Secretary of Justice in the Republic of Mexico.
My dear Mr. Calero:

According to our agreement before I left Mexico in keeping with my promise I went immediately to Los Angeles and called on Flores Magon. Mr. Cannon whom you met in Mexico accompanied me. The editor of "Regeneracion" their organ, was present with one or two others. I approached the subject to them, by asking them if it would not be more logical for them to go into Mexico and carry on their agitation there, as the Government permitted free press, free ballots, and a free discussion of the issues of the day. They would not accept any proposition that Mr. Cannon or myself made to them. They charged everyone with being a traitor, but themselves. I stated to them that I had been down in Mexico, had met some of the public officials and I considered them very able statesmen. They replied to me that I was very much deceived in them. I said "You mistake the person you deal with. I have dealt with men in every avenue of life nearly; I can form an average estimate of a man's principles and honor when he makes a statement". We discussed the matter pro and con for an hour, but they believed only in direct action, the taking over of the lands. That seemed to be the question on which they based their contention. I made the statement to them that they could not take the land over by force and hold it, unless the law of a nation so permitted them. I thought it was much more advisable for them to go into Mexico, go into the Legislature, and make the laws to reclaim the lands legally and legitimately. I stated to them that I did not believe in force, as it was the last resort of intelligent people. But they stated they were already taking the land over and that it was only a question of time until Madero would be overthrown. I told them that I found Madero a very broadminded man, and that he would carry out the laws of justice as far as he was able to. He said that already there was several states in revolt, but I said "You know in every nation that has had a Revolution it takes some time to settle down to a normal condition". It certainly will be so with Mexico, and if they would only act on reasonable lines I thought they would do a great deal of good for their people. After an hours discussion pro and con with Mr. Cannon myself and those men, I concluded it was useless to reason with them any further. We bid them good-bye and went away.

I then thought I would make another move. I took their Attorney Mr. Harriman,[2] who is now candidate for Mayor of Los Angeles, Before I went he told me he was afraid we would be unsuccessful but he said nevertheless, I would accompany you and explain things as clearly as I can. On Thursday, the 19th of October, I made my final visit there. Mr. Harriman put it up to them in this way: "Now suppose the Mexican Government permits the Mexican working man to organize, and guarantees safety to the organizers. Wouldn't it be better for you boys to go down into Mexico with a guarantee from the Government that you could carry on a legitimate educational agitation, than to remain here." Neither Mr. Harriman or myself could get them to accept any proposition that was made to them. In closing I said to them "Now, I want to say to you you have one of two alternatives, and I want to be honest with you. You cannot go into Mexico by force and take the lands, for the United States is a friendly nation to Mexico. They will not uphold any violation of International laws. There is one of two things before you. You will either go into Mexico, accept the proposition of the Government that is given to you here today, or you will be arrested by the American Government and handed over to the Mexican Government. I am not prepared to say what will follow after that." And I said to them "If you are again [ar]rested the labor movement will take no hand in your defense. It has done everything honorable for you. It has delved down into its Treasury and defended you when you needed a friend." So I bid them farewell.

Mr. Harriman said to me after we left "I don't think I will continue as their lawyer, or have anything more to do with them."

Attorney Cleary of Bisbee Ariz., who defended them in Tombstone when they were brought from Los Angeles called on me while I was in Los Angeles, and I discussed the matter with him and told him my mission in Los Angeles. I stated to him that I had been to see those fellows but was unsuccessful in convincing them in their mistaken methods. I asked Mr. Cleary if he would go with me and see if he could influence them and show them the error of their ways. He said to me "I would not go near them", but after talking with him for a while he said "Well I'll consent to go with you, but" he said "I would not have anything legally to do with them again. They have no appreciation for those who sacrificed for them at the time they most needed friends.

I missed seeing him at the hour appointed, so I did not have the pleasure of his company.

I went around among the labor unions, their committees and officials. They do not entertain a very kindly feeling towards them. I exacted a promise from them that they would not in the future by any means permit the qualified labor unions of Los Angeles to render any aid to those men, for the reason, when men are granted the rights to agitate within the border and under their own government, I don't consider that they have any right to come and do that agitation at long range, across the border under another Government. The officers of the labor unions agreed with me that I was perfectly correct. I learned that they receive considerable money from the Anarchists of Italy and Spain. How much truth there is in that I am not prepared to verify.

Now then Mr. Calero, so far as my promise to you goes, I have carried it out to the full extent of my ability, and in the future any services that I can honorably render to you in the interest of the oppressed class, I am ever and always at your service. Accept from me my deep appreciation of your courtesy to my comrades and myself while in Mexico. I shall always remember it with great pleasure. I shall send a copy of this letter to President Madero. I understand that he had been a friend to them in their hour of need. I consider them one and all a combination of unreasonable fanatics, with no logic in their arguments and when people tell me that these fanatics are honest I cannot agree with them. Fanaticism has never won anything permanent for humanity's cause.

I am

> Very Sincerely and Loyally yours,
> Mother Jones

Printed letter (in Isidro Fabela, ed., *Documentos históricos de la revolución mexicana* [Mexico City, 1966], X, 371–73)

1. Manuel Calero (1868–1929) served as minister of justice in the provisional government of President Francisco Leon de la Barra, and as foreign minister for President Francisco I. Madero. He was later ambassador to the United States and a senator.

2. Job Harriman (1861–1925), a clergyman turned lawyer, was active in Socialist organizations from 1890 on and had been Debs's vice-presidential running mate in 1900.

To Ricardo Flores Magón

> Denver, Colo.,
> Nov. 4, 1911.

Mr. Flores Magon,
914 Boston St.,
Los Angeles, Calif.
Dear Sir:

In looking over the last two issues of your paper I find some misstatements as to my visit to you and colleagues. I cannot conceive how you could so misrepresent the object of my visit. First you state "Not for sale", I believe that was the heading. I had nothing to buy you with or for. You stated, I had just come from President-Elect Madero with a proposition to you which you would not accept. It was not true. Mr. Madero never mentioned your name to me or any one else who was with me, whether he did not consider it worth mentioning or not I am not prepared to state. The Vice-President of the United Mine Workers, Mr. Frank Hays, Mr. Joe Cannon, representing the Metal Miners, accompanied me on my visit to President Madero. We found President Madero a gentleman in every sense of the word, a man with the most remarkable grasp of the economic struggle and the underlying causes. We discussed the matter after we left Mr. Madero and said to each other how remarkably well posted he was. It is not often that we find a man in his position with so deep and clear a conception of the wrongs of the people and the causes that produce them. The only person who mentioned your name while I was in Mexico was your own brother, a gentleman in every sense of the word. He expressed his deep appreciation for the work done for you and your associates during the closing years of ex-President Diaz reign. He said "I will remember you through all the years of my life for saving the lives of my brothers.

You say I knew nothing but what Villareal told me, again your statement is false. I did not have the pleasure of meeting Villareal while I was in Mexico, which I much regretted.

You say "that I knew nothing of Mexico." I must have known something of the conditions in Mexico under which the people suffered or I could not go before the President of the United States nor could I have brought the matter up before Congress. You should have told me all this before I went to Washington with your case and not placed me in such an embarressing position before the President of the Nation and Congress.

Then again you attack the American Federation of Labor. You should have refused the $4,000 that they donated if they are what you represent them to be. You should have notified me not to accept a dollar from them or their colleagues to defend you. Many of those braves after voting me a hundred dollars, would say to me: "We have left our treasury in debt Mother, but go and save the lives of those poor fellows." The immigration commissioner is a member of the American Federation of Labor. When your colleagues were arrested under the immigration laws and held for extradition, I went to San Antonio and held five meetings for your people there. I investigated the matter and immediately wrote to the Immigration Commissioner at Washington, and stated the cases to him. The United States Marshall was present at all the meetings. The victims were released.

I hope Mr. Magon, that this explaination will be satisfactory to you and convince you that the American Federation of Labor after paying all the bills, are not such a criminal combination as you might suppose them to be. I hope this convinces you that my mission to Los Angeles was not at all in keeping with the statement in your paper. Neither my colleagues or myself shall ever again insult you by taking any money from the American Federation of Labor to defend you if you should again get into the clutches of the law.

I am, Sir
Most respectfully yours
Mother Jones

TLS (Ramos de Revolución Politica Interior, Correspondencias Varios, 1910–1919)

To Thomas J. Morgan

Kofa, Arizona,
[1911?]

Dear Comrade
How did you like the Magazine article   I don't think they framed

that in the National office Orders are coming in from all over letters complimenting the Editor are pouring in.

The fight has just comenced I think Germer wished he was off the Com. here are a few subs every one makes another discontended The movement is filled with people who have no [idea?] of the Revolution. They are a lot of hero worshipers take it for grant.

Barnes put his when he brought the B mailing to cover up his durt he is not so slick after all he & his Harry Orchard will get cleaned up before this thing is ended

What a rotten gang that want endorsement from a drunken bum from Indiana they will wish they had never started the fight it will not end untill the party is cleaned up Write me how you feel about the Magazine

Loyally
Mother

ALS (Thomas J. Morgan Papers, Chicago, box 1, folder 7)

To Thomas J. Morgan

[1911?]

My dear Comrade Morgan

Barnes wrote to ONeil to advertise in the Magazine that the [stenographer's?] report would be furnished for 50 cts. O my God, what ONeil wrote back to him will never be hung up in the Young Socialist Hall.

I am going to send you one Doz of the next No of the Miners Magazine ONeil have Tore the gang to pieces there is going to be Hell. Keep up the

AL fragment (Thomas J. Morgan Papers, Chicago, box 1, folder 7)

To [Thomas J. Morgan?]

[1911?]

Will you tell me how eight Deligates happened to be sent to Copenhagan Were they elected by the Congress or a referadom vote did anyone protest Give the history correct ONeil is going to get after them

My God there is going to be hell to pay after Berger reads this weeks Magazine he will go up in the air don't forget to send the Provokers

Send me the Christian Socialist since the 25. I don't hear a word from Miss Flaherty. I am on the war path here for the Miners trying to get them to understand where there at

AL fragment (Thomas J. Morgan Papers, Chicago, box 1, folder 7)

To [Thomas J. Morgan?]

[1911?]

are doomed If Berger opens his mouth there is going to be Something doing   No matter what comes they must get out   The Movement have got to be cleaned up of the leeches. Get them to give you five cents apiece for the Magazine   We must flood the Locals everywhere

Can you by any means get a list of the locals so that we can send the Magazine   it is going to tear things to Pieces

Loyally yours
Mother

ALS fragment (Thomas J. Morgan Papers, Chicago, box 1, folder 7)

To Thomas J. Morgan

Grand Hotel, Cincinnati,
[1911?]

Dear Comrade

Don't [know?] when I will be in Chicago   these fellows are all O. K.   Mrs. S[1] spoke here Sunday   So did I   She got sore because the Trades Union wanted me to speak first   The Socialist are sore at her   She took $20 for forty minutes talk an got mad beside   have not a minute to spare or I would write more   I have lots to tell you

Mother

I leave in a few [minutes?]

ALS (Thomas J. Morgan Papers, Chicago, box 1, folder 7)
   1. Probably May Wood Simons (ca. 1885–1948), an economist, editor, writer, and Socialist lecturer who married Algie M. Simons, editor of the *International Socialist Review* and other socialist journals.

To [Thomas J. Morgan?]

Youngstown Ohio
[1911?]

Dear Comrade

I met with Local Youngstown last night & I opened their eyes   There will be something doing here soon. Why the Comrades were shocked They had a letter from Gobel, who wanted a date here but the last time he was here he was selling Wilshire Stock   They refused to take him   When a member of the Ex Board of the Socialist Party draws his revenue both ways it is time to stop the game   I am fixing things as best I can for the Cause that should be dear to all. Comrade don't flinch   You are getting a following   The Comrades are beginning to get their eyes opened I dont care if I am without a cent   I will show up the corruption in our Movement   They have their machine but right will be heard in the end. I am going to E. Liverpool Ohio tomorrow   Send my mail there untill next Monday.

I see they are starting a minstrel show for the daily   Six of them are to tour the country to gather Strickland[1] the all for Jesus guie is the leader. They fell down when they went out for S. H.   Now the campaign is over there must be a new source of revenue for the leeches   Strickland is the fellow who married the [*two words illegible*] to a ex Catholic priest after a Socialist meeting one Sunday afternoon in Anderson Ind. The Chicago Herald says if you don't like one man get another   The ex priest goes by her name   *Nice clean movement*   I will go up to the Central Coal field in Pa do a little agitation then I go to New York from there to Washington.   don't fear   There will be something doing in the next six months the only fear I have is that my strength is going but I am going to keep at it. I had a big meeting here last Sunday at New Castle in the afternoon   There is more hot air than real Revolution

I am always with you for a clear cut Movement of the Workers

Mother

Send mail to 308 Market Street E Liverpool Ohio untill Monday

ALS (Thomas J. Morgan Papers, Chicago, box 1, folder 7)
1. Frederick Guy Strickland, ordained in the Disciples of Christ, combined pastoral appointments in Ohio, Illinois, and Indiana with active participation in Socialist party affairs, including service as party secretary in Indiana.

To Thomas J. Morgan

Denver Colo
[1911?]

My dear Comrade Morgan

Your letter came in time but I have been rushed with work   I have cut out all dates, will be in on the 21st. I feel that gang of grafters who have lived at the Socialist pie counter for years will take a back seat   The Movement today is nothing more or less than a crib to get the foder out of for a few   I am going to clean up that two-faced Goebel I'll throw it into that fellow   he will wish he keep quite   that fellow have been playing his cards for some years   I think his days are numbered   I am going after them if I die   When they undertake to put you out of the party there will be a lot more go out   They have sucked the blood out of the Movement If you did not O K their rotten[nes]s why you must go I am going to raise H——with that gang

> Yours for the fight
> Mother

Will be in Tuesday

ALS (Thomas J. Morgan Papers, Chicago, box 1, folder 7)

To Peter Joseph Conroy

[1911?]

you must keep up courage even if the storm is fierce— Keep the children at school by all means. Tell Joe to be good and take good care of the Mama I hope you some one who will take care of the house. She alway had a home for everyone. I certainly felt at home & I wish I was there now to help her.

I hope the strike is pulling out to an end We have a hot time here they killed one of men a few days ago They women would have killed a half dozen scabs if the Sherif had not come along and saved them. I may be in Greensburg soon if the boys let me go

[*Illegible*] Joe tells James Brady to be good the world will be his sometime.

> Mother

ALS fragment (Historical Collections and Labor Archives, Pattee Library)

To Caroline Lloyd[1]

Charleston, West Virginia
Nov. 27, 1912.

Miss Carrie Lloyd,
New York City
My Dear Miss Lloyd:

Pardon me for not writing to you befor but I have had so much to do since I got back. I cannot give you any advice on coming down here just now owing to the fact that we have marital law here including military desperatism, and I am afraid it would be only a wast of money on your side because you could not go into the strike field   it is all we can do who are familiar with the field to get in there. I cannot express to you how deeply I appreciat the interest you have taken however if I were you I would try to make some arrangements with some magazines so that when the opertunity came you could avail your self of it to do good for the cause. That certainly was a tiresome night when we sent to Brooklin, I hope to have the pleasur of meeting you in the near future.

Sincerely yours,
Mother Jones

TLC (Henry Demarest Lloyd Papers)
1. Caroline Lloyd (1859–1940), sister and biographer of Henry Demarest Lloyd.

1913

To William B. Wilson

[February 1913]

My [dear] Mr. Wilson

here I am for the last week locked me in military prison   The civil officers picked me [up] on the streets of Charleston threw me into an auto   brought me 22 miles [to] the marshall law prison   The war[r]ant was not signed by the Squire untill after I was arrested   anarchy   if you can find anything [to] beat this in Mexico

Get this note to Senator Borah type writ[t]en and give to Senator Borah   Correct it where it needs [it.] They have over a hundred of our men in military [prison.]

O the Villians   they shot a man dead while [he] was takin[g] his wife to the S[h]elter   She gave birth to a babe while they were bur[y]ing him   Shot a woman through the leg   Talk about brutality   heavens this beats anything   That was after they went to bed

have Senator Borah's letter copy by Agnes   They do not allow anyone to speak to me

When I get out I will give them H——

Mother

I am just [scribbling?] this to you

ALS (William B. Wilson Papers)

To William E. Borah[1]

Pratt. W. Va.
[ca. 20 Feb. 1913]

To the Honorable Senator Borah, U.S. Senate.
Dear Sir:

Permit me to extend to you in behalf of the crushed and persecuted slaves of the coal mines of West Virginia my deep felt gratitude for your resolution[2] demanding and [sic] investigation by the National Government. The wretches have pleaded with the State to do something for them but in return they got the jails and bullets from the public officials.

I am in confinement now for a week at the age of 80 years. I am a military prisoner. This is just what the old monarchy did [to] my grandparents 90 years ago in Ireland.

Senator, do what you can to relieve these wretches and the coming years will call you blessed.

Gratefully yours,
Mother Jones
Military Prison, Pratt, West Virginia.

TLS (William B. Wilson Papers)
    1. William Edgar Borah (1865–1940), senator from Idaho.
    2. Borah had introduced a resolution to investigate conditions in West Virginia in the preceding session. It was resurrected and pushed through the Senate on 29 May 1913 by John W. Kern of Indiana, and is usually referred to as the Kern Resolution.

To Terence V. Powderly

Pratt W Va
Military Bastile
3–3–1913

My dear friend

You no doubt have heard of my arrest by the hounds of cap[italist?] pirates They have me in close confinement There are two military guarding me day and night No one is alowed to speak to me. The Supreme [Court] squashed all constitutional rights and handed us over to the military. here I am The first thing I will do if [I] am turned loose will be to go up and see you

Tomorrow at ten oclock we will be taken before the Military Court for trial They charge me and 3 other national organizers besid the Editor of the Argus a local labor paper Neither one of us was in the Marshall Law zone They picked me up on the streets of Charleston kidnaped me rushed me with 2 others down the military camp. here I am now for 22 days. Not allowed to speak to anyone or see anyone just think of it I have lived 80 years and never before charged with any crime Now I am charged with stealing a cannon from the military. Inciting to riot putting dinamite under track to blow up a C-O road We were not there at all Just think what the tools of the alagarchy can decend to I know they are death on me for I have cost them hundreds of thousands of Dollars

They came to me yesterday wanted to get a lawyer & witnesses I refused to get either. I said if I have brok[en] the law of the State or nation I do not want any lawyer nor witness one fellow said I should be drummed out of the State I have a lot to tell you when I see you God spare me the Heart to fight them Love to my dear Emma Tell her not worry I'll fight the Pirates to [the finish?]

Mother

ALS (Terence V. Powderly Papers)

To Caroline Lloyd

Pratt W. Va.
Military Bastile
17—3—1913

My dear Miss Lloyd

Your very kind note reached me yesterday handed over by the rep-resentives of the Spanish Inquisition   how deeply I appreciated your thoughtfulness   Yes We are held for fighting against the most infa-mous system of peonage   There is over a hundred of us up before the most infamous Court since the Midel Ages. I see that Michelson did not get his stuff in to the American. If it was anything against the workers every paper & magazine would be filled with falsehood.

And our Socialist papers are filled with thrash with what Vic Burger did in Congress and he never did a thing only boost Burger   how little they realize what this class war means   They have 3 sqare meals Thats about all they care.

here is the most far reaching thing that has ever taken place in this country   if the people stand for it, the death of human liberty have been sunded

I refused to recognize the court   I so stated to the military.   it was to me a [species?] of Fudalism a part of the Spanish inquisition   it was unAmerican   a disgrace to our age   They may chain me shoot me put in prison for life. I will never [one word illegible] that for a moral I recognized.

I am scraching this off in a hurry. It goes out underground   I am watched on all sides of my room   My old [three words illegible] this off   I am writing it blindly for I have to watch the windo I'll take no back water for the Pirates   Will write you again

fondly
Mother Jones

If you write don't send mail to   Send to Mrs Isable Carney   Pratt W Va   She brings my meals

ALS (Henry Demarest Lloyd Papers)

To Caroline Lloyd

Pratt West Va
Military Bastile (In Russianized America)
[Apr. 4, 1913][1]

My Dear Miss Lloyd

Your beautiful letter reached me yesterday. It takes some time for a letter to reach me unless the Corperation mules read it   I do not give them the Satisfaction of Seeing my mail if it is possible they woul[d] get that Satisfaction.

I miss your dear Brother So much with his Master Pen how he would put the State of West Va on trial at Bar of the Nation   I do not know what is [the] matter with the Socialist papers   I do not expect much from the Call   It has no grasp of these mighty Conflicts   We are up against a condition here that cannot grasp the situation

Your beautiful letter brought me such an inspiration in this lonely Bastile   I am writing this on my knees for the blood Hounds are watching every move   When I know my doom I will Tell   I was tryed 4 weeks ago by the Drum Head Military Court   I have not recd. my Sentence yet do not know what they pirates will give me   If I would sign a paper to leave the State they would let me, but I sign no paper accept no favors from Governor nor any one else   I'll die fighting the Crew of Pirates

Long live the Industrial Revolution   I have drawn the attention of the nation to their crimes   O if I could tell you the things that disgrace the nation that have existed in this God Cursed State   It's a disgrace to any peopl[e] & civilization   You cannot expose [*one word illegible*] putting salve on the ulcer   You must tear the ulcer open let the world see the root & what produced it   When I am out I will go to see you
fondly yours in the fight for freedom

Mother Jones

ALS (Henry Demarest Lloyd Papers)
  1. In another hand.

To William B. Wilson

Pratt West Vir
Military Bastile
April 5th 1913

My dear friend

Just going to drop you a line.   on the 12 Feb they picked me up on the streets of the Capitol brought me down handed me over to the Military. I have been guarded day and night ever since by the Bayo-nots   Not one moment have I been left alone. If a report hopes to speak, through the window he is arrested & thrown into the bull Pen. 5 weeks ago they took me before a Drum-Head Military Court. I refused to recognize the right of that Court to try me stating that I had done or said nothing but what I had done or said all over this country would go on fighting for Liberty all my life. When they concluded the Judge Advocate their was not Sufficient evidence convict me on, but they have kept me hemed in. I have not been outside the gate in 8 weeks only when they took me to the court room. from close confinement I am Suffering with headachs. I know they would let me go if I would go out of the State but I will die before I give them that Satisfaction wont you write to this gov & tell him it does not speak very highly of America to hold a woman 80 years incarcerated with no charge against her and Senator Lafolete to write to him with you I think after he gets a Letter from you he will act. this feller have been in about 5 weeks but he made no move to let me go. you know the mine owners are the Government they have Ten more of our boys in Clarksburg jail of all the black pirates that ever ruled a State they are here. Act just as soon as you get this Note. Sen Lafollette also I am insane for the want of air and exercise

Mother

Printed letter (Philip S. Foner, ed., *Mother Jones Speaks* (New York: Monad Press, 1983], p. 592)

To Caroline Lloyd

Pratt, W. Va.
Military Bastile,
April 27, 1913.

Caro Lloyd
Nutley, N. J.
My dear Miss Lloyd,

Your two volumes of Mr. Lloyd's Biography came to me and was received with a great deal of pleasure. As I opened the package and saw what it contained, I, for a moment felt down hearted. I looked at Mr. Lloyd's beautiful picture, so natural, as I saw him the last time in Pa. I remember it so well the statement he made on the floor of the convention in 1896 at the Populist's convention when they nominated Bryan and were cheering. I said this looks like a complete sell out and he said to me in reply, "Mother, this is the last of the Populist movement, this is its funeral." How true indeed was his statement, how far seeing was his vision. He seemed to grasp that the traitors had gotten hold of the movement and in that he was right. We have not since resurrected from that. I appreciate your kindly offer to me of coming to your quiet home to visit. I don't know that I could visit, there is so much to do for the cause and so little time to do it in and so very few who are willing to do. I don't know, dear comrade, what effect a letter from you would have upon this Gov. He is strictly owned by the coal barons and I don't know whether he would pay any attention to it or not, however, it would do no harm to put it up to him. What we should do, is go after the socialists, if your brother was alive I would not be here now as he would long ago have taken steps to get me out. We miss him in more ways than one. We are short of such great characters.

I got a letter from the Trades Union Women in N. Y. and all of the cold, sentimental documents that ever I read it was one of them, fortunately for me I have never mixed with them and I certainly shall not waste postage or paper in replying to them.

Now dear Comrade, I am still fighting away and perhaps I am doing just as much good within these prison walls as I would outside.

I think Leonard Abbot[1] sent me a clipping from the call. It was exceedingly thoughtful of you to put that article in. If they cannot grasp this great and mighty struggle, let them go by the waysi[d]e

Mother Jones

TLC (Henry Demarest Lloyd Papers)
   1. Leonard Dalton Abbott (1878–1953) edited the *Literary Digest, Current Literature,* and *Current Opinion,* and helped to establish the Rand School.

To Maude Walker[1]

Pratt W. Va.
Military Bastile,
Apr. 27, 1913.

Mrs. Walker,
150 W. 104th St., N. Y.
My dear Mrs. Walker:

Your letter of the 19th reached me a few days ago. I was glad to hear from you and glad to know you at least thought I was still alive. This is a very serious situation we have here and is not grasped by the outside world and God knows when it will be. I have been in here about eleven weeks. No word of protest has gone out from our dear Socialists. If Victor Berger or Wilford or any of those or any of their Jesuses was in here what a howl would go up but there are 12 of us poor devils, 11 men and myself, one of them the editor of the Socialist paper in Charleston, the other one of our speakers, John Brown with his wife and three children left to perish outside. We hear the cry of their little ones for their father, we hear the groans and sobs of his beautiful wife but the dear well fed socialists don't care for that. They can tell us what they are doing in the Balkan war or something of that kind, they are very much like the capitalists they will take us many miles across the ocean to see misery and overlook the horrors of home. I don't care much for myself because my career is nearly ended but I think of my brave boys who are incarcerated in Harrison Co. jail in Clarksburg and not a voice of protest raised in their behalf. They have been brave and true. They are now paying the penalty of what they have done but it matters not, this fight will go on and the workers themselves will have to take hold of the machinery and pick out the sky-pilots and lawyers and quit feeding them and giving them a job. I have been fighting this machine for years with scarcely any help.

I hope Ryan will be home soon, tell him I am still in the fight and the pirates can't shut me up even if I am in jail watched by the bloodhounds.

Mother Jones[2]

TLS (Haldeman MSS. II)

1. Maude Helena Davis Walker (d. 1925) was a radical journalist and with her husband Ryan Walker, a free-lance labor cartoonist, was later associated with the New York *Call*.

2. The signature is not in Mother Jones's handwriting, and another hand has added a note: "edited as follows by Appeal editors, probably Warren." As edited, the first ten lines eliminate invidious references to Socialists and read: "My dear Mrs. Walker: This is a very serious situation we have here and is not grasped by the outside world and God knows when it will be. I have been in here about eleven weeks. There are 12 of us poor devils, 11 men and myself, one of them the editor of the Socialist paper in Charleston, the other one of our speakers, John Brown with his wife and three children left to perish outside. We hear the cry of their little ones for their father, we hear the groans and sobs of his beautiful wife but the dear well fed people don't care for that. I don't care much for myself because [*remainder of letter follows the original*]." This edited verson, dated 25 April 1913, was published in *The Appeal to Reason,* 10 May 1913. A third and even more distorted version, or a letter using many of the same phrases, is quoted at length in the New York *Call,* 30 April 1913.

To Terence V. Powderly

Pratt, W. Va.
Military Bastile,
May 1st, 1913.

Mr. Terrence D. Powderly,
#502 N. W. Quincy St.,
Washington, D. C.

My dear Mr. Powederly:

I wrote you two letters but I have never had a line from one of them and I know that is not like you I think they have been held up by the Military sewer rats. I have been here 11 weeks, tried by a military drum-head court, kidnapped on the streets of Charleston and brought into the martial law zone and turned over to the military and I refused to recognize the drum-head court and I have been held here with 11 others for 11 weeks and dont know what for. No sentence. I wrote to Wilson but he dont seem to do anything although he is a member of the cabinet. There is 11 of us held prisoners but I am the only one in the Military camp. I know if you had received my letters or I would have received your there would have been something done long ago because you don't fool with things and don't make promises and not fulfill them. They have me held up for stealing a cannon from the coal company is one of the charges against me and the other is for making incendiary speeches. And of all the brutal gang you ever saw, it is down here. No where in the country could you find more brutality than you do here. Men have been shot down in cold blood. The children have been starved to death, some of them. About four weeks ago they took 11 of the boys away from here. You should have heard the wails of their children and their wives. But it did not pierce the heart of a cold blooded pirates of the ruling class. The martial law is taken off here now and they are getting ready to move the militia. I don't know just exactly when they will get out but I suppose when they get out they will turn me loose.

If you write me, write to the Fleetwood Hotel Charleston and if I am here it will be forwarded to me.

I wish you would see Senator LaFollette.[1] I know that he would write to this Governor at once and tell him if he don't take action that the Senate will, do you understand.

Give my love to Emma and all at home. I can't write a very long letter because I am tired. I have been sick for some weeks.

Sincerely,
Mother Jones

TLS (Terence V. Powderly Papers)
1. Robert Marion La Follette (1855–1925), former Republican governor of Wisconsin, and one of the leading progressives of the era, was currently serving his second term as senator from Wisconsin.

To John Worth Kern[1]

Hansford, West Virginia,
May 4, 1913

Senator Kern
Care Senate Chamber
Washington, D. C.

From out the military prison walls, where I have been forced to pass my eighty-first milestone of life, I plead with you for the honor of this Nation. I send you groans and tears of men, women, and children as I have heard them in this State, and beg you to force that investigation. Children yet unborn will rise and bless you.

Mother Jones

Telegram (*Cong. Record.* Vol. 50, Pt. 2, 1403)
1. John Worth Kern (1849–1917), of Indiana, majority leader of the Democrats in the U.S. Senate.

To Caroline Lloyd

Pratt, W. Va.,
Military Bastile,
May 7th, 1913.

Miss Caro Lloyd,
Nutley, N. J.
My dear Miss Caro:

Your letter reached me a few day ago but I was very sick with an abcess in the ear and was unable to reply. I certainly appreciate all the efforts you have been making. You seem to be the one woman in the U.S. that is taking hold of the question and doing what you could do to force it into the public eye.

I am still holding the fort in the prison although the great Governor says I am not in prison. I would like to know what he calls this place. I have been here three months incarcerated in one small room with a lounge to sleep on and no place to wash you face without going out on the porch and I am beginning to suffer with severe headaches which I am afraid will prove fatal one of these days. How brutal those men in authority are. They never reverse the condition of others and wonder how they would feel if their wives or mothers were placed in the same condition. I know that the May Day celebration would not have touched this subject had it not been for you. You have indeed so much of your brother's nature in you that every letter you send me brings him so vividly to my mind. I looked upon him as one of the great men of the age but unfortunately he passed away a little too soon.

When my emancipation takes place you will be one of the first that I go to visit and to see. I got a letter from Mr. Northrop[1] telling me that the single taxers had passed resolutions and I see your name among them. How strange it is indeed that you and he should be the two who are leading the battle in that location but it always takes some one to get the people started in any direction. I wont make this letter as long as I would like to for the reason that I have been suffering for several days with severe attacks of head ache and I presume it is from close confinement.

Write to me when you can as your letters are always an inspiration

115

and I never read them but what they bring back the memory of your brother. I am

Always yours,
Mother Jones Per M. D.

TL (Henry Demarest Lloyd Papers)
1. W. B. Northrop had written Woodrow Wilson as early as 18 March 1913, urging him to intervene in the West Virginia strike (Northrop to Wilson, 18 March 1913, National Archives, RG 174.)

To Members of the *Appeal* Army

Washington, D. C.
May 21, 1913.

To the Members of the *Appeal* Army:

Greeting—Permit me to express my deep appreciation for your generous response in behalf of myself and my colleagues who are now in the iron hands of capitalism.

It is to you I owe to a great extent my freedom today.

But you cannot let up your zeal and interest in behalf of human freedom until such time as my eighteen comrades are out of the clutches of the industrial pirates of West Virginia. I would have gladly written to each and all of you, asking you to carry on the battle for my imprisoned colleagues if it were not for the pressure of urgent duties that are demanding my time and energies.

To the brave women of the country, and especially to those of Oklahoma and Washington, I tender my deep respects. The number of letters and their tone show that they were alive to the importance of the issue.

The fight must be kept on. The workers must be aroused.

Continue to spread the light with the dear old *Appeal.* Do not rest even if congress orders an investigation. It will be a fairer and squarer investigation if the senators know that you are watching them.

The fate of the prisoners and the starved wretches of West Virginia is in your hands. Will you do your duty?

Yours for the emancipation of the workers.

Mother Jones

Printed letter (*The Appeal to Reason,* 31 May 1913)

To Eugene V. Debs

Indianapolis, Ind.,
July 5, 1913.

Eugene V. Debs,
Terre Haute, Ind.
My Dear Comrade Debs:

I so much regretted that I did not see you when you were in West Virginia, but I had so much work to do in Washington, when the pirates left me out of the bull pen that I was unable to meet you. I have been so busy since I got out that I have not had time to write you a line, much as I wanted to.

I very much regret the sad incident that that fellow Simons and the Appeal. I expected nothing else when he went there. I think that Warren will learn when it is a little too late. I told him about Ricker and about Rogers, I told him about Shoaf.[1] You know that we are living in a peculiar economic age, and self interest comes to the front instead of principle or a cause. When I was going into West Virginia, to take up the battle of the poor slaves, I stopped off to see poor Wayland in Girard. He was not there but I saw Warren; Simons said he hoped I would get lost in West Virginia, and never return. When a man is so cold and brutal as that there is nothing in him for a great cause. I have known Simons for some few years, and he has done just what I expected to the Appeal. But there is an unfortunate phase in our movement.   that if you undertake to give people any warning they generally put you down as a knocker. I just read in the morning paper which prompted me to write you that you took a girl home when the court said that you would have to either keep off the street or go down to the red light district. If that judge would not have exhibited his ignorance as he did the public might have more respect for him. If he would study the causes that bring those effects into society it would be far more to his credit as a member of the judiciary. That poor girl was a victim of a horrible system that is more brutal than the world has ever known, and God grants that we have more Eugene Debs, to protect such people from the depraved lions of capitalism.

I am on my way to Washington, to work among the Senators, and explain to them the horrors of West Virginia. I shall be going through next month, to Texas, and I shall try to stop off at Terre Haute, and see you.

Give my regards to Mrs. Debs, to Theodore and his family.

I am, always yours in the great struggle for the race,

Mother Jones

TLS (Eugene V. Debs Collection)

1. George H. Shoaf, who reported the McNamara trials in Los Angeles for *The Appeal to Reason,* was charged by Ernest Unterman with seducing his daughter; controversy over the incident within the Socialist party reached the National Executive Committee. Ricker and Rogers were presumably also *Appeal* reporters who caused trouble.

To William B. Wilson

Charleston, W Va.
July 30, 1913

W. B. Wilson
Washington, D. C.

Arrange soon as possible go to Michigan, Calumet, Tuesday.

Mother

Telegram (Labor Department Records, RG 174 16/013, National Archives)

From William B. Wilson

August 4, 1913

Mother Mary Jones
Charleston, West Virginia

He [Woodrow Wilson?] agreed to meet you shortly after you left. Notice was too short to communicate with you. Have not yet been able to make second arrangement for interview. As his time is very much taken up, arrangements could be made better when you are here on the ground.

William B. Wilson

Telegram (Labor Department Records, RG 174 16/013, National Archives)

To William E. Borah and James E. Martine[1]

Denver, Colo.,
Sept. 9, 1913

Senators Borah and Martine,
United States Senate Chamber,
Washington, D. C.

Colorado miners join with me in tendering sincere congratulations for the splendid manner in which you handled the workers' cause when in controversy with the Wheeling sky-pilot.

Mother Jones

Telegram (Terence V. Powderly Papers)

1. James Edgar Martine (1850–1925), Democratic senator from New Jersey, was well known for his labor sympathies.

To Terence V. Powderly

Trinidad, Colo.,
Sept 20, 1913.

My Dear Mr. Powderly:

I just write you a few hurried lines. I was not able to get to Washington to the hearing. I had to go to Salt Lake to raise some money for the poor fellows in Michigan.

What a proposition that sky-pilot[1] made about putting the bible under our heads. How a man in his position could display such a lack of knowledge of the economic struggle, is more than I know. He has very little grasp of the affair in West Virginia, and cares less. He was fed and entertained by the exploiters of labor. When he went up Cabin Creek he was entertained by Charlie Caball,[2] one of the biggest exploiters on Cabin Creek. Charlie Caball brought four negroes, a couple of Italians, and a Slav that he had working, to tell the bishop how good they were treated and what fine money that made. But Chas. Caball did not tell the sky-pilot that he bought potatoes for 50 cts a bushel and sold them for $1.50 to his slaves, two hundred per cent profit. That is the christian doctrine of today. I almost broke down after I got back from Salt Lake. I have been wanting to write to you for some time, but when I get a moment I feel like I must rest.

Give my love to them all at home, and when you see Mr. Hughes, tell him I always think of him.

See how that fellow Nugent falsified things about Keefe. What a terrible thing those judas's within our own ranks. That fellow Nugents was an organizer for the miners in West Virginia. He took their money and betrayed them. So did that fellow Kennedy.[3] He was President of a District once and everything belonging to him scabed, and his whole rotten carcas inside is full of scabs. They are sending me all sorts of threats here. They have my skull drawn on a picture and two cross sticks under neath my jaw to tell me that if I do not quit they are going to get me. Well they have been a long time at it.

I would liked to have been at the hearing. I wish you let me know when the peonage question is coming up. I would like to go to Washington and hear that discussed, because I was the one who started the investigation in Washington.

Well, give my love to them all, and save for yourself and Emma a great portion.

I am always yours, not for the revolution, but in it.

Mother Jones
Toltec Hotel   Trinidad

TLS (Terence V. Powderly Papers)

1. Patrick James Donahue (1849–1922), bishop of Wheeling, agreed to preside over a citizens' committee appointed by Governor William Ellsworth Glasscock to investigate mining conditions in West Virginia; the report of the committee, published 27 November 1912, did not please union leaders, although it criticized mine owners for employing armed guards and overcharging at company stores.

2. Charles A. Cabell, president of the Carbon Coal Company, was a director of several other companies in the Kanawha field.

3. Duncan Kennedy (1873–1947) in 1902 had been president of District 17, UMWA, but later became a mine owner and secretary of the Kanawha Coal Operators Association.

From Frank J. Hayes[1]

Denver, Colorado
Nov. 28, 1913.

Mother Jones
Washington, D. C.
Dear Comrade:

I am in receipt of your kind favor of recent date, and was indeed pleased to hear from you.

We are still battling away out here, and, considering the obstacles we are up against, we have the situation well in hand.

I appreciate very much the good work you have done in Washington, especially in the halls of congress, and feel sure you have aroused a splendid sentiment in favor of our cause.

I will communicate with E. Knockels,[2] of Chicago, requesting him to do everything he can to influence Congressman Mann to withdraw his opposition to the Keating resolution.[3]

We have a serious situation out here at this time, and the operators are doing everything imaginable to break the spirit of the men, and have their agents in all the large cities, for the purpose of importing strike breakers into this field. So far we have been able to prevent the success of their plans in this direction.

We have been doing everything we can to arouse a favorable public sentiment in support of our strike, and have had considerable success along this line.

I just concluded a tour of the principle cities of the state, addressing large meetings in each town visited.

Keating tells me that he is going to make every effort to have his resolution considered by congress. I sincerely hope that he will be successful, and I know that you have done all you possibly could to create sentiment in favor of his resolution. If this situation is investigated by the Federal Government I feel sure it will produce results very favorable to our strike.

With kind personal regards, in which all the boys join, I am, as ever,

Fraternally yours,

Frank J. Hayes

TLS (Terence V. Powderly Papers)

1. Frank J. Hayes (1882–1948), vice-president (1910–1917) and president (1917–1920) of the UMWA; later lieutenant governor of Colorado.

2. Edward N. Nockles (1869–1937), secretary of the Chicago Federation of Labor (1901–1937); founder and manager of the pioneering WCFL, the radio voice of labor.

3. On 21 October 1913, Edward Keating introduced into the House a resolution calling for an investigation of conditions in the Colorado coal fields, paralleling the previous session's Kern Resolution regarding the West Virginia fields. Edward Keating (1875–1965), journalist, editor, and publisher, served as a Democratic congressman (1913–1919); defeated for a fourth term, he became editor and manager of *Labor,* the weekly publication of the railroad brotherhoods. James Robert Mann (1856–1922), Republican congressman from Chicago (1897–1922), was the minority floor leader of the House in the Sixty-third Congress.

1914

To Terence V. Powderly

Denver, Colorado
March 22, 1914

Mr. T. V. Powderly
Washington, D. C.
My own dear son:

I am just going to drop you a line or two so that you will know I did not forget you even in the military bastile. Last Monday morning I closed five months and one week in the military bastiles of America out of ten months, so we can boast of our republic. In the last nine weeks which I spent in the military bull pen, I never got a glimpse of a newspaper or a letter and the only human being, outside of the military, that I saw was my attorney Hawkins.[1] He came three times during the nine weeks. The sisters permitted their religious institution to be turned into a military prison. I never saw more moral cowards in my life than those sisters were. It is a sais [sad?] comment[ar]y on a religuous institution. They are simply owned body and soul by the Rockefeller interests. The priest would go by my window in the morning and take his hat off to the uniform murderer and not notice a poor wretch who was digging in the gardens with his legs off.

How they have prostituted Christ's holy doctrine. Five big burly uniformed murderers with their guns on their shoulders and a belt of bullets around their stomachs and a saber hanging to their sides, came up every night at 6 o'clock to put in 24 hours watching an old woman 82 years of age. Four of those military were in the hall outside of my door and one outside the window and the entire military was just a block away facing my window. The Sisters and priests stood for all that insult. My God how can he stand for the cold blooded hypocrisy of today. Men have no regard for human life. Right on the ground with that convent those uniformed murderers drilled every afternoon to learn how to become experts in the shedding of human blood. The military now is turned on to the working class and priests and presidents and ministers endorse the crime. Oh when the judgment day comes what a reckoning there will be. Tell Emma I have thought of her often in my lonely cell during the last weeks. As soon as this fight is over, I am going to Washington to write that book. It will be dedicated to your labor in the early days of the struggle. I would not undertake it, if it were not that I want to show some people up and

Sketch of Mother Jones, 1914. Maurice Becker Papers, Archives of American Art

Mother Jones marching in a strikers' parade, 10 August 1913. Archives of Labor History and Urban Affairs, Wayne State University

vindicate the real hero of the labor movement. You and Martin Irons shall have the pleasure of seeing your name on the front page. The history of this thing, since I have been out here I cannot relate until I see you. I have so much to tell you, it would take pages and pages to relate the brutality. And the churches have stood for it all and endorsed it.

I leave again tonight for the field of battle. I suppose that just as soon as I get to Trinidad I will be arrested. They searched the train the night before last to see if I was on it. I presume they will do the same tonight so you can watch the papers. I wish you get the Appeal to Reason of the 21st. Villa, the revolutionary general in Mexico gave Wilson and the Democratic party a terrific slap. Wilson ordered Villa to turn loose the wealthy Mexican who was held in Chihuahua and the Mexican said whenever you turn loose the 82-year-old woman that your military hold incommunicado I will comply with your request. She got protection in Mexico. No one would dare imprison that woman in Mexico but the brave soldiers of the American Revolution held her for nine long weeks.

I will have to close because I am getting a little nervous. Tell Emma to keep well until I see her. I guess the headlines of the papers will notify you what's happening down here.

I am always yours in the cause of freedom.

Mother

TLS (Terence V. Powderly Papers)

1. Horace Norman Hawkins (1867–1947), a leading member of the Denver bar, supervised the many defenses of UMWA members indicted in Colorado.

To the Public

Walsenburg, Colo.
Military Bastile
March 31, 1914.

To My Friends and the Public Generally:

I am being held a prisoner incommunicado in a damp, underground cell, in the basement of a military bullpen at Walsenburg, Colorado. Have been here since 5:30 a.m. of the 23rd of March, when I was taken from the train by armed soldiers as I was passing through Walsenburg. I have discovered what appears to be an opportunity to smuggle a letter out of prison, and shall attempt to get this communication by the armed guards which day and night surround me (me, a white-haired old woman eighty-two years of age).

I want to say to the public that I am an American citizen. I have never broken a law in my life, and I claim the right of an American citizen to go where I please so long as I do not violate the law. The courts of Las Animas and Huerfano are open and unobstructed in the transaction of business, yet Governor Ammons[1] and his Peabody appointee, General Chase,[2] refuse to carry me before any court, and refuse to make any charge against me. I ask the press to let the nation know of my treatment, and to say to my friends, whom, thank God, I number by the thousands, throughout the United States and Mexico, that not even my incarceration in a damp, underground dungeon will make me give up the fight in which I am engaged for liberty and for the rights of the working people. Of course, I long to be out of prison. To be shut from the sunlight is not pleasant, but John Bunyan, John Brown and others were kept in jail quite a while, and I shall stand firm. To be in prison is no disgrace. In all my strike experiences I have seen no horrors equal to those perpetrated by General Chase and his corps of Baldwin-Feltz detectives that are now enlisted in the militia. My God—when is it to stop? I have only to close my eyes to see the hot tears of the orphans and widows of working men, and hear the mourning of the broken hearts and the wailing of the funeral dirge, while the cringing politicians whose sworn duty it is to protect the lives and liberty of the people crawl subserviently before the national burglars of Wall Street who are today plundering and devastating the State of Colorado economically, financially, politically and morally.

Let the nation know, and especially let my friend General Francisco Villa know, that the great United States of America, which is demanding of him that he release the traitors he has placed under arrest, is now holding Mother Jones incommunicado in an underground cell surrounded with sewer rats, tinhorn soldiers and other vermin.

Mother Jones

Printed letter (*Miners Magazine,* 9 April 1914)

1. Elias Ammons (1860–1925), governor of Colorado, 1913–1915.

2. John Chase, adjutant general of Colorado, had also commanded troops during an earlier strike when James Peabody was governor.

To the *Appeal* Army

May 9, 1914

Dear Comrades:

John Kenneth Turner's[1] articles on Government by Gunmen should receive the widest circulation. Government by Gunmen must go. From my experience in the labor movement I am convinced that our worst enemy today is the private guards of the mine owners and the other exploiters. The injunction judge was our worst enemy yesterday. Today the capitalists hire murderers and cutthroats to do their dirty work. When I was in Washington last week I urged members of congress to have a federal law passed against the employment of private armies by individuals or corporations. I find some of them willing to pass such a law. But they will never act if the working people do not insist that such a law be passed. The pressure must come from the people. Turner's articles, I am sure, will arouse the people to demand action from congress. Let us avenge the massacre of the women and children of Colorado with a lawful destruction of Rockefeller's private army of gunmen. Let us restore to this country the constitutional rights and liberties of the people.

Down with government by gunmen! It has no place in the United States in the twentieth century!

Mother Jones

Printed letter (*The Appeal to Reason,* 9 May 1914)

1. John Kenneth Turner, a Socialist journalist and author, was probably best known for his analysis of the Diaz regime, *Barbarous Mexico.* Along with Mother Jones he had testified in behalf of Mexican revolutionaries before a congressional committee in June 1910.

To John D. Rockefeller, Jr.[1]

[Union Square Hotel
New York, New York
May 12, 1914][2]

John D. Rockefeller, Jr., Esq.
26 Broadway
Dear Sir—

As you may have noticed in the newspapers, I am visiting New York for the purpose of directing public opinion in mining conditions in Colorado.

Before going before the public in a series of meetings now being arranged before civic bodies, trade unions, single tax leagues and other representative societies, it occurs to me that, out of fairness, a personal visit to you for the purpose of laying before you the exact facts in the entire matter would be in order.

I feel quite sure that I have in my possession facts and data which you have not been provided with, and which I would take great pleasure in laying before you in the course of an interview, if you make an appointment within the next day or two.

No "demonstration" is intended, and I merely wish to present to your fair minded consideration the entire truth of the Colorado situation.

As evidence of my intentions and good faith—should such be required—I will be accompanied by Hon. Alfred J. Boulton, a well known Brooklyn official, and Hon. William Lustgarten, the distinguished single taxer and real estate investor. I would like them to be present at our interview.

Trusting you will see fit to make this appointment, preferably for 11 o'clock Wednesday morning next, I remain very truly yours.

Mother Jones

Printed letter (New York *Call*, 14 May 1914)

1. John D. Rockefeller, Jr. (1874–1960), had in 1911 taken over from his father active management of the Rockefeller interests, which included extensive investments in Colorado coal lands and companies.

2. Heading and date are inferred from the highly circumstantial account in the New York *Call*, which tells of the rejection of the registered letter when it was delivered at 26 Broadway.

To Caroline Lloyd

Washington D. C.
6—5—14

Miss C Lloyd
My Dear friend

Your kind letter reached me a week or two ago It had to wait a week or ten days before I rec. it. I have been driven to Death Since I came out of that Military Basti[l]e which apology I make for not expressing my appreciation of your kindness. I over worked. but I have to keep at it. how much I would [like?] to be near you at times there are so few in life we can cling to in this great struggle.

I droped your Post Office order in Waterbury Con. one day last week Will you notify the P. M. to Stop the Payment

I am going up to see you before I go west I never know when they will lock me up to stay. The Pirates are after me.

How much I would give to have a few hours with you I will be in New York in a few days again Will be at the Nenius Square Hotel

fondly
Mother Jones

ALS (Henry Demarest Lloyd Papers)

To the Editor of *The Appeal to Reason*

[11 July 1914]

Editor, *Appeal to Reason,* Girard, Kan.:

On behalf of the Colorado strike sufferers and the United Mine Workers of America, I wish to extend sincerest thanks to the many loyal ones throughout the country who responded to my appeal in the Appeal to Reason for shoes and clothing for the striking miners and their wives and children. The response was immediate and generous, and many have been benefited, but many are still in need.

I only wish that I had the time to answer personally the many letters I have received in connection with these donations, but I have had such a heavy volume of work falling on my shoulders in carrying on the fight against the industrial slavery in Colorado that it is impossible for me to do so.

Yours fraternally,
Mother Jones

Printed letter (*The Appeal to Reason,* 11 July 1914)

To Caroline Lloyd

Indianapolis, Ind.,
July 21, 1914.

Miss Caro Lloyd,
Little Compton, R. I.
My Dear Miss Lloyd:

Your beautiful letter reached me in New York, and I immediately complied with your directions. I saw the post master last Saturday in New York. He said to ask you to get the post master at Nuttley, N. J. to issue an order payable to me in Denver Colo. He said there was no danger of any one duplicating that order and said they could do nothing further about it in New York. It must come from Nuttley.

We had a beautiful meeting in New York on Friday night, the 17th.[1] I was wishing that you were there. I will enclose you one of the bills with this letter. Nothing would give me greater pleasure than to be with you for a day or two in the woods so we could talk things over. I met your dear nephew in Chicago. He urged me to go home with [him?] for that evening, but it was utterly impossible, much as I would love to have gone. You know I always feel when I am conversing with a member of the family that I am talking with Mr. Lloyd. He died many years too soon.

I shall write you from Denver soon, and hope it will not be long until we meet again.

Mother Jones

TLS (Henry Demarest Lloyd Papers)

1. The meeting had a list of blue ribbon sponsors, including Amos Pinchot, William Dean Howells, Max Eastman, John Reed, Ida M. Tarbell, and many others. Resolutions calling for the nationalization of the mines in Colorado were adopted.

To *The Appeal to Reason*

[8 August 1914]

In the cause of the striking miners in this country I have been illegally held in jail three months in West Virginia, nine weeks in Trinidad and twenty-five days in Walsenburg, and my heart goes out in sympathy to Bob Uhlich[1] who has been held in the Trinidad County jail seven months without trial and refused bail. I am heart and soul with the Appeal to Reason in its fight to free Bob Uhlich, an innocent miner, who was jailed by the enemies of organized labor because they were afraid to have at liberty a fearless man.

Mother Jones

Published telegram (*The Appeal to Reason*, 8 August 1914)
1. Robert Uhlich was an official of the UMWA and of the Colorado Federation of Labor.

To the Editor, *Miners' Magazine*

Denver, Colorado,
August 13, 1914.

To the Editor of the Miners' Magazine:

I have received a few letters from Butte, Montana, from parties who were formerly identified with Butte Miners' Union No. 1 of the Western Federation of Miners, but who are now members of Butte Mine Workers' Union. I have not answered these letters owing to the fact that I cannot give my approval to the lawlessness that disgraced the greatest metal mining city of America—a city that has been lauded as the best organized mining camp in America.

Two of the parties who have written letters to me have stated that the Butte Mine Workers' Union would seek affiliation with the United Mine Workers of America. It seems to me that the time has come when it is imperative that every man and woman who is interested in the cause of labor should speak in no uncertain language relative to the situation that presents itself in Butte, Montana. I feel positive that the United Mine Workers of America will not court the admission of a local union that was born in dissension and promoted by disrupters who seem to have no scruples, as they destroyed with explosives a temple that stood as a monument to the pioneers who laid the foundation of Butte Miners' Union. The United Mine Workers of America has never given its sanction or recognition to dual unions, and the coal miners of this continent, believing in the strength and power of labor solidified, will scorn to accept an organization that came into the world heralded by explosions of dynamite.

The Butte Mine Workers' Union can have no standing with the bona fide labor movement of this country. The members of the Butte Mine Workers' Union can only come into, or become a part of the United Mine Workers of America through the Western Federation of Miners, and if any members of this dual union are laboring under the delusion that they can become affiliated or become a part of the United Mine Workers of America, they should get rid of the deception immediately, for the United Mine Workers believe with all their hearts and souls in that solidarity of the working class that will one day be able to grapple with the hosts of greed. If the Butte Mine Workers' Union ever becomes a part of the United Mine Workers of America, it must come under the flag of the U. M. W. of A. as members of Butte Miners' Union No. 1, W. F. M., or remain outside the pale of the labor movement. The United Mine Workers of America will demand that those seeking affiliation or amalgamation shall come in with clean hands, not as secessionists, but standing under the banner of the Western Federation of Miners—an organization that for more than twenty-one years has fought the battles of labor in Western America, and though defeated in a number of battles has never been conquered.

I have fought for the men of the coal mines for many long years. I have helped to establish the United Mine Workers, and my voice shall be raised in protest against the taking into its folds men who have seceded from the metal miners' organization. I know the Western Federation of Miners. I have also fought its battles, and shall continue to do so, and I now serve warning on all who would seek its destruction that it will find no place in the United Mine Workers of America, unless it be as members of the Western Federation of Miners. If they have grievances against the management of their local affairs, let them go to work like men and adjust them, and not spend their time in an effort to destroy an organization such as the Western Federation of Miners, which will go down in history as second to none in fighting the battles for the emancipation of the toiling masses.

Mother Jones.

Printed letter (*Miners Magazine,* 20 August 1914)

From James Lord[1]

Indianapolis, Ind.
Oct. 9, 1914

Dear Mother:

I have just written to Frank [Hayes] relative to what has transpired since you left.

There is nothing to add to the situation, [it] is as it was when you were there.

I waited until after the cabinet meeting, and as we feared, they had got the President to believe that he could not close the mines legally, that is, he was afraid that he could not, but he stated to Wilson plainly that he was not going to surrender to John D., and that he had refused to answer their correspondence at the present time and was going to seek further light in the matter and proceed in such a way that Standard Oil could not come back at him. W. B. seems confident that Pres. Wilson has got a plan whereby he can force them to accept his proposition, and I sincerely hope and trust that he is right. He said that he expected that he would make his final answer in not more than a week.

John Brown went over to see Louis Brandeis and get his opinion relative to putting the flag on the mines under the circumstances.

I am going to Illinois and make another attempt to raise some money. If I can get enough to take care of the Eastern Ohio situation from them, then we are safe in Colorado, and I am still confident that that proposition adopted by the Trinidad convention is going to be put into affect.

Address your mail to Farmington, Ill. for the time being, as I will be in Illinois for sometime.

Hoping that you are in the best of health, I am,

Yours truly,
[James Lord]

TLC (AFL Papers, Mining Department)
1. James Ravell Lord (1878–1941) for many years headed the Mining Department of the AFL.

To James Lord

Denver, Colorado,
Dec. 23, 1914.

Mr. James Lord,
Washington, D. C.
My dear Lord:

I have been trying to write you ever since you went away, but I have not had the time. I have been down to the Southern coal fields and the conditions are frightful. I went all through Segunda, Aguilar, Delaqua and Ludlow and several other places and the poor wretches are in a sad plight. However, we are encouraging them all we can. I suggested to Frank that while the Industrial Commission is in session in New York it would be well for us to have meetings in Brooklyn, New York, Jersey and all around to keep the thing alive while we are going. We must let Rockefeller know and the government in Washington that the working people are demanding to be heard.

By request of Mrs. Harriman,[1] I spent a couple of hours with her before she left for Washington. I had quite a long conversation on Industrial conditions with her. I look upon her as a very strong character and hope for something to come from her ability in the future. I have been down all through the coal fields in the south and I leave again tonight. Lord, the conditions that confront us here in Colorado are beyond description. These poor wretches have nothing, at best, and now that the relief is being restricted, it is creating a spirit of discontent and we have to meet it as best we can. They beat up Street down in Routte County. They gave him an awful hammering in the head. They threatened everybody but me and I presume they will begin to threaten me, by and bye. I will be in Washington about the first of the year. I will talk things over with you at that time. I hope you are feeling better. You looked miserable when you left here and I regretted to see you leave that night. Frank went east on Sunday night. He went to Indianapolis. I think they are having a meeting there to discuss the Ohio strike. I want to have a long talk with you on some things when we get together. I feel sorry for Frank. He seemed to have the blues when he left. There is no use in our getting discouraged about anything. The storm and sunshine comes and goes and the fight must still go on.

I wrote to Mr. and Mrs. McBride today and if you see them, give them my regards.

Are you going home for Christmas? I see that Farrington has got to the helm in Illinois. Now there is going to be war, unless the thing gets straightened up by next April, and it don't look as if it will. You know McDonald has no use for Farrington,[2] and then Germer has his machine, and between the whole of them, the office seekers and glory hunters, the poor wretches off of whose backs they live will have to pay the bill. Strange that men cannot feel for those who trust them. I want to tell you that unless this thing is cleaned up and the leeches are put where they belong the Miners' Organization will go to pieces.

Well, I must close, as I am tired and must leave tonight for Trinidad.

Loyally yours,
Mother Jones

TLS (AFL Papers, Mining Department)

1. Florence Jaffray Harriman (1870–1967), was the only woman member of the Commission on Industrial Relations, 1913–1916. She later served on the Democratic National Committee, and as minister to Norway, 1937–1941.

2. Frank Farrington (1873–1939) had just been elected president of District 12 (Illinois), a position he was to hold for twenty-six years. Duncan McDonald served as secretary-treasurer of District 12 during part of Farrington's tenure as president.

To John D. Rockefeller, Jr.

Trinidad, Colorado,
March 15", 1915.

Mr. John D. Rockefeller, Jr.,
5" Avenue & 54 Sts.,
New York City, N. Y.
My dear Mr. Rockefeller:

The sympathy of one whom thousands of men have called "Mother" is with you at this time when your heart is filled with sorrow for her who called you "Son". Grief brings us to a level, and the highest level, perhaps, that we shall reach here. For, in this hour, all hearts beat the same.

I am sure that you will understand, at this time, I voice the hope that you will pay the highest tribute to a mother's love by being all she prayed for you to be. The mothers of the race fix all standards of life. The mother love preserves it. He who justifies that love will find consulation for every sorrow of life.

I am sure that you will not resent these few words from one who has felt a mother's love for all boys and men, who has shared the sorrows of those in the ranks of toil, and finds in her heart the same sympathy for you, in this, your hour of greatest grief.

Mother Jones

306 German-American Trust Bldg.,
Denver, Colorado.

TLS (Rockefeller Papers)

To Walter Watson Stokes[1]

Denver, Colo.
March 17, 1915.

Mr. Walter Stokes,
66 Broadway,
New York City.
My dear Mr. Stokes:

Since I left New York, I have been very anxious to write to you. I regretted that we did not discuss matters more thoroughly. Never, in the history of industrial conflicts, in this country, has a more serious situation arisen than here in Colorado. It depends upon how we get together and discuss the question. The future of the state and her people depends upon our understanding each other. We must put our financial and social position entirely aside and work on the humane side of the question.

I have been in conversation with Mr. Randolph Walker, several times. To me he is a very broad, fair-minded character. Has a clear grasp of conditions as they are out here. He is rendering all the service he can to break down this horrible bitterness that has grown out of the confict. I have a great deal of confidence in his judgment and much respect for his manhood. He leaves aside all personal and selfish interest for the good of a cause that needs great men and women, just at this hour. I gave him my impression of young Mr. Rockefeller. I believe the human is very deeply planted in his breast and when he understands the conditions under which his people suffered here, he will do everything to remedy the wrongs. I do not expect that these conditions will be changed all at once. They did not grow over night; it has taken years of wrong to develop the conditions that exist in Colorado. I know his tender heart would be touched if he heard the baby ask the father: "Oh, where has mama gone?" These pathetic scenes that we witness in these great conflicts here touch the better side of our nature. I wish it were possible, indeed, for Mr. Rockefeller, himself, to view it from his own personal investigation, but owing to the loss of his mother, I fear it may delay his trip here. These superintendents, as a rule, have developed the side of brutality in their nature and are accordingly expressing it to the poor father who goes to appeal to them for work in order to get a chance to get bread for his little ones. One mother, a few days ago, took a crust of bread out of her trunk and put it in water to give a starving child. The child died of pneumonia. In my own heart, I believe it died of hunger. I know Mr. Rockefeller would not stand for this for one moment, if he knew it. I am convinced that he would rather lose all his wealth than have anything such as that recorded in the calendar of the future. We only pass through this life once; let us do all the good we can for humanity, making it a better place for those who come after us to live in.

I expect to go to New York sometime the early part of April and without wanting to infringe on your time, I should be very glad indeed, if I could spend an hour with you. You have won my confidence. I believe that nature has gifted you with a kindly humane tendency. True indeed, our position in life makes us view things only from the standpoint of the conditions that surround us. But in the better days to come when men and women will reach that grander height we will meet each other as human beings; no class distinction will draw the line. Let me call your attention to why I am out here. They have arrested many of my boys and are trying to send them over the road, away from their loved ones. In these great industrial conflicts, we all do things that in calmer moments we appal. You have never made the world better by crushing the higher aspirations of the human being.

I will not tire you with a longer letter, and I hope you will accept this in the same spirit in which the writer sends it. We must work for peace on earth and good will to all mankind.

Mr. Stokes, there are thousands of men, women and children now starving to death in the Colorado coal fields.

I hope Mr. Rockefeller will keep his word to me and not delay in his visit to Colorado to see for himself the actual conditions.

I am,

most sincerely yours,
Mother Jones

TLC (Rockefeller Papers)
1. Walter Watson Stokes (1881–1960) was a New York stockbroker and a close associate of John D. Rockefeller, Jr.

To James Lord

Denver, Colorado,
March 23, 1915.

Mr. James Lord,
Ouray Bldg.,
Washington, D. C.
Dear Lord:

I have been wanting to write you for several weeks but you know how I am up against all the time and my feet have been troubling me for so long and I haven't had the time to go to a chiropodist. I am going to go to one this afternoon no matter if the sky falls. I was down in the Southern Coal fields and the poor fellows are in a horrible condition. There is hunger and suffering and misery on every side. Things are going all right though in the court. They are trying to get Zankenelli.[1] They have a jury impanelled. It is not everything we want but the best we can get out of the gang. I will go down again before I go away.

MacKenzie King[2] is out here. He is coming to see me this afternoon at 2 o'clock. I had a party go and see him yesterday and had a long talk with him. I told this party to tell him to keep away from the Chamber of Commerce and other crook institutions if he expected to do anything for Mr. Rockefeller in this state. I have been working the game very quietly without letting any of them know what I was doing out here and I think we are going to clean house in this state. I am inclined to think a good many of the Rockefeller representatives will get their walking papers. He is digging into things here and I have got the right people going to see him, not out of the Labor Movement. I think before I get through we will be able to organize the southern coal fields. I expect to go to Christopher, Ill. for the first of April and from there I am going to Chicago to get in touch with the hearing there. As the open on the fifth of April. None of the boys here have seen MacKenzie King, here. I am going to wait until I have my talk with him this afternoon. I sent young Rockefeller a letter of sympathy on the loss of his mother. I believe we should touch the human side everywhere we can. I spent last evening with a member of the Guggenheim firm. I got a very urgent invitation to spend the evening at their home. The fellow seemed to have no grasp of what they were doing in the southern coal fields. Tell Brown that I am going to West Virginia. I am going to stop off at Charleston. I want to get a line on the situation there because if we don't straighten things out the I. W.'s are going to tear down all the work that we have done. I must try and straighten the matter out between Tom Haggerty and Boswell. Tom has got his head swelled a little bit since that pill peddlar of a governor has been patting him on the back. He doesn't seem to realize that the fellow is using him. He went up New River and in his speech he made a statement that the Governor was his personal friend and he was the Governor's personal friend. Such statements are very suicidal to the cause of the workers and particularly to the miners. No man, if he wants to respect himself and save himself from condemnation and criticism can afford to make those statements. Governor Hatfield in my estimation is a political rattle snake and Haggerty has fallen into his tracks. Tom has no conception or grasp of the philosophy of class war. I sometimes think it would be a fortunate thing for us if we had some of the old fighters back from the grave. I don't know Lord, what the outcome of things are going to be, if we don't wake up to the fact that wer facing a crucial hour in the Labor Movement of this Country, but I have hopes we will be able to bridge the chasm successfully. If I can succeed in getting the Southern Fields organized I will be willing to go way back and watch the future. It means so much to the Labor Movement of the west. I want to have a long talk with you when I get to Washington That will be the middle of next month. Give my regards to Frank Morrison,[3] he is one of my old good boys.

The Free Press[4] is doing a lot of fine work in the Southern Fields. We got our candidate nominated at the primaries for mayor of the city of Trinidad. Northcutt and his cut throat sheet was all up in the air. This Mrs. Thomas[5] went out with another trollop from Ludlow to campaign for the C.F. and I candidate. They carried a bottle of whiskey into the homes of the men in order to bribe them to vote for the C.F. and I I hope that the Labor Movement will learn one lesson from the past, particularly in Colorado, to make those women keep their place. It is a terrible tale that can be told of the blunders that can be told.

Well, Lord I will have to close. Give my love to Minnine when you write, and the same share to yourself and John. I am ready for fight. I can't keep still.

Believe me always, yours in the fight,

Mother

TLS (AFL Papers, Mining Department)

1. Louis Zancanelli, an Italian striker, was charged with, and later convicted of, murder of a company guard.

2. William Lyon Mackenzie King (1874–1950), later prime minister of Canada, was serving as an adviser to John D. Rockefeller, Jr., on labor matters.

3. Frank Morrison (1859–1949), a member of the typographical union, became secretary of the AFL in 1897 and held the post for the next forty years.

4. The Trinidad *Free Press* was subsidized by the UMWA; Judge Jesse Northcutt, publisher of a rival newspaper, was a local political leader.

5. Mary Hannah Thomas, wife of a miner, was arrested for leading demonstrations at Ludlow and Trinidad; how she happened to be campaigning for a candidate of the Colorado Fuel and Iron Company is not clear.

From John D. Rockefeller, Jr.

[March 1915]

"Mother" Jones,
306 German-American Trust Bldg.,
Denver, Colo.
My dear Mrs. Jones:

I am deeply touched by your beautiful letter of sympathy with me in the death of my mother. Never did man have a purer, braver, nobler mother than mine. It is largely to her blessed influence that I owe whatever I am or may be. That I may be true to her teaching and worthy of her is my earnest prayer. ¶Her love and sympathy went out to all alike. She was no respecter of persons. To her all men were brothers. She was deeply interested in my meeting with you. I gave her a full account of our pleasant conference, telling her of your fearless devotion to the cause to which you have given so many years of earnest work.

Again I thank you for your letter.

Very sincerely,
J.D.R., Jr.

TLC (Rockefeller Papers)
1. A right-facing paragraph symbol has been inserted in ink. The letter was probably retyped, for a copy with the paragraph correction and omitting the typed initials of the signature is to be found in the William Lyon Mackenzie King Papers in the National Archives of Canada, along with a typed copy of Mother Jones's letter of March 15. King was serving as a labor adviser to Rockefeller.

From James Lord

April 3, 1915

Mother Jones,
Care U. M. W. of A.,
German-American Trust Building,
Denver, Colorado.
Dear Mother:

Yours of the 23rd received and very glad to hear from you. I thought you had passed us up altogether. I hope by the time this reaches you that you are rid of that trouble with your feet.

I note what you say relative to the Southern coal field and you know how I feel about it, but I still have the feeling that the thing is going to turn out in the end to be a victory all along the line.

Let me know what transpired at your interview with McKenzie King. White and I slipped over to New York with a view to meeting McKenzie King and John D., Jr., but just missed them by a day. However, we did succeed in meeting Starr J. Murphy[1] and your dear friend, Ivy Lee.[2] I think that was a good card you played in sending young Rockefeller a note of sympathy on the loss of his mother. I expect it hurt him just as bad as if he had been a coal digger.

I have not heard anything from Haggerty lately, but will probably write him today or tomorrow.

The proposed amalgamation of the Tunnel and Subway Workers of New York with the W. F. of M. is coming along nicely and I expect application will be made by the Machinists to the Mining Department in the next few days. I appeared before their Executive Board yesterday and we went over the ground pretty thoroughly, and they have decided to apply for membership.

Brown is still here and feeling better than he has felt for years, he says, but is restless and wants to get back into the work somewhere. There seems to be some influence at work to keep him out of West Virginia, and just now I know that he is badly needed in the New River field. I am going to take this matter up with Haggerty.

Take good care of yourself and keep me posted as to your where-abouts all the time.

> Yours sincerely,
> [James Lord]

P.S. I agree with what you say about the Free Press and want you to use all the influence you have to have that paper continued indefinitely by the U. M. W. of A. I feel sure that White and Hayes will be guided by your judgment in this matter.

TLC (AFL Papers, Mining Department)
1. Starr Jocelyn Murphy (1860–1921) served as personal counsel to John D. Rockefeller, Jr.
2. Ivy Ledbetter Lee (1877–1934), a pioneer public relations specialist, entered the service of John D. Rockefeller, Jr., in January 1915.

To Mary Field Parton[1]

> Denver, Colo.
> 10 June 1915

My dear Mary:

I want to drop you a line or two to say that I have not forgotten you, now will I ever forget you. I meet so few like you, in all my [work?]. You were married some time before I heard of it. I think Mr. West[2] of the Industrial Relations Commission was the first who told me. I want to extend my congratulations to you and express my hopes for happy years for you and your companion in life. May the bitterness that surrounds us forever disappear from your life and the sunshine surround your home and loved ones in every hour of your future history.

I expected, dear Mary to go west. Was to start tomorrow, but I am called on to go east to hold meetings of protest against the horrible, unjust decisions of the court in dealing with our people. I hope, though, that later in the Summer I will be able to go west and see you and a few more friends I have there.

Give my regards to Tiedemore[3] when you see him. He is one good, brave, soul, that I have admiration for.

I wish you would gather a few copies of Everyman and send him to me. I saw Mr. Darrow at Washington, at the hearing. He always speaks of you warmly, but I never have much time when I go through Chicago.

I close, Mary, not finally, because I shall write to you again and ler me assure you of my devotion to you and wherever I can be of service to [you?], let me know.

I am always yours until death closes my eyes.
Warmest wishes to your devoted companion in life.

[*One word illegible*] Sincerely
Mother Jones

ALS (in private possession)
1. Mary Field Parton, a journalist, later collaborated with Mother Jones in producing the *Autobiography*.
2. George West was one of the staff investigators of the Commission on Industrial Relations.
3. Possibly Olaf A. Tveitmoe of the California Federation of Labor.

From John P. White[1]

Kansas City, Mo.,
Coates House,
October 8, 1915.

Mother Jones,
Washington, D. C.
Dear Mother Jones:

I am in receipt of your favor of the 4th inst., containing money order for $37.45 from Warren Ohio meeting, I am forwarding it to Secretary Green's office with the necessary instructions.

I will give the matter referred to in your letter my thoughtful consideration. I have a committee in Colorado now dealing with the internal matters that have been so annoying to us for some time.

I see by press reports that Lawson[2] has been given his liberty. I suppose this means that he will not be tried again.

In my judgment, it would be unwise for you to go to Cumberland, B.C. at this time, as things generally throughout Canada are in bad shape and I do not believe you could do much to help the situation there just now.

With best wishes, I am

Yours very truly,
John P. White
President.

TLS (Terence V. Powderly Papers)
1. John Phillip White (1870–1934), president of the UMWA, 1912–1917.
2. John R. Lawson, president of District 15, UMWA, was freed on bail before his murder conviction was overturned by the Colorado Supreme Court.

1915

From William B. Wilson

October 19, 1915

Mother Jones
Morrison Hotel
Chicago, Illinois

Do not deem it wise for the Department of Labor to investigate garment makers' strike at the same time that the City Council committee is making investigation. We have representatives of the Department quietly watching the situation in order that we may keep in touch with the developments.

W. B. Wilson

Telegram (Labor Department Records, RG 174/280 33/390, National Archives)

From Thomas J. Mooney[1]

San Francisco, California,
December 15, 1915

Mother (Mary) Jones,
Denver, Colo.

My dear Mother Jones:

Your letter of Nov. 7, arrived in due time, and the contents was duly noted. I was very much pleased to learn of your willingness to help the International Workers Defense League out of its present difficulty, if the circumstances would permit you to do so. The Members of the Defense League are active in the world labor movement, and are watching every move of Labor everywhere. Therefore they realize how busy you are and where you can do the most good in the movement. It is not the desire of the League or its members to have you stop your work in the interest of the miners if you would, so as to permit you to come to the coast for the benifit of the League.

When the Delegates and Visitors and press representatives of Calif., returned from the A. F. of L. convention, they gave out the information that in your address to the Convention, you deplored the tendency at the present time in the Labor Movement toward Dual and Secession movements, that you said you had refused to come to the Coast to speak for one of the dual or secession movements on there last year. Now we are led to believe that you in your remarks to the Convention had in mind the International Workers Defense League, whom you said you refused an invitation to come and speak on the Coast for such a moment. We first thought you might have had in mind some other organization on the Coast that asked you to speak for them that we

142

know nothing about, but after reconsidering the whole matter, some of us came to the conclusion that maybe some one of the Calif. Delegates misinformed you as to the true character of the Defense League and what it is composed of.

The last time I wrote you, I duplicated the letter, sending one to Denver, and the other to Indianapolis, in hope of sure communication with you. I sent one of the League's latest financial reports in your letter to Indianapolis and I don't know if you ever received it or not. This letter will give you some idea of the Defense League's work, the character of the organization, and its makeup, and the various organizations that compose it and support it in the defense of labor men involved in Labor troubles. I don't know if you received that letter containing this financial report, but to avoid delay, I am sending you a second copy hoping you will find a few spare minutes in your long busy life to look it over, and if this is done, from what I know of you in the labor game of the past, you will be satisfied that the defense league is doing good work, and at the same time not interfering with the regular course of the Labor movement. In short, the Defense League confines its activities to the defense of men (Labor) who get in a jam during times of Strikes, Lockouts, Boycotts or any labor trouble. Similar Leagues were formed all over the Country during the Meyer Haywood & Petibone episode. This league was organized during the Meyer Haywood Petibone trouble and was again reorganized during the Ettor & Giovanitti-trials, and after that it organized for good and all time under the International Workers Defense League. A delegated body, at the present time with about fifty organizations most of which are regular A. F. L. trade unions affiliated with their Respective Internationals, the Calif. State Federation of Labor, the San Francisco Labor Council, San Francisco Building Trades Council, etc. Most of the active delegates in the League are also the representatives of their respective unions in the various councils of Labor in San Francisco, and California. This League is in no wise dual or secession, but it more truly represents the militant, than the conservative element in the Labor Movement. Most all of the League's Delegates believing in staying in the A. F. L. and developing that organization into a real world force in the Labor Movement. We are convinced that the best results will only be produced in the Labor Movement through solidarity, and not the kind that proposes to start one more organization (One more division) of labor so-called in order to bring about this thing called solidarity. There are some men in the labor movement of Calif. as well as other states who have more or less control of labor organizations, but not always in the interest of those organizations as the respective members see it. This difference belongs to each organization. The

Defense League lets each organization of labor take care of its own troubles and differences, and even to the extent of not defending men if his organization desires to carry on the defense itself.

Many of the Leaders of the Labor organizations in this city, and some in the city are opposed to the Defense League secretly but not in the open, as they have no good excuse. The principle reason they are opposed to the League is because it is Militant in Character and its makeup is of the ideas and ideals that have been the impelling motive in your whole life work, the things which you have worked for for years. I suppose of all the organizations in this city, the Defense League will be most thoroughly able to appreciate your work, as they themselves are trying as near as their ability will permit them to do the things that you have done and which has won for you the respect of the Labor movement of the entire world which you are more than justly entitled to. I am a member of the International Molders Union of North America since I was 19 years old, and I am at present 32 years young. I toured the Country on the '*Red Special*' with Gene Debs in 1908, and have carried a card in the Socialist Party since then. I am personally acquainted with Adolph Germer and Frank Hayes. I don't want you to think I am trying to misrepresent to you the International Workers Defense League, as I think too much of you and also of the League to lie to you about an organization which I love for many reasons, and mostly because it was responsible for the victory of keeping me out of Jail.

The California Light and Power Council called a strike against the Pacific Gas and Electric Co. one of the largest and most powerful corporations in this state. The Pinkerton Detective Agency was put on the Job by the Gas Co. At the time I was out of work and I at all times feel it my duty to do all in my power to aid and assist any or all aggragations of workers on Strike for better conditions. Many labor leaders used the pretext that the strike was by a dual or secession bunch and should not have the support of the Labor Unions. The truth of the matter was that the council of the Light and Power industry looked like a great power and some of the Labor leaders were not in the circle of power so it was not the best thing for Labor, despite the fact that 1500 Union men in that line of work went on strike after taking a referendum vote on the question of the strike. Five of them were sent to the Penitentiary of this state for periods of from one to five years on evidence secured by Pinkertons. The Building Trades Council of Calif. fought with the Gas Co. and aided in the Defeat of the strikers when the entire state Federation of Labor was supporting morally and Financially the strike.

There was several hundred thousand dollars worth of property of the

Gas Co. destroyed by the strikers in various ways. I was in hiding for four months myself and finally arrested kept in Jail for five months going to the highest court of the state on habeas corpus, and then three Trials on the first Charge (Having High Explosives in my possession unlawfully) at Martinez, Calif. *with two of the best and highest paid criminal lawyers prosecuting me for the Gas Co. and then the fourth trial at Sacramento, Cal. all finally resulting in my release.* The Defense League carried on the defense in my behalf, and were it not for such a league I would be in San Quentin with the McNamara boys today and unable to write you as I am doing at this minute. The Pinkertons said if I did not tell all I knew they would Press three charges against me which would bring me fourteen years (14). They tried me four times on two charges and let go on the third because it was in the same county as the first where I received three trials, and was acquitted at the last trial.

The Defense League would like to have you come out here to help it pay off its debt that was incurred in my defense and also the defense of Ford and Suhr who were convicted of Murder in a strike on the Hop fields, and were sentenced to life at Folsom Prison, Cal. If the miners need you, stick, but if you can spare a few weeks in Calif. in the early Jan. you will enjoy it and at the same time lend a helping hand in a good cause as you have always been doing.

With Best wishes and the Kindest Regards to You, and Your Co-Workers (The Miners) in the Cause of the Working Class.

Fraternally

Thos. J. Mooney.

D (Thomas J. Mooney Papers)
1. Thomas Joseph Mooney (1882–1942), within the year was charged with murder after the explosion of a bomb during the San Francisco Preparedness Day Parade in July 1916, beginning what proved to be a twenty-year fight for freedom.

From John H. Walker

May 29th, 1916.

Mother Jones, c/o Chas. Moyer, Denver, Colo.
Dear Mother:

I am writing, to advise you that we had an enormous meeting at Decatur on the 20th, which was a week last Saturday. There was at least thirty thousand people at it. I never did see such a large turnout for a town as small as Decatur. They were all very much disappointed at your not being there. However, I explained that at the request of President Moyer and President White, who believed that you could do more than anyone else in the country in this particular matter; that you were in Arizona to do what you could to assist Governor Hunt,[1] who did so much for the Western Federation of Miners, in the Clifton Morensa strike, and whom the Copper Mine Owners were trying to destroy for that very same reason, and it was because you felt you could do more good for the movement by doing that work, than addressing the meeting at Decatur, was the only reason for your not being there.

I am writing this letter Mother, as you know it was through me that you suggested that date for the meeting yourself, and that you agreed to be there, and for fear that you might have forgotten that agreement, there is a newspaper man in Decatur, that is trying to discredit men who are making a campaign there, to organize the workers there, and it is just possible that he might write you, asking whether or not you had agreed to be there, and put it in a light that might influence you to say something to him that he could use against Carbine[2] and the rest of the boys who are trying to organize that town.

He poses as editor of a labor paper—that is his own personal paper. He and his paper have been repudiated by the Central Body there; I understand he has been expelled from the Printers Local Union there, so you know he must have been pretty bad when that organization threw him out.

He gets it printed on scab paper in a non-union shop, and is playing the game for the crooked politicians all the time whenever they will pay him for it; and for the price of an advertisement, he sells his paper to every business and employing interest that is fighting the labor movement, and I wanted you to have these things in mind, so that if he would write you, you would understand and be able to avoid saying anything to him that he could use to injure the labor movement in Decatur.

Personally, I am very sorry that you were not at that meeting. It was the greatest of its kind that I ever attended in a small town of 30,000, and I know that if you would have been able to do an immense amound of good if you could have been there at that time; still I know how important it is after what he done, for us to, if we can save Governor Hunt and even make him stronger so that not only he will be able to continue to do that kind of work and feel like doing it, but also for the effect it will have on men in public official positions everywhere in the country in the future.

I hope too, Mother that you will actually acknowledge to yourself, that you are not as strong as a steam engine or a battle ship any more, and that you won't allow your love for the cause and your desire to work, let you injure your health.

Take care of yourself; we need you, and you owe it to the labor movement as well as to yourself to stay with us as long as you can, which you can only do by taking care of yourself.

With all the love in the world, I am,

Yours,
[John H. Walker]
President.

TLC (John H. Walker Papers)
1. George W. P. Hunt (1859–1934), first governor of the state of Arizona, who was elected to six subsequent terms.
2. Ed Carbine, an official of the Illinois Federation of Labor.

To G. W. P. Hunt

Los Angeles, Cal.
June 12, 1916.

Mr. Geo. W. Hunt
The real Governor of Arizona
Phoenix, Arizona.
My dear Mr. Hunt:

If I can render you any assistance during your campaign in Arizona, do not hesitate to call upon me, because the Miners are more than anxious to have you returned to the Executive Chair. I will be at your service whenever you call on me.

Mail will reach me at 1106 Merchant's National Bank Building, c/o United Miners Office, Indianapolis, Indiana.

With many good wishes,
Ever sincerely,
Mother Jones

TLS (George W. P. Hunt Papers)

To G. W. P. Hunt

Los Angeles, Cal.
June 12, 1916.

Mr. Geo. W. Hunt,
The real Governor of Arizona,
Phoenix, Arizona.
My dear Mr. Hunt:

I hope that you will not take my silence as indifference to your kindness to me when I visited the Capitol City of the State of Arizona.

I have no words to express to you my deep appreciation for the kindly treatment I received from you. It was so foreign to the treatment I get as a rule from Governor's of States where I enter to educate the workers to their own class interests. Generally speaking, the bayonets are sent to receive me. They are usually the flowers that our modern Statesmen send when you go to carry the message of hope to the exploited and robbed.

It is my desire that every State should duplicate a man of your type and make-up as their Chief Executive. It would be far more to the honor of the State and nation and to the protection of life and property, and while the "high-class burglars" may not make so many dollars out of the life's blood of their fellow beings, they will at least be making for a higher and nobler civilization.

I regret that I did not see you the last day I was in Phoenix, but hope it will be my good fortune in the near future to meet you again, and let me say to you, that as long as life remains, I shall feel there was one man that followed in the footsteps of Jefferson, Patrick Henry, and Lincoln. They thought more of human life and the honor of the State and nation than they did of service to the interests.

Your administration will live in history when the administrations of Hatfield, Ammons and Peabody, and others of their type will go down in the black pages.

I have the honor and extreme pleasure to sign myself as one who shall always remember you,

Ever sincerely,
Mother Jones

TLS (George W. P. Hunt Papers)

From G. W. P. Hunt

June 14th, 1916.

Dear Mother Jones:

I have read and re-read your notes of the 12th inst., in which you express approval of the course which I have pursued, and extend your whole-hearted co-operation.

I need hardly assure you that I deeply appreciate the tribute which you have paid my humble efforts to be an Executive representative of all the people rather than the privileged few. You and my other friends may rest assured that, notwithstanding the repeated onslaughts of a certain corporation coterie in Arizona, my purposes will remain unaltered and my intention to work for the best interest of the great majority will be steadfast.

I am personally grateful to you for your generous proffer of assistance, and I will keep your friendly statements in mind, with a view of counting later upon your co-operation.

With assurances of my high regard,

Yours sincerely,
[George W. Hunt]
Governor of Arizona

TLC (George W. P. Hunt Papers)

To Edward Crough[1]

Denver, Colo.
June 30, 1916.

Mr. Edw. Crough,
General Delivery,
Bisbee, Arizona.
My dear Ed:

I received your letter of June 23rd in Trinidad. I realize the work you are doing and I know our trip was not in vain. While we did not see the results while we went, for we were irritated at the way things looked. I was worn out when I went to Arizona because the strain on me before that had been so great that I had begun to feel it. No doubt our meeting in Miami [cut the posturings?] of the ambitious pie-counter hunter. When I think of what an insolent, empty brained thing that fellow was to have the audacity to have the ambition to become President of a great growing organization, it was nasuating. And then to think that Joe Hanson would stand for a thing like that, I don't know Ed, whether it is indifference or treachery that makes men so indifferent to the welfare of the workers, but the result is the same to us.

I shall always think of you, Ed with the affection of a mother, because you were so kind to me and were so loyal and true to the cause. Take care of your health more than anything else because we are short of men of your makeup. I am glad you told that fellow de Lara what you thought of him [*Torn*] is there for what he can get out of it. It is a hard road to travel Ed, at best and when our own people should stand by us shoulder to shoulder that they are ever got their knife out filled with slime, not to stab the system that is ruining childhood, womanhood and manhood, but to stab everyone who dares to take the bit in their mouth and go forward for a better civilization. But we had a good meeting in Bisbee anyway. I had a very good letter from the Governor and I prize that letter highly, he sent it to me with his photograph and autograph. I shall never forget how kindly he received me it is so foreign to what they generally do. I generally am met with the bullets and bayonets, but here is one man who will be in history if I live long enough to put it there. I am going to Arizona this fall to work there and we have move heaven and earth to put him back.

Well Ed, I leave for Chicago tomorrow night and you can send my mail to Ed Nockles, Chicago Federation of Labor.

I am fondly and Loyally yours and always ready to do anything for you.

My love to all at your home, and give my regards to the True Blues and tell the leeches they can go to Hell.

Yours
Mother Jones

TLS (in the possession of W. K. Crough)

1. Edward Crough (1878–1951) held offices in the Western Federation of Miners and, later, the AFL.

To John H. Walker

Denver, Colo.,
June 30, 1916.

Mr. John H. Walker, President
State Federation of Labor,
Springfield, Illinois.

My dear John:

Your letter of the 29th reached me a day or two ago when I arrived in Denver, there is no one that I feel more glad to hear from than you, because I know when the sentiment is expressed it is meant.

I saw Frank P. Walsh[1] yesterday, he says that he has exonerated Alec Howitt[2] and the man from Oklahoma. It was a glorious event as the knife was out in several quarters to stab Howitt. I was indeed glad to see the feeling that Walsh had about it, he felt as if it was the greatest victory that Labor has ever won.

Now, John so far as anyone writing to me, do you know that I have as keen an insight in discovering a trickster as anyone else and if anyone in Illinois had written to me about that meeting and wanted to know why I was not there, I would have immediately went to a notory public and taken an oath and made him swallow it. No one regretted my not appearing at the Decatur Meeting more than I did, but under the circumstances, John, there was very important work to be done in the West. I also went to see the prisoners Caplin Schmidt. I found the boys looking well with good heart.

I also went up to see the boys in San Quintin. I saw Clancy, the McNamaras and Ryan. I hated to leave, poor Ryan he stood by and when I looked back he stood there wiping his eyes. The warden extended a good deal of courtesy to me which I appreciated, so did the boys. I regretted more than anyone could have regretted, that I could not attend that meeting, but the circumstances that arose forced me to take the steps that I did. We must choose between the most important position for the Labor Movement always. It was nine o'clock Friday night when I got into Coffeyville, Kans., I had to drive 19 miles from the railroad station into Coffeyville. When I got on the platform I was still tired, John, but nevertheless I delivered the goods, and I had a packed audience from beginning to end. I had to leave next morning early, and it was Hell at both ends. They were after Moyer hot and heavy, but during my campaign, I changed the whole thing, I think the other side, the tools of the interests, got a blow they will not get over in a hurry. The Governor of the State[3] extended all the courtesy that he could and I received a fine letter from him since I left.

John, would it be possible for you to be in Chicago next Sunday afternoon, I want to have a long, long talk with you alone, you know John, I would write to you so often, but when I get through with these campaigns I am kind of tired and I cannot do much writing and I cannot always have a stenographer near me. Take care of yourself because some of the rats have the knife out for you, but you have more friends than any man I know in the Labor Movement. Here is a letter I am going to send you for Lord[4] and I wish you would forward it to him, if I sent it to Washington it is generally there two or three weeks before he gets it, he should have some arrangements for having his mail forwarded, that thing of having mail laying in an office for weeks and weeks will not do for it might be that some important matter should be attended to immediately, and again, John, it does not register good business tactics.

I visited Frisco and the Building Trades there gave me a royal reception. I addressed their meeting one night and got a very warm reception from every member, and for the four days that I was in the City they devoted their time to giving me some enjoyment   Never before in my life have I been treated with such warm feeling as they received me in Frisco, you know John I am usually hammered but the thing was so different with the boys in Los Angeles and Frisco that I could not help but feel it to the depth of my soul. There is one thing about it, John, that we sometimes find good men who are not corrupted. When I left Frisco I was feeling fine.

I will say goodbye and hope to see you in Chicago.

With all the warm regard and esteem I have for you,

Mother Jones

TLS (John H. Walker Papers)

1. Frank P. Walsh (1864–1939), a prominent St. Louis lawyer with labor sympathies who was chairman of the Commission on Industrial Relations.

2. Alexander Howat (1876–1945), a belligerent radical in the UMWA leadership, was president of District 14 (Kansas) for many years; power struggles with John L. Lewis, which Howat lost, marked his career in the late teens and twenties.

3. Arthur Capper (1865–1951), governor of Kansas, 1914–1918, and senator, 1918–1949.

4. James Ravell Lord.

From John H. Walker

July 1st, 1916.

Mother Jones,
c/o Morrison Hotel
Chicago, Ill.

Dear Mother:

Just got yours of the 30th ult., and was glad to hear from you. Yes that was a great victory that Walsh won, under almost impossible circumstances. It required a superhuman effort almost, to do what he has done. It was about as low and vile and sinister a conspiracy as has ever been hatched by man. I sincerely hope that Moyer[1] will be re-elected president.

There is a little local union at Rosiclare, Ill, Hardin county, of Fluespar miners where they are putting up a splendid fight, that I think sent in 250 votes for him.

By the way Mother, it is a strike that should be won and if it is not, it will be because of lack of a little finance, and there is so few in number, and they are conserving the resources in such a manner and fighting the battle so heroic that it will be a shame and a crime if it is lost, and ther[e] won't be over a hundred families that will have to be kept at any time.

If you could only have gone down there and held one meeting, so that you could understand the situation, I know there would be no trouble for you to raise enough money to enable them to win that strike; and I know too, that you could not help doing it, after you went down there and saw and understood the situation.

It is in Hardin County, southern Illinois. There are no railroads there. You would have to go from Chicago to Vincennes on the C. & E. I. and if you was in there on the early morning train, you can catch that 7:10 I. C. to Dekovan, Ky., then get the Kack from there to Caseyville, which is about three miles, and then take a boat from there to Elizabethtown. It is not so very far and the Rose hotel is right at the landing at Elizabethtown, and I know they would make you comfortable and they would take you to and from Rosiclare in a machine.

Wm. Sneed is there in charge of the strike. A fine young fellow; clean, square and able. He has done magnificent work, and you can trust him implicitly. He would be tickeled to death to arrange for a meeting for you, if you went down there, and would take you there and bring you back in a machine or a gasoline launch; and I know your presence there would inspire those men in such a way as nothing else would.

You did not enclose Lord's letter to me, so that I have not got it. He was here yesterday. I think he is going to Farmington for the 4th of July and from there, go back down to Rosiclare for a day or two.

I understand Mother that the three International Board members from the anthracite, want me to make the race for International President of our organization, and that other Board members from the different districts where I have been uncertain before, want me to make the race also; this would make a certainty that I would be elected, if I was a candidate, and the conditions are so deplorable within our organization, that I am very strongly tempted to make that race, although we have our movement here in Illinois in such fine shape and doing such splendid work, and the prospects for doing greater work in the future are so bright, that I hate to leave it; and I am afraid my leaving it now, would disarrange our organization within the state and maybe retard things for a little while.

I am very sorry I can't meet you Sunday Mother, but I have a meeting at Pekin for Sunday; all arrangements have been made and I just can't disappoint them now.

Sincerely yours,
[John H. Walker]
President.

TLC (John H. Walker Papers)
1. Presumably Charles Moyer, longtime president of the Western Federation of Miners.

To Ed Nockles

Indianapolis, Ind.,
July 7, 1916.

Mr. Ed Nockles
Sec'y Chicago Federation of Labor
Chicago, Ill.
Dear Ed:

Am leaving for Washington and send my mail to the Atlantic Hotel, Washington, D. C. Sec'y Green[1] of the Miners, will go with us to Washington, so I think you had better write him an invitation. The more powerful the committee is the more effect it will have on the other side. I have to go to Atlanta, Ga., tomorrow but will be in Washington Monday. Have to go up to the prison there to do some work for the national office. Take care of yourself and give my regards to Olander[2] and Fitzpatrick.[3]

Yours sincerely,

[*Holograph note*] I looked for you at Hotel untill late you never showed up

Mother Jones

[*Holograph note by Ed Nockles*] Friend John   Am sending this letter for your information   will try and phone or wire you next monday or tuesday   consequently keep me posted where you are and be ready to leave for Washington on a minutes notice   (I am being hounded to death with work)   Ed

TLS (John H. Walker Papers)
  1. William Green (1873–1952), secretary-treasurer of the UMWA, 1912–1924, president of the AFL, 1924–1952.
  2. Victor A. Olander (1873–1949), who held several offices in the International Seamen's Union, became secretary-treasurer of the Illinois Federation of Labor in 1914 and occupied that position until his death, despite a period of blindness; his sight was restored by a cataract operation.
  3. John Fitzpatrick (1871–1946), president for forty years of the Chicago Federation of Labor, was probably best known nationally for his chairmanship of the Steel Organizing Committee in 1919. He was one of the executors of Mother Jones's will.

To Edward Nockles

Washington, D. C.
July 20, 1916.

Mr. Edward Nockels,
166 Washington Street,
Chicago, Ill.,
Secretary, Chicago Federation of Labor.
Dear Ed:

I received your letter yesterday and your telegram the day before   I have made all arrangements with some very influential people in Washington to lend their hand. I am all ready paving the way. I have lost no time since I have been back from Atlanta. I think that we had best all stay at one hotel, so that we would be altogether, as there are some Senators and Congressmen who will want to see us and talk this thing over before we approach the President. I suggested that we ask for no parole, but a complete pardon and exoneration for the men, and influential persons that I spoke to agreed with me. They were glad to know that a few people were taking up the matter. If you get here on Tuesday then we can all meet and outline our policy collectively, so that there will be no blunders made. When we act we will have a clear understanding of what we wanted. Things are moving pretty well as I would like to see them. Of course I am not getting up in the air, Ed, because if I was knocked down I would feel it keenly, but I am very hopeful of the outcome of this move. I have been watching that strike in Illinois and was somewhat surprised of the Governor sending the troops there even at the request of a corporation sheriff.

Things will be so arranged here that you will not have to lose any time. If you get in at 1:30 Tuesday we will have the afternoon and the next day to work. We can arrange to have the President meet us on Wednesday. You telegram to me the train that you leave on and I will meet you at the depot. Give my regards to Olander, Fitzpatrick Pretty hot here Ed, and you will need all the summer clothes you can bring. I am loyally yours for a damn fine fight.

Mother Jones

TLC (John H. Walker Papers)

From John H. Walker

August 9th, 1916.

"Mother" Jones,
c/o Western Federation of Labor
Denham Bldg., Denver, Colo.
Dear Mother:

After thinking over the matter of what you told me about the future program of our organization on the part of some people and what it was likely to result in, and then giving consideration to the earnest appeals that have been made by different men in our movement everywhere in the country and taking into consideration the statement of what settlement represents, I finally decided to become a candidate for International President of our organization in the coming election.

Now, I know what your position is Mother, and I would not want you to do anything in the world that would jeopardize yourself, but I wanted you to know that I am going to make the race, because I am convinced that I owed it to our organization to do so. Personally, I would much rather to have remained in the position I was in, but if things had developed, such as you said that you feared they would, I would have felt in a way responsible and never would forgive myself.

The prospects are exceedingly good for a good, big, substantial majority. However, I don't underestimate the strong and unscrupulous oppositions that will have to be met and over-come.

Trusting that this finds you in your usual good health, I am,

Yours,
[John H. Walker]

TLC (John H. Walker Papers)

From Marguerite Prevey

Akron, Ohio,
Oct 26th 1916

Dear "Mother Jones"

We have been informed that you are campaigning for the Democrat Party in the 5th Indiana Dist.—the District from which the Socialists expect to elect Debs. I should be pleased to have you either deny or verify this report.

I can hardly believe you would use what influence you have with the workers to deafeat Comrade Debs for Congress.

Sincerely yours
Marguerite Prevey

ALS (Terence V. Powderly Papers)

From Katherine L. Schmidt[1]

Los Angeles, Cal.
October 29, 1916.

Dear Mother:

This is Sunday afternoon—I am here all alone trying to get some of my work straightened out. I was elected Recording Secretary of the Woodrow Wilson League when it was organized, and doing the balance of my work in conjunction with that, keeps me pretty busy. Of course, the Wilson position will be a thing of the past next week, and then I can settle down into the old harness again.

Mother, this has been a most interesting fight. It would do your heart good to see John Murray[2] manage some of these people. When we called for volunteers to sell papers on the street (women) I told some of the men that I would bet my money on the women, providing they did not have to fight the entire family in order to come out. And much to my astonishment Chas. Myers wife—Secy. of the Central Labor Council, and Mrs. Drake, wife of the editor of the Labor paper joined the rest of us, and it was a good stunt. I am enclosing clipping from last Sunday's Times, so you will please note we have acquired reputations via the Times route. Some of the leading club women came out with us—we had about 100 all told.

Last night the women had a big meeting in the Trinity Auditorium and it was packed to the doors. Mrs. Fremont Older[3] and two other women came from Frisco. Mrs. Older was the best of the three—the other two were about as good as I would be. As John Murray said, the audience was stupid, so they got away with their little talk. These semi-society ladies are about the limit no matter where you put them,

157

dont you think so Mother? May find an occasional worth-while one, but generally speaking it is a waste of time to bother with them.

Caplan's[4] trial started last Monday—the 23rd. It was to start on the 16th, but we could not raise enough money to get Coghlan here from Frisco. He never got a cent in the other trial of Caplan's, so after many sleepless nights we got Appel (Mexican lawyer) here to take the case. So far they have selected ten permanent jurors. Mother, the quicker we can rid our labor movement of some of these pesky politicians, the better it will be for us. We did not have one red cent for the trial, and as a last resort I wired Fay Lewis[5] for $1000. (Please note my modesty) but there was no other way out of it, and I for one could not sit by and see the boys deserted. I realize this is a miserable year—the election, and the Prohibition fight has demanded so much of the time and money of the working people, so the boys have been forgotten as it were for the time being. No-one in Frisco ever does a thing but O. A. T.[6] Poor dear soul, I feel sorry for him at times.

Mother, I have been thinking seriously of starting out for myself to raise money for the boys, and I think this would be a good time to start while Caplan's trial is on. These d—— lawyers all insist upon having money and it does not stop with them—some of our dear workers are just as bad, and I thought I should like to go to the [AFL] Convention at Baltimore and take the matter up with the men individually—not on the floor of the Convention, and then start out and do something. I wondered, Mother, if we could not start sort of a woman's movement to free all of our labor prisoners—not alone my brother and Caplan, but all of the poor wretches that are behind prison bars. I believe the women would do something providing they were sufficiently aroused. Not that I am an orator, but I am Mathew's sister, and that will help some. I thought I'ld like to talk this over with you and get your advice, as you have been in the fight so long you know all of the angles. I had planned to borrow some money from Fay Lewis to make the trip if you deemed it wise—providing you are going to the Convention, and if not, I could route myself any other way so I could reach you and talk the matter over.

One thing, Mother, if I go out it wont take a small fortune to get from one place to the other. Some of our men when they go out they must have big dinners, joy rides, sporting women, etc., so they eat up about all they collect. Dont you think, Mother, we could do something with our own sex? They have become very active on behalf of Wilson and Hughes, and we might be able to divert their attention to the other when election is over. Really, Mother, I am heartily disgusted with some of our men, and something will have to be done for the boys in jail—all of the boys.

I am enclosing an article about some of our prominent men, and thought they would be a drawing card—in that way at least some people would respond—knowing the formost men of the county were interested. Now tell me what you think of it, and if you deem it wise for me to undertake a trip to Baltimore, etc.

Mother, it was a real pleasure to meet Sec'y of Labor Wilson. Isn't he wonderful? Those deep set kind eyes of his. He delivered a splendid speech here at the Temple, and we had a fine audience. He got in here at 7:50 in the eve and left again the next morn. John Murray got up bright and early so as to have breakfast with him.

By the way, Mother, that little John Murray does some good work, does'nt he? Very recently he did a good stroke—I cannot tell you about it on paper. He works a person to death, but yet I learn a great deal being with him. He is going to the Convention at Baltimore as a delegate from the council here—paying his own expenses.

I am going out to see Miss Flaherty just as soon as election is over and I have a few minutes to spare. Yes, isn't she a fine girl? John Murray said he would like to come with me—said he knew her when she used [to] live in Chicago, and spoke very highly of her. We may be able to go ere he leaves town.

No, you can rest assured I am not wasting much of my time or money entertaining some of these people here. Miss Dean (the girl you met at dinner) would pester me to death if I let her, but I need all the rest I can get and like to be alone—I cannot afford to have guests, and then my time is worth more in another direction.

I go up every day to see the boys. Mathew had a fine letter from Jim Lord the other day. They have not sent in a penny from Arizona as yet. John Murray had a letter from Ed. Crough saying they were collecting the money in Bisbee and some other place, but we have not seen it as yet. It is so depressing, Mother, to go up to that old prison day after day and just wait and watch. I do hope Dave wins this time. Mathew's appeal was postponed to January 27th. I would rather go to jail myself than keep Dave there much longer. Some of the jews can make a thundering lot of noise, but they are'nt the best fighters in the world.

Mother, it is lovely of you to take the time to write to me. I cannot tell you how much it means to both of us to get an encouraging letter from you now and then. Smidie says, and so do I, that we'd bet our last cent on Mother Jones—you have got more ginger in you than all the men in the country put together and they all know you cannot be touched with money, and you dont want a political job, so they cannot reach you nohow. It amused us when we got a letter from one of the girls at the Madison University. She was just having a spasm about your activities in New York, and I think every student in the college heard about you through her. Smidie and I have told her a great deal about your good work, and then, of course, she is a reader and thinker, so knows all about you, but surely Mother Jones was the topic of conversation at the University for some time. I bet, Mother, you could tell them more real facts in one hour than those professors will drill into their noddles in a year.

I will keep you posted on the Caplan case as it goes along. I have not been in the Court room, but expect to attend more regularly when election is over.

Be sure to let me hear from you, Mother, and tell me what you think about my plan to raise money for the boys. Honestly, I was nearly besides myself wondering and worrying trying to find a way out. I can always rely upon Fay Lewis to come to my rescue. He certainly has been a real guardian angel to me. Really, Mother, he is one of the most beautiful characters I have ever known.

I had a letter from Mrs. Darrow recently, but Mr. D. is kept pretty busy. I understand he is out making speeches for Wilson and doing all the boosting he can. He is a dear good soul. In a way, Mother, he did not deserve all the criticism he got out here. Some of our men should have remained here with him and lent a helping hand. Perhaps some of this H—— could have been averted.

Many good wishes from both Smidie and I, and let me hear from you soon again.

Curley Grow[7] was out talking against the Prohibitionists. He is a brick. Really, Mother, he is the only real labor man we have in this whole town. I would bet my last cent on him.

Much love,
Katherine Schmidt

TLS (Terence V. Powderly Papers)

1. Katherine Schmidt, a member of the office employees' union, was the sister of Mathew Schmidt, who was convicted as an accomplice in the bombing of the Los Angeles *Times* in 1910.

2. John Murray (1865–1919), a follower of Tolstoi, devoted his life to various labor and Socialist causes and edited the *Los Angeles Socialist*.

3. Cora Baggerly Older (c. 1873–1968), reporter and author, was the wife of Fremont Older, editor of the San Francisco *Bulletin*, and later of the San Francisco *Call*.

4. David Kaplan was implicated along with Mathew Schmidt in the Los Angeles *Times* bombing of 1910.

5. Possibly Lafayette Arthur Lewis (1888–1966), a prominent lawyer of Whittier, California.

6. Probably Olaf A. Tveitmoe.

7. Probably Cyrus F. Grow, business agent for Local 311 of the International Association of Machinists in Los Angeles; he ran for local offices as a Socialist in several elections.

To Marguerite Prevey

Oct. 31, 1916.

Mrs. Margaret Prevy,
140 High St.
Akron, Ohio.
My dear Mrs. Prevy:

Your letter reached me yesterday. Permit me to say to you that whoever wrote you the falsehood should take a day off and learn to tell the truth. I went in to the mining districts of Indiana to have Senator Kerns returned to the Senate, because he saved me from serving five years in the state penitentiary of West Virginia with twenty-one of my fellows. I think the miners of this country owe him a debt that they should pay by returning him to the Senate. If we did not do it we would be ingrates. No political party in this nation ever paid me five cents. I was not there in the interest of any political party. I was sent there by the United Mine Workers to explain to the miners why they should return Senator Kerns. I had nothing to do with Debb's campaign. I was not sent there by the National office to inter-fere with any party affairs. Senator Kerns befriended me on more occasions than one in Washington. I could always go to him in behalf of those who needed assistance.

The socialists in their whole lives never gave me a dollar. I have given them a good many. I know how they treated Miss Flaherty and others who served them in the days gone by. They are not runing my affairs and they don't own me and they had better learn to quit slandering people if they are going to revolutionize the nation. They had better revolutionize their own brains first. The democrats did not bring me there nor would I go out for any political party. I went out for the Labor Organization that I am directly interested in. The politi-cal parties don't bother me very much. It is the individual. I have no apologies to offer to any member of the Socialist Party for any act of mine. If they would clean house they might have many more members. I have no earthly use for people who are forever digging up the actions of other people and overlooking their own. I hope this explanation will be satisfactory to you. The socialists of Terre Haute brought me there some eight or ten years ago. I had to pay my own railroad fare and pay my own expenses. It was a May Wood Simons, or a Lena Morrow Lewis or people who had never been in the trenches nor ever in their lives fought one of labor's battles and the only interest they had was to bleed the wretches who were putting up the money, they would have been highly entertained and been paid generously, but whenever you go in the trenches and face the bayonets of the comon enemy against the gang, they have nothing to say. I want to say here that I owe the socialists no apology, nor will I offer one to them. I have seen enough of their treachery to those who have fought the battle and want to keep the party clean; but one of these days, Margaret Prevy, we are going to clean house and we will have a real revolutionary socialist movement and we will see that neither lawyers nor sky pilots are running our affairs.

With love to Mr. Prevy and you, I remain

> [*Torn*] in the struggle for better days,
> [Mother Jones]

TLC (Terence V. Powderly Papers)

From Tom Mooney

> San Francisco, Cal.
> Nov. 25, 1916.
> County Jail No. 1, Cell No. 29.

Mother Jones,
Care of United Mine Workers
Indianopolis, Ind.
My Dear Frind & Comrade:

The last time I wrote you I was asking your aid to help dig some other fellow out of the Bosses Bastille.

This time it is to try to enlist your support moral, financial and economic to the end that I my wife and three others may again walk in free air, to fight in labors ranks once more.

We are all indited on eight charges of murder, as a result of the bomb explosion that happened during the preparadness parade in this City on July 22, of this year.

I might write at length on the details of this fight for your special benifit, but you know the struggle well enough. It is the same old story in this case. Though some try to make it a little different.

This is one time that they have made the whole frameup, out of the whole cloth, and apparently they intend to make it stick, or at least they did so far. One of [our?] Boys Warren K. Billings,[1] was convicted and sentenced to Life imprisonment as a result.

I am the next to be tried, Jan. 3, 1917 is the date set for the battle to begin.

We have been very fortunate in securing the services of the formost attorney of the Country Bourke Cockran[2] to take up our case free of charge as a result of Frank P. Walsh, interceeding for us in a measure.

It will devolve on the defense to at least pay his personal as well as his court expenses which will be very high.

Frank P. Walsh is also comming to the Coast to take up our cases, and Geo. West, Special Investigator, For the U. S. Industrial Relations Commission will soon start to write up the police conspiracy frame up for all of the labor papers as well as all others that will print what he will write. West arrived in town a few days ago.

We are making a desperate effort to gain a new trial for Billings which all takes lots of money and the Defense is at this time depleated.

I wrote John P. White Pres. of the United Mine Workers, about the cases and he never answered my letter. I asked him if he would send me a list of the names and addresses of the Secretarys of the locals of the Mine Workers throughout the Country so we could give our cases the desired publicity and appeal for funds. I have not heard from him at all.

Mother, I am enclosing you some of the Publicity gotten out by myself also some put out by the Defense League. I hope you will find time to give what ever help your health and energy will permitt you to when you read this stuff, I am sending you.   as we sure need not only your help but the help of all others.

I wish it were possible for you to come to the Coast to look over the situation and take up the platform in the larger Cities at advertised meetings as a forerunner to other work needed in order to insure success in our coming trials.

I wish you would make an effort to get the United Mine Workers Local Union Secretary Directory.   and if you have any influence with Adolph Germer, Sec'y of the Socialist Party at Chicago, to get from hi if it is possible the list of the addresses of the Socialist Party locals in all parts of the Country. So they can be circularized by our publicity committee and at the same time an appeal for funds. I have been a member of the Party for the last nine years and an active member at that.

I went thru the country on the Red Special with Debs in 1908 and while on that trip I met Germer and Frank Hayes on the train while it was in the state of Illinoise.

The Socialist Party Here is not much, as they tried twice to help the corporation to send me to the prison in the way of putting me out of the party when I was in jail and charged with crime and the corporation was bending every effort to get me with the aid of two of the ablest lawyers as special prosecutors working with the Dist. Atty. and compelling the Sheriff who was such for 25 years in succession to sit at the Dist. Atty.'s table to aid in the selection of the Jury, that would convict. The only reason that I was not put out of the Party was that I was a member of the Hungarinag Branch and they said if you put

Mooney out, You will have to put the whole branch out.

Debs has written an article about our case in the Rip Saw and the Melting Pot. The Appeal to Reason will carry a story about our case on Dec. 2, that will be this Sat.

I have written to Pres. Mahon[3] of the Street Carmens Union and he has not even answered my letter. One of the greatest reasons for my being in jail today is the fact that I tried to organize the carmen of this city, and failed in my effort just one week before the bomb went off.

I am enclosing you other matters of detail about my own as well as the general league publicity gotten out in our behalf.

I hope your health and tireless spirit will permit you to lend us a helping hand, for we sure need it. The defense treasurey is at this writting depleated.

I go to trial Jan. 3, and no money on hand to do many kinds of very necessary work. This is one time that Labor has all of the facts with it. We are absolutely innocent, of the crime or any Knowledge of it.

Hoping to hear from You.

Fraternally and Sincerely Yours in Labors Fight.
Tom Mooney

TLS (Mother Jones Papers)
1. Warren K. Billings (1893–1972), president of the shoe workers' union, was charged and convicted in the Preparedness Day bombing case.
2. William Bourke Cockran (1854–1923) divided his time between politics, which included seven terms as a Democratic congressman, and a lucrative law practice in New York.
3. William D. Mahon (1861–1949), one of the founders of the Amalgamated Association of Street and Electric Railway Employes, was to become a member of the AFL executive council and a vice-president of the organization. At this time he had just returned from an investigation of municipal ownership of street railways in Europe and attendance at the British Trade Union Labor Congress, representing the AFL.

From Charles Batley[1]

Charleston, W. Va.,
November 28 1916

Mother Jones,
Washington, D. C.
Dear Mother:

I was glad to get your letter but sorry to learn you were worn out with your work here tho I was not surprised for as you say the meetings were very poorly arranged and I know must have been a great strain on you. I know from experience that the annoyance of such badly managed meetings is much more exhausting than the speaking itself.

I agree with you that many of the leaders in the labor movement do not fully realize what they are up against hence it is the blind leading the blind and if they do not soon open their eyes I fear the leaders and the lead will fall into the ditch. The average labor leader has never given any study to the financial system that the industrial masses have got to combat. The only thing that they give any study to is their own personal and slfish interests and how can such so called leaders educate and systemize a thorough industrial organization to meet the requirements of the present situation.

I trust you will be successful in your efforts to get the boys out of the penitentary because I know how you feel about those things and there is no one in the United States who has more experience along these lines and has given more time and energy in helping those who were forgotten by the ones they had tried to help.

Everyone in the labor movement knows that you have given your life to the cause and the upbuilding and educating of the workers in every branch of society and it can never be said by anyone that Mother Jones has failed to do her duty.

Mother, Senator Chilton[2] was defeated and so was Judge Robinson,[3] the Watson gang of the Fairmont field and the Vinson gang of the Norfolk and Western field and the McKell gang of the New river field accomplished their purpose by defeating these two candidates who stood by labor in West Virginia, even the Cabin creek district cast their votes against Judge Robinson, who proved their friend in the cricis of 1911–12. This is only example of the workers ignorance in supporting their enemies and distroying their friends.

I see in tonights "Charleston Post" that Chiltons usefullness is not going to be lost to labor. There is a rumor that he is to be appointed in President Wilsons cabinet to secretary of commerce and labor Littlepage[4] and Neely[5] were returned to congress. Of course know you will have learned of the defeat of Kerns of Indiana and Martine of New Jersey. I believe however that President Wilson will take care of both of them so their influence will not be lost.

The Rush Run arbitration case is still on and it will be about a week before a final decision. Congressman Littlepage was chosen as final arbitrator.

Mrs. Batley joins me in good wishes and expresses the hope that she may meet you again soon.

I told George Hargrove[6] to forward your mail if any came to Atlantic Hotel Washington, D.C.

Affectionatly,
Chas Batley.

TLS (Terence V. Powderly Papers)
1. Charles H. Batley, originally a miner from Missouri (Districts 14 and 25) served for many years as an international organizer for the UMWA.
2. William Edwin Chilton (1858–1939), publisher of the Charleston *Gazette,* served as Democratic senator from West Virginia, 1910–1917. Even after defeat he remained a power in state politics.
3. Ira Ellsworth Robinson (1869–1951), who had served on the West Virginia supreme court of appeals, 1907–1915, lost the contest with John J. Cornwell for the governorship.
4. Adam Brown Littlepage (1859–1921) represented West Virginia's Third District in Congress, 1910–1916 and 1918–1921.
5. Matthew Mansfield Neely (1874–1958), who relied heavily on the support of organized labor, enjoyed a political career that included a decade in the House of Representatives, twenty-five years as a U.S. senator, and a term as governor. He was serving his second term as a Democrat in the House.
6. George Hargrove later became president of District 20 (Alabama).

From Henry Hagelstein

San Francisco, Cal.
Dec 1st 1916

Mother Jones,
Washington, D. C.
Dear Comrade:

Enclosed please find receipt for $10.00 your contribution to the defense of our imprisoned comrades.

The next trial, that of Tom Mooney of Moulders Union #164 is fixed for the 3d of January. We anticipate a fair trial, seeing that the professional jury system and the hired witnesses of the prosecution have been thoroughly exposed. The Hon. W. Bourke Cochran of New York has volunteered to act as chief counsel for the defense, a fact very conclusive in itself of the absolute innocence of the accused.

The San Francisco Building Trades Council, the Chicago Federation of Labor, The Bay District Councils of Painters and Carpenters and all the largest unions of San Francisco are united, demanding fair trials for those so unjustly accused of the bomb outrage.

We thank you for your aid, which we sincerely appreciate and ask your further co-operation towards securing the freedom of our comrades. We are,

Yours fraternally,
International Workers Defense League
By Henry Hagelstein Secy.

TLS (Terence V. Powderly Papers)

To J. Clancy

December 2, 1916.

Mr. J. Clancy,
San Quentin State Prison,
San Quentin, Cal.
My dear Mr. Clancy:

I have just returned from Leavenworth Prison, where I had Ryan and all the boys apply for pardons. I brought the documents back with me and Mr. White and myself will present them to the President and do all we can for you and the boys in Leavenworth. The boys are well and looking well in Leavenworth, and I hope you are feeling well. Keep up courage, for I think the dawn of your freedom is here. Give my regards to Albert Ryan and tell him some day I am coming to California to work for him. I assure you I will leave no stone unturned to get your freedom with the other boys. Give my regards to the Warden and the Deputy Warden for they are both good, true men in that position. The American Federation had their Convention, and it was really the most progressive and most radical that I ever attended in my life, although I was there for only two hours on a couple of days.

I am sincerely and loyally yours to the end.

P. S. Please sign the inclosed application for pardon and return as quick as possible to me at the Atlantic Hotel, Washington, D. C. Lose no time.

TLC (Terence V. Powderly Papers)

To Edward M. House[1]

Atlantic Hotel, Washington, D.C.
Dec. 9, 1916.

Colonel Edward M. House,
115 E. 53rd st., N. Y. C.
My dear Col. House:

I hope you will pardon me if I take the liberty to write you in behalf of the structural ironworkers who are incarcerated in Levenworth prison and who have been separated from their homes and families and from society for several years. I write you because I know your abiding faith in the goodness of human nature and because of your close relation with the President who I know, is a man of kind heart and tender sympathies. The men for whom I appeal were convicted under stress of public excitement and it is not unfair to say that the mind of the court and the public was inflamed against them.

If in desperation over real or fancied wrongs men commit acts of violence, who is there to say that there is no extenuating circumstance? We do not all entertain the same viewpoint towards society Imagine men engaged in the hazardous work of erecting iron and steel for tall buildings. Suppose one of them fell to the ground and was crushed, who would take care of his family? You can realize that these men do not earn enough to insure the future let alone provide sufficient for the daily needs of themselves and their families? These men cannot entertain the same beneficent attitude of men in easier and more comfortable circumstances. And who shall say that these men are not more sinned against by society than sinning?

We all go through this life but once my dear Colonel and it behooves us all to render as much aid to our fellow-beings as we can while here. If we could raise up all humanity and obviate all strife, what a glorious world this would be. But constituted as it is, society inflicts many hardships on those least able to bear them.

When I visited the penitentiary a few weeks ago, one of those whom I am trying to help asked me "Mother, will it be possible for us to see our families at home this Christmas?" I responded that I thought it might be and I said this in the hope that my appeal in their behalf would bear fruit. The world is growing better in spite of the terrible slaughter on the other side, or maybe because it is awaking people to "man's inhumanity to man" so aptly described by Pope. We should try to raise this country above the Greed for Gold that has produced such horrible disaster abroad. In my long years I have seen many men sacrificed on the Altar of the Dollar and I hope that the last of such sacrifice in this country has been made. Let us all work for a better day when this nation will stand forth as an exemplar for the world; when Greed will be banished and when the strife for gain will no longer afflict us.

With faith in the humane interest of the President and confident that he will aid me in the effort to restore these men to their families, and to society, I remain

Yours faithfully,
Mother Jones

TLS (Woodrow Wilson Papers)

1. Edward Mandell House (1858–1938), a Texas Democrat, was President Woodrow Wilson's intimate adviser.

From John P. White

Indianapolis, Ind.,
Dec. 9, 1916

Mother Jones
Atlantic Hotel
Washn D C

Expect to be in Washington Monday morning early   Will meet you at Department of Labor about ten oclock   Unable to secure Walsh as he was reported out of the city

John P. White

Telegram (Terence V. Powderly Papers)

To Joseph P. Tumulty[1]

December 13, 1916.

Hon. J. P. Tumulty
Secretary to the President,
The White House.
My dear Mr. Tumulty:

I enclose application for Executive clemency for Eugene A. Clancy, one of the men in whose behalf I saw the President on Monday. At that time I left with you several other applications. The enclosed application for Mr. Clancy reached me from San Francisco the day after I saw the President. Will you please be good enough to place it with the others, to be acted upon with them.

I want to take this occasion to express to you my most sincere thanks and appreciation of your kindness to me in this matter.

Sincerely yours,
[Mother Jones]

TLC (Terence V. Powderly Papers)
1. Joseph Patrick Tumulty (1879–1954), lawyer and New Jersey legislator, served as President Woodrow Wilson's secretary, 1913–1921.

To Tom Mooney

Washington, D. C.,
December 15th., 1916.

Mr. Tom Mooney,
San Francisco, California.
My dear Mr. Mooney:

Your letter of the 25th ultimo reached me a week ago. I have already got my hands full, but nevertheless I have been watching the trend of things in California. I realize that the enemies of society are not on the working man's side, but on the side of those who rob the workers in the interests of dollars.

I am opposed to violence, because violence produces violence, and what is won today by violence will be lost to-morrow. We must ever and always appeal to reason, because society after all has made all the progress it has ever made, by anyalizing the situation carefully and bringing the matter before the public with reason on its side. Humanity as a whole is right, if they only learn the truth and the way out. The taking of human life has never settled any question. And the wrongs eventually revert back to those who commit them. I am not afraid to say that I probably, in the great industrial struggles that I have been in have prevented more blood shed than any other person in America. I felt in this case, as I read it, there was a hidden wire somewhere, that has not come to the surface. I cannot believe that the workers in California would resort to any crime of the kind. The people have a right to have a preparedness parade, if they wish, without being molested, or interfered with in any way. And we must be generous enough to concede to every citizen the rights we claim for ourselves. I feel that you boys have been the victims of this diabolical crime and are innocent from the beginning. I will do everything that I can do to help you. You refer to Mr. White, President, he will render you all the assistance that can be rendered in your defense. He is waiting for a meeting of the Executive Board to act, and do never be afraid of him to act in a great cause. No man in America is more anxious to see justice administered than he is. So far as President Mahon of the Street Car Men, he has been up to his shoulders in struggles of his own craft. He has just returned from Europe, and had a terrific strike in New York; and you must remeber that these men have but one brain and the responsibility of their craft is on their shoulders. Keep up courage for right and justice will finally prevail. I am going to Chicago on Sunday and I will ask them to take up your case. I dont think that they ought to be asked; I think that they ought to do it themselves. Give my best wishes to all the boys. You have got a good man in Robert Minor,[1] and no better man could go to the post George West. I am yours in the struggle for a nobler civilization.

[Mother Jones]

TL (Terence V. Powderly Papers)

1. Robert Minor (1884–1952), a journalist, headed the organization to free Mooney, 1916–1918; he later helped establish the Communist party in the United States and edited the *Daily Worker*.

From Emma T. Martin

56 West 13th St., Atlanta, Ga.,
December 27, 1916.

Dear Mother Jones;

I have been waiting and hoping that you would return to Atlanta so that I could talk to you about what is on my heart, but as it seems that great things keep you away, I am writing to ask if you will not come here before a great while and let me write *The Life of Mother Jones?* I know I could do this to your satisfaction and there are millions of people who would buy the book. We would divide the profits and I believe each of us would have enough to *do things with.*

If you will come here as my guest we can talk things over and you stay with me while I am getting all the facts you wish mentioned. I have talked to Mr. Jerome K. Jones[1] and to Mr. Louis Marquard about this desire of mine and they think as I do that you are the most interesting and unique character this country has ever produced, hence the importance of writing your life. Wont you come and wont you let me write this book?

Hoping to hear from you at a very early date I am,

Sincerely yours,
Emma T. Martin.

TL (Terence V. Powderly Papers)
1. Jerome Jones (1855–1940), editor of the Atlanta *Journal of Labor* for forty-two years, was a friend and adviser to Samuel Gompers.

From Tom Mooney

San Francisco, Cal.,
Dec. 28, 1916.

Mother Jones.
Any Where in the Country.
My Dear Old Freind:

Your most welcomed, and long looked for letter came to me the other day. It was in its self great encouragement to me and my codefendants.

It is with in the last few weeks or a months that our case has cause very much comment, or received publicity to any great extent on a national scale. And even now, it is not one hundredth part as much advertised as it should be.

I am enclosing you a letter that was just sent to all of the Molders Locals and the Officers, It gives the latest developments in our case, I have just been informed that the Court has ordered drawn 200 names from the Regular Jury panel box, which contains the full list of names that are thrown into it each year by the different judges. My jury will be drawn from these two hundred.

This is not much of an improvement over the Billings selection. and the ones drawn are no better than those that convited Billings. They are tools of the Police, Prosecutors, and the Judges, and ready and willing tools of the Corporations against Labor Men, on trial for their activities in the Labor Movement.

Make an effort in every locality to get the different labor papers to take up the news of our trials and the case in general. Get all of the central Labor Bodies to endorse our fight.

Fraternally and Sincerely Yours in
Labors Fight.
Tom Mooney

P. S. Have written John P. White, & Wm. Green with a hope that they will have the U. M. W. Executive Board do some thing at their next meeting in Jan.

TLS (Terence V. Powderly Papers)

1917

To Mr. and Mrs. John D. Rockefeller, Jr.[1]

Denver, Colorado,
January 1, 1917.

Mr. & Mrs. John D. Rockerfeller,
26 Broadway,
New York City, New York.
My dear Mr. & Mrs. Rockerfeller:

I wish to extend to you my best wishes for a peaceful and Happy New Year, 1917.

May the coming year bring all classes together for a greater nation and a more humane people.

With my sincere wishes that you may have a Peaceful and Happy year, I am

Sincerely yours,
Mother Jones

TLS (Rockefeller Papers)
  1. Mother Jones met Rockefeller when he testified before the Commission on Industrial Relations; there is no evidence that she ever met Abby Aldrich Rockefeller (1874–1948).

From Samuel Graham

Department of Justice
Washington, D. C.
January 2, 1917.

Mother Jones,
Care of U. M. W. of A.,
Merchants Bank Building,
Indianapolis, Indiana.
Dear Madam:

Mr. Tumulty has referred to the Department applications for executive clemency in behalf of Eugene A. Clancy, Frank M. Ryan, Michael J. Young, Frank C. Webb, Phillip A. Cooley, and J. E. Munsey, which you sent to him, together with printed copies of the general applications for pardon, and a separate petition in the case of Frank C. Webb, and a general statement regarding the cases by Martin J. Wade.[1]

The pardon attorney informs me that when you were at the Department and secured forms of application, which were filled out, describing the petitioners as your boys, he did not understand that they were the present applicants whose petitions for pardon have already been considered by the President and denied by him. This being the case, and since the President has already passed [*one or more lines missing*] upon a statement of new and material facts. The applications are not entitled, therefore, to presentation to the President.

> Respectfully,
> For the Attorney General,
> Samuel Graham
> Assistant Attorney General

TLS (Terence V. Powderly Papers)
  1. The applicants had been convicted in a trial in Indianapolis in 1912 of illegal transportation of dynamite and other charges connected with the bombing of the Los Angeles *Times* building in 1910; most of them were national officials of the International Association of Bridge and Structural Ironworkers.

From John D. Rockefeller, Jr.

January sixth, 1917.

Mrs. Mary Jones,
Denver, Colorado.
Dear Mother Jones:

Mrs. Rockefeller and I greatly appreciate your New Year's Greetings, which we warmly reciprocate, and thank you for your friendly rememberance.

> Very sincerely,
> John D. Rockefeller, Jr.

TLC (Rockefeller Papers)

To the editor of the New York *Call* Forum[1]

Indianapolis, Ind.
[January 1917]

Editor of the Forum:

My attention was called to an article that appeared on December 9 in The New York Call, written by one Edward Meyer. It seems that he had a spasm and called for house cleaning in the Socialist party. His criticism was entirely misleading. He said that while languishing in the prison cells I had asked the Socialists to secure my liberty. I have never in my life asked the Socialists for any personal favor, and I have never received any that I know of.

He further said that I solicited votes for Woodrow Wilson. That is not true. I made some speeches in Indiana coal camps for Senator Kern. I would do it again, if every one in the United States stood against me. In my opinion he is one of the truest and noblest of men within the walls of the nation. I did incidentally pay my respects to President Wilson for leaving the White House and going down to the Senate and notifying the committee that they could not adjourn until the child labor bill was passed. I would do that again and apologize to no man.

The child of today is the future citizen of tomorrow; and any man, whether he be president or otherwise, who considers the welfare of the child against dollars will receive my indorsement to the end.

Coming back to the jail question, I have never been molested by the civil authorities of this country, except once, in Clarksburgh, W. Va. in 1902, for alleged violation of an injunction issued by a federal judge. I was taken 84 miles to the courthouse, appeared before the federal judge, was tried and acquitted. I refused to pay a fine, and it was either to acquit or jail me. I was acquitted. I answered the court that I had no money to pay a fine, and that I would not permit any one else to pay it for me.

Every time that I have been arrested it was done by the military on order of the governor of the state. In every instance I could have secured my liberty had I compromised my principles in yielding to the wishes of the dominating powers, and they would willingly have paid my transportation to get me out of the strike zone. My life has not been, nor will it be, spent in the parlors of tea parties or of midnight diners and revellers, but in the trenches, with my boys, facing the machine guns. And I expect to close my eyes in these battles.

When the hounds of vested interests put me into bull pens and their military prisons midst rats and vermin, I never made any appeal to be released, nor would I allow any one to make it for me. In one instance the military court appointed two lawyers to defend me, but I declined their services. I fought my battles alone, ever suspicious of the capital-istic tools and hirelings.

When the aforementioned writer charges President Wilson with fail-ure to intercede in my behalf when I was languishing in jail, I want to remind him that I was not a federal prisoner, but a military prisoner of the state, and the president had no jurisdiction over my case.

My whole life has been spent on the economic field fighting the battles of the workers, and it will close there. Inexperienced critics will not sway me from my work to help the needy and exploited wherever I can, and in this particular I have got to use my own judgment.

If proper analysis were made of my activity on the economic field it would be discovered that I have rendered greater service to the Socialist philosophy than the highly-paid star orator, who in some instances receives a hundred dollars a lecture for telling all about economic determinism to the half-starved, overburdened wretches who, because of their physical deprivations are not mentally equipped to grasp abstract theories.

Mother Jones

Printed letter (New York *Call*, 21 January 1917)

1. The New York *Call* Sunday magazine section regularly carried a Forum department for letters to the editor. Meyer's letter actually appeared in the issue of 17 December 1916, not the 9th, under the heading "Time to Clean House."

From John H. Walker

July 12, 1917.

Mother Jones,
Beckley, West Va.
Dear Mother:

I am returning letter which you left with Ed Nockels for me. It is to say the least, a deplorable state of affairs, and I sincerely hope that some means will be found of adjusting that matter on a decent basis, that will work out to the best interest of the organization. I would be willing to go to almost any extreme to accomplish this; it is pitiful, that the present opportunity can not be taken advantage of, for the best interest of the men who work in the mines and their families.

Just received a letter from Frank Kasten.[1] He was released on the 28th of June, and he says that our meetings in Brazil, without question, were largely responsible for his being released at that time. He really believes the things that we said about Judge Anderson[2] that were true, the things that we advised those men to do with reference to him, brought that gentleman to the place where he thought it might be him that would have the punishment meted out to him in the near future, unless he changed his attitude.

I know it will give you a good deal of pleasure to know that your influence helped Frank in that instance, for there is no finer or more decent fellow living, there is no better officer in the Labor Movement anywhere, and his organization needs him badly at this time.

May say too that they have got every plant tied up as tight as a drum, and their prospects are better now for getting a favorable adjustment of the strike, than at any time since it began.

It will no doubt be a source of gratification for you to know that the Street Car and Power House men at Bloomington, have got an adjustment of their trouble. The Power House men got a straight eight hour work day, with ten hours pay; the Street Car men (motormen and conductors) got an average increase that will give them about 45¢ a day; they got recognition of their union, and everyone of the old men were taken back to his old job. It was a grand settlement in the face of the situation that existed there, and your influence had, in my judgment, more to do than that of any other one who had anything to do with it, in bringing about that result.

I was sorry I did not get up to see you, but I had just got in late that day from Christopher where I had spoken at a Mooney meeting July the 4th, and I was about all in, and could not have gotten up there in time anyhow.

With sincere good wishes, I am,

Yours,

[John H. Walker]

TLC (John H. Walker Papers)

1. Frank Kasten (1878–1946) followed his father into the brickmaking trade and rose through the ranks of the union to become national president of the United Brick and Clay Workers, 1916–1946. His leadership of a long and divisive strike in Brazil, Indiana, had entailed a jail sentence.

2. Albert Barnes Anderson (1857–1938) served as federal district judge in Indiana, 1902–1925, and on the U.S. Circuit Court of Appeals, 1925–1929. He had presided over the dynamite transportation conspiracy trial of 1912.

From John H. Walker

July 19, 1917.

Mother Jones,
Beckley, West Va.
Dear Mother:

Enclosed you will find list of local unions and the number of votes in each, for candidates for President, that, according to the judgment of my watcher, Brother Scheafer, and that it is obvious on the face of the returns themselves, were cast illegally in the last International election.

It is rather interesting to note, that in a good many local unions, practically the same vote went for everybody who got a vote at all, and no vote for the others. It is most illuminating, as it applies to auditors, tellers and delegates to the A. F. of L convention.

I have a number of affidavits that are rather interesting and I think maybe would furnish the basis of a startling statement to the membership. If I can get a few more that are positive and reliable, I think maybe I will make that statement to the membership and it is just possible that it might upset the present situation and even yet, have that election settled on an honest basis.

I am enclosing you a few of the affidavits. May say that the Providence local of Ky. is a sample. That local was organized on the 29th of November, 1916, and the election took place December 12th, 1916, just fourteen days from that time.

The vote is supposed to be on the average membership for per capita tax that has been paid for the month of November. There were eight men who were on strike, and some of them, there was a question mark before that strike, that were initiated as charter members, along with two International organizers, who put in their cards.

You will note that that local cast 175 votes for White and none for me, and 175 votes for every other candidate that got any vote, and they were on the slate of the International office, and nobody else got any, and that is only a sample of what took place throughout the entire country.

This is a rotten situation. A man who will steal a job, will steal anything else, and nobody can expect the ordinary working man to have any respect for a known public thief, a fence who receives stolen goods from thieves, who is surrounded by a bunch of petty larceny thieves, and before our organization can be made much better, that kind of a condition has got to be eliminated, and without regard to who gets the positions, provided they are honest and competent, every real friend of our union must do what they can to wipe out this situation, and put the organization on an honest basis.

Yours,
[John H. Walker]

TLC (John H. Walker Papers)

To John H. Walker

Charleston, W. Va.,
[1917]

Mr. John H. Walker,
801 Commercial St.,
Danville, Ill.

Dear John:

I am going to write you a few lines. We had a convention here yesterday of the New River miners to accept an agreement that the distinguished officers made in Cincinnati. I mean the vice President[1] and Johnie Lewis[2] has become the general Jesus of the movement. Hays made a speech. I wish you could have heard that fellow. He has become what you call a self conceited empty brained dictator. In the conference in New York he struck the table with his empty fist and he told the operators that they had to come across that he had the goods on them. and he would get them before the Federal Government. And they told him to go to it that they had the goods on them and were very anxious for him to make the brake. Just imagine men putting themselves in the position to take that water I dont know John what the future of this organization is going to be, but if they continue doing business as they have I doubt very much of its destiny And the other fellow, Lewis He represented John P.[3] in the conference. There is nothing to that fellow but an empty piece of human slime. I get so disgusted sometimes that I feel like giving up the whole field, and going away off some where. If the organization ever gets into the hands of this fellow that is the end of the miners Zimmerman the board member from Ill. is in here, and Valentine from Iowa. I think he is the best of the lot. F. J. [Hayes] gave the revolters the right to sit in the convention and President Keeney[4] of the District forced them to get out at the point of the pistol and altho he was a big gun in his own estimation, the local officer carried the day. as for orarty and logic John, there is none in that individual, and is imposition on civilization to have the miners money paid in salary to such ablily. No wonder the operators get the best of them. If I was an operator I would sit back and laugh at the things that come across However, there are a few brave men here that will take the bull by the horn and do business regardless of who oppose them and who doesn't. That was a good meeting we had at Brazil, Only I am a little afraid they are going to loose that strike. John, the Sec'y of Central labor Hutchinson in Brazil, was a detective for seven years. He is a very smooth guy and the unsufiscated would fall for his philosophy. Would fall into his traps. I am a little afraid of him, and if there is anyone in Brazil that you can trust you better put them next to keeping an eye on him. He drops in Terra Haute quite often and meets someone there, that he comunicates with when a man has once been in such organizations I am ever afterwards weary of them because a man with a principal will die before he will ever render service to a machine as rotten as the detective agency. They are organized for no other purpose than to destroy the welfare of the human family. I dont know when I will see you again I am going to Henderson Kentucky for Labor day. I dont think I will be out of this state before then. There is so much to do and so few to do it. But you send my mail to Beckley, W. Va. and when you see Nockles[5] and Fitz Patrick[6] give them my best regards. They were not put on the defence committee. They were not the kind uncle Sam wanted I mean uncle Sam Gompus. John, the whole labor movement is becoming an inactive institution. It is falling in to the mesh of interest. and welfare leaders are lending their hands to the game and the poor wretches are paying the bills. I look for the most despotic system of industrial slavery after the war the world has ever known. they are putting the breakes on us now. and paid officials are rendering them faithful service. Just see the committee they sent to Russia. The slickest rottenest. Despirte on the soil of America. George E. Russell, the intelectual socialist, and Duncan president of the granite workers, and ultra conservative. I am a little afraid that Loyd [Lord?] will get under their influence in Washington, We have not what I term a good watch dog in all of Washington to keep an eye on what these pirates are doing. I leave tomorrow for New River and expect to be up ther all summer Take good care of your self until I see you again. and give my love to them all at home.

Always yours,
Mother Jones

TLS (John H. Walker Papers)
1. Frank J. Hayes.
2. John Llewellyn Lewis (1880–1969), president of the UMWA, 1920–1960.
3. John Phillip White.
4. Frank Keeney, president of District 17 of the UMWA.
5. Edward N. Nockles.
6. John Fitzpatrick.

To John H. Walker

Fairmont W. Va
Augst 25—1918

My Dear John

I have been trying to see you but every time you were gone Just missed you by one day

On my return from Colo you had just left for Penn. I had some thing of importance to tell you. John this organization is in the hands of the mine owners   When could I see you or where   I am going to Washington after Labor day   I wish you [could] be in Washington that week   Some time I am sick at heart about the poor Devils that are betrayed   This [is] the rottenest age

[*Remainder of letter missing.*]

AL fragment (John H. Walker Papers)

From John H. Walker

August 29, 1918.

Mother Jones
Fairmount Hotel,
Fairmount, West Va.
Dear Mother:

Yours of the 25th received. Very sorry that I did not get to see you as I wanted to very much. I know something about the situation down yonder, and like yourself, I fear for our organization in the future if it continues in the hands of the men who are deliberately betraying it to serve their own personal ends at this time. That condi[tion] is not alone true in West Va., Maryland, Old Virginia, Sommerset County Pa., and I am almost sure as I am living, that it is also true of the Coke regions in Pa., and in some of the places that are at least on the surface, organized.

They are going to desperate extremes to prevent their defeat. At the same time, I really believe that it is going to be impossible for them to get away with it this time, because the miners everywhere are begining to have an inkling of what the situation really is. This, coupled with their absolute inactivity, with the maudlin, idiocy, drunkenness and egotism of the one, the brazenness and domineering blatant dishonesty, some cunning and intelligence, but no real ability in the other, it is having the effect that at least I am hopeful will enable us to root them out of there in this coming election.[1]

If we could be sure that the Ohio man would be clean and square and refuse to permit himself or his office to be used dishonestly to serve their purposes, there would not be any question about it at all. Of that however, I am not sure, because it seems that they must either have some hold on him, or he considers his interests bound up with them, or else he has some other motive—at least he is not standing out in the open, being counted and fighting as he should be.

There is a lot of real information I could give you Mother, that would make the thing look a little better to you, if you had it, altho it don't appear on the surface.

I am going to be in Byesville, Ohio, on Labor Day and I could meet you in Cincinnati on my way back,—could possibly go even further, just so I can get back and meet an appointment here on the 5th which will enable me to possibly get an increase in wages for some poor devils who are working in the Smelter at Springfield, and incidentally, strengthen the Mine, Mill and Smeltermen's organization.

Anyhow when it is over, I will have the satisfaction of knowing that I did my damndest to straighten the thing out right, and if we don't make it right in this election then By God! the fight has only started. We will clean it out before we get through and put our movement on an honest clean wholesome basis.

With love and the highest and most sincere regards, I am,

Yours,

[John H. Walker]

TLC (John H. Walker Papers)

1. Walker was seeking the presidency against the incumbent, Frank J. Hayes, whose vice-presidential running mate was John L. Lewis.

To Miners and Other Working Men of Colorado

Fairmont, W. Va.,
Aug. 31, 1918.

Dear Brothers:

In the struggle for justice I wish to remind you that the 10th of September is registration day in your state. Let me impress you with the necessity for each and every man to go to the polls and register and cast your votes for men who stand for real democracy against those who stand for the dollar interest. Remove from the statute books of your fair state that constabulary law that was passed to enslave the workers by those who stand for dollars instead of humanity. I urge you to redeem your fair state so that the generations of the ages to come will not have to stop and ponder on the sad days of old when you roasted the babes of Ludlow in the interest of your god-cursed gold. The state's history is already printed by indelible impression on the minds of the nation's people and the pages of the records of the state scarred by the accounts of the charred bodies of mothers and babes that were burned in the tent village of Ludlow; the account of the deaths of the miners who were shot down by the cossacks who represented the dollar interest.

While our boys are spilling their blood on the battle field of France, to make the world safe for democracy, let the working men of Colorado rise in the power and might of their franchise and vote for men who will stand for the same democracy for Colorado that our boys are fighting for across the ocean.

Let there be no autocratic rules of Hessian constabulary laws remain on the statute books of your fair state. There must be changes made in the law-making body of your state; you should select men who will do so.

Permit me here to make a statement to you. In the halls of congress, you are represented by one of the noblest, truest men, who stands for human justice over whose honor dollars have no control. In all the statesmen that stand on the floor of Congress, Edward Keating soars above them all, and I hope you will show the dollar interest that Colorado can produce men whose honor cannot be bought by their god-cursed coin.[1]

Let me suggest to you to duplicate Governor Hunt of Arizona; in doing so you will redeem the state from the blot that has been placed upon the pages of the past. Thomas Tynan is going to run for governor of Colorado.[2] He will fill the bill to perfection. I watched his course with a great deal of interest, as I have others in public life in Colorado. He would stand for justice to all, regardless of class, and I have no doubt he will repeal that infamous Hessian law that the dollar interest has placed upon your statute books.

It is your duty as a citizen to let the nation see that you stand for real democracy and not corporation autocracy. We are fighting the Hessians abroad to overthrow their rule, let us fight some of the Hessians at home by repealing the imported laws that have been placed on our statute books.

Hoping you will wake up and tell the powers that be we are marching to the sunlight of a grander civilization, I am, yours for real democracy of industries.

Most sincerely yours,
Mother Jones

1918

Printed letter (*Miners Magazine,* September 1918)
    1. Keating was serving his third term in the House; he was defeated in 1918.
    2. Thomas J. Tynan (b. 1874) gained some measure of fame as an innovator with his system of rehabilitation while he was warden of the Colorado State Penitentiary, 1909–1927; he, too, was defeated in 1918.

To Walter Wayland[1]

Charleston, W. Va.,
November 15th, 1918.

Mr. Walter Wayland,
Editor of the Appeal to Reason,
Girard, Kans.
My Dear Walter:

I have been for some time wanting to write you to know how Julia and Edith are, I have had so much to do, that I have been unable to get around to that part. What has become of George Brewer and Grace,[2] I think they made a great mistake when they left the Appeal. I don't hear much of the party that they joined, it seems to me it went to pieces just as it rose. It certainly did not figure in the last campaign.

I hope that you will put some fire into the Appeal now that the War is over, the Appeal once was the best paper in this country, that is so far as the worker were concerned, but it has of recent years lost that fire, you must get a hold of some Editor who understands the reconstruction period for there is no doubt that there are stormy days ahead of us, and the Appeal can do more good than any other paper in the country if it is properly edited by men with the fight in them.

What has become of Copeland,[3] I don't hear of him only that he went across the water, did he return? Even Copeland did not have the fire in him that was so necessary to keep the Appeal going, that is to interesting readers, it was one of the papers that struck the angles in the right place.

I am going to the Illinois State Federation in a week or so, but you send those books here. I want Voltaire's Greatest Work, Candide, you know he is a very great wrighter, he and Victor Hugo and Tom Payne were my favors, when you[r] father and myself used to set up at night and talk these over. Perhaps some day I will go down to Girard and see you again.

Give my love to the girls and to John   tell them I love them just as I did in days of old.

Sincerely yours,
Mother Jones

PS I hope the coming year will be a prosperous one for the coming year.

TLS (Haldeman MSS II)

1. Walter Wayland succeeded his father, J. A. Wayland, as publisher of *The Appeal to Reason,* which during the war supported pacifist views.

2. George D. Brewer was associated with the Waylands, father and son, in various capacities in the publication of *The Appeal to Reason.* His wife, Grace, managed a Socialist speakers' bureau.

3. Louis Kopelin, assistant editor, and briefly editor of *The Appeal,* in June 1918 joined a delegation of Socialists who supported the war on a trip to Europe to express solidarity with other Socialists in Allied countries.

To Sara J. Dorr

San Francisco, Cal.
Dec. 16, 1918.

Mrs. Sara J. Dorr, President,
Womens Christian Temperance Union,
3 City Hall Avenue,
San Francisco, Cal.
Dear Mrs. Dorr:

Permit me to extend to you the deep appreciation of Organized Labor the country over for the stand you have taken in behalf of justice. It is not a question of Thomas Mooney—the question goes further than Thomas Mooney. The great issue now before Organized Labor and the thinking American people is the integrity of the courts. They are the bulwark of our institutions and their integrity must be preserved, for once the workers lose faith then all hope is blasted and no one can be responsible for the outcome.

It is the duty of every citizen to awaken to the fact that not alone is America interested but the eyes of the world are focused upon the courts of California and it is really up to her noble womanhood whether the terrible stain that is cast upon them in the Mooney case shall remain unchallenged.

The light is breaking. The maps of the world are being changed. A new world is in the making and our American woman can participate in that making. She can make it a safe and happy place for the generation yet to come to dwell in.

If thru our indifference, suspicion has been placed upon our courts then it is thru our vigilance and our spirit for love and freedom that we must transform them and surely the women of California will not let this issue die.

I shall convey to Organized Labor the world over that the women of

San Francisco, particularly the members of the W. C. T. U. are the first to demand a revolution in our courts and your action I am sure will awaken other women of our nation. It was the Dreyfus case in France that changed the spirit of the people and to you fair women of San Francisco all honor shall be due.

With deep appreciation for your good work, I remain

Sincerely yours,
[Mother Jones]

TLC (Mother Jones Papers)

To John H. Walker

San Francisco, Cal.,
Dec. 18, 1918.

John H. Walker, President
Illinois State Federation of Labor,
Springfield, Ill.
My dear John:

I arrived here pretty tired but the train men were very good to me coming out and I got them all so interested that they wrote a vote of appreciation to Fremont Older, Editor, of the San Francisco Call.[1]

I saw the Governor[2] last Thursday. I was accompanied by Mr. Scharrenberg[3] so as to be safe and I don't know of any safer person I could have taken with me. I didn't get any satisfaction out of him but he gave me a hearing any how but I have been keeping the newspapers busy since I came here. I will enclose you a number of the clippings.

How did things go in the election? I haven't heard a word out here any more than the papers carried that Frank Hayes won out by 60,000. Its all right. Let him win. Things will shape themselves pretty soon.

I am going down to the oil fields to talk to those poor fellows on Sunday next. Then I shall leave for Los Angeles and from there I will go to Kansas City and try and see Howat and have a talk with him. Under no circumstances surrender an inch to those fellows. The fight is only begun, John.

I am visiting the unions at night to urge them to send a delegate to that Congress at Chicago on the 14th of next month. You have got to make that a success. Some of these pirates out here are getting a little alarmed. We want to give them a shaking up and let them know we are not asleep.

My regards to all the boys, and take good care of yourself. We will stand together till death. The brave and true die only once. Cowards and traitors die often and they have some horrible deaths at that.

I'll close up now because I have a lot to do this afternoon, I am

Yours,

Mother Jones

TLS (John H. Walker Papers)

1. Fremont Older (1856–1935), crusading editor of the San Francisco *Bulletin* and *Call*, championed the cause of Tom Mooney from the beginning.

2. William Dennison Stephens (1859–1944), Republican congressman and lieutenant governor, succeeded to the governorship when Hiram Johnson resigned to become senator. He was elected to a term in his own right, 1919–1923.

3. Paul Scharrenberg was secretary of the California State Federation of Labor.

To John H. Walker

Los Angeles, Cal.
2759, Marengo St.,
Dec. 28, 1918.

John H. Walker,
State Federation Office,
Springfield, Ills.
Dear John:

I received your telegram forwarded to me from San Francisco. It was not very plain owing to the transmission but it gave me to understand that you were elected president but I warn you now to keep close watch or they'll count you out as they did in the last election.

You know, John, you're dealing with a terrific, powerful combination and the interests will do anything and spend any amount of money to keep you from getting control of the United Mine Workers Organization. They know they can't play the game with you and when you do get in, I hope to God you'll have a housecleaning. The leeches that those poor fellows have carried on their back for years, [if?] they themselves knew it and understood it, I'm inclined to think they'd shake the nation and all thinking people would endorse them.

I read just a few days before where they said you were beat by sixty thousand. I knew, John, the statement was false, but the honest men that read it, regretted that you failed to take charge of the destinies of those poor hounded and deceived slaves. The pirates now will sit up and take notice and I slept good that night when I read that telegram.

I did not get the full meaning of it, I concluded that the victory was yours. There's a new day breaking for the Workers and you, no doubt, will help to bring the sunlight to the poor wretches who have been deceived, robbed and plundered by their own people that they were paying

I probably would have been back in Chicago by this time only the Oil Workers in Taft, held me up and after I spoke in Taft, they urged me to remain with them for a week or ten days and tour the Oil Fields so I concluded that I would comply with their desires. After all, John, it makes no matter where we do the good. They told me they'd pay my expenses. I told them that was not the question—the question was, could we bring them together into the organization and they said that if I toured their Oil Fields they knew that 95% of them would be in the Union. I am also working to get them to join the United Mine Workers. for their industry in reality is mining. They mine the oil while the subterranean miners mine the coal. It's a wonderful field, John. I think we must consolidate the workers and put an end to these jurisdictional disputes.

I have not heard fro Olander since I left. I hope he is [feeling?] better. He's a valuable man and we can't afford to lose him. Such men are rather scarce, John, in these days.

I will not be in Chicago for that Congress that's going to meet but the Densmore expose[1] has stirred things up on the coast here. They squashed all the endictments against Nolan. I could not get anything out of the Governor—more than that he said he was giving me a hearing. But Sharrenburg said that I said a great deal more to him than any man would dare to say—The Governor is a perfect tool of the interests—he has no love for the workers.

I'll close by wishing you and all at home the happiest New Year and Prosperity to all around us.

Mother Jones

TLS (John H. Walker Papers)

1. Secretary of Labor William B. Wilson sent John B. Densmore, a departmental employee, to investigate the conduct of the cases arising out of the Preparedness Day parade, including Tom Mooney's. With the aid of a planted dictaphone, he was able to obtain evidence of improprieties in the prosecutor's office; Fremont Older published the transcript, with expletives deleted, in the San Francisco *Call*.

1919

From John H. Walker

January 8, 1919.

Mother Jones,
2759 Marengo St.,
Los Angeles, Cal.
Dear Mother:

Yours of the 28th of December received. It is just as you have said. There were returns from over 130 local unions reached the national office after the 23rd of December; some of them as late as the 31st., notwithstanding the fact that the district officers had the tabulated returns in district one, which showed that I carried it by 1,000. Hayes beat me there 409 votes and in district 2, he beat me 1009 votes,— with 2/3ds of the votes counted in district 5, he beat me 8,000 votes which means a 12,000 majority.

It is going to be pretty close under those circumstances; the chances are they will steal it by some means. In the event they do, if I get sufficient proof to warrant me in believing I have a fighting chance, I am going to give them a fight for it. However, I don't expect to fight otherwise.

Glad to know that you are feeling so well mother. I know a month or two out there will do you good. I am very very sorry to say that poor Vic[1] has got diabetes, and that every physician I speak to about him, holds out no hope for him; they say if he was a little older ten or 15 years that there would be some hope, but that in his case he don't know of a single individual who ever had it as he has, that ever recovered.

Just got a letter form him this morning. We sent him to Seminole Alabama. I know if you would write him it will make him feel good, and as this may be the last chance we will have. I am doing the best I can to make him comfortable, and happy.

With the fullest measure of love and assuring you that no matter how it goes, or how long it lasts while I am living, I am going to continue plugging away and do the best I can.

Yours,
[John H. Walker]

TLC (John H. Walker Papers)
1. Victor A. Olander.

1919

To Ed Nockles

January 14, 1919

To Ed Knockels,
166 Washington St.,
Chicago, Illinois

To the delegates in Convention greeting. May your resolutions be tempered with reason. Courts of our country must be exonerated. Convention must demand courts be cleansed of corporation judges. Place men on bench who will consider justice before dollars. Blot must be removed from courts. If the workers lose faith in courts then where are they to turn for justice.

Mother Jones

Telegram (Terence V. Powderly Papers)

To John H. Walker

Charleston, W. Va.
February 5, 1919.

Mr. John H. Walker,
Springfield, Ill.
My Dear Mr. Walker:

Enclosed find my bill of expenses there is no charge for services outside of the real expense concurred in railroad fare and Hotel bill.

I learned a great deal since I came here and have a good deal to tell you that I can not write,   I will be in Washington the last week in this month, perhaps something may bring you there. I see that Gem [Jim] Lord has been notified by powers that be that his services is not needed any longer

I stopped off at the office and never in the History that I [*holograph note in margin:* was I][1] received with such courtesy, I coulden't tell myself what was up, but I know what they meant alright [*holograph note in margin:* John they walked over me]   I cannot imagine that men who draw their salaries from the rank and file that stood for the things that I have learned since I came in here. However, someday there will be a reckoning, only I am afraid it will be a sad one for the rank and file.

[*Holograph note in margin:* J L asked me to go to Pitts to the Steel Workers   they wanted me]

I sent a satchel by parcel post when I was in Chicago, but they notified me that it was unmailable, I can't understand what objections they have to it, but I wrote to Knockles to get it and send it to me by express, but for fear he would not be in Chicago, you had better telephone to him. [*Holograph note in margin:* Wish you would have it sent Here]   I can't write you anymore, so I will have to wait until I see you.

With good luck, I am,

Yours sincerely,
Mother

[*Holograph postscript:* John its rotten]

TLS with holograph notes (John H. Walker Papers)
   1. Only rarely did Mother Jones indicate corrections in typed letters; in this instance, she wrote in the margin but did not designate a place for the emendation or addition. The editor has inserted the marginal notes on the bases of their location in the margins and the sense of the passages.

From John H. Walker

February 7, 1919.

Mother Jones,
Box 246, Charleston, West Va.
Dear Mother:

Yours of 5th with enclosure received. I have o.K'd. it and sent it to Asst. Secretary Towers,[1] and you will no doubt hear from him within two or three days.

Yes, I understand that the governmental authorities have advised Lord that since the war is over and the work for which he was appointed has ended, his services are to be discontiued. I understand in addition to that, that the "powers that be" in our organization expect to discontinue his services in the capacity of president of the Mining Department at the very first opportunity.[2]

Well Mother, I hate to see this happen, and particularly because I know that it was on account of his friendly attitude to me that they are doing these things to him,—however, it seemed like that there was a chance to put our organization on a decent, honest basis again, and that means so much as compared with the situation that obtains now, that we would have been less than men if we did not attempt to take advantage of it and do the best we could no matter what price we had to pay,—and while I feel sorry that that thing is being done to Jim and his family, maybe there could not be anything that would happen that would make me feel worse, than to have them do the same thing to you, still, feeling as I do, I could not do anything else only what I did, and I would not want either you or him, and a number of other friends, to have done anything else.

I want you to know that I not only appreciate as much as a man can, what you have done, but I feel too, as proud of you as it is possible for one to feel.

With every good wish in the world and hoping that there are better things coming, I am,

Yours,
[John H. Walker]

TLC (John H. Walker Papers)
1. Alois Towers, a molder from Belleville, was a vice-president of the Illinois Federation of Labor.
2. James Ravell Lord had served on the Committee on Labor of the Council of National Defense and also on the National Coal Committee; Walker's prediction that he would be eased out of his position as head of the Mining Department of the American Federation of Labor came true.

From John H. Walker

February 11th, 1919.

Mother Jones,
Charleston, West Va.
Dear Mother:

Further reference to yours of recent date, I don't believe I am going to be able to get to Washington on any official business before the end of my term of office, and of course, will be more unlikely to get there after that than before, and I do not believe I can afford to go there personally, but if possibility develops you may be sure I will take advantage of it and will advise you just as soon as I know definitely that I can go.

Yours,
[John H. Walker]

TLC (John H. Walker Papers)

To Terence V. Powderly

Charleston, W. Va.,
June 19, 1919.

Mr. T. V. Powderly,
502 Quincy St., N. W.
Washington, D. C.
My Dear Friend:

I am just going to drop you a line to let you know that we are having awfully hot weather down here, I came back a week ago from Illinois, where I had some tremenduous meetings. Went to Ziegler, the mines belonged to Joe Lighter,[1] eight years ago, when I went there they turned two machine guns on me, this time I went in on a special train and was met at the depot by the Mayor of Ziegler and a delegation there, and the Mayor is a Miner and I was their guest at his home that night, next morning I left and got the truck car and went to Christopher and there I got the Train for Sentralia, where I also had a tremenduous meeting. Then I came back to Fairmot, West Va., and had a parade of 14000 miners, there were no sky-pilots or no politicians or nor pike counter hunter speakers of that day the speakers all were from the rank and file. Ex-Senator Watson[2] gave them a park to meet in. fifteen months ago if you would have gone in there in any mining camp in that district you would have been asked what your business was and put you out at the point of the gun even if your own brother would have been there, what a change has taken place, so we are making progress, but I had to leave there that night for Pittsburgh and from Pittsburgh I went back to Herin, Ill, then came into Chicago, and held three big meetings there with the cigar and Shoe workers,   I have not had a moments rest until the last week, I have not been working very hard, so I am beginning to geather up my strength again. I see they are having a great convention up on the sea-shore.[3] I don't know what the out come will be this week, but I am looking for some pretty hot times., but perhaps they will get weakning, I don't look on the labor movement of this country with very much enthusiasm for the people, they have not the men at the helm, and to tell you the truth going over the country as I do, if a revolution started tomorrow I don't know where they would get a leader, and I think the capitalist have got that down fine. however, we have to keep on pounding and hammering away.

I don't know when I will get to Washington, tell Mr. Powderly to take caer of himself this hot weather.

With best wishes to everybody in the house, I am fondly,

Yours,
Mother

TLS (Mother Jones Papers)

1. Joseph Leiter (1868–1932), the son of a partner of Marshall Field, presided over wide-ranging financial interests which included the Ziegler Coal Company.

2. Clarence Wayland Watson (1864–1940), president and chairman of the board of Consolidation Coal Company, was elected senator from West Virginia in 1911 as a Democrat, filling an unexpired term for two years.

3. The AFL convention was meeting in Atlantic City, New Jersey.

1919

From A. Mitchell Palmer[1]

Washington, D. C.
July 11, 1919

Dear Madam:

I have caused an investigation to be made of the question whether there are any Federal prisoners confined in the Sissonville Road Camp.

I am advised that there are no Federal prisoners there and therefore I do not know of any ground on which the Federal Government could institute an investigation. I suggest that complaint should be made to the Governor of West Virginia if you think the local county authorities are not dealing adequately with conditions.

Yours very truly,
A. Mitchell Palmer
Attorney General

TLC (Justice Department Records, RG 60, File 203233-3, National Archives)

1. Alexander Mitchell Palmer (1872–1936), attorney general of the United States, 1919–1921, had not yet embarked on the search for subversives for which he is best known.

To Ryan Walker[1]

Charleston, West Va.
December 12, 1919.

Mr. Rine Walker,
c/o New York Call,
Fourth Avenue,
New York, N. Y.

My Dear old friend Rhyne:

I wanted to see you while I was in New York and have a long talk with you about old times. The last time I was in Kansas city I stopped off a day or so with Snyders[2] at their hotel, most all the old warriors are gone or dead, you can't meet scarcely any of the old force. Plamer is dead, Page is dead, Putnam is out in California. I had a letter from him a year ago, and from what I learn I don't think he is the happiest man in the world. What faithful loyal workers those men were in their days, then Wayland is gone and the element that is in and around Kansas city today so far as the revolutionary is concerned don't amount to a row of pins. It looked at one time that we were going to make wonderful progress, but it lookes to me as if that time has passed. When Wayland passed away another element got a hold of the pier, and it hasen't amounted to a row of pins since. I don't read it

194

anymore. The only papers I read now are something that I get from Australia or from England. How much I would like to have an hour or two with you and talk things over. You know Ryne, I am going all over the country, and I don't tak up much with the vulchers, that have lead the movement for their own pockets. They can go on with a lot of star sentamental oratory, but that have never touches the core of the workers pains, it gives them a little soothing syrup but if the [*subsequent page(s) lacking*].

TL fragment (Walker MSS)
1. Ryan Walker (1870–1932), a labor cartoonist, grew up in Kansas City in the 1880s, and later worked on newspapers in Kansas City, St. Louis, Boston, and New York.
2. Ten years earlier, J. E. Snyder had been secretary of the Socialist party in Kansas; T. E. Palmer of Kansas City had been party secretary in Missouri.

To Otto Branstetter[1]

Charleston, W. Va.
Jan 26, 1920.

Mr. Otto Branstetter,
2845 Wilcox Street,
Chicago, Ill.
My Dear Mr. Branstetter:

Your letter with the postal order enclosed I received while in Pittsburgh. Let me express to you my appreciation. I needed it badly owing to the many poor souls that were suffering, and it came in at the proper time to reliev people that are not up against those things, have no realization that the suffering means. Things are all torn up side down. I see they are after your Reds in Chicago, well that things are all ablock, don't you know they make those reds, those reactionary statesmen do, but we have got to keep up the fight. Nevertheless, remember that the days are true, die only once pike counter hunters die often and they have some horrible deaths at that.

Tender my regards to Mrs. Branstetter, I shall be in Chicago the last of this week on my way to California. I have a severe attack of rheumatism, and want to get rid of it.

With best wishes, I remain,
Yours very sincerely,
Mother Jones

TLS (Mrs. Philip Taft, collector)
1. Otto Branstetter (1877–1924) served as secretary of the Socialist party, 1919–1923.

To John H. Walker

Los Angeles, Cal.,
Mar. 9, 1920.

John H. Walker,
801 Commercial St.,
Danville, Ills.
Dear John:

I regretted not to have been in Chicago when you got there but I was all in and had to get away. You know I had three months of awful hard work in the Pittsburg[1] and I gave out and I had such a desire to see you, John, before I left for there were so many things I wanted to talk to you about.

I have found out in New York that John L. has $500. worth of stock in the Casy-Adams Magazine.[2] That John P. has $500. more and God knows how many more of them had their hands in it. It's so rotten, John, that one hardly knows where to begin on.

I don't know what that convention did in Chicago with all of you people. I had very little hope in the R. R. men's striking and I so said to them in the office in Chicago because there's so [no?] strike in 'em, John. There's a great deal of begging from the Masters but the Railroad men are not fighters and they never have been to my knowledge. They don't even lend a hand to other men on the fight and ra[r]ely ever do you hear of them donating any sum to any of our great conflicts. However, John, we've got to keep on the fight.

They made some vicious attacks on Foster[3] and if you read the Machinist's Journal you'll find even the enemy within making this attack. John, I want to tell you something, I don't look with that hope for the Labor Movement that I did three years ago. The workers of this country are the most backward for action than any body of workers in any country in the world—Even China is ahead of us to-day

The Ways and Means Railroad men may strike, but I doubt it. The fellow who gets fourteen thousand a year and expenses, will hardly take any chances.

In my opinion it is a very great mistake to pay those high salaries but we have nothing to say about it—they will have to go.

I wish I could have seen you before I left but I shall go down to Springfield when I go back to Chicago and see you if you won't come up to Chicago.

I wouldn't have much to do with that political movement if I were you. Keep your hands out of it. I don't think, John, it will have the effect that the boys thought it would—However, let us hope for the best.

I leave for Frsilo, tomorrow night so send my mail to Box 95, San Francisco, Cal   The metal workers there are on a strike and they have a very ugly situation. They revolted here and went into One Big Union—they got sore at their officials and of course they had to pull out when they could not overthrow them. Instead of claning house inside, they went outside and weakened their forces.

I shall hold till I see you   I have a good deal to talk to you about, John.

The boys here did not speak any too well of Jim Lord's and that fellow davis' settlement in the Oil Field. It's a very weak instrument as I read it. Of course I didn't say anything because I thought it best not to.

Take care of yourself. I suppose you go into office the first of the month and if you can, come up if I telegraph for you.

Love and regards for all those at home—

Sincerely yours,
Mother Jones

TLS (John H. Walker Papers)
1. In the recent attempt to organize the steel workers.
2. K. C. Adams, regarded by some labor leaders as a henchman of A. R. Hamilton, a Pittsburgh industrialist, edited *The American Miner* in Indianapolis, *The Labor World* and the *Coal Trade Bulletin* in Pittsburgh, and eventually the UMWA *Journal*. The stockholders mentioned are presumably John L. Lewis and John P. White.
3. William Zebulon Foster (1881–1961), who later became one of the leaders of the Communist party in the United States, had led the unsuccessful effort in 1919 to organize the steel industry.

From John H. Walker

March 16, 1920

Mother Jones
Box 95, San Francisco, Cal.
Dear Mother:

Yours of the 9th received and was very sorry I did not get to see you before you went west, although Ed told me what I knew before hand, that you were pretty much all in and you had to have a rest and you were going there to try and have a little breathing spell.

I take it from your letter however, with reference to that fight that is on with the Metal Workers, that you are doing exactly what I said you would do, no matter how tired and worn out you were, if there was a strike on you would be in the middle of it as long as you lived.

I am not surprised about that information that they all have an interest in the newspaper that the coal operators furnish them money, from under the guise of paying for advertising, when in reality it is paying them for betraying the Miners' Union and the labor movement, that was T. L. Lewis' method, and they are all a part of the same arrangement.

I was not at that Chicago Labor Party convention the last day, and up to that time they had acted fairly sensible. On the last day however, they fixed it so that the labor movement could not support them, which means that they acted in such a manner that there can be no help come for the labor movement from political sources, for sometime.

The enemies of labor are going to be in all the positions of government, legislative, judicial and executive.

With reference to the railroad men not striking, I think it is only fair to say that the spectacle of the national officers of the Miners' Union, the biggest organization in the country, with the reputation of being the best fighters in the country, surrendering and bowing in abject submission, allowing the men to be driven back into the mines like cattle, without a fight at all, not only demoralized them, but has taken the heart out of the whole of the rest of the movement. It will be sometime before they will recover again.

That same action was responsible for encouraging the other side to pass the Esch-Cummings bill and to embolden all the Injunction Judges in the country into breaking more strikes, and by more vicious injunctions than ever before.

It is a tragedy to think that an organization with members of the makeup of ours, who would be willing to fight until they died rather than be put in that position, if they could help themselves, being deliberately used in that manner to destroy the liberties of all the people, it makes the decent Mine Workers who understand what it means, blush with shame and hang their heads; and I hope they may get an opportunity to redeem themselves sometime in the near future, with the right kind of leadership.

If they knew what was done to them and who did it, it would be "God help that bunch of traitors!" They would do a good job for them.

I am not taking much to do with the political movement. The action of the Executive Council after that rotten action of that convention on the last day of its session has simply fixed it so that there is no hope for years, from that source, and all a person can do is get himself into trouble if he mixes into it at this time.

I don't [know] what the situation is in the oil fields, but I am satisfied that Lord did the best he could with what he had to deal with and the opposition he had to meet.

If it is possible at all, and I think it will be, I will be in Chicago to see you as you go through, if you will only let me know in time.

With best wishes, I am,

Yours very truly,
[John H. Walker]

TLC (John H. Walker Papers)

To Otto Branstetter

Charleston, W. Va.
April 21, 1920.

Mr. Otto Branstetter,
2845 Wilcox St,
Chicago, Ill.
My Dear Mr. Branstetter:

Your letter mailed from Chicago reached me here in Charleston when I arrived. I regretted it very much indeed that you did miss me in Chicago. There was so many things I wanted to see you about. The $25.00 dollars came in good time, for I had to send part of it to California, they are trying so many of our boys on this Syndicalis law that they passed there, and many of the poor fellows haven't got a dollar.

These are stormy times and there are stormy times ahead let me tell you. If the party had of stood loyal to the principal of the working class in the past, you would of had one of the greatest organizations in America today. but there were so many within her ranks that were traitors to a wholey cause, and when I would rebell against those things, every leach and blood sucker in the movement with the ax out to take my head off, but I am still at the front fighting the battle of the workers.

I will be in Chicago about the 19th of May, I expect to go down to Peoria to speak there, and I would like very much to see you then, I am,

Most sincerely yours,
Mother Jones

TLS (Mrs. Philip Taft, collector)

To John H. Walker

Charleston, W. Va.
April 27, 1920.

Mr. Jno. H. Walker,
Springfield, Ill.
Dear John:

It looks as if I am never going to see you again. I did not hear from you all of the time I was in California, and you know I get lonesome when I do not hear from you personally. You and Ed Nockles are the two I look to.

These are stirring times, John, and I don't know what the outcome is going to be. I am not as well and strong as I was when I saw you last, but however, I am still able to go out. I had a terrific meeting last night down at Kanawha city, it is so pathetic to see those wretches, they are the common laborers and there has never been very much done for them. I had to amuse them John, as well as educate them, because giving them the dry stuff, they did not understand as so many of those organizers, do, you could have not got any response from them. Those who preceded me in speaking told them about paying their dues, joining the union and then they are wise guys get $50.00 for it. John, these organizers ought to be trained before they are sent out, but they do really more harm than good.

They have a terrible time of it out on the coast they have a ship yard strike and the medal workers and they have a railroad strike, from mail I get from there, and the whole country seems to be torn to pieces.

We have not got any statesmen today that understand how to handle the situation, and I don't know John whether the labor party will bring the results they they boys hope for. I would give a great deal to see you and hope to be able to reach you some time in the near future. I expect to go up to Washington tomorrow or next day. Even Lord I don't hear from him any more.

I hope your wife and little one is alright and you try and get up a meeting there somewhere so I can go and address it and then have a long talk with you. I don't want to go to Chicago to expressly to meet you, I don't want to spend the money for that purpose.

I am not feeling as well John as I used to, and I won't be able to do the work I have been. I hope you are going to have a successful year in your administration and that things will come out victorious for the workers.

Write to me when you get a chance, I am always devotedly yours,

Mother Jones

TLS (John H. Walker Papers)

From John H. Walker

May 4, 1920.

Mother Jones,
c/o Box 1332,
Charleston, West Va.
Dear Mother:

Yours of April 27th received and glad to hear from you. Am very sorry I was unable to get to see you the last two times you were by this way going through Chicago, but in each case I had arrangements made for meetings sometime ahead; everything had been procided for and you know how disappointed they are when they make arrangements of that kind and you fail them at the last moment,—and that little bunch about Byesville, Ohio seem to be a decent little bunch of fellows and they are having a devil of a struggle. There is something over there that don't seem to be just right, and I wanted to encourage them the best I could.

I can understand your situation in Kanawha,—that is about the same situation everywhere. If the organizers were only honest they would develop the knowledge and experience to do the job properly, but under the present administration in our union, I doubt very much that they would want an honest organizer or that they would permit one to work for them any length of time, if they felt safe to discharge them. It seems to be a worse situation now than it ever was. A. R. Hamilton[1] has gotten complete control. Nockels was showing me a telegram from Schmidty's sister in which she said that you were, while perhaps not as strong or rugged physically as you had been, still in pretty good health, I was pretty glad to hear of it.

I wish I could go out there and spend a month or six weeks with you. We are moving from Danville to Springfield. Everything is torn up and my wife and girl are stopping at her mothers in South Danville. They will get over here when Esther finishes the school term sometime next month.

If you can possibly do it, the first time you are through this way again, write or wire a couple of weeks ahead. In the meantime, will try and arrange for a meeting sometime where we can be together. I have twenty meetings arranged now and other work until it makes your eyes dance in your head.

Am feeling pretty good physically, but between working and riding on trains, losing sleep, I get sometimes rather tired myself.

With love and best wishes I am,

Yours very truly,
[John H. Walker]

TLC (John H. Walker Papers)

1. Alfred Reed Hamilton (1872–1927), a Pittsburgh industrialist with interests in steel, coal mining, and banking, published the *Coal Trade Bulletin*. Walker, and other opponents of John L. Lewis, charged that Lewis was a puppet of Hamilton and received income from investments in Hamilton-sponsored publications.

From Terence V. Powderly

June 15, 1920

Dear Mother Jones

I am inclosing with this a letter from Brother Nockels. I suppose it relates to the money you sent him while here. I thought I would open it but thought that I could do no good by doing so and am burdening you with it.

I received an acknowledgment of the letter which accompanied the money from the editor of the New Majority, so that instance is closed.

We talk of you every day and express regret that you did not remain at home until fully recovered and strong enough to take up the burden again. Somehow I feel that you ought to make arrangements to stay home for at least a month, and the next time you come here I think I will chloroform you so that you can't get away.

As you know, the girls occupy the South porch evenings, and last night they had some kind of a sewing-bee out there and needed a tall light so I borrowed yours for the occasion, but will gladly return it the minute you come home again.

Emma and all the rest of them send their love to you, mine included, with the hope that you will keep well, but if you don't feel just exactly right switch off and come home at once.

Faithfully yours,
[T. V. Powderly]

TLC (Terence V. Powderly Papers)

To John H. Walker

Charleston, W. Va.,
June 18, 1920.

Mr. Jno. H. Walker,
120 So. 6th Street,
Springfield, Ill.
Dear John:

Every time I have gone in and around Chicago I have tried to see if I could get a line on you, but it is utterly impossible to do so, but when I was going to Southern Illinois to speak with you, I took sick on the train going into Washington, but was unable to keep my engagement, which I very much regretted.

I wish you would get one of those fellows to bill a meeting there some where, so I can get a chance to see you, sometime in July I sold three hundred of the New Majority, in the meeting I held in Illinois, but I got thirty dollars for them to help them out there is a great deal could be done John in that direction, if there was a system, but when we hold meetings and leave nothing with them to think about afterwards, it is almost useless work. You know the Journals of today are not educational, I mean the Labor Journals. But the new Majority is a pretty good paper, in fact it is about the best one I know of, there is many things I want to discuss with you that I cannot write to you about.

I hope you are going to settle down in Springfield, you know it is too much of a strain to be going in home in a hurry and in coming away in a hurry, you have no home life   if you get no time with your family, and you are one of the fellows that are out most of the time. We [are] having some hot times over in West Virginia, politically and industrially, I don't know what the future is going to be the laws that are made in the last four or five years in Washington have been suicidal to the labor movement, even tho their head-quarters of labor is there.

There is something wrong John somewhere, and I am afraid that Labor is going to pay the penalty dear and let me tell you that the labor organizations are up against all over this country. There is nothing in Utaugh ther is nothing in Mexico and the few they have in the northern coal field and in the western don't amount to much, ther is a terrible dissatisfaction there, they boys have time and again to come to me and beg me to come out there and stay with them, I was down in Louisville the first of April and O. My God!   It was sad to hear those men complain about those National organizers, they said they were going to have a Policy meeting in Louisville and they were going to telegraph to attend it, you know John I could not do much if I did go, and it was useless to spend the money on railroads and there is so much to be done here and the poor devils need every penny of it, and the poor boys have a burden on their shoulder here they are almost broke down and the fellows that come in from the National and there is only one here that can be relied on that is Old Batley.

The boys in Frisco were awfully good to me, I went out to St. Quinton to see Schmitty and the MacNamara, the warden told me that is the Deputy Warden, that they had eighteen hundred and fifty-four prison[er]s in that one prison alone, and he said to me Mother Jones, do you see that door, every man that has gone in that door, and that is closed behind them in the last year has been a young man under thirty, some years under thirty. What an endictment John against us, there is something wrong in the whole social struggle.

We have 120,000 legal hold ups that is lawyers, and 132,000 men and women in behind the bars in the penetintery not speaking of the local jails, there is a terrible endictment against our churchs and a terrible endictment against the Rockefellers church fund. I get terribly discouraged at times but then again I feel the fight must go, and I can't give it up John, as long as I am able to go. I am not as well or as strong as I used to be, but I have just as great a desire to keep on fighting, and you must arrange a meeting soon so that I can see you. These poor officials here have all they can carry on their shoulders.

Take care of yourself and don't be carried away with that weakness of yours, doing a special favor for every fellow that want[s] to work on your favor. The favor must be done for the million women and children and not for the individual. I don't care particular for Carbine billing meeting for me, I want to talk to you about it when I see you.

Well you give my love to the little ones at home and tell them some day I am coming down to visit them, with best wishes and take care of your self for you are the one lone human being that I want to cling to until death. We have known and worked together John many long years in this desparate battle, and I hope to be near you somewhere when the last hour comes.

With best wishes and loyal devotion to you, I am,

Yours sincerely,
Mother Jones

TLS (John H. Walker Papers)

From John H. Walker

June 25th 1920

Mother Jones
Charleston, West Virginia
Dear Mother:

Yours of the 18th received and I wish that I could be with you. I know how you feel because I sometimes feel that way myself but all we can do is fight on. It is a great relief to talk to someone who understands. On the first suitable occasion I will arrange for a meeting and will advise you in plenty of time ahead.

We moved to Springfield but are living in a rented upstairs in a rather cramped condition. We expect however to get a place to ourselves as soon as possible and I think I will be settled for sometime. When we do have a place, I hope that you can make up your mind to come and stay with us.

Phoebe and Esther send their love and best wishes

Sincerely yours,
[John H. Walker]

TLC (John H. Walker Papers)

To John H. Walker

Charleston, W. Va.,
July 21, 1920.

Mr. John H. Walker,
120 So 6th St,
Springfield, Ill.

Dear John:

I was sadly dissapointed in Westville, for not meeting you. I thought surely you would show up at that meeting. I wanted to see you so much, there were so many things I wanted to talk to you about. You left Chicago the night that I got in, I got in on Thursday night. What a geathering you had there of high-brows and know it all, who had no more conception of this death struggle that we are in than a lot of school children, I saw them geathered around of that Hotel lobby, I don't know John, I got all disgusted when I saw that geathering of high-brows, intelectual no-nothings.[1]

We are coming to a crisis anyhow, I see the railroad men are up against it.[2] After waiting for sixteen months, they have got nothing hardly. I am sick and tired of your meators, your whole system is eating up the vitals of the people, never in human history, will be pass through anything so treaterous as we are going through now.

I suppose the change will come and propably come faster than we realize, I would have given a great deal to see you John, because there are only a few of us that stand close together. I am going to Missourra for Labor day and if possible I'll go away a week ahead so as to see you on my way.

I see that Harlen and Howet[3] are going to look for the higher-ups Well it will be doubtful indeed if they can ever get there. I did not have much time to talk to Nockes, I did not see Fitzpatrick, I saw Foster[4] for a few minutes. We went out together and had dinner. They are going to get after Fitzpatrick, mind what I tell you, he is too honest a man too up-right to stoop the inner circle.

My strength is failing, John, I don't feel able to do the work I did, but the boys are good to me here they don't over work me, the fact of the matter is they let me come and go as I want to. I put in some very strenous years for the last ten years, it has not been easy sailing for me, but however, I have lived to see things moving.

Give my regards to them at home and I am glad you have got that new stenographer in Ester. Take care of yourself, with devotion, I am

Always yours,
Mother Jones

TLS (John H. Walker Papers)

1. In July 1920, John Fitzpatrick's National Labor party sponsored a conference in Chicago to establish a national Farmer-Labor party, but factional quarrels prevented the participants from achieving more than nominal unity.

2. A series of wildcat strikes on the nation's railways began in April and continued through the summer.

3. Alexander Howat of District 14 and Robert Harlin of District 10 had announced their candidacies for president and vice-president of the UMWA in the election of December 1920.

4. Probably William Z. Foster.

From John H. Walker

August 4, 1920.

Mother Jones,
c/o Box 1332,
Charleston, West Va.

Dear Mother:

Your letter of the 21st ultimo received. I was very sorry I could not get to Westville myself. I did not know that you were going to be there, although you had been billed for it, or I would have been doubly disappointed, because I could not go. At the same time, arrangements had been made a month before that, for me to speak at Streator on that date. A mass meeting had been called,—every local union in the city had planed to join the demonstration. We had some bands out and it was made a gala day, and I could not possibly have disappointed them after all those arrangements had been made. Carbine[1] billed me in good faith, I expect but he did not let me know until after it had been done. He figured that I would have no engagement for that date, and that I would go to Westville, which I would, had I been free to go, but it was impossible under the circumstances.

There were a lot of the kind of people that you mention at that meeting in Chicago,—high-brows, intellectual know-nothings. Most of them were disappointed at its outcome. A considerable number of them have gone where they belong, over to the Republican-Democratic parties. It is a very difficult situation in our organization, the intricacies of the machinery within the movement which the big corporations have set up through which they can perpetuate their paid hirelings in high official positions of dominating power, by having them resign. When they get discredited, one of their puppets go into higher position through law or the constitution, from Vice to President; then have another one of their puppets appointed in their place, which enables them to use all of the powers, influences and machinery of the organization to do whatever they please.

They corrupt and steal elections, and where they are not successful by that process they baldly trample the law under foot and set the elections aside; they make agreements binding the membership without consulting the membership, in opposition to the membership's wishes,—and then use the machinery of the organization and all the power and influence of the corporations and political organizations that they are serving, added to the strength of the union to crucify anybody, member or officer that protests.

However, it is about to the exteme now. I don't believe that the membership will stand for it much longer. There is a revultion of feeling on, and I believe the day is at hand when these modern, cheap judases posing as labor's representatives, being paid by labor, while they betray them, will be rooted out of every phase of our life and made moral lepers of publicly, so that every one can guard themselves from them.

At any rate I am hoping for it, and I am doing my best to that end and expect to continue as long as I live. When I go out, if I have nothing else left I will have a clear conscience on that score.

I think in an honest election, Harlin and Howat would defeat those other two. However, the representatives of the International Union are going the rounds of every local in the country now, employing every prominent, active, influential man that they can to go on as organizers just after the election takes place. This means of course where they fall for it, that they will support the men that are giving them their jobs in the coming election. Most of them will not get the jobs, but of course that will be after the election is over and they will have done their work,—a few of them will really get jobs.

Strikes are being called to enable the organizers to vote the paper membership, and I suppose they will steal and count the votes of all of the membership in the partially organized districts whether they vote or not, or regardless of how they vote, and even although they get the proof, those gentlemen will have the convention packed with two or three hundred of their paid men to control it, and there will have to be an exceedingly great revultion of feeling and rebellion and a representation of honest men who know, at the convention, if they are prevented from stealing it. Even then I believe they would destroy the organization rather than let honest men get in those jobs.

A. R. Hamilton, the Steel Trust and Boise Penrose,[2] the Political Boss of the Steel Trust has got complete absolute dominition and control. They are not going to give it up and leave the organization intact. However, I am going to do what I can for Harlin and Howat.

The larger the vote is for those two men, the more it forces the others to do, in the interest of the rank and file, and the more it prevents them from doing what is rotten and wrong and against the interest of the rank and file. I believe Harlin and Howat will get a majority of the votes cast.

With love to the end, I am,

Yours truly,
[John H. Walker]
President.

TLC (John H. Walker Papers)
1. Ed J. Carbine of the machinists' union served as vice-president of the Illinois Federation of Labor.
2. Boies Penrose (1860–1921), a Philadelphia lawyer, served in both houses of the Pennsylvania legislature before being named U.S. senator from Pennsylvania in 1897 for the first of four terms.

From John H. Walker

August 13, 1920.

Mother Jones,
c/o Box 1332
Charleston, West Va.
Dear Mother:

I am enclosing check for three hundred dollars ($300.00) Sometime ago I needed this money very badly and took advantage of that occasion and took the matter up with Jim Lord of having him return that three hundred dollars if he could spare it at that time. He did so.

I am able to get along without it now and am sending it to you, as I thought it might be possible that you would need it. In the event you need the other two hundred at any time, just drop me a note and I will see to it that you get it.

I hope this finds you in good health. We have had a terribly hot summer. It has been raining for a couple of days which sort of makes it more pleasant and cooler.

Yours,
[John H. Walker]

TLC (John H. Walker Papers)

To John H. Walker

Charleston, W. Va.,
Aug 17, 1920.

Mr. John H. Walker, Pres,
State Federation of Labor,
E. & W. Bldg, 120 S. 6th St,
Springfield, Ill.

Dear John:

I received your letter yesterday, I was glad to hear from you. I send back check to you that you sent me, you had better hold it and take care of it, if I have it, it won't last two weeks until it is gone.

I will be going to Missouri in a week or ten days, and I will then stop off at Springfield and see you, and have a talk with you. Things are pretty lively over here, we are doing business. I had a meeting at Princeton, West Va., yesterday the first labor meeting ever held there. It was only five miles from Bluefield, the head-quarters of the Baldwin Thugs.[1] I must have had six or seven thousand people, there were seven wagon-loads of Baldwin Thugs at the meeting, but John, I licked Hell out of the whole crowd. I put a new life and a new spirit into the wretches, certainly it was taking my life in my hands, because I had to come back thirty-two miles, over rough lonely roads along the mountains, with only one man and he was a lawyer, and the Schaufer with me, every one was afraid they would follow me and murder me, but we bluffed them and took the wrong road. It was near eleven o'clock when I got into Hinton, but after I crossed the river, I felt safe. I got into Charleston at four o'clock in the morning, had no sleep for twenty-eight hours. I had to go thirty-four miles over that rough road and back the same and then speak for one hour and a half to that tremenduous audence, but John, I sowed the seed anyhow, the voice of labor should not be raised there before, it was just as bad as homestead, but anybody else would have got killed.

Give my love to them all at home, I will let you know when I start for Springfield so you will be in town.

Sincerely yours,
Mother

TLS (John H. Walker Papers)

1. The Baldwin-Felts Detective Agency frequently supplied the mine guards and undercover agents employed by mine owners.

To Theodore Debs

Charleston, W. Va.,
Aug 18, 1920.

Mr. Theodore Debs,
Terre Haute, Ind.
My dear Theodore:

I received your letter of the 16th. this morning. I must say that I was more than glad to hear from you. I have been thinking of you for several days, and I am going west in a few days and will stop off at Terre Haute and have a talk with you about some things.

Poor Gene, he works on my nerves everytime that I turn my thoughts to Atlanta, and I cannot conceive how they could keep a kindly soul like him locked up, he woulden't harm a little kitten.[1]

I am worried to death sometime about a number of people that are going to jail and how cold blooded they are getting. I will telegraph to you as soon as I arrange to go to Terre Haute, so you can meet me.

With love to Mrs. Debs and your beautiful sweet girl, I remain,

Very sincerely yours,
Mother Jones

TLS (Eugene V. Debs Papers)
1. Eugene V. Debs was in the federal prison in Atlanta, having been convicted of violating the Espionage Act.

From John H. Walker

August 18, 1920.

Mother Jones,
c/o Box 1332 Charleston, West Va.
Dear Mother:

This is to acknowledge receipt of yours of the 17th returning check. I am mighty glad to know that you were able to break the ground at Princeton.

I know nothing in life will give me more satisfaction than that knowledge. I think I could have been with you, although I expect possibly you did better without me. Be sure and stop off in Springfield while you are going through and drop me a note before hand letting me know what time you will be here so that if it can be done at all, I wil arrange to be here with you during the time of your visit.

Yours,
[John H. Walker]

TLC (John H. Walker Papers)

1920

To Ryan Walker

Charleston, W. Va.
Sept 21, 1920.

Mr. Rhyne Walker,
New York Call,
New York City, N. Y.

My dear Ryan:

I received your letter some time ago, owing to the pressure of work, I was unable to reply to it. I would have been glad to wrote you a few lines for Labor day, but the pressure was so hard, I could not find the time.

I see you are up against it in New York. The papers say that they are going to turn down the men that were elected by the people to the State Legislature. If they can do away with those things, then farewell to Liberty in America, there is very little of it left anyhow.

I was in Kansis City on the 13th of this month   I went up to see the Snyders, most all the old timers have gone from there, they are very few of them left, that is of the old warriors, one of the Snyders died in Oklahoma, very suddenly and the other brother is attending to their business in Kansis city,   they are just as true and loyal as they ever were; but the movement there is practically dead. It is only a reminent of the old timers, are keeping it going and they are all going over to the Labor party.

Well there are stormy times anyhow, it is hard to tell what the future will bring forth. It looks as if that old spirit is dead in the people. They have no more street meetings in Kansis city, and I don't know that it will ever be reserected or not.

You know Ryan there were a great many sentementalist that got into our movement, and they are perretical educators, others got in and used it for what they could get out of it for their pockets, and the wretch below had to bear the burden.

We have a terrific fight in the southern end of the state. I don't pay very much attention to the political phase of it. I know the future battle of it is is going to be in the field of industry, and this fellow has got to be educated to his power. University Professors and the power orators have no grasp of this thing. A great many are using it for themselves.

I hope Mrs. Walker is well   I don't know when I will get to New York. I have not been really well for the last two months, but perhaps some day I will try and see you.

Give Mrs. Walker my best wishes, and tell her I hope to see her if I do get to New York.

You must come up and see me and spend an Hour with me   I want to talk over old times with you. Write to me sometijje and send me the call, we don't get it here nowhere on the stand.

With best wishes to you and Mrs. Walker, I am,

Sincerely yours,
Mother Jones

TLS (Walker MSS)

To Terence V. Powderly

Charleston, W. Va.
Dec 14, 1920.

Mr. T. V. Powderly
Department of Labor,
Washington, D. C.
My dear Mr. Powderly:

The bearer of this letter, Mr. Fred Mooney,[1] Secretary-Treasurer of the United Mine Workers, District No. 17, I consider it quiet and honor and pleasure to be able to entroduce him to you, and vouch for his manhood.

Any favor that you can do for him, will be deeply appreicated. Try and get his pass-port, give him any service you can, and that service will be well rendered.

I don't know just exactly when I will leave for Mexico. I'm feeling better than I have been for several days.

With deep appreciation, I remain,

Sincerely yours,
Mother Jones

TLS (West Virginia Collection)
1. Fred Mooney (1888–1952) served as secretary-treasurer of District 17, UMWA, 1917–1924.

To Woodrow Wilson

December 16th. 1920.

Hon. Woodrow Wilson,
President,
Washington, D. C.
My dear Sir:

In the spirit of the season I come to you with an appeal addressed to your heart and conscience in behalf of a fellow-citizen who languishes in a federal prison.

Without in any manner questioning the wisdom or justice of the punishment that has been meted to him for what he has consistently contended has been a rigid adherence to his inherent rights, I do respectfully represent that the cause of justice has been completely vindicated, and from my mother's heart comes only horror and repugnance when the laws of a great nation are liable to be subverted to the ignoble demands of vengeance.

Those of us who know this prisoner best are absolutely convinced that he is incapable of harming his government—of harming any living creature. I have been associated with him for thirty years and make this statement without reservation. His life has been one of unceasing devotion and heavy sacrifice to those principles which he has deemed to be worthy and righteous. If he has erred it has been at the urging of a great love for his own kind.

In the name of that broad humanity for which you, too, have suffered; in the name of all those who are downtrodden and oppressed; in harmony with the universal aspiration for "peace on earth, good will to all men," I earnestly and humbly petition you to exercise the gracious perogative of pardon that you alone possess and bestow upon Eugene V. Debs his freedom and restore him to his family before Christmas.

Sincerely yours,
Mother Jones

TLS (Woodrow Wilson Papers)

From Terence V. Powderly

Washington, D.C.
December 28, 1920.

Dear Mother Jones:

The inclosed copy of what occurred in Carbondale forty-seven years ago, as it appeared in our old M. & B. Journal for January 1874, will, in part, illustrate the folly, if not worse, of letting land on ninety-nine year leases.

The Delaware and Hudson Canal Company began operations about ninety-eight years ago or in 1823, I am not positive as to date. The mining of anthracite was in its infancy and buying land from which to mine the coal would be a risk, some of the land was bought outright by the company, much of it was obtained from those who had ninety-nine year leases on it.

The real reason why lots were not sold to the miners in the beginning was, because the compnay could not give title to land it held on a ninety-nine year lease.

In order to obtain some sort of title the company endeavored to have some of the squatters sign five year leases and then have the land revert to the company, that was done to wipe out the claim of the squatter, in the first place by recognizing the right of the company to the land, as the signing of such a lease would do.

You will also note that the two years in which efforts were made to intimidate squatters into signing leases were 1857 and 1873. Panics had occurred in both years, many were idle and every one lived in dread of worse to come. So at a time when men were going through hard times the company endeavored to over awe the workmen and oblige them to surrender land they had held possession of without let or hinderance for over thirty years in one instance and fifty years in another.

In two years, 1923, the lands obtained in the first place under ninety-nine year leases will revert to the original lessors. *Where are they?* Not one now living of course and there is no one to go back over the records to find out how they obtained their leases in the first place. The dead do not boast, brag, defend or explain, they have passed beyond the reach of earthly inquiry. No man can make a lease for ninety-nine years and live to see the lease expire by lapse of time.

The means by which ninety-nine year leases are obtained are always hazy, no one can testify and frequently—as is the case with many Pennsylvania leases—the records have been burned.

A corporation lives on but as I understand it the idea in Mexico is to give the individual settler a secure claim to his land while allowing the title to remain in the State.

The best plan is to make short leases with right of removal, without expense to the lessee in case the lessee or heirs wish to renew, the land to revert to the state on the expiration of the lease in case the lessee or his heirs do not care to continue in possession.

There should, of course, be safe-guards thrown around to making of leases so that sharpers, swindlers or land grabbers could not get hold of land.

In all cases the state should retain the sole right to mineral deposits, improvements on land belong to man under certain well defined rules or laws, but no human hand did or could place the minerals in the earth, they were made and placed in the earth by God for all the people, through their own Agent the State should control them.

Short term leases with right of recession vested in the State are safest.

No man living in 1922 can testify to the terms of a lease made in 1823.

No trace of such a lease can be found in the archives at Harrisburg for most of the old land records were destroyed by fire.

No man living in 1922 cares a rap for what men did in 1823, and you and I have seen too much of indifference to welfare of the children of yesterday to place any reliance on the present generation being anything but indifferent to the dead and gone men of one hundred years ago.

I hope this will be of some little vervice to you and when you see M. Villa extend my compliments to him and say that I hope his administration will redound to the good of the people of Mexico.

With love and blessings,
[T. V. Powderly]

TLC (Terence V. Powderly Papers)

To John H. Walker

Charleston, W. Va.
Dec 28, 1920.

Mr. John H. Walker, Pres,
The Illinois State Federation of Labor,
E. & W. Bldg, 120 So 6th St,
Springfield, Ill.
Dear John:

I am dropping you a line or two. I haven't been well since I saw you, and I leave for Mexico city the first of the week with Secretary Mooney. Perhaps the change of climate will be a benefit to me. You know there is so many of those revolutionist that I saved from being extradicted during the Deistz administration that are now a part of the Mexican government and they want me to come down there, so I am going to leave the first of the week.

I would like very much to see you before I go away but I cannot go by way of Chicago. I see they have won out again in Indianapolis   Searles telegraphed the associated Press in Washington that they have won over whelimngly.[1]

I am not going to write much John.

With best wishes for a Happy New Year, and love to all at home, I am,

Most sincerely yours,
Mother

[*Holograph postscript*] R C Adams who is a member of the Co told Hag that you won by 20000 votes over White   Said he was Whites manager. Safe organization when such rotten Practices are resorted to and they boast about it   He told Hagerrty

TLS with holograph note (John H. Walker Papers)
1. Ellis Searles was editor of the UMWA *Journal*. Mother Jones probably is referring to the recent election of John L. Lewis and Philip Murray to the leadership of the UMWA. The postscript, however, refers to the 1918 election, when Walker ran against Frank J. Hayes.

From John H. Walker

December 31, 1920.

Mother Jones,
Hotel Hagerty,
Charleston W Va
Dear Mother:

Your letter of the 28th instant received and glad to hear from you. I think however, that Searles sent out that telegram not because it was based on facts or truth, but to set the stage for their trying to steal that election again. Howat is elected by such an enormous majority that I doubt very much that they can get away with it. Nevertheless A. R. Hamilton will not permit his men to be put out of control of our union, if by any desperate measure he can retain them in office. Harlin is also elected by about 20,000 majority easily, and if they can be prevented from stealing votes either for themselves that were not cast for them, or from Howat or Harlin that were cast for them, there is no question about the defeat of Lewis and Murray. Lewis got 22 votes in the local union where he held his membership for ten or twelve years, in Panama Illinois, and where his father and four brothers and all of the rest of his family lived for about the same length of time. Not a single member of that union comprising about 700 members would rise to their feet in the sight of the others and place him in nomination for reelection. The 22 votes he got I am convinced he received from men who knew nothing of him and only voted for him because he was at the head of the ticket.

It is the most sordid narrative of robbery and betrayal of human beings that worked for a living, men, women and children, injured men and the dead men and their widows and orphans that I have ever known anything about, and this is no hearsay Mother, you can go to Panama and get the sworn statements involving him and his family.

Four of them were compelled to put back about a thousand dollars that they were caught with the goods on them so strong and conclusive that there was no escape for them, and that they were not entitled to. John Lewis' bosom friend and closest political associate and campaign manager William MacDonnell was proven as having been on the payroll of the company getting fifty dollars a month for betraying men who were injured in the mines, when their cases were settled under the law, at the same time he was posing as their representative and as an official of the local union.

He also did the same thing for the widows and orphans. Collusion was also clearly obvious between them and the mine management, the management refusing to hire any one who opposed the gang and discharging any one opposing the gansters in the Local Union who were robbing and looting the treasury and betraying the membership, injured men, widows and orphans. On the other hand the gang let the management refuse to hire anybody that he did not want to hire, and to discharge anybody for any or no reason at all, that he did not want to work there.

They threatened and intimidated and beat up a number of men that opposed them in their machinations and more than one man was found dead the next morning who was seen in their company the night before, usually robbed. One man who confessed, had been forced into accepting the money and becomming one of them, because of his concern for his wife and nine children (he was the only bread-winner and he did not have any money to leave town and he did not want to get beat up) He later was made Sub-District Secretary, but it preyed on his conscience so that he confessed, gave up his office as Sub-District Secretary-Treasurer and blasted his standing with the membership for life, rather than continue to be a party to it.

It is horrible to think that such men get in powerful positions in the labor movement. The last year that John Lewis was one man committee man at this mine, there was over $81,000 checked off those men for local expenses. After this rottenness was exposed and the membership rose in arms John Lewis as International Vice-President, sent a National Organizer from the Anthracite fields at the expense of the International Organization for wages, hotel, railroad and other expenses, whose purpose (stated by himself under oath) was to electioneer,—to keep these traitors and thieves in office, and prevent the membership from putting them out.

It is too horrible to describe or even contemplate. I sincerely hope that everybody who loves humanity and the movement, will take a chance on doing everything they can to clean this rottenness out of our union and to put clean, honest men in the official positions again. It is not only a cancer eating the heart out of our organization but it is corrupting and diseasing and be-foulling the whole labor movement of our country, and spreading that same rotten influence over the whole world to the injury and disgrace of the whole human race and to the detriment of not only our generation, but future generations everywere on earth.

I hope you have a pleasant trip and that it benefits your health. I know it will give you a good deal of satisfaction to see those men again that you helped save their lives who are now working and fighting in the interest of humanity. The Lord keep you and spare you to humanity for many more years.

With best wishes and love from us all, I am,

Yours
[John H. Walker]

TLC (John H. Walker Papers)

From George W. P. Hunt

Bangkek, Siam,
Feb 15, 1921.

My Dear Mother Jones:

Your splendid letter of December is before me, it takes a long time for mail to come, and after the elections, and while I felt that Nationally there was not much hope, but to see my beloved State, which was for so long the real progressive state to turn down all that was good for labor made my heart sick, as in breeding over this like the golden lining to the black cloud came your letter, so it gave me hope for with your cheer and that spirit that will never die, would that some of our so-called labor leaders in Arazonia had some of it. It seems strange that one who has always been so democratic as I should be representing my country in the only despotic court left in this world. Well in a measure, I am glad for it has made me just the stronger for the things that I have always stood for.   hoped for and worked for, but as you so wisely remark there is a dark period ahead for labor in America, and I pray that time will do better than I hope for.

The other day I was shown through the Railway shops. I saw men naked to the waist hammering the steel getting in our money 40 cents a day, but what made me think mad was to see women like men and they were getting fifty savages a day, which amounts to in our money twenty cents a day. So this 25 Santang Piece that I am enclosing you with the King of Siam on one side and the White elephant on the other and in value is worth 10 cents our money is what a woman gets here working in the machine shops here in the city of Bangkok.

I have gathered a lot of it lately, and I hope that some day when I return can make use of it. As there is no English schools here for my daughter to attend, I am sending them back to Arazona. No doubt, some G. O. P man will be anxious to get my job, but I will be just as anxious to get back to Arazona, and hope that I will always have your spirit, so with many thanks for your fine message and may the good lord protect you and keep you in the prayer of your friend

Gov. W. P. Hunt,
American Legation, Bangkek

TLC (Terence V. Powderly Papers)

To John H. Walker

Box 1332, Charleston, W. Va.,
March 22, 1921.

Mr. John H. Walker, Pres,
State Federation of Labor,
Springfield, Ill.
Dear John:

I have been wanting to write to you for sometime, but I have been held up, I have not been very well. I got a letter from Ester[1] sometime ago, and do you know for two or three days, I could not locate who it was, and all at once it dawned on me, I did not dream of her being in Indiana at school, but I wrote to her yesterday to let her know that I did not forget her. She is a very beautiful girl, that is she was a very beautiful child and no doubt raised by the mother that she had, she coulden't be anything else but a real democratic woman.

I am not well, John, but I am going west soon in sight of a couple of weeks and I want to stay a week with you down in Springfield, before I go to San Antonio, Texas, on my way to Mexico. The boys won the fight here in Mingo, they came out victorious yesterday, but it is an outrage to see the way of the courts of capitalism do business, and how they spend the Tax-payers money to carry on capitalist rot. I want to stay with you a few days; there is so much today to talk over about Mexico and other things that we don't have any time meeting each other and going away   Lord and Wallace will be here tomorrow night, to talk on the Kansas Court Law. I don't think either one of these fellows can handle that question as it ought to be handled just now, owing to the fact that the Legislature is in session here, and no doubt they will attend the court to hear that lecture. You know it takes more powerful men than either one of those, with a deep personality to impress the people of today. Johnson was to come, but I don't know he left out. I see that Hearst is getting after Gompers, or rather Gompers is getting after Hearst. I think it was rather a mistake, John, for Gompers, to open up the battle with Hearst, you know there isen't a more powerful newspaper man in the country than Hearst is, and Gompers can't hold his own within.

Well, I read an article of Howat yesterday in one of the local papers and it was a very good explanation, he is a remarkable man he stood the fire for years, and it has not been all of the open enemy, a good deal came within the ranks of those who should have stood by him at all times and all hours. However, you know John, we have a whole lot of people in office that have a much deeper desire for the odor coming from the flesh-pot of capitalism than they have for their children desteny of the future of the nation. The labor movement will never be wrecked from out side, John, the wrecking force will be from within.

I have not had anytime to talk with you, but I am going down to tell Mrs. Walker that I want to stay four or five days with her, as I want to rest up. With best wishes, to you and all of yours, I am,

Sincerely yours,
Mother

TLS (John H. Walker Papers)
1. Esther Walker, John's daughter, was attending Indiana University.

From John H. Walker

March 24, 1921.

Mother Jones,
Box 1332, Charleston, West Va.
Dear Mother:

This is to acknowledge receipt of yours of the 22nd. Glad to hear from you although sorry to learn that you are not in your usual health. Will tell Mrs. Walker today of your coming and will be glad to have you for the week. We live at 626 Fayette Ave. If you let me know what train you are coming in on, will arrange to meet you there. In the event there is any misconnection, just get a taxi at the depot and ask him to take you to 626 Fayette Ave., and he will take you there alright.

We are having a desperate battle here too. There are four bills in here that the enemies of labor are pushing strongly. Either one of them if enacted into law will do away with the present open form of trade unions in our state and compel us to go back to the meetings after midnight and try to work without being known, and there is too grave a danger of their passing to suit me.

However, we have a fighting chance to defeat them, and we are strongly hopeful of defeating them.

Anticipating the pleasure of meeting you in the near future I am,

Yours,
[John H. Walker]

Give my regards to Mooney[1] and the other real fellows in the West Va. portion

TLC (John H. Walker Papers)
1. Fred Mooney.

To Terence V. Powderly

Charleston, W. Va.
April 5, 1921.

My dear friend Mr. Powderly;

This is a copy of a letter that I found when I returned here. It will show you what is going to happen to me when I go to Mexico, and I know that no human being will enjoy this letter more than you and Mrs. Powderly. I also received a very fine letter from Governor Hunt of Colorado [Arizona], who is the American Legation of Bangkek, Siam, I will send you a copy of his letter also. I won't leave here before Friday and I may write to you again, but I could not leave without sending you and Mrs. Powderly a copy that I received from Mexico that I received on my arrival here.

With sincere love to all, I am,

Sincerely yours.
Mother

PS: When I go to mexico I got some information that I am going to dig up which I will send you, but has got to be kept strictly secret.
[*Holograph note*] Tell Margurete I miss that medecine

TLS (Terence V. Powderly Papers)

To John H. Walker

Charleston, W. Va.,
April 5, 1921.

Mr. John H. Walker, Pres,
State Federation of Labor,
Springfield, Ill.
Dear John:

I have just come down from Washington, I will be with you next Sunday. I have a good deal to talk to you about on the future of the labor movement. I think that there is a good deal that you ought to know. I have not been well John, since I came back from Mexico, I have had rheumatism so much, and it is kind of playing on me. I will stay two or three days with Mrs. Walker on my way to Mexico city. I'll explain matters to you when I get there.

Things does not look very bright to me John, you know every where they are passing bills to crush labor, and it seems that the thing has been staged for a long time what they were going to do, I won't say much in this letter, but will talk it over with you when I see you.

I leave Thursday night sometime, and will leave Chicago Sunday morning, I will get Ed Nockles to telephone to you on Saturday. I had a letter from Ester and do you know John, it was a whole week before I could think who sent me that letter from the College, and all at once I woke up one night and it just dawned on me that it was Ester, so I wrote her a letter to let her know that I received her She is a very beautiful girl and I hope she will live to be a duplicat of her mother.

With best wishes for you and your home, I am,

Sincerely yours,
Mother J

TLS (John H. Walker Papers)

To Terence V. Powderly

Charleston, W. Va.,
April 6, 1921.

My dear Mr. Powderly:

I am just writing a few lines. You can read carefully the enclosed document and as soon as you read this carefully, you send it back to Box 1201, Charleston, W. Va., Mr. Frank Snyder.[1] Say nothing about this to anyone.

Hoping this will find all at home well. Don't forget to send this back. With love to all at home, I am,

Most sincerely yours,
Mother

TLS (Terence V. Powderly Papers)
1. Frank W. Snyder (1874–1953), editor of the *Labor Argus* and the State Federation of Labor journal, held several offices in the West Virginia Federation of Labor and served as state commissioner of labor, 1939–1941.

From Terence V. Powderly

April 9, 1921.

Dear Mother Jones:

In compliance with your request I am returning the "Echoes of the Pan-American Labor Congress". I have an idea that the statement of the bar-tender of the Hotel Princess may have been exaggerated a little bit for I do not see how less than half a dozen men could get away with from $50 to $75 worth of liquor in one night. I would not advise you to rely too implicitly upon that bar-tender's statement. At the same time I feel that men representing a movement so important, so far-reaching and so fraught with possibilities of good or ill to humanity, should be very careful how they expose themselves to criticism. I know how apt every little thing a labor man does is magnified into mountainous propositions. You and I have both suffered from the unguarded tongue of the thoughtless critic and I would not advise that anything be said or done in relation to this matter.

By this time you will be ready to start for Mexico and I ask you to always bear in mind that there is only one Mother Jones. I doubt if the world has seen her like before and while I hope for the future, sadly feel the world will not see her like again. Be careful then of her health, remember that the covering of the soul you carry is frail, that time has not dealt too kindly with it and every precaution of yours should be taken to guard it carefully and well.

With every good wish for your safe journey to Mexico, a pleasant stay there and a safe return to us again, I am,

Affectionately yours,
[T. V. Powderly]

TLC (Terence V. Powderly Papers)

From Roberto Haberman[1]

Apartado 1855,
Mexico, D. F.
[April 1921]

Dear Mother Jones:

This is Good Friday, I think. It is good because of the fact that I am sort of conversing with you, and because I know that soon you will be with us again.

Your letter of February 28th was sure a welcome news. As has been your letter of a couple of weeks ago to general Villarreal. He passed on the latter to me for translation, and also to answer it, which I will do tomorrow.

Have written a letter to Jim Lord trying to trace the five hundred dollars that Villarreal sent you. You write to him too. It surely is funny that you did not get this money yet. Will also try to trace it through the banks.

We are all expecting you down within a few weeks. Gen Villarreal has a house ready for you, and a prettier place cannot be imagined. Also servants, and an automobile. The only bad thing about all this is that you will have my wife and I hanging about your place in our spare time. I am going to try to get the General to furnish you with some Felts hounds to keep us off.

Then don't forget that Felipe Carrillo[2] expects you to be down in Yucatan for the Socialist Convention the second week in May. He does not think that he can be Governor unless you are down here.

Our work is going on splendidly. Morones[3] is sure a great labor leader. The so-called "Communists" are as damnable a lot of whelps as they were when you were down here, but they do not amount to anything, and we don'[t] pay any attention to them, anymore than does any worker. Gale[4] is doing fine work.

How is Fred Mooney? He never writes, he is worse than I am. Lincoln Stephens [Steffens] is here, and with his usual fine spirit and judgment manages to have loads of fun. He was received royally by everybody. Great man.

Please let me know the whereabouts of the five hundred dollars as soon as you get any news of them.

Loads of love from wife, baby, Mary Doherty, and Lincoln Stephens, and me.

To the Red Dawn!
Roberto Haberman

TLC (Terence V. Powderly Papers)
1. Roberto Haberman (1883–1962) emigrated from the United States to Mexico in 1917, founded the Federacion de Trabajadores de Mexico, and held Mexican civil service appointments during the next forty years.
2. Felipe Carillo Puerto (1872–1924), Yucatan agrarian leader and follower of Emiliano Zapata, was elected governor of his province and served until his death during the Delahuertista rebellion in 1924.
3. Luis N. Morones was a leader of the Casa del Obrero Mundial and later served as minister of industry.
4. Probably Lynn A. E. Gale (1892–1940), an antiwar propagandist who moved to Mexico from the United States during World War I; he later returned to the United States and was convicted of publishing seditious materials.

To John Fitzpatrick and Ed Nockles

Mexico City,
May 16, 1921.

Mr. John Fitzpatrick,
President of the Chicago Federation of Labor
Ed Knockles,
Secretary of the Chicago Federation of Labor
My dear friends:

Your very beautiful telegram of May the first reached me on May second. I don't know of anything I received in years that so deeply affected me for the time being. I hope you do not think or have the impression that I was unappreciative for your humane consideration of me in a far off city. I have no words to convey to you and your associates in the great struggle for justice the deep appreciation that I feel.

My reason for not acknowledging your message at once was that I was not well, but I am now beginning to get back my old fighting qualities. On the day your message arrived, I was down in Orizaba, a strictly manufacturing town. I addressed a large meeting there with several diputatos, or congressmen also. It was the most remarkable meeting I addressed in years; the spirit was so marvellously fine. The town was thoroughly organized and the spirit they possessed was an inspiration. One got new hope for the future. They had a union band with the finest music I ever heard in a labor display. The building was a municipal building, very large, tendered by the public officials to the Labor movement. There was no uniformed police there, either at the entrance or inside of the building. This was something marvellously new to me, because with us in the United States, in the great American Republic, you know the outside and inside would have been multiplied by the uniformed representatives of the high class burglars. The meeting continued until nearly twelve o'clock. Not one human soul left the hall. All were deeply interested to my surprise, a flag representing the murder of the so-called anarchists in Chicago of '86 came marching in side by side with the national banner. Everyone of you would have been put in jail for the next ten years if that occurred in Chicago. The congressmen, most all of them, referred to it in their speeches, the tribute paid to that banner as it entered that hall was the most remarkable demonstration I had witnessed in all my years in the industrial conflict. The next morning as the train pulled in and stopped on its way to Mexico City, the workers came out of the shop and jumped on the train and no one could keep them off. The came in and urged me to come back again. I promised them to do so and fell just in fine spirit now to return to them.

After all one's life is not in vain when they witness the beautiful conception of industrial freedom that is taking possession of the souls of the workers. Here they are making wonderful progress and they are not bothered with a lot of police and capitalist henchmen. But we have a good many so-called Cominist freaks here that want to rule and dictate. God help the day that those fanatics should ever get to the helm, we'd be worse off than we were under the rule of a Wilson. The workers went up to the Camara of Deputados last Friday, May 13; walded into the Congressional Hall, planted the Red flag and notified the Congressmen that they were not getting a square deal from their representatives and told them it act for the interest and honor of the Nation and the future destinies of the children yet to come. Of course the kept-press howled a little. There was no violence, nothing rough or loud—it was simply a practical and logical demand of their representatives. They returned in peace. If such a thing had happened in Washington, all the machine guns within a hundred miles would be called in and turned on them. They are making marvellous progress here in the Labor movement. If they only keep their heads level for the next few years, they will give an example to the world of what can be acquired in a peaceful manner instead of by force.

I expect to go to Yucatan inside of a week. The only one danger that there is here to interfere with their progress is that religious issue. If that can be kept out of the Labor movement, there will be marvellous progress made here.

Give my best wishes to Olander and Knockles. When you see Walker tell him I shall write to him soon.

They are going to have a Labor Convention here on the first of July. I am going to stay over for that. One of those refugees that I got out of jail during the Diaz administration called to see me and told me that the Mexican government would extend all the hospitality to me while I was in Mexico, and they would spare nothing to make my stay here pleasant.

I hole that things will go along smoothly. This awful unemployment question I am afraid will bring on trouble in the United States. It looks as if the greed for money and power developed during the war, and they want to continue the game, but then the labor movement did not take advantage of the opportunity that they had.

Well you will hear from me again soon, and give my deep appreciation to all the delegates. Tell them the future is ours if they only stand like men to-gether.

With best wishes, I am

Sincerely yours,
Mother Jones

TLS (John Fitzpatrick Papers)

To John H. Walker

Apartado 1855
Mexico City, Mexico.
May 27, 1921.

Mr. John H. Walker,
Pres, of the State Federation of Labor,
Springfield, Illinois.
My dear John:

I have been trying to write you ever since I came down here, but I have not been very well. I wrote to Mooney but the loafer has never given me an answer yet. He sent me a copy of the Federationist. I saw where you received an invitation to address the Convention in Huntington and I was glad indeed to know you were one of the crowd. I saw that Riley[1] got elected President and he is by far the best to have that job. I was afraid one of the political crooks would get in.

Weve had some stormy times down here since I've been here. You know they have an element of so-called revolutionists here that are doing their best to destroy the Labor movment. No they are not well on their feet yet here. They don't understand the danger they are up against with those fellows. You know as well as I do the enemy gets his tools inside our ranks and once they get their poison in it is not easy to apply the chemical to undue it. There is another phase, John, that the heads of the Labor movement of Mexico do not understand the background and treachery of the common enemy. They have got good men, but you know here they have gone through a twelve yrs. turmoil, torn to pieces with scarsely no organization and no education on the industrial field. They had just entered the kindergarten when this political, this communist and religious question began to be injected into them. They got to fighting each other and you know John those freaks that see the light breaking out of heaven for their interest are the most dangerous sewer-rats we can get. They imagine God Almighty never gave any brains to anyone but them and they are going to solve the whole problem with the sole of their shoes. And even the fellows working for Jesus take a hand in the game. Last Sunday in Morelia the sky-pilot delivered a sermon after Mass and aroused the peoples' passions against the Reds in the Labor movement until the whole congreation went out, men and women and stoned the building where the socialist paper was published. That was Christ's philosophy filled up with capitalist swill. I wonder what Jesus will do to that dam pirate when he gets his claws on him— I want to be round. Unfortunately John, these poor fellows here have been crushed for centuries and they are just emerging from that oppression. It seems so sad that they should be interfered with, but such runs the stream of the vicious philosophy of the capitalist vultures.

Well I see that Brofy[2] is coming to the front in District 2 of Penn. I wish we had more like Howwatt—I am going to write to him to-day. I shall see you on my way back John and tell you all and you tell that brick maker that brought that bottle of tonic when I was in Springfield that I've been praying for him ever since, If I dared to risk it I would bring him some tonic from here. Well I have a lot to tell you Jack but I am kind of tired, I am not well. I think the altitude is too high. I hope that Esther and Mrs. Walker are well. Had a good time in San Antonio. I met some of my old friends and they left nothing undoe to make it pleasant for me. But John there is no life in the movement there and the organizers and officials have no life in them. They can't stir the animal up. They are of the conservative dog type and I don't consider such people worth wasting time with. I see they are after Tobin.[3] What in hell do those fellows know John about the great struggle. I never had any use for him since he took that job away from that old man in Bloomington. They have lost out in Alabama entirely and I'm afraid they are going to loose out in Mingo because they haven't had the man to handle that strike at the beginning. There is an unfortunate in the Labor movement and some of the officials to-day. They like to have a slate and they think more of "my individual friend" that they do of the destinies of thousands of men, women and children.

Well I'm going to close until I find something to send you. I have a whole lot but I can't write it. Give my love to Mrs. Walker. I hope her mother is better. Try and keep your health for you will be needed in the near future,

Sincerely,
Mother Jones

TLS (John H. Walker Papers)
1. James Riley was elected president of the West Virginia Federation of Labor at the Huntington convention at which Walker spoke.
2. John Brophy (1883–1963), president of District 2 and an advocate of nationalization of the coal mines, tried unsuccessfully to unseat John L. Lewis as president of the UMWA in 1926; later, the two were reconciled and Brophy was named national director of the CIO.
3. Probably Daniel Joseph Tobin (1875–1955), head of the teamsters' union, 1907–1952, who was currently under attack in the UMWA *Journal*.

From John H. Walker

June 6, 1921.

Mother Jones:

Enclosed you will find letter and copy of my reply which explain themselves. Kindly return them to me for my files after you have read them. Make any use of them you care to.

Yours truly,
[John H. Walker]
President.

TLC (John H. Walker Papers)

From John H. Walker

June 6, 1921.

Mother Jones,
Apartado 1855,
Mexico City, Mexicao.
Dear Mother:

This is to acknowledge receipt of yours of May 27th. Glad to hear from you. I was at the Huntington convention, and I think I helped reelect Riley President. After I got there, I understood the significance of your request and did what I could, and Riley agreed that I helped.

Sorry that conditions are as they are in Mexico, but because of what they have gone through and thier limited opportunities, I think they are really doing well, and I sincerely hope they may be able to keep a grip on things, maintain what of progress they have made, and in spite of the traitors and ignorance inside, and the enemies outside, continue to make progress.

Yes, Brophy seems to have developed a little backbone latterly. I hope he continues to. Howat is making a great fight. Will tell President Casten [Frank Kasten] of the Brick Makers the first time I see him, of your letter.

Legislative matters are in such shape that I doubt that I am going to be able to get to the A. F. of L. convention until the last week of it, maybe not even then. We have been able to prevent the enactment of proposed laws that were inimical to us. I think we have them all killed, but we cannot be sure until they have adjourned.

We have not been able to make very much progress for ourselves, but I think that if we hold our own during this period, we are doing fairly well. All the folks are well and send their love.

With best wishes I am,

Yours truly
[John H. Walker]
President.

TLC (John H. Walker Papers)

To John H. Walker

Apartado 1855
Mexico City, Mex
June 21, 1921.

Mr. John H. Walker,
Pres. of the State Federation of Illinois,
Springfield, Ill.
Dear John :

I shall inclose the letter you received from the World To-morrow in a few days. I have already given a copy of it to one of the Cabinet officers. I regret very much that you were unable to attend the convention in Denver. It would have given you a chance to get next to things from the opening of the convention, because you know we never get the same grasp of any subject by merely being told of it or reading.

I see you have deafeated the Hessian law, the constabulary. If you didn't do anything else for the workers in Illinois, that of itself was a marvelous victory. Although Pennsylvania is the greatest industrial state in the Union, that law was passed in 1903 just after the anthracite strike and working men from Pittsburg went down and lobbied for it, and you will agree with me that in all those years they have not won a strike of any importance. They've got it in West Virginia and they have had nothing but war ever since the bill passed. But I couldn'd convince Keeney at the time that if they didn't take pretty drastic steps, they'd pull that law over. But these men don't seem to have a grasp of the methods that the Capitalists use to enslave their class.

I have not been well John since I came here. I have not seen a well day in the two months that I have been here. I am leaving next Friday night for the East and I'll have to stop off at San Antonio on a mission—also at Denver. Then I shall go right on to Chicago and I want you to try and meet me there.

Those fellows are having a hard fight in West Virginia, but to some extent it is somewhat their own fault. Have not had a line from Lord since I left Washington, altho I've written to him three different times.

Things are not just as bright here as I would like to see them, John. But I hope the future will clear things up. You know they are up against it with those oil pirates and the gov't is doing all it can to render assistance to the workers. But they are up against a powerful machine.

I am going to close and I hope to see you in Chicago on my way

East. Love to Esther and Mrs. Walker, and save for yourself a large portion. Remember me to the brickmaker.

With devotion to you and the cause we are both engaged in,

Sincerely,
Mother Jones

TLS (John H. Walker Papers)

From John H. Walker

July 20, 1921.

Mother Jones,
c/o Fred Mooney,
Charleston, West. Va.
Dear Mother:

I am enclosing a lot of correspondence which explains itself. Mallen wants an endorsement from me to lecture about Mexico. As I guess you know I would be glad to do anything I could to help Mexico, and I would dislike very much to do anything that might injure them, and as you are in touch with the situation, I would like very much to know whether or not it will be in the best interest of the Mexican Government for me to give Rafeal Mallen a letter of endorsement.

Would like to hear from you as early as possible on this matter.

Yours,
[John H. Walker]

TLC (John H. Walker Papers)

To Ephraim F. Morgan[1]

Washington, D. C.
Aug 29 1921

Governor Morgan
Charleston WVA

Can [*Torn* I?] be of any assistance in restoring order[2]   Answer 502 Quincy Street NW Washington D C

Mother Jones

Telegram (Ephraim F. Morgan Papers)
1. Ephraim Franklin Morgan (1869–1950), Republican governor of West Virginia, 1921–1924, later served as a solicitor in the Department of Commerce, 1927–1933.
2. Widespread violence in the southern West Virginia coalfields did not end until federal troops were sent in.

1921

From Ephraim F. Morgan

August 29, 1921.

Mother Jones,
502 Quincy Street N. W.
Washington, D. C.

Situation still tense   May have to call on you   Certainly appreciate your offer of assistance.

Morgan

Telegram (Ephraim F. Morgan Papers)

To John Fitzpatrick

Charleston, W. Va.
September the tenth
1921

Mr. John Fitzpatrick,
Pres. Chicago Federation of Labor,
166 West Madison St.,
Chicago, Ill.

My dear Mr. Fitzpatrick:

I am writing you a few lines. Would you have the kindness to send me Clarench Darrow's address? We have some hot times over here and it looks as though you are going to have some hot ones in Chicago too. I was in Pennsylvania for Labor Day with the miners of District Two. They have some very fine officers and are doing well making progress. I don't write to Ed because he is never in the office or in Chicago anymore and I have entirely lost connection with him. I am inclosing a copy of a document to you which will give you some inside information as to the brutality as to the high class burglars in this part of the country. I hope it will be of some service to you.

With best wishes to all, I am

Yours for the Cause,
Mother Jones

TLS (John Fitzpatrick Papers)

To Terence V. Powderly

626 Fayett Av
Springfield, Illinois,
November 23, 1921.

Hon. T. V. Powderly,
502 Quincy St., N. W.
Washington, D. C.
My dear Mr. Powderly:

I have been slow in writing you, but I have got a severe attack of rheumatism and I am laid up here in Springfield, Illinois. I want to go to St. Louis to a specialist there. I have been informed that he is an expert at this disease and I will go and get some treatment from him as soon as I am able to. I am suffering severely, and unable to do anything outside of moaning about my troubles.

I had a letter from Father O'Donaghue.[1] He has a remedy he says to cure the trouble that we are going through now. I am very much afraid that it is more enthusiasm than any scientific medecine he has got. You can't remedy those troubles that exist until you destroy the system. The ulcer must be first removed, and as the moneyed power rule Washington and the government, we are going to have some job to remove the ulcer. It is going to take people of fare more experience than Father Donaghue.

This affair in Kansas is a very ugly thing.[2] I am going to send you one of the papers from there so that you will be able to see whats going on. They have suspended the whole organization and they have put Howat in jail and his vice-president.

Well it is a pretty hard problem to solve when your own national officers stand behind the enemy and put you behind the iron bars, it is not very encouraging for men or women either to fight the battle of labor. Makes no difference if Howat made the mistake. He was fighting the enemy of labor. He was fighting the most damnable infamous law, the Kansas strike law, that a capitalist governor had pulled over, and the conditions of that jail I am informed is terrible, and when any set of men even though Howat made a mistake, even though he is wrong, stand in line with the capitalist to crucify labor there is something rotten in the background.

It does not give very much encouragement for men to go forward when your own class stands with the common enemy and puts you behind the bar and tears you away from your family.

I received my things alright and thank Daisy very much for her kindness. I am in a terrible condition and hope to get alright soon. I hope Kerwin, Mrs. Powderly and all are well. Tell them I am coming home when the spring comes.

John Walker is down in Kansas fighting the battle of the miners. He sends you his best wishes and hopes the next time he goes to Washington to see you.

Give my love to all at home and tell Margaret I am suffering for that tonic that is in the cellar. I don't know whether I will send a special messenger after it or not, but then it will be well developed when I get back. and under no circumstances give anybody one single drop of it until I do get back. With a happy thanksgiving to everyone, Mrs. Myers and Mrs. Barret and the whole family, and tell Kerwin that I send him my best wishes. If you see Lord tell him you had a letter from me and that I send him my regards. I am, sincerely yours, in the battle for freedom.

Mother Jones

TLS (Terence V. Powderly Papers)
1. Probably Denis O'Donaghue (1848–1925), rector of St. Patrick's, Indianapolis, chancellor and later auxiliary bishop of the diocese of Vincennes; from 1910 to 1924 he was bishop of Louisville.
2. Events in Kansas confirmed the supremacy of John L. Lewis in the UMWA. Alexander Howat, his rival in the 1920 election, defied a court ruling to order men on strike back to work; Howat was sentenced to a year in jail and appealed. Meanwhile, the executive board of the UMWA, after investigation, ordered Howat to send the men back to work and he refused. The supreme court of Kansas confirmed the lower court's ruling, and a convention of the UMWA upheld the order of the executive board. Howat went back to Columbus, Kansas, to begin serving his jail sentence, and Lewis seized the opportunity to annul the charter of District 14 and install his own officers. Continued resistance brought expulsion for all dissident locals and UMWA members, including Howat.

To William Green

626 Fayette Av.,
Springfield, Ill.,
12/ 27, 1921.

Mr. William Greene, Sec-Treas.,
United Mine Workers of America,
Indianapolis, Indiana.
My dear friend Mr. Greene:
I received your letter but I was too sick to answer it. It is not alone the physical sickness that is breaking me down, but it is the thoughts of the internal trouble among ourselves within our own ranks. I dread the future of the organization, from what I see now. It looks so dark to me. There is nothing but throwing daggers at each other. I wish to God that thing could be stopped. It makes me tremble at the thoughts

of men fighting each other when a great principle is at stake. This is the time we should have harmony and we should stand shoulder to shoulder and go in a room and fight out our personalities.

It seems to me that those people have very little thought of the men lying in their graves who paved the way for them, who have good offices, good salaries and every other comfort they need, while they gave up their lives, and their bones lie bleaching along the highways of the industrial fields of America. I look at the men of Stanaford mountain. I look at the heroic battle they fought, I look at their brave wives and little children standing together with them, hoping for a better day. I am heartsick and weary of the world that seems to have no human outside of their own interest

West Virginia bid fair to me in the days to come, to be one of the best states in the Union. It never has had good officers to my knowledge. In the 21 years it has never had the men who understood the peculiarity of the state and the makeup of her people.

Unfortunately you know as well as I do, today it is a pie counter age. Every fellow is looking for the pie counter but he has no thought whether he has the ability to digest the pie that the poor devils fought for, after he gets it. If the right man had been placed in charge of Mingo at the beginning of that strike, it could have been settled, and the hatred that has developed would not show its hand as bitter as it has today.

They had no knowledge of handling the strike. They had no knowledge of what the other side of the house would do. They had no knowledge of the way he plays the game and you could not tell them anything or try to teach them anything, because immediately they thought you were dictating to their brains. They were men of cheap brains without any power of analysis. If a man like Fowler had been put in charge of that field in the beginning that strike would have been ended a year ago. I know all those people in there. I know how they play the game. These fellows had no grasp of it—they were not students. As Thomas Moore said "far dearer the grave of the prisoner illumined by one patriotic name, than the trophies of all who has risen on liberties ruins to fame.

I am far from being well. I am not as nervous as I was some weeks ago, but the rheumatism still tortures the life out of me, but perhaps it may ease up soon.

I want to extend to you, my deep and greatful appreciation of your beautiful Christmas gift. There are few men in your position that give me any thought. But all I can say is this—that from the first day I met you until this very hour, I have clung close to you believing always that I was dealing with a man of honor and principle, and that no matter what came or went, that high sense of honor still remains. My deep interest in the cause has made enemies for me,—those who did not understand me, but the destinies of these miners are more to me than all the tributes and all the money in the treasury of the miners or any other organization. I love those souls that lie moulding in their graves. I know what they have suffered and sacrificed for their men's future welfare. And to see how little it is appreciated by this generation is a sad indictment.

I wish I could see you and talk things over with you. Let me say a word to you. You tell the editor of the Miners' Journal to stop that low business of throwing daggers out. Our Journal must soar high above those small methods of assassination. Big men don't do those things. Men who love the organization don't stoop to that method of assassination. That is an educational Journal, not an assassinating instrument. Those things bring no harmony,—they don't drain the ulser, they only irritate it. And to me it indicates a very small mind. With no broad vision of the great economic conflict that we are going through. The destinies of thousands of men women and children are of far more interest to me than all the office holders within its ranks. You get him to cut that trash out, for when the world reads it the other side immediately conclude that we are nothing but a combination of assassinating office holders. There is a certain dignity that our Journal must attain regardless of who is hurt or who is not.

Well I am a little tired this morning and I won't tire you. Accept my deep devotion to your noble manhood.

I have had so much to tell you that I never had the time in the office, because you were always too busy.

With deep friendship and best wishes for your future welfare, I am,

Sincerely yours,
Mother Jones

[*Holograph note*] Many happy & Peaceful returns of the coming year

TLS (William Green Papers)

To Ephraim F. Morgan

626 Fayette Av.,
Springfield, Illinois,
December 27, 1921.

To the Honorable E. F. Morgan,
Governor of the State of West Virginia,
Charleston, West Virginia.
My dear Governor:

The clipping you sent me from the New York Times I deeply appreciated. It was the work of a humane thoughtful mind. I certainly have to express my deep appreciation to Mr. Tumilty, Secretary to President Wilson. He was the most courteous, kindly man I ever met in that position, and I have met most every President from Cleveland down. Some one asked Mr. Tumilty one day, what brought me so often to the White House, and he replied, "the doors are always open—she never comes for herself, it is always for some poor suffering person or the safety of the nation". But like yourself, those type of men are very scarce at this time.

It would be far more to the nation's advancement, if such broad minds were in the majority in public life. I have not been well Governor ever since I left. That shock was so sever that I had a nervoud breakdown from it and a severe attack of rheumatism, and I have been here under the care of a specialist physician for the last four weeks. I am improving a little but not as rapidly as I would like to.

I hope things are a little more peaceful than they were. I don't get any direct information from the field. Occasionally I read a little article in the evening paper here, but you know the papers are very unreliable in giving the truthful information to the public.

There is such an upheaval all over the world and in fact all over our own country too, that every loyal citizen should do their part to inaugurate a reign of peace instead of brutal war. I regret war more than I have words to utter,—the terrific mistake that was made in West Virginia,—there was some evil hand behind it, and those young fellows, void of any experience in the great industrial conflicts, were carried away thinking they could change the world over night. They will not be able to change it with guns and bullets. It has got to be done through practical, fundamental, patriotic education. The incomes of certain individuals have got to be curtailed and limited. In fact in my estimation the money they made during the war, they should be made to turn it all into the treasury of the U. S., and give them ten percent of their investment. The nation and her future destiny are of far more importance to me than the dollars of certain men or certain parts of society.

Well I hope to hear of you having a successful administration of peace and prosperity through the state. Any effort of mine governor that you can use, don't hesitate to call for that end. Those poor unfortunate boys had no bad intentions—they were simply carried away with excitement, and I hope the poor fellows who were misled, that the court will be merciful and lienent to them. I think of their wives and little children every time I wake up in the night. I think of the battles that were fought in the past and won. I think of the little children as they cry for bread, that money that was spent uselessly should have been used for their nourishment now.

I wish the Department of Labor would take up that matter in the

Mingo field and see if it could not be straightened out. My best wishes to Mrs. Morgan,—say to her I send her a New Years greeting and hope there will be peace and happiness in and around her home.

With best wishes to Mr. Sullivan[1]—he is a clean upright man and the right person in the right place at this time

With best wishes for a happy New Year and God alone knows I hope it will be far more peaceful to you than the past,

I am most sincerely, with best wishes,

> Yours in the great struggle.
> Mother Jones

TLS (Ephraim F. Morgan Papers)
1. Jesse V. Sullivan served as Governor Morgan's private secretary; he later became secretary of the West Virginia Coal Operators Association.

To [John H. Walker?]

[1921]

that W. V. thrown out of court They had 3 or 4 concilliators down there Gover Hatfield[1] that fellow that kept us all in the B Pen in 1913. Ill get on to the thing latter on   At the last trial those fellows tried to bribe the foreman of the jury. The fellow who offered the bribe is in jail They tried to get the Gov[2] to have me supenaed as a witness the Gov replied No then they would tell the world she was a Judas. She did her part   had he left that woman alone there have been no trouble   Now they want to send her grave milnged & vilified to save themselves   They have already done all they could to her

My hand trembles when I write   I am nervous   I have a lot to tell you   If I could see   I will you a checgh for the amount   Keep what you have for me   Say nothing to no one. O God if I could only see you   you & Nockels are the two I rely on   I am going to close I have so much to tell you

> Loyally,
> Mother

ALS fragment (John H. Walker Papers)
1. Henry Drury Hatfield (1875–1962), governor of West Virginia, 1913–1917.
2. Ephraim F. Morgan.

To William Green

626 Fayette Av.,
Springfield, Ill.
March 4, 1922.

Mr. William Green, National Sec.,
United Mine Workers,
Indianapolis, Ind.
My dear friend:

For such you have always been to me. I am writing you these few lines before I leave Springfield. I leave tomorrow for Chicago, and from there I shall go to Washington. I hope some day that I will see you in Washington and have some time to talk things over with you.

I am astonished at the way Phil Murray used that gavel on that table that day. It seems to me he is not a reader of men. Did not he know under the present pressure that the more he hit that table with that gavel the more they rebelled against him. It was a crucial hour. He, nor others will never know what it was perhaps.

I wanted to see you before I left Indianapolis but I could not. You have got to get after the high up officials and tell them to put their personality and prejudices and dictatorship aside. This organization was not built on roses. It was built on the agony and suffering of men and whose bleaching bones they are living on today. The men who paved the way for this organization had no salaries—they had no offices—they faced rage and snow storms—they faced blizzards at night to carry the message of hope to their fellow beings. Oh, what a sad indictment against our present officials. If they don't give those men who are molding in their graves some appreciation of what they did.

They faced hunger, and I know what they went through because I am one of those who helped to build this organization. Not in offices nor not in hotels, we marched many weary nights, and spent all our Sundays perhaps in the woods or in a section house talking over the future of the little children to come.

It is a sad indictment against our officials that they will permit their personality to go ahead of the destenies of a great organization. In the long years of the past, I drew no salary. The miners fed me, and I have seen this organization grow from its infancy to its manhood and it grieves me more than I have words to express, to see its very foundation undermined today. I do not like the methods that were persued in that convention and no organization can stand the test that will endorse it or stand for it. We must be able to go before the public with clean hands. There is too much rotten politics has entered into the organization. It will not be wrecked, but there will have to be a house cleaning. I attended that meeting on Sunday in the machinists hall in Indianapolis. I took note and I felt we have got to handle the future with care.

I am not feeling any too well, but from different parts they are calling on me to come to them and I see Colorado is gone Utah is gone, New Mexico is gone, Alabama is gone, part of Tennessee is gone and I am afraid it is going to be long years of strenuous work to build up your organization in West Va. West Va. has not had the men who understood the background of this great upheavel that is going on in the industrial world. There is too much pie-counter hunting today, and not enough of sincere honest work done for a cause. If they could digest the pie that the poor devils paid for it would be somewhat encouraging but they digest it in their own interest but not in the interest of the rank and file.

There is no organization in the world has more sincere honest men within its walls than the miners have, but it is an unfortunate statement for me to make, they are betrayed by the very men they pay. It makes no difference to me how you cut my throat whether you have an intention of doing it or unintentionally, it is done just the same.

I am sick at heart, I am broken down, but I shall always look to you as one whose heart beats in sympathy with the poor wretch below. I know your position,—I know your surroundings there—I know you cannot do all that your heart beats and throbs to do, but anyhow keep up the battle, you can always rest assure that as long as breath remains, this heart of mine will beat in gratitude for your kindness to me. You were one great soul that I could always look to. Let us keep up courage and the future probably will be ours. I am

Most sincerely and devotedly, yours,
Mother Jones

TLS (William Green Papers)

To Ephraim F. Morgan

March 4th, 1922.

Governor Morgan,
Charleston, West Va.
My dear Governor:

I have been wanting to write you for sometime, but owing to the condition of my health, and other conditions also in the industrial field, I have not been able to settle down long enough to communicate with you.

I notice that they have not let up on you yet. I will be in Charleston in side of a week. I hope to have the honor of meeting with you and Mrs. Morgan and that dear sweet Boy Albert.

I have much to talk to you about, and hoping that your courage keeps up and that you are not at all affected by the dagger of enemies, I am,

> Most sincerely and respectfully yours,
> Mother Jones

TLS (Ephraim F. Morgan Papers)

From William Green

March 8, 1922.

Mother Jones,
Springfield, Illinois.
My dear Mother:

I received your letter of March 4th today and note thereby that you are going to Chicago and from there to Washington. May I suggest that you conserve your energy and take good care of yourself because you can be so easily overcome by travelling too much and by undertaking to do too much work.

I am sure you appreciate how deeply concerned I am over the present situation within the organization. It is most deplorable and fills one with feelings of apprehension. We ought to be solidly united instead of divided by internal dissension. I am doing my very best to harmonize the situation and will continue my efforts. You can rest assured I will do everything that lies within my power to bring about solidarity, understanding and cooperation. It is not an easy task to do this when men become embittered through hate and enmity. When such a condition is reached personal interest becomes paramount to the common good.

I will endeavor to see you when in Washington if I have an opportunity to be there while you are in Washington. I know how you feel about the condition of the organization, especially when you observe that in fields where you worked and sacrificed there is a lack of proper appreciation and understanding of the principles of the organization and economic problems. Be assured, however, that the work you have done will live. Nothing can destroy it and even though we must suffer temporary set-backs, due to our own inherent weakness, the time will come when we will learn and understand better how to control and govern ourselves. Take good care of yourself. Let me hear from you at your convenience. Be assured that I will never betray any confidence which you may wish to place in me.

With every good wish, I am,

Sincerely yours,
[William Green]
Secretary-Treasurer.

TLC (William Green Papers)

From John H. Walker

March 18, 1922.

Mother Jones,
c/o T. V. Powderly,
502 Quincy St. N. W., Washington, D. C.
Dear Mother:

I sent your two grips this morning. One of them by parcel post and the other by express. The one I sent by express was the suit case which you had locked before you left here. The man in charge of the parcel post told me that on account of your locking it with a key if it went parcel post, it would have to go at the rate of first class mail—two cents an ounce. It weighed a little better than 35 pounds, and at the rate of 32 cents a pound that would amount to $11.20, and so I sent it by express. I hope that you get both of them alright.

Everything is just the same as when you left here. Give my regards to T. V. Powderly.

Yours,
[John H. Walker]

TLC (John H. Walker Papers)

To John H. Walker

502 Quincy Street N W
Washington, D. C.,
March 20, 1922.

Mr. John H. Walker,
626 Fayette Street,
Springfield, Ill.
Dear John:

I have been trying to get a chance to write to you for the last week, but I have been unable to do so. I have not been well since coming here. I expect to go to West Virginia soon. May be this week or the fore part of next week. I did not go from Chicago as I did not feel that I could do the work I wanted to do successfully. I think I will be able to make good next week.

I called the attention of a party in the office to cut the slime out of the Journal.[1] The Journal was not established for any such tactics and if he did not do it, I would make a move so that he would have to do it. The Journal was not meant for his use to send out poison ivy. I told James if he did not stop it, I would.

Things do not look very good to me. I think the anthracite will come out all right but the bituminous fields look rather week.

Give my love to Mrs. Walker and tell her how much I appreciate her kindness to me. Tell her I will write to her soon. When you write to Esther give her my love.

I have not yet received my trunks and you know all my clothes are in them. I hope you insured them.

I was out to Lord's house yesterday.

Give my regards to Farrington. When you write to Howat tell him I am going to write to him soon.

With best and warmest wishes, I am,

Yours to the end,
Mother Jones

TLS (John H. Walker Papers)
1. The UMWA *Journal* had contained a number of personal attacks on Walker.

From John H. Walker

March 23, 1922.

Mother Jones,
502 Quincy St., N. W.,
Washington, D. C.
Dear Mother:

Just got your letter of the 20th and glad to hear from you, although sorry to learn that you were not as well as you might have been. You are going to have to take exceedingly good care of yourself, Mother, if you are to avoid illness.

I appreciate very much your effort to get the JOURNAL straightened out, although I have become reconciled to it now, and it don't bother me any personally,—and in the long run I think it will do more good than harm. At the same time, for the sake of the Miners Organization, our official JOURNAL should not be used in that way. However, as long as we have vermin and rats acting as editor, we are going to have filth for their surroundings—that is their nature.

I wrote you about the trunks. I expect you will have them by this time.

I hope the anthracite field does come out alright   I am fearful of the whole situation however.

Just received a card from Howat this morning. He is in Eastern Ohio at that convention and addressing meetings in that territory. He said that the officers are very sore and that the miners are all very enthusiastic and strong for the Kansas miners.

All the folks are well and send their love.

With sincere regards and best wishes I am,

Yours truly,
[John H. Walker]

TLC (John H. Walker Papers)

To John H. Walker

Washington, D. C.,
March 29, 1922

Mr. John H. Walker,
626 Fayette Street,
Sringfield, Illinois.
Dear John:

I received your letter of the 23rd. I was more than glad to get it. You know the old-timers have a feeling for each other that no one but the old-timers can understand. Terrence V. Powderly and I spent last night going over the terrific struggles we have left behind us but they don't compare with the struggle ahead of us, and he said, Mother, you and I have walked over the stormy days of the past and there is no one in the labor movement that understands its struggle more clearly than we do. For forty odd years, he says, I have known you and you have been up against the guns all the time. Its a sad indictment against us, John, that at this crucial hour we must be fighting each other and fighting corruption in our own ranks and the enemies' guns turned on us, but notwithstanding I think we will all come out ahead yet, right and justice must prevail.

I have had some letters from the poor fellows in Colorado, begging me to come to see them, and I had a letter from West Virginia telling me that things looked dark. Use your influence to keep Illinois within the organized labor; under no circumstances let them pull away; if we are divided we are ruined. Keep up your spirits, we will yet come out victorious. I have just seen Wallace and he sends his love to you, and I send mine to Mrs. Walker, and tell her that I shall always appreciate her kindness to me; I think she saved my life. I got the trunks all right but you have not learned to be a good burglar, you could have pulled down that little clasp and then it would fly open; I never had a key, and I thought surely you were on to the game, but the other fellow can burglarize you, and hold you up, but you don't get even with him. However, I am going to send this letter and in a week or so I am going to write you a longer letter, for I have a good deal to talk to you about.

With my love to Esther, Mrs. Walker and yourself, I am,

Always yours,
[Mother Jones]

The thing is so rotten I fear there is no [*one word illegible.*]

TLS with holograph note (John H. Walker Papers)

From John H. Walker

April 6, 1922.

Mother Jones,
c/o 502 Quincy St. N. W.,
Washington, D. C.
Dear Mother:

This is to acknowledge receipt of your letter of the 29th. Glad to hear from you and to know that you received the trunks alright. Mrs. Walker told me about that grip not being locked after it was sent, but it was too late.

Glad to get the good word from Wallace.[1] You need not be afraid of Illinois Mother. Illinois will not pull out of the labor movement, except to save itself from destruction, and I don't think that it is going to have to make that choice.

Give Powderly and Wallace and other friends my best wishes. Hope that this finds you well and that you are really trying to take a little care of yourself.

Sincerely yours,
[John H. Walker]
President.

TLC (John H. Walker Papers)
1. Possibly Edgar Wallace, who five years earlier had been one of the editors of the UMWA *Journal*.

To John H. Walker

Washington, D. C.
Apr. 22–1922.

Dear John

Just came back from W Va   The Poison that has been sown there against you Howat you and Farrington beat anything—There is going to be some terrable squeelling at the trial begins next Monday   I cannot write all I uncovered   The main question that I went down for I did not get quite at [*three words illegible*]   get a promise it would be dug up   Am weak not strong but better [than when] I left Springfield   perhaps my strength will come back some time   My God the corruptness in that state beats all I have ever seen   I am tired can't write much

Tell Mrs. Walker I will write her soon   I will remember kindness in my grave.

Most Sincerely Yours
Mother

ALS (John H. Walker Papers)

From John H. Walker

April 27, 1922.

Mother Jones,
502 Quincy St., N. W.,
Washington, D. C.
Dear Mother:

This is to acknowledge receipt of yours of the 22nd; also got the one with the clippings from West Virginia. Will convey the information to that party.

It looks black Mother, from every angle, but I guess it has got to be blacker before the membership will realize what the situation really is. I hope they wake up before it is too late.

Everybody is well at home and send you their love.

Yours,
[John H. Walker]

TLC (John H. Walker Papers)

To John H. Walker

502 Mercantile Bld
Denver, Colo.,
June 26, 1922.

Mr. John H. Walker,
626 Fayette Street,
Springfield, Illinois.
Dear John:

I have been wanting to write you ever since I came out here but I haven't been able to do anything. I have a little quiet home to stay at with Mrs. Langdon's[1] daughter but I don't seem to regain any of my old time strength. I am just as weak now as I was some time ago although they are doing everything they can for me out here. The boys are just as good as they can be. Moyer and Mills and the officers of the State Federation still I don't get back one particle of my old time strength.

That terrible blow that those idiotice brained gave me in West Virginia the work and sacrifice of years was wiped out almost over night. The mines are all working nearly on a non union basis and open shop. There was no check off they have spent all the money that they could lay their fingers on.

The acquitted that fellow Blizzard[2] but there was no jury that could convict him because he didn't know what they meant by treason. If you asked him he would tell you it was some town or county in the United States some where.

But there will be some convictions over there. I see they have already convicted the Minister and his son is going on trial now.[3] It seems a very queer thing John to me that poor Howat and Dorchy[4] and the Executive Board should be sent to jail for fighting the most infamouse law that could be placed on the statute books against labor.

And yet those officials that forced the men to break the contract at the point of guns there was not one word of reproach against them.

I cant understand the background of that. I wish you would find out for me whather Howat is in Columbus jail or in Gerard. The miners of Herrin deserve the support of every man woman and child in the United States they did the job and did it right.[5] They didn't spend hundreds of thousands of dollars I wish we had more men such as they have in Herrin.

I have a clipping that I must send you that I took out of the papers here. Wilkinson[6] had to jump into the press and accuse the officials of Illinois, hold them responsible for that move.

Tell Mrs. Walker I am not an ingrate even if I have not written to her I have the most deep appreciation for her kindness to me and always will. I suppose Esther is home from school and enjoying her Mother's Company.

She is a very beautiful girl and I know will be a wonderful comfort to you and her Mother in the years to come.

John keep your head level watch every one you talk to. You know the world is most treacherous today than it has been in all history.

I see the gang is getting after Foster.[7] Foster is a student and a very deep one. He realizes that the make up of the labor movement has got to changes its methods or else it will be driven to the wall.

You can see that the capitalists are amalgamating all their forces against us and we don't seem to keep pace with the great changes that are taking place.

Write to me as soon as you get back. Give my real love to them all at home.

I am picking up notes to write my book and I want you to help me a little. I can't let that thing go. I wish you could get MacDonald[8] over into the forces with you he is a food boy but that paper of his doesn't amount to a row of pins.

Give my love to them all at home and tell Mrs. Walker I am going to write to her some day.

I remain yours, John as in days of old a sincere friend,

Mother Jones

TLS (John H. Walker Papers)

1. Emma Langdon (1875–1937), author of *The Cripple Creek Strike,* was active in Colorado labor and Socialist circles.

2. William Blizzard (1894–1958), president of Subdistrict 4, District 17, UMWA, was acquitted on a charge of treason, 27 May 1922, at a trial in Charles Town, West Virginia.

3. The Reverend J. M. Wilburn and John Wilburn were convicted of murder in the trials in Charles Town, West Virginia, in the spring and summer of 1922.

4. August Dorchy, vice-president of District 14, UMWA, had been convicted along with Alexander Howat in the Kansas strike cases the preceding year.

5. Herrin, Illinois, was the scene of extensive mob violence, 21 June 1922, when miners in retaliation for the shooting of two of their number fired on armed guards and strikebreakers, killing twenty men and wounding many others.

6. John Wilkinson, president of District 21, UMWA, for six years, resigned 10 November 1922 to go into the mine insurance business.

7. Probably William Z. Foster.

8. Probably Duncan McDonald, whose career as a labor leader in Illinois was declining.

From John H. Walker

Mother Jones,
502 Mercantile Bldg.,
Denver, Colorado.
Dear Mother:

This is to acknowledge receipt of your letter of the 26th which I just received this morning. Glad to hear from you altho very sorry to learn you are not getting your strength back. Was glad to know that you were stopping with Mrs. Langdon. She is a fine woman. One of the real kind of which there are so few in this world. I know that she will do everything she can for you.

Yes, it is too bad the way things are in West Va. I saw Tom Tippet Monday and he told me that he had just gotten back from West Va., and that he had been in every district in it and practically all of the mines were working there every day on a non-union basis; that the situation there was hopeless.

It has not alone been blunders—it has been much worse than blunders. It is no blunder what they are doing to Howat and Dorchy and the Executive Board of District 14. I think it was planned deliberately, with knowledge of what it meant. I think too that they are being paid for it by the coal operators of that territory.

Those coal operators paid one man by the name of Hazen, thirty thousand dollars according to the confession of their president under oath in court to destroy Howat. They hate him even worse now than they did then, and the thing that has been done to him is so raw, that I know no man with any intelligence would do it, that ~~are~~ [*holograph correction* was][1] honest and that dishonest ones would not do it unless they were paid, and of course those kind of men would not say anything to others, or about others who violated the contract, violated the law, or did anything else if they were friends personally of theirs for the time being,—that is the situation as I see it.

Very sorry for what happened in Herrin. Two of our men, defenseless and unarmed, were killed. That provoked the rest to do what they did.

We had labor's proposal adopted in the constitutional convention on Tuesday morning before the news of that situation was carried in the newspapers. A proposal which would have safeguarded us largely from injunctions in the future, and would have given us the absolute constitutional guarantee of peaceful picketing. In the afternoon when those papers came out, the enemies of labor were able to defeat that section and now I am afraid, that they are going to be able to use that occurrence to pass the State Police or Constabulary bill, here.

Wilkinson is at the very best, a swine. I think however, that it is much worse than that.

I am trying to protect myself but you have got to take some chances.

Esther is home from school and she told me that she is going to make her own living from now on. She put in her application here in Springfield to teach school and has been given a job, starting in about two months.

I think Foster is honest and I think his purposes are good, but I believe that the methods he has adopted, instead of helping, are hurting.

As to the other (Mac) I have, all my life, tried to help him, and have helped him when he needed it sorely, at times altho I did not want to tell him about it, and on some occasions he has made a splendid fight in the right way, but he seems to have an unfortunate disposition, and besides, he has no faith in me—to the contrary—I think he has hatred for me, I believe growing out of disappointed ambitions.

I know some things that have been said that could not be said by any decent fellow, and while I shall not go out of my way to injure him at all, I would rather help him than to hurt him, at the same time I could not give him my confidence Mother, and feel that I could not depend upon him, and to work with him in all the vicissitudes that surround men and women who are giving their whole heart in this work.

The paper he is editing is pretty much a whining snarling dog-in-the-manger assassination of people that he don't like personally. That is about all it amounts to.

Esther and her mother are in Danville this week, will give them your letter when they get back. I know they would be glad to hear from you.

Give my best regards to Mrs. Langdon.

With all the good wishes in the world, I am,

Yours sincerely,
[John H. Walker]

TLC (John H. Walker Papers)
1. Three similar holograph corrections are made in the later text without notice.

To John H. Walker

Washington, D. C.
July 27, 1922.

Mr. John H. Walker,
626 Fayette Street,
Springfield, Ill.
Dear John:

I have a letter from those boys in the southern part of Illinois asking me to go down for Labor Day. I picked up the wrong letter this morning and as I do not remember the address, I ask you to convey to them my appreciation for the invitation and say that if my health permits, I will be glad to comply with their request, but as I feel at present, I could not promise them to be there. It would be only spending the money for nothing and increasing the wealth of the railroads.

Well, John, things do not look very encouraging as I read the papers. Lord left last night for the West. Maybe it was best. He could not do anything here and the Western Federation of Miners are practically out of business, John. As things look to me they will not get better in a hurry. They have not got the officers that will put life into them.

I hope to see you soon and that something will bring you to Washington. After I left you in Chicago, I went to Charleston. There are many things I want to talk to you about. That Blizzard has four more indictments against him, and I am a little afraid of the future trials. I got next to many things when I was there. I also saw this morning in the Washington papers that Wilkinson of District 21 ordered all the pumpmen and the orders that keep things in condition have been ordered out. If that is true he has made a blunder because the government can sue them for wilfull destroying property. That is something that should be looked after before it is acted on. In my opion it would be wiser if they had made agreements with the mine owners that were willing to meet them and then the others would soon follow. However, I hope it will all come out right in the end.

Give my best wishes to all at home. Things look anything but bright in West Virginia.

With love and devotion to the cause, I am,

Sincerely yours,
Mother

TLC (John H. Walker Papers)

From John H. Walker

August 1st, 1922.

Mother Jones,
502 Quincy St., N. W.,
Washington, D. C.
Dear Mother:

This is to acknowledge receipt of yours of the 27th. Glad to hear from you. Will let the boys know at Sandoval as requested. I was sorry to learn that Lord had to go. It may be for the best, but with all of his faults, Jim was square, could always be depended upon, stood for the thing that was right all the time, and did the best he could. There are so few of those kind of men in the world now that I don't like to see any of them being hurt. At the same time they have made it impossible for him to stay. I suppose they will protest at the end of the three months against his being continued in the A. F. of L. I hope by that time, he will have gotten something that will enable him to make a living for himself and family.

The whole thing is being made a mess of and unless they are able through some intrigue to work something out of it, I doubt that anything eill come out of it but disaster, although the men are standing firm, making a heroic fight and they deserve better things.

I am being kept exceedingly busy at the present time.

With sincere regards I am,

Yours truly,
[John H. Walker]

TLC (John H. Walker Papers)

From John H. Walker

August 8th, 1922.

Mother Jones,
c/o 502 Quincy St., N. W.,
Washington, D. C.
Dear Mother:

I am enclosing letter with enclosure, also copy of my reply all of which explain themselves. They are a bunch of good boys down in that place and I know if you can be with them a day or so they would appreciate it very much. However, if you feel that you cannot go, when the time comes, if you will send them a telegram advising them to that effect, then they can read it and the people will know that you would have been there if you could.

Everything seems to be up in the air at the present time. We are hoping for the best.

Sincerely,
[John H. Walker]

TLC (John H. Walker Papers)

From Katherine [Schmidt?]

San Francisco Calif
Sept 4 1922

Mother Jones
520 Quincy St. Northwest
Washington D C
Dearest Mother
  No word from you am anxious to know how you are   Do you want
me to come to you   Have some one wire me P O Box 95   I will
arrange somehow if you want me   Boys join in sending oceans of
love   Everybody well

Katherine

Telegram (Mother Jones Papers)

From Federated Shopcrafts and Brotherhoods of Texas

Houston Tex
Sept 6 1922

Mother Jones
Care Labor Department 17th and G Sts
Washington D C
  Our hearts throb in love and sympathy for you   May Gods peace be
with you restore your strength and keep you our true councilor friend
defender

Federated Shopcrafts and Brotherhoods of Texas

Telegram (Mother Jones Papers)

From Ephraim F. Morgan

State of West Virginia
Executive Department
Charleston
Sept. 6, [1922]

Dear Mother Jones:
  I notice in today's paper that you have been seriously ill for some

time at the home of Mr. Powderly. This is to express my deep interest in your condition and hope for your early restoration to health.

Very sincerely,
E. F. Morgan

ALS (Terence V. Powderly Papers)

From Dan W. Stevens

Minneapolis Minn
Sept 7 1922

Mother Jones
Cr of Terrence Powerly
Washington D C

The Minneapolis Trades and Labor Assembly expresses its deepest sympathy for you in your illness and hopes for your speedy recovery Your service to the labor movement is most highly esteemed and appreciated and we hope that we may soon have the pleasure of your visiting Minneapolis

The Mpls Trades and Labor Assembly
By Dan W. Stevens Secy

Telegram (Mother Jones Papers)

To William Green

Washington D C
Oct 2n 1922

My Dear Mr Green

This the first line I wrote in three months. Since I Saw yo I have been at Deaths Door. If I had not been with such loyal friends I would be sleeping in the Clay long before this I long to see you but my wishes are blasted I have so much you know that I cannot trust anyone else with

I had to send this bill for I knead the money

I have so much to say but my hand Trembles

Overlook this letter   When I get strong will write

With deep friendship I have to close

Mother

ALS (William Green Papers)

To John H. Walker

Washington D C
Oct. —4—22

Dear John

I was dreaming of you last night I hope there is nothing wrong. I have not heard from you for such a long time it seems as if you have forgotten me. I am slowly getting back on feet. It is so slow John owing to the severe attack I had   I am fortunate to get along as well as I have

If I had not been lucky enough to be with the old time friends I would be sleeping in the clay today. They left nothing undone they had 3 Proffessional nurses   The best D in the City   The left nothing undone to save my life

We have many men like Terence V Powderly   he would morged [mortgage?] the Home if I needed it.

Tell Farrington I more than appreicate the kind the resolution he offered in the Convention

That was more than the other fellow offered in the Convention in Walkersburg Pa   he lay back exausted asked the reporters to let him rest   John there are some storys out in that field about some and miners themselves are to blame   See the way they allow themselves to be swayed in that Convention

Look at the money that is spent for lawyers in West V.

My God John is there no sense of honor in the Miners Organization   Look at the Journal   It has not said a word about those poor boys at [*word omitted*] but they will tell you about Pres Lewis

I am just scraching this   I have to stop   Write me   Love to both loved ones at   I have to stop but I have so much to tell you   Write me   I have been nervous all day for fear you [were] sick or them Dam Vilians were making some attack on you

fondly
Mother

ALS (John H. Walker Papers)

From John H. Walker

October ninth 1922.

Mother Jones,
Washington, D. C.
Dear Mother:

This is to acknowledge receipt of your letter of the 4th. Glad to hear from you and to know that you are on the mend again. I have been keeping as closely in touch with your situation as I could, through Powderly, Nockels and some others, and was a little worried. I was afraid that you could not stand it. And knowing how the situation has taken the heart out of you, I was fearful of what might happen. Glad to see that you came through it and hope that you may be able to gather your strength again and get back your old spirits and be in good health. Will surely be glad to convey your word to Farrington.

They are not making any open attacks on me at the present time Mother, although they have been doing that until recently. They have however organized and are making the most capable campaign they can to defeat me in the coming election, and personally, I have got to the place where I really don't care much. In view of what they have done to Howat and our organization has stood for it and let them get away with it, as well as the kind of things that have been going on in the last three or four years, which were done openly and everybody knows what they meant, I have not got the same feeling in the matter that I used to have. I expect however to continue on doing the best I can until the end, no matter what is done or what happens, but I confess I have not got the same faith and confidence that I used to have, and to know that such a man as Powderly, in his generation, was treated in the same way, and that Martin Irons got the same treatment, and you could go on down the line and name hundreds of others, the finest men that ever drew the breath of life, who did magnificent work in behalf of the workers and the cause of humanity, and then were crucified, deliberately, cruelly and publicly, and the movement itself did nothing for them,—permitted it to be done, it rather tempers a person's enthusiasm. It does weaken their faith. That may be a sign of weakness—I guess it is. The fact that they have gone on through and did the best they could, ought to rather encourage us and inspire us, but there is so much of it and it is so rotten that at least at times I cannot help but be affected by it.

The only reason that gang have not done it to you publicly is because they are afraid of their own political welfare. The whole thing is so rotten, that I would be glad to forget it if I could for a while. However, there is only another thing we can do and that is to keep on doing what we can. We have got to do that to retain our own self respect and we have got to realize that those poor devils, even the worst of them don't know any better,—they never had a chance,—they have been born with crooked dispositions, that has made them do what they are doing, they are really not to blame, and if we are big enough to measure up to the requirements, we will not get embittered,—we will have that much more power, and sympathy for them, we will be that much better pleased that we were able to see the thing clearly and give all we have as long as we are able to, cheerfully, to help them, with the knowledge that in doing it we are really helping the great cause, the most that it is possible for us to.

Of course we have got to use what influences we can to safeguard the movement and to guide it right.

Mother if there is anything you want that it is possible for us to get for you, if you will let me know, I know we will be able to get if for you. Mrs. Walker has had a very bad cold for about three weeks, practically pneumonia. She seems a little better this morning. Esther is well and both inquiring for you. We all send our love.

Yours,
[John H. Walker]

TLC (John H. Walker Papers)

From William Green

October 13, 1922.

Mother Jones,
Washington, D. C.
Dear Mother:

I was touched very deeply when I returned to the office this week and found your favor of October 2d awaiting me. I could tell from the character of your letter and the outstanding evidences therein that you were weak and ill. I am glad, however, that you were able to write me a letter with your own hand.

I truly hope the check I sent you reached you safely and that your health is improving. I feel sure if you will remain where you are with your friends and do not worry ultimately you will be restored to your usual health. I have been thinking of you very much and have told a great many of your friends about your illness. All have expressed very great solicitude over your condition.

I expected to be in Washington ere this but it has been quite impossible for me to do so. I expect I will be there sometime during the month of November. You can rest assured I will call and see you. Take care of yourself, do not worry, rest and build up your strength and health before you attempt to do any work.

With kind personal regards and best wishes, I am,

Sincerely yours,
[William Green]
Secretary-Treasurer.

TLC (William Green Papers)

From Ephraim F. Morgan

October 20, 1922

Mother Jones,
3700 Fifth Street,
Washington, D. C.
Dear Mother:

Thank you very much for your esteemed favor of recent date and assure you that same is appreciated.

It was certainly very thoughtful in you in giving me this information.

I certainly hope that you are on the road to a speedy recovery.

Cordially yours,
[E. F. Morgan]
Governor

TLC (Ephraim F. Morgan Papers)

From John H. Walker

October 22nd, 1922.

Mother Jones,
Washington, D. C.
Dear Mother:

This is to acknowledge receipt of yours of October 15th. You may be sure that I was exceedingly glad to learn that you were recovering, even if it were slowly and I know that you are not anything like your old time self. I hope that you may get back your health and strength again because although you have been badly needed all your life, I think perhaps you will be needed worse in the immediate future than at any time in all your history.

I agree with you that things are rotten. The enclosure is enough to break the heart of any man who knows the sacrifices that were made to establish and build up our organization. I don't know what can be done about it but I expect to try and get definite conclusive proof if that can be done. If it is then to take what steps we can to mend the situation inside of our organization. I expect though that it will be rather difficult because they are shrewd capable gentlemen, they will not overlook very much and they have the resources to take care of anybody that can be handled. They too have the available resources to do almost anything else and they will stop at nothing.

The convention is on. I guess I have been overdoing myself. I could not speak the day before yesterday but I am getting better now, and although it is a rather stormy session there are some stories going ahead. I think, taking it all in all we will be able to accomplish some good for the movement.

With sincere regards and best wishes I remain,

Yours sincerely,
[John H. Walker]

TLC (John H. Walker Papers)

To John H. Walker

Washington, D. C.
[October 1922]

Dear John

I wrote you over three week Sent you enclosed a little information I have not heard a word from you not even wheather you won in the Election I was a little anxious about that letter for there was some important information in it.   it is almost to send anything to those offices   That stenograph is not overly careful I dont get that Ill Miner untill it is three weeks old I see they are after Farrington What will they resort to next They will stoop anything

Just think of putting Seales on the Com. to deal with the coal question with the Pres Coal Commission Kennedy & Jack Moore out of John the thing is so [curious?]

I am not able to do much writing more scribbling half the time I can't remember how to spell Write just as soon as you this Let know if you got my last letter if it got into the hands of those villains they would hang me Love to all at home Will write Mrs Walker soon Write me just as soon as you get this

Most sincerely
Mother

ALS (John H. Walker Papers)

From John H. Walker

November 7, 1922.

Mother Jones,
c/o 502 Quincy St., N. W.,
Washington, D. C.
Dear Mother:

This is to acknowledge receipt of yours of recent date. Got your letter alright with the enclosure. Got it at the convention in Rockford and immediately answered that letter. I don't know whether it was improperly addressed or not, but you should have had it before this time, and as it has not come back to me I am rather under the impression that some one has got it or it has been delayed in the mails.

That outfit are out to assault and destroy everybody in every position in the labor movement, everywhere that refuses to become a part of A. R. Hamilton's machine, and that they cannot control, and if they are successful they will get control of the whole labor movement in addition to the Mine Workers Organization, and Mr. Hamilton is a pretty shrewd, capable gentleman that knows the game thoroughly and has unlimited resources in the way of finances, trained stool pigeons, newspaper publicity and organization. They are going to make it mighty disagreeable for everyone that refuses to knuckle to them, or that they cannot destroy.

However that is the kind of a game I have been up against with them for over twenty years and I expect to continue as long as I am able to.

They tried to get me in the last convention but their trap turned on them. They laid their plans for doing it in the recent co-operative convention but they got away with nothing at all.

It is making the work doubly difficult however and the Lord knows there is plenty of it without that added complication. At the same time it is pretty nearly positive proof when they give so much time, spent so much of their money, use so many of their tools to injure a man, that he is really doing, so I have that consolation anyhow.

Mrs. Walker has been pretty sick with a severe cold for the last six weeks or such a matter. It was practically pneumonia. I just took her to the hospital this morning.

Esther is working every day. We are all glad to hear from you and hope that you will continue to get well.

With love from us all I am,

Yours sincerely,
[John H. Walker]

TLC (John H. Walker Papers)

To John Fitzpatrick

3700 Fifth St., N. W.,
Washington, D. C.
December 5, 1922

Mr. John Fitzpatrick, President
Chicago Federation of Labor,
166 W. Washington, St.,
Chicago, Ill.
My dear Mr. Fitzpatrick:

I am enclosing a letter to Mr. Chas. Darrow and I would appreciate it very much if you will forward same to him for me as I have not his address.

I shall write to you in a few days as I am too tired to write to you today as I would like to do. I am improving very slowly.

With best wishes to you and all the boys, I am,

Most sincerely,
Mother Jones

TLS (John Fitzpatrick Papers)

From John H. Walker

December 12, 1922.

Mother Jones,
Washington, D. C.
Dear Mother:

Just a few lines to let you know that I received both your letters at home. Glad to hear from you and to know that you are improving. Mrs. Walker is home and almost fully recovered. Her sister is stopping at the house, she is a nurse I think that has helped some. Esther is working every day teaching school.

I have been out of the office almost continuously for the last six weeks which accounts for my not writing you sooner and everybody has been burried with work in the fight against the proposed new constitution, which if adopted, would destroy the last vestige of whatever there is that is good in our American form of government in this state.

I think we have it beat. I sincerely hope so.

Will try and reach that other party and advise him of the danger indicated. However I think he is aware of it. Yes, that is about as cruel a thing that a man could do. It indicates the caliber of that outfit that done it to him. They wrecked the mining department of the A. F. of L. for no other purpose than to get Lord's job. I don't think he would have hesitated to have wrecked the A. F. of L. for the same purpose. The things they have done not only shows the inhuman cruel and unscrupulous nature of that gentleman, but it also shows how little he cares for the labor movement as well. It means nothing to him except as it may serve his own personal purposes. It will take about a week or more to get things cleaned up now, the work that has accumulated. By the end of that time the legislature will be in session again, so that I doubt that I will be able to get away. I had hoped to pay a visit to Washington.

Howat is doing good work and may clean out our organization. I sincerely hope he does.

With sincere regards and good wishes I am,

Yours,
[John H. Walker]

TLC (John H. Walker Papers)

To John H. Walker

Washington, D. C.
Dec. 20 1922

Dear John

Got your letter It was like a ray of sunshine I think the world looked dark before I got it. Your the one human soul I looke to when the cold world is freazing. John the Labor Movement looks dark

There's nothing hardly in the West. After the lives and money that have been spent I am not gaining strenght as I had hope to. The way that Mooney & Keeney treated me made a total wreck out They are dirty and treachrous a group of Vultures as could be found They would cut the throat of Jesus Christ to save themselves. I wish you would see Darrow about that book he has wanted me write If will not write it let me know for 20 years he has been after me now I am ready for I cannot do anything else

I am so glad Mrs. Walker on the road to health a that is home I don't like Hospitals you know she the best nurse in the country in Harriet I am enclosing some mail, that will put you nex to thing but send the mail right back to me

Tel Mrs. W. I wish I could spend Christmass with her Kiss her for me I hope the poor Devils in Herrin will come out all right it was an unfortunate affair Just at the time it Hapned. I have a lot to tell you but I cannot write our organization in the A. F. L. have droped from 100 000 to 30 000. poor Jim what a cold blooded deal he got from the organization in which he was born Talk about Morgan & J D. R. They could do nothing more rotten than that Some day the workers will wake up if it is not too late

Dont forget to try & see Darrow at once you know after the attack I had I will not go back to my old [one word illegible] Keeney gave me my Death blow I saved the lives thousands of men Those Lap Dogs of Al Hamilton left nothing undone to crucify me Look at what they did to poor Howtt You know I helped to build up West Va I waded creeks to get meeting I faced machine guns I spent months in Military Prisson I was carried 84 miles in the night taken in to the

Federal Court I fough my own case the miners never spent a Dol for a Lawyer for me nor did they ever pay me one penny for all the times I was in Prisons   I spent most of what I got from back for you know how the poor wretches suffered in these [*one word illegible*] Lewis never did that

Merry Chrismass to Edith & all. I must tell you Houston came for me to go on the stand to save Keeney   Then the State came   The Dr. would not let one of them see me   I have so much to tell you

Loyally
Mother

I would give anything to see you   See Darrow & I will go to Chicago

ALS (John H. Walker Papers)

To William Green

Washington D C
Dec. 24–1922

My dear friend

For such you have been to me at all times. I have no words to express my heartfelt gratitude for your beautifull token of Friendship   It is the Spirit that so deeply [inspires?] me   I am not in a Condition to write all I wish to

It is a Terriable Inditement against us the Condition in W Va When I look back at the years gone bye when I walked 19 miles of a night Counted [*two words illegible*] there was no Side walk after I would Organize poor wretches between Rocks and often helped to Pay for their Charters It is heart breaking to see the Condition they and their Children are   Those Traitors made no Sacrifices they have had easy Sailing   read the Inclosed   Send them back to me Just soon as you read them   They are *Strictly Confidential*

ever devotedly & gratefully yours
Mother

May the Coming Years be happy ones for you

ALS (William Green Papers)

From John H. Walker

December 26, 1922.

Mother Jones,
Washington, D. C.
Dear Mother:

This is to acknowledge receipt of your letter of the 20th. Glad to hear from you although sorry to learn that you are not regaining your strength as it looks like you might, because you are needed worse in the labor movement than you ever were during all of your life. It does look black. At the same time, one cannot tell how things are going to go. Just about the time it begins to look the blackest, usually it stirs the heards of many good men and women who, when things were going well, did not interest themselves, so that it might mean that there will be a change in time yet.

We defeated their infamous new constitution. It meant the end of American government in Illinois and I think the beginning of the end for American Government all over this nation, at least without the bloody revolution to either save it or reestablish it.

I just received a letter from Lord. It was the rottenest deal ever put over. It shows how brutal and consciencless Lewis really is. There is not a particle of human feeling or decency in him.

Lord is taking it philosophically. He has no work out there, and he is going to have to take the first thing that he can get, to make a living for himself and family.

Those fellows in West Virginia I think have gotten completely under the control of Hamilton and his minions. It is too bad, because I think in the beginning they were honest but once that monster gets men in his clutches, he not only corrupts them, but gets the proof so that he can destroy them, and then drive them to the utmost depths to save him, and I suppose they become hardened and desperate.

Will try and see Darrow at an early date, and will write you just as soon as I do. The folks are well again. I wish you could have spent Christmas with us.

I am returning those two letters as requested. Thanks very much for sending me the information. Glad to see Hunt elected governor of Arizona. He is one real fellow.

Everything is going on about as usual here, except the legislature is about to convene and we are in the midst of our effort to get our proposed legislation in shape to introduce, and of course to try and get elected a speaker on the different committees that will be friendly. It obviously don't show, at the same time, it is a rather delicate proposition to handle, and it takes a lot of tedious pain staking work.

Sincerely hoping that this may find you getting stronger and better health, with sincere regards and the seasons good wishes I am,

Yours sincerely,
[John H. Walker]

TLC (John H. Walker Papers)

From William Green

December 29, 1922.

Mother Jones,
Washington, D. C.
Dear Mother:

I was pleased to receive your favor of recent date. I note with very great interest the newspaper clippings which you enclosed, also the letter. You can rest assured the same will be treated in strict confidence.

The situation in West Virginia is distressing indeed. I know how you feel about it and how deeply concerned you are about the welfare of the miners and their families throughout West Virginia. Let us hope that out of the trials, troubles and tribulations through which the poor mine workers and their families in West Virginia are passing there will come a better and brighter day for all. We must keep up the fight until this purpose is achieved.

I am returning the enclosures which you sent me. I thank you for submitting to me the information contained therein.

Please take care of yourself these wintry days and do not worry and fret over conditions over which you have no control and for which you are in no way responsible.

With assurances of kind personal regards, I am,

Fraternally yours,
[William Green]
Secretary-Treasurer.

TLC (William Green Papers)

1923

From Thomas Francis Cairns[1]

Charleston, W. Va.
Jan 2, 1923

Mother Jones
Washington, D. C.
Dear Mother,

I received your letter a few days ago and was delighted to hear your health is improving. This is indeed a good sign as you will be needed this Spring as you were never needed before. The organization is crumbling to pieces, and it is not through any effort on the part of the coal operators, because they only sit quietly by and watch it fall. The trouble is all on the inside of the union. Enclosed find clipping which tells about Geo. Barrett going to the Pen. Others will follow soon. I am informed the officers of district 17 are making arrangements to turn over the property bought to establish a hospital to their attorney Tom Townsend to pay him for his services. He will in this way get property worth Forty thousand dollars for one years work. It is also said Mr. Huston will get the property on Summers St. where the offices are located. It is further rumored on the quiet the officers, that is Keeney and Mooney will never come to trial as they intend to collect as much money as possible, by disposing of the property and collecting all the cash they can and leave before the trial come up. This, of course, seems to be a rather far fetched question, and I am only giving you underground reports, but part of it is absolutely true, especially that part concerning the hospital property, because this case came up before a commissioner appointed by the court, and the commissioner happens to be the partner of their attorneys his name is Mr. Bock, law partner of Tom Townsend. This looks queer. Another curious thing is they won't pay the bills of the merchants who supplied the striking miners with goods. They owe Geo. Ort of Charleston over Forty thousand dollars and he says he can't collect a cent. This is also true with numerous merchants all along the Kanawha river and on the Creeks throughout the coal fields.

If these men stay here they are going to prison for not less than ten years. This is as certain as the Sun shines. The evidence is overwhelming against them and lots of men are turning states evidence. I saw Kennedy and he was very glad to hear you are better. He sends his very kindest regards. He also informs me they have not got the completed figures for 1922, but there was collected in 1920 and 1921 over two and a half million dollars in dist. 17 The miners are compelled to pay from 5 to 7 dollars a month dues and beleive me they are raising a howl as they are only working one and two days a week. Wll I will close with my love and hope you will continue to improve in health.

Sincerely yours,
Tom Cairns.

ALS (Mother Jones Papers)
  1. Thomas Francis Cairns (1875–1949), president of District 17, UMWA, 1912–1917, was one of the founders of the West Virginia Federation of Labor.

From John H. Walker

January 3rd, 1923.

Mother Jones,
c/o 502 Quincy St., N. W.,
Washington, D. C.
Dear Mother:

This is to acknowledge receipt of yours of recent date. Glad to hear from you and hope that you may have gathered strength and improved since writing the letter.

I have written Darrow, but have not heard from him yet. I appreciate your feeling about staying in one place all the time, particularly in Washington. I know you would be glad to get out of there for a while and particularly to get into Chicago where you can meet Nockels and a good many other friends up there for a while.

In talking things over today, Mrs. Walker asked me to invite you, while out here to come to the house and stay a while with us, or as long as you can stand it. We will all be glad to have you.

It is great news from Kansas. They have elected all but two of the fellows who were friends of Howats forces. The two that they did not elect, was the Secretary-Treasurer and the Strip Pit Board Member. They elected all the others. That must make Howat feel good. I know it makes his friends everywhere feel that way. The boys are making a great fight in the Pittsburg district. It begins to look like they have a little chance to get control there although I cannot conceive of Hamilton giving up the Pittsburg district, if by any conceivable means whatever, he can keep control of it.

Trusting that this finds you in better health and good spirits, and hoping to see you in the near future, I am,

Sincerely yours,
[John H. Walker]

P. S. I am returning the letter you enclosed. JHWa

TLC (John H. Walker Papers)

From John H. Walker

January 9th, 1923.

Mother Jones,
Washington, D. C.
Dear Mother:

This is to acknowledge receipt of your letter of the 4th. Glad to hear from you. Sorry to hear of Powderly's having been compelled to go to bed. Yes, he is getting old   Time is beginning to lay a heavy hand on him and he has had to battle against heavy odds all his life. The treatment of the movement too has not helped him any. Very sorry, but it seems that is the way with those who are clean. They have got to put up with the opposition of the other side and the demagogues and crooks, and those who don't know, on our own side. It takes a strong character to stand up against that sort of thing. There are not many who do, but it is those who do, that, have made all the progress that has been made in the world, although usually they get little credit for it and much crucifixion.

I sincerely hope that you get stronger and better and that you may be able to complete writing that history of colaboration with Darrow and other capable friends. The message that it will carry is needed badly in our country now. I am returning letter you enclosed as requested.

Yours,
[John H. Walker]

TLC (John H. Walker Papers)

To Emma Powderly

Springfield, Illinois.
February 23, 1923

Mrs. T. V. Powderly,
3700 Fifth Street
Washington, D. C.
My dear friend:

I think you have cast me down as the ingrate but you must change your opinion. I have not been very well the last two weeks but I am getting ready to do my work. I came down with Mr. Walker to spend a few days and to rest up. I miss home very much and all the old friends about it. I intend to write to Mr. Pwderly soon and I appreciate his kindness in sending me the letter he did. I will not be here but just another week. Send my mail to 166 Washington Street, Chicago, Illinois. I shall go there very soon. I would like to be home again and sit down in the evenings with the family but then you have rest since I have been gone as you do not have to doctor my knees every night. I do not think I will be back before the first of May anyway, and tell Mr. Powderly I hope he is making progress in the Smith case in California. If that poor boy could only get out to see his dear mother and be with her before she passes away, it would be one grand deed in history. I am not going to write you a long letter, I am just writing this to let you know I am still alive.

Give my love to Daisy and all the family, and also to poor Aunt Lizzy, tell her I am going to write to her one of these days. With best love and deep appreciation of your kindness to me, as it will go along the stairway of time until I enter my grave.

Yours,
Mother Jones

TLS (Mother Jones Papers)

To Terence V. Powderly

626 Fayette Av.,
Springfield, Illinois,
March 1st, 1923.

Mr. T. V. Powderly,
3700 Fifth St.,
Washington, D. C.
My dear friend:

I received your letter. Have no words to express how much pleasure it gives me even to get a line from you.

I more than regretted the sad information of Kerwin's misfortune. He is too noble a fellow to be injured. He is too useful to a great cause, and particularly in the position that he is in.[1] I hope though by this time he has somewhat improved.

I know that he will make every effort to regain his strength and health. Nelson got elected to the city council of Chicago. That is one hope we have that we are making entrance into the enemies ranks. I suppose you know who Nelson is. He is one of the conciliators in Chicago, representing the Dpt. of Labor. He is a very shrewd good boy, and no doubt will do his good work for the toilers.

I hope Mrs. Powderly is well, and moving along nicely. Give my love to all the children at home, and tell Aunt Lizzie that some day I will be back.

I am going to speak at Fort Wayne, Indiana on the 7th of this month. I am feeling better, but I won't hold many meetings for I won't take any chances, but those poor shop men have been out since last July and I feel if I am able to crawl I owe them a duty to give them a word of encouragement.   and let them know the sunshine of hope still throws out its rays.

Things don't look very bright to me as I survey the labor movement as I go along. I hope you have got in touch with Golden[2] on that coal question.

I will close by wishing all good health and good luck. I do get lonesome a little while for the crowd.

With warm wishes to everyone in the house I am.

Yours to the end of time,
Mother Jones

TLS (Mother Jones Papers)
  1. Hugh L. Kerwin was director of conciliation in the Department of Labor.
  2. Possibly Christ J. Golden of Shamokin, Pennsylvania, president of District 9, UMWA.

To William Green

29 March [1923]

Dear Friend

When can you see me   I have very Important Information for you. I cannot go to office. You mention the Time I will meet you at the Spencer House   Wire me to this Hotel.[1]

Mother

ALS (William Green Papers)
  1. This letter is written on stationery of the Hotel Washington, Chicago; it bears a receiving date stamp of 30 March 1923.

From William Green

March 30, 1923.

Mother Jones,
Hotel Washington,
Chicago, Illinois.
Dear Mother:

Your letter of March 29th came to hand this morning. I am leaving the city for Kentucky where I am going to attend some meetings and make some addresses early next week. I expect to return about Thursday, April 5th, although this is uncertain. In fact I cannot exactly tell about my movements next week.

However, if you come here by Thursday I will call for you providing, of course, I return to the city at that time.

I was glad to hear from you and hope you are well. I trust I may have the pleasure of seeing you soon.

With sincere personal regards and best wishes, I am,

Very truly yours,
[William Green]
Secretary-Treasurer.

TLC (William Green Papers)

To William Green

Chicago Ill
Apr 4—1923

My Dear Mr Green

In reading over your letter I concluded it was best to wait your return. You can wire me when you will be in the city for a few days Then I will leave The Information I have is of Importance to you for the future of the organization That was built on the agony & suffering men who are sleeping in the Clay to day

Mother

ALS (William Green Papers)

From John H. Walker

April 4, 1923.

Mother Jones,
c/o Ed Nockels,
Chicago, Illinois.
Dear Mother:

This is to acknowledge receipt of your letter of recent date with enclosure, which I have read through carefully. I am returning same. I am kept pretty busy. Hope to be able to come to Chicago some time to see you. The folks are all well and send you their love.

Yours truly,
[John H. Walker]

TLC (John H. Walker Papers)

From Ephraim F. Morgan

April 10, 1923

Mother Jones,
c/o Ed Nockels,
166 Washington Street,
Chicago, Illinois.
Dear Mother:

I have made an investigation in regard to those confined in jail at Logan charged with having participated in the recent insurrection in West Virginia and find that they have all been released except three; Savory Holt, Buck O'Dell and G. C. Hickey. They have not been in very long and have not yet been indicted. I presume they will be at this term of the court and then some disposition will be made of their cases.

You remember that Holt was one of the real active participants and made a speech at Lens Creek urging the crowd to go on after it had decided in response to your request to return to their homes.

Hoping you are still improving in health and with best wishes, I am,

Very cordially yours,
[E. F. Morgan]
Governor.

TLC (Ephraim F. Morgan Papers)

To Ephraim F. Morgan

Chicago, Illinois,
April 16, 1923.

Governor Ephraim F. Morgan,
State of West Virginia,
Executive Department,
Charleston, West Va.
My dear Governor Morgan:

Your letter of April 10 was received. I was very glad indeed for the information it conveyed—the release of those poor fellows in jail. I know that many of those men were unwilling to join that march, but were forced in against their own judgment and will. It is a good thing for West Virginia that she has a governor who looks at the human side of questions as well as the executive side.

So far as that poor fellow, Holt, is concerned, I do not believe governor, that he is altogether right. And if the fellow is convicted, I hope you will use a little human consideration in his case. You know he blows off a lot of steam, without ever considering where it is going to land or what effect it is going to have. I know, governor, that it is not a very easy position to be governor of West Virginia. You were handed a very ugly ulcer upon your entrance into office. I perhaps know the condition of West Virginia and its elements about as well as anybody in West Virginia. I have been twenty-three years going all over that state from one end to another. I felt, governor, when I first met you that if we worked in harmony we could put the state on the map of America and remove that black spot which she has been carrying for years. I know well what you have had to go up against, and I believe you know me well enough to know that I will not stand by a governor whose interest is not in the welfare of the state and her people. I hope to live to see these disturbing elements in the state laid on the shelf. I have no ax to grind—I am not looking for any office. But I have always felt a deep interest in the state ranking as high as any state in the Union which she could have done if we had the right element on both sides.

You know, governor, as well as I do that the tyranny of power is a dangerous thing to be in the hands of undeveloped minds. I am yet in hopes that before your term expires that you will leave a record that will live in history—a record that the children of the future may sit up and read with pleasure and gratification.

I notice they are referring to the money that was put up for your campaign. I wish you to see Duncan Kennedy, the commissioner of the Kanawha Coal Company, and get the figures of the amount of money he paid over to the people who are finding fault with you, and after you get the figures ask them what they did with that money. It didn't belong to them—it was the hard earned money of men, women and children who deprived their tables of the necessaries of life, and it was squandered for campaign purposes. Demand an investigation of that when they are attacking you.

Well, I am not going to write much. I am slowly improving in my health and hope I shall have the pleasure of seeing you and Mrs. Morgan. She is one noble, democratic woman for whom I have the deepest respect.

Believe me very sincerely yours for the welfare of the state and nation and her people.

My best wishes to your lovely boy, and tell him perhaps someday when he grows into manhood the world will be better.

> [*Holograph*] With deep friendship
> Mother Jones

TLS (Ephraim F. Morgan Papers)

To Ephraim F. Morgan

> Chicago, Illinois,
> April 17, 1923.

Hon. E. F. Morgan,
Governor, West Virginia,
Executive Department,
Charleston, West Va.
My dear Governor:

I forgot to enclose this clipping[1] to you yesterday. They are circulating this article through all the labor papers. That is why I called on you to give the civil liberties something else to talk about, when you get those figures that I referred to yesterday.

Enclosed find some figures of the amount paid into the office in 1921.

> With best wishes, I remain
> Yours sincerely,
> Mother Jones

(Confidential)

TLS (Ephraim F. Morgan Papers)
1. A brief note of a letter from the American Civil Liberties Union charging Morgan with failure to uphold civil rights in West Virginia.

From Ephraim F. Morgan

April 19, 1923

Mother Jones,
c/o Ed Nockels,
166 Washington Street,
Chicago, Illinois.
Dear Mother:

Thank you for information and suggestions contained in your communication.

Am enclosing you herewith copies of letters recently written to Mr. Ward, Chairman of the American Civil Liberties Union. Of course, he is not anxious to make these public and I presume you have not seen them in the papers.

Very sincerely yours,
[E. F. Morgan]

TLC (Ephraim F. Morgan Papers)

To Robert Watchorn[1]

April 1923

Mr. Watchorn
Oklahoma City
My dear Mr. Watchorn:

Mr. Powderly handed me a statement made by you to him in a letter you wrote to him. Permit me to say that when I read it I don't know when anything so affected me.

You know we usually have stones thrown at us and rarely ever a kind word, and when I read that article over and over again, it draws tears from me. It had been so many years since I had seen you I had lost entire track of you, but not but what I often referred to you and wished it was possible to have more men of your type. But the labor movement is not producing such men. Honestly I do not look with very great hope on the future of the labor movement in America. The men are not at the helm who can grasp the changes that have taken place and the evolution that is going on in the economic field.

The Labor Movement of today has become more or less of a pie counter institution. Everyone is looking for office whether he has the ability or not to fill that office for the benefit of those who pay him and trust him. I would like to see you personally and talk over the situation with you, but money is scarce and railroad fare is high. Every fellow in office today has a machine thoroughly lined up and equipped to fight for his interests.

The affair in West Virginia is a very sad indictment against Labor leaders. What little grasp they have of the evolution that is going on day or night in the industrial world. The tyranny of power has grown to be a frightful disease among them. There should be some way to educate them. The man who is running the Miners Journal was never in a mine in his life. He has no grasp of what the men are up against. The articles in the Journal are not understood by the rank and file and those who do understand them do not need instructions from editors.

Al Hamilton's machine dominates the national office. He gets his men in office and even if he has nothing to do with getting them in he knows how to handle them when they get there. There is not a vestige of organization in the New River field of West Virginia today. For twenty-three years I have been going in and out of there, I have helped to organize these men three different times but they have never elected officers who understood dealing with the common enemy.

One of those fellows who has been a board member for about twelve years bought coal in Indiana. When he got that office his toes were out through his shoes and his pants were patched all over. And now they have a fine home, automobiles, their wives decorated with diamond rings. It is too sad to repeat when you think of the men and women who are moulding in their graves that took the thorns out of the pathways of those office-holders of today.

Well I am not going to tire you with reading this. I hope some day to see you and have a long talk with you because I think there is some way out if we can only get together. Permit me to convey to you my deep felt gratitude and appreciation for that humane tribute you paid me. The first day of next month I will have walked over my ninety-third milestone. I do not know how many more milestones I will have to travel. However as long as life remains I shall try to take the thorns out of the homes of the little children yet to come.

With sincere friendship, I am

Yours in the battle for justice
Mother Jones

TLC (Lillie May Burgess MSS)
1. Robert Watchorn, first secretary of the UMWA, held a number of civil service posts, including commissioner of immigration, until 1907, when he entered the oil business which eventually brought him wealth.

To Terence V. Powderly

Chicago, May 3, 1923.

Mr. T. V. Powderly
3700 Fifth Street,
Washington, D. C.
My own dear friend: (for such you have ever been to me)

Your letter gave me some distress and kept me awake nights, when you made the statement in it that you did not expect to stay very much longer. Just close your mind to that—don't be looking forward to the day you go away, you will be there long enough—look forward to the great grand work you have done in the past and the work there is to be done in the future. Don't be dwelling on when we are going to take our final rest, we will have time enough there to think of it. Then you have left a record behind you that will live in history. Your faithful work to the poor wretches who needed your advice and counsel and service most. So far as leaving anything behind us, I don't want as much as ten cents in my possession when I travel to the grave—I want no fine coffin—there is too much heathenism about this display—they'll hammer us when we are alive and then march after us to the grave when we are dead. I want the tributes paid while we live. I hope that Emma is well, and don't be so despondent for it discourages her—you know she has responsibility enough on her shoulders to attend to that house without you throwing one word of discouragement in her path. I'll be home sometime soon, I am working away—I can't work very fast—the boys are good to me here. I am going to send you a document, that is a copy of it, which you can read and you needn't return it because I am only sending a duplicate copy which will open your eyes to the rascality and villiany that is used today upon the poor unfortunate wretches and I wish you would let Kerwin see this document. I went down to Charleston—I saw the Governor, I had a talk with him, and all the prisoners that were in jail in Logan were turned free, all but three, and I think I will be able to get those three out. I told him it didn't look well to see the leaders going about in automobiles and drawing room cars and living in $10,000 houses, and these poor wretches paying the penalty of their crime. I asked him to picture to himself his little boy sitting on his mother's knee in the dead of night and asking why papa wasn't home, and the tears almost filled into his eyes when I told him the mother's reply was that he was behind the iron bars. Morgan is a good Christian man, but that gang has given the man a dirty deal. I will write no more, because this letter will explain a great deal to you. Tell Emma I am longing to get home to get a good look into her face—she was always true to me and only for her tender heart, I know that I would be molding in the clay today.

With my warm love to everybody in the house

I am, as ever yours,
Mother Jones

TLS (Terence V. Powderly Papers)

To William Green

166 West Washington Street
Chicago
May 18, 1923.

PERSONAL
Mr. William Green,
Merchants Bank Building,
Indianapolis, Indiana.
My dear Mr. Green:

I sent you a letter some time ago and I marked it personal. I hope that no one else in that office got that letter but you because it was very important that it should fall into your hands only. And something else I want to ask your advice on—would you advise me to go to that convention of the miners that is going to be held in Pittsburg the second of June.[1] I have been asked to go there but before I move I wanted to get your advice. I don't think we ought to overlook the fact that there is an element that perhaps is not on the surface that is trying to break up the miners' union. I, for one, know the struggle, the sacrifices, the blood shed, the hunger and misery and suffering that the men went through who undertook to build up that organization. Any effort of mine that can be used will not endorse anything of that kind. I know the men who are sleeping in their graves who gave up their lives who hadn't a cent when they closed their eyes on earth, their whole desire was to bring a greater sunlight for the generations to come. Your advice will be of value to me in this case. I think that I could use some influence against any division that the enemies might bring up on the floor. However, I will subject this entirely to your advice and if you endorse I will go and if you don't I will continue my work. And write to me as soon as this letter reaches you. If you can send it special delivery.

I am with confidence and sincere best wishes,

Yours,
Mother Jones

TLS (William Green Papers)
1. A group calling itself the Progressive International Committee of the UMWA and associated with William Z. Foster's Trade Union Educational League issued the call for a convention; the UMWA Executive Board later denounced it as a Communist front.

From William Green

May 21, 1923.

Mother Jones,
166 West Washington-st.,
Chicago, Illinois.

Dear Mother:

Replying to the inquiry contained in your letter of May 18, I received the letter you sent me a short time ago marked "Personal". I did not acknowledge receipt of the same because I took it for granted that you would understand that it reached me. I have it my possession and you can be assured that it will not pass from my control.

I have no hesitancy in advising you that, in my judgment, it would be better for you to remain away from the meeting called in Pittsburgh, June 2. I have several very strong reasons why I give you this advice and because of these very good reasons there is no doubt in my mind that you, of all persons connected with our organization and the labor movement, should remain away from this meeting. Your enemies would seize upon your presence there for the purpose of injuring you and your friends would be placed at a disadvantage in explaining why you attended this meeting.

Work at the mines throughout the Western Districts is very poor. Many of the members of our Union are idle altogether while some others are only working 1 or 2 days per week. I hope you are well and that you are successful in your work.

With kind personal regards and best wishes, I am,

Very truly yours,
[William Green]
Secretary-Treasurer.

TLC (William Green Papers)

1923

To William Green

166 West Washington Street
Chicago
May 24, 1923.

Mr. William Green,
Merchants Bank Bldg.,
Indianapolis, Indiana.
My dear friend:

I received your letter yesterday and I read it with a great deal of interest and care. I certainly will follow your advice because I know the best and purest motives were back of it when you sent me the letter although I feel somewhat restless about that convention in Pittsburgh. You know the agony and suffering and privations men made who are in their graves today and to feel it is going to be wrecked almost keeps me awake nights. However, I hope that they will use a little common sense and judgment and you know and I know that Pittsburgh is the very last place a convention of that kind should be held.

I have not been feeling any too well for the last few days. That letter that I sent you came from a railroad man who is in a position to get next to most everything that is going on. He is a whole-souled good character and every statement he makes can be relied upon. He sees and knows the sufferings of those poor women and children that those inhuman monsters are living the bones and suffering of those women and children. However, we must only live in hopes that a better dawn will come. I am not afraid to confide in you and I will always to continue to send any information I have to you but I was a little nervous that that letter fell into the hands of someone else and all you have to do is to let me know that you receive it and then I will feel contented.

With my most sincere wishes, I am

Yours in a great cause,
Mother Jones

[*Holograph postscript*] I am frightfully nervous

TLS with holograph note (William Green Papers)

To Ephraim F. Morgan

166 West Washington Street
Chicago
June 9, 1923.

Governor Morgan,
Charleston,
West Virginia.
My dear Governor:

For some time I have been trying to get an opportunity to write you and I was determined this morning to ask you for a special favor. I am writing a book and I would like to get your photograph to put beside Governor Hunt of Arizona. I want to do some vindication and the picture will give me a better chance.

I more than thank you for letting those poor fellows out of prison that you. The future will compensate you for your humane act.

I won't get over to Charleston until after the 4th of July for I have a great deal of work to do here and then I have the railroad shopmen of Indiana calling for me and I must respond to their call.

I want also to make another request to you. If you have any appointments to make on the factory inspection I don't know of a more efficient man, a more honorable man than Tom Cairns. I want to ask you as a special favor to put him on and you will never regret it. I want to get Tom's assistance to counteract some of the forces at work and if he doesn't come up to my estimate of him, hold me responsible. He is true, he is loyal, he is a man in every sense of the word.

I am going to write you a longer letter by and by and I want to see for I have a great many things to talk over with you that I cannot very well write.

Give my best wishes to that noble woman, Mrs. Morgan. I'll be over to see you sometime in July and I want some time when you won't have interruptions to talk with you.

I am sincerely and gratefully yours,

Mother Jones

Don't neglect to put Tom on!

TLS (Ephraim F. Morgan Papers)

1923

To Emma Powderly

Chicago Ill
June 11—23

My own Dear friend

I cannot sleep nights fearing there is something wrong at Home   I hope you & Mr Powderly are well   every day I looked for a line   it never came   I am getting so D—— tired writing this book only for that grand human soul who have stood by me in all the fierce storms I would not bother   I want to make the assasns take back water before I die. This work I am not used to, but I am nearing the end. You should hear Darrow talk about that great soul   Write me if only 2 lines   Love to all   Tell Aunt Lizzie I am lonesome without her

Mother

ALS (Terence V. Powderly Papers)

From Ephraim F. Morgan

June 19, 1923

Mother Jones,
166 West Washington Street,
Chicago, Illinois.

Dear Mother:

Complying with your request of June 9th I am sending you under separate cover photograph.

I believe that we will be able to take care of Mr. Cairns as requested by you, and hope it may be of benefit to the situation here. Things are coming on very nicely.

I was unable to induce the legislature to pass the mine guard law. The Senate was republican and the House democratic. The leaders in the Senate agreed with me to pass the bill if it were passed by the House, but I could not, although I made every effort possible to get them to do so, get the Senate to take the initiative. On motion of one of the labor leaders in the House, the bill was referred to a committee where it remained until the close of the session. I have never fully understood why the labor people in the House assumed the attitude they did in regard to the bill. I was very anxious indeed that it be passed.

284

Trusting you are enjoying good health, and with kindest regards, I am,

Very cordially yours,
[E. F. Morgan]
Governor.

TLC (Ephraim F. Morgan Papers)

To Ephraim F. Morgan

Chicago,
July 12, 1923.

Governor Morgan
Charleston, W. Va.
My dear Governor:

I received your letter with your photograph. The photograph impressed me wonderfully. There were no airs or posing about it, but just the natural position. I read with interest the reference you had with reference to the mine guards. It is just exactly what you might expect from those fellows. They had no grasp of the value of that bill when they referred it to the Committee, but one thing they are experts in and that is personal abuse to one who does not cater to their insane ideas. I read some clippings that were sent to me and they don't speak very well for the people who are in court today. I was also glad when they made that fellow Montgomery acknowledge that he wrote those resolutions. That shows the double dealing that has been going on in the back ground.

Governor, I owe you a debt of gratitude that I don't think I can ever compensate you for. If you had not sent me down to stop that day I would have been the victim of it all. Slander and villification would have gone out through the country against me. I have put up with more insults for the sake of the poor wretches that they might see a brighter day for their children. Those fellows had no respect for womanhood—the only thing they respected was their pocket and glory. It is not much to their credit to go flying around in sedans and the poor wretches paying the bills. That fellow Grant Scott and the others went down to Townsend farm where he has 275 acres and there they were hunting wild chickens for a whole week and drawing the blood out of the starving wretches to pay their salaries and expenses. They were as dirty bunch of blood-sucking leaches as ever cursed any state, Governor, and no one knows them any better than I do. I did everything I could for those fellows to try to advance them for the sake of the men they represented. I suffered every insult that could be suffered from their vile tongues and pen, but there is a day coming when the whole thing will be uncovered. In the twenty-four years that I have been going in and out of West Virginia you are the one man I could approach for the sake of the poor helpless man who had been exploited and robbed. I think yet, Governor, that good deal of those moves that were made had a silent hand behind them. They were made to embarrass your administration, but I shall clear you before the world and for those who are going to come after us. I will put you in the right position. No doubt they will howl at me like a bunch of mad dogs, but I'll stand the howling for a principle. No one knows better than I do what you have to go up against, and you saved me from destruction and the world and the generations that will come after us will know it. I don't know when I will see you but I will drop you a line occasionally. Governor, wherever there is a poor helpless wretch in jail, through the blunders of their officials, I hope you will use your good influence and let them home to their families.

Write and let me know what the outcome of the trial is, although I have no desire to tax you any more than you are taxed, but I have some desires to find out what the ending is. Let me express my appreciation to you for appointing Tom Kearns [Cairns]. You will find him a good, honest loyal defender and whenever you anything done don't fail to ask Tom, he will do it with a heart filled with gratitude.

Give my best wishes to Mrs. Morgan, one noble, grand democratic woman. and Dear Albert.

With deep devotion and gratitude, I am your friend,

Mother Jones

TLS (Ephraim F. Morgan Papers)

To William Green

166 West Washington Street
Chicago
July 23, 1923.

Mr. William Green,
Indianapolis, Indiana.
My dear friend:

For a week or ten days I have been trying to get to feeling like I could write to you on a very important question. When I attended the Farmer-Labor Party convention there was a woman delegate there who originally lived in Philadelphia. She was a member of the Communist Party. She went down to Illinois and the Zeigler delegates told me that she got $500.00 from that local and other locals just the same all along through Illinois. She was sowing the seed of her philosophy which is not very wholesome for those unsophisticated men. I learned from the delegates that she must have taken ten thousand dollars out of Illinois from the locals there. She was one of those who was up in St. Joseph with that Ruthenberg[1] on trial. In the present condition of the miners I think they will need every dollar they have got for themselves and their families and if they have any money in their treasuries it should not be donated for that purpose. As individuals why of course they give what they please but out of the treasury I think that thing should be stopped. You cannot tell what that money is going to be used for or what is back of it. I intended writing to you before but I haven't felt extra well. Take some steps to stop that thing of giving their money away as they have been doing. There is no organization so exploited as the miners. I write this then I have some other information that I want to give you but I can't write all of it and sometime in the future I will try to see you and tell you of it.

I haven't been feeling any too well. I hope that peace will come to the organization. God knows that for the last two or three years it has gone through a terrific turmoil. There are some things that I want to tell you that I can't write to you.

With my best wishes to you,

I am going to send you a bill tomorrow or next day because I am broke. I know you have been under a terrible strain.

With best and warmest wishes I remain

Always yours in the cause,
Mother Jones

TLS (William Green Papers)
1. Charles E. Ruthenberg, executive secretary of the Communist party and its successor, the Workers party of America, testified extensively at the trial in St. Joseph, Michigan, of William Z. Foster for violation of the Michigan criminal syndicalism law.

From William Green

July 25, 1923.

Mother Jones,
Chicago, Illinois.
Dear Mother:

I acknowledge receipt of your favor of July 23. The informa[tion] you give regarding the woman solicitor who has been collecting funds from Local Unions in Illinois is similar to other information we have received at International Headquarters regarding others who, like this woman, visit Local Unions of the United Mine Workers of America and collect large sums of money. Incidentally these parties sow the seed of Communism and dissension among members of our organization. This is one of the problems we are facing because, as you know, our Local Unions are so sentimental that they give out of their Local Union treasuries freely, when people ask for money. We are trying to devise some means by which this can be stopped. If an end could be brought to this practice the Mine Workers and their families dependent upon them would be benefitted. It is true, as you say, our poor miners and their wives and families need the money these solicitors collect and it is a sacrifice which they make when the money is turned over to these solicitors.

I am sorry to hear that you were not well but I hope that your illness is only temporary. I trust you will be strong again soon. Send in your bill and I will send you a check in payment of the same. We are working very hard meeting, as you know, some very trying situations and doing the best we can to promote and preserve the best interests of our membership.

With every good wish, I am,

Very truly yours,
[William Green]
Secretary-Treasurer.

TLC (William Green Papers)

To Terence V. and Emma Powderly

November 10, 1923.

Mr. & Mrs. P. B. Powderly,
3700 5th St.,
Washington, D. C.
My dear Friends:

I am anxious to hear from you all I have not heard for so long that I begin to get a little nervous. I hope Mr Powderly is well   there is a case I would like to take up with him as soon as arrive there regarding a fellow in Gary, Ind.,   Old Geo. Anderson took his citizen paper away from him and registered him for deportation   I know him a long and know he is a good forward Citizen   I hope you are all well because when I don't hear from you I think wome one is not well and Mr. Powderly is not as strong as he used to be. I was talking to a gentleman the other day he said he had never had the pleasure of meeting Mr. powderly although he wished to he said that he had studied his face very often when he saw it and came to the conclusion that he was deep sincere and reasonable and before he acted analysed the question closely he paid his wife a tribute although he had never met her. Well when you get this letter write me two lines and I will feel happy. With love to every body in the house   tell Aunt Lizzi that I often think of her and hope she is well.[1]   poor Dear good soul   I hope you are well   Take care of yourself

TL (Terence V. Powderly Papers)
   1. The remainder of the letter is in Mother Jones's hand but is unsigned.

To William Green

November 23, 1923.

Mr. Wm. Green,
Merchants' Bank Bldg.,
1106,
Indianapolis, Ind.
My dear Mr. Green:

I Have been wanting an Opptunity to write you for sometime but I have been so tied up between my rhumetism and other things that I have been unable to write. In [Sept.?] I went to Cal. and tried to get poor Mathhew Shcmitt out of the San Quentin prison. Govenor Hunt gave me very nice letters of introduction to every public official in California. The treasurer of the State Mr. Johnson, a very fine man, made an appointment with the Governor of California[1] in Sacramento to meet me and he said to me "Just make a social visist mother, and don't refer to the release of those prisoners just yet." I followed his advice because he seemed a very open minded man. He took me to the Governor in his automobile and brough me back for the train. I had the commissioner of Port with me and Joe Marshall of the Bldg. Trades, both very fine men. They were very surprised at the very cordial and friendly reception the Governor gave me   He has the reputation of being a very reactionary and cold-blooded individual, but mey expereince has been that even such men have human blood. I had quite an audience with the Attorney-General and he agreed with me that even if those boys were guilty they had suffered enough now. I got the wires going with every political office-holder in the state nearly to get the Governor to commute the sentence to ten years and the next meeting of the pardon board would probably pardon them. I saw the warden of the pententary, San Quentin, and he was very kindly disposed. I had quite a long visit with the boys and the guards did not restrict my time and the priest for the warden came in and introduced himself to him and said that the captain of the guards had told him I was in there and we had quite a visit. They wanted me to see the owner of the Los Angeles Times[2] but I thought I would use a little discretion and keep away from him until a little later on. I am all crippled up with rhumetism and I am going to leave for Washington Sunday. I had a letter from Charleston telling me that those fellows bribed the foreman of the jury. Mr. Green, will we ever change our leaders? They seem when they get into power they do not use common judgement they become egotistical dictators, My God, going to bribe the forman of a jury don't that prove your guilt? I would die within the prison walls before I would stoop to such a thing or go on record for such an act. There isn't a single organized labor man In Cabin Creek now and twice I organized that place from top to bottom and made it all closed shop. No one is to blame for that but the leaders   They had a poor fellow the name of Bell he could hardly speak any English, they had him out here to collect. Nockels got a lot of clothing for him and I asked for $25.00 to pay his way home and I got it. I didn't have the money or I would have paid his way myself. I [hope?] to God the next convention will reconcile all factions for the labor movement. is up against it. They are honeycombing local unions with the K.K.K. and if they don't bury the hatchet and stop throwing insinuations at each other I am afraid the labor movement will be wrecked and the little children and innocent women will be victims of the most cruel treatment from capitalism in the ages past. I am rather pessimistic about the labor movement   I did not see much life in it in California and I notice, too, that that women that I referred to you sometime ago had been up in Alberta bleeding the organizations for money. She is now in California entertaining them about Soviet Russia. We have enough to do at home without bothering our brains across the ocean   I am not goin to take up your time much longer but I am going to send you a bill for some money because I am broke and when I am hungery I shall always appeal to you.

Sincere friendship for your future peace and happiness, I am alwasy your friedn,

Mother Jones

TLS (William Green Papers)

1. Friend William Richardson (1865–1943), newspaper publisher, state printer, and state treasurer, served as governor of California, 1923–1927.

2. Harry Chandler (1864–1944), one of the leaders of the conservative Republicans who put Richardson in the governor's seat, continued at the Los Angeles *Times* the antiunion stance of his father-in-law, Harrison Gray Otis.

From William Green

December 4, 1923.

Mother Jones,
3700 5th–st., N. W.,
Washington, D. C.
Dear Mother:

I acknowledge receipt of your favor of November 23. I note your explanation of your visit to California in the interest of certain prisoners and your efforts to secure their release. I feel sure your visit will be productive of good results.

I can see by your letter that you are keeping in touch with the situation in West Virginia and elsewhere. We are all deeply concerned over the situation there. We can only hope that eventually we will get out of the litigation and strife and cost so that our organization may carry forward the work it is called upon to perform, namely, the economic betterment of the workers.

I am very busy getting ready for our convention which will meet in January. I will wait until some future time when I can write you more fully. Send in your bill and I will forward you a check in payment thereof as promptly as possible.

With every good wish, I am,

Fraternally yours,
[William Green]
Secretary-Treasurer.

TLC (William Green Papers)

From John H. Walker

December 8, 1923.

Mother Jones,
3700 Fifth St., N. W.,
Washington, D. C.
Dear Mother:

Just received your letter with enclosures.[1] will take the matter up at an early date and I think will be able to get it adjusted. There is not a particle use of your worrying over this matter, as there is no possible danger of any trouble developing out of it, and I am writing to Green for detailed statement of your income for that time, as salary, with the items separated for expenses, so that just as soon as it is possible, I will be able to give Paulen the facts and they will have the matter adjusted. Just as soon as I get things cleared up, will write you.

Yours,
[John H. Walker]
President.

TLC (John H. Walker Papers)
  1. The Internal Revenue Service charged Mother Jones with failure to pay her income tax, and Walker undertook to clear the matter up, as several subsequent letters show. Green was William Green, treasurer of the UMWA; Paulen was the internal revenue agent with whom Walker dealt.

To Ephraim F. Morgan

Washington D. C.
Dec. 9. 23

Gov E F Morgan
My Dear Gov
  I was at the Dept of Labor on Friday I found Sam Montgomary–Ex Gover Hatfield with 3 other conciliators holding a conference with Sect I did not see Sam nor Hatfield but the other conciliators were miners from Iowa & Pen They said both sides were getting tired of making attorneys rich Strange they did not of this before
  Hatfield is going to run for Gov again If he don't make a better job of it than he did when he held the job before then Sam the Pre Cossack [hunter?] would be [Senator?] I have some sugestion to make to you but I cannot do it in writing

Most truely yours to the end of time
Mother

ALS (Ephraim F. Morgan Papers)

From Ephraim F. Morgan

December 11, 1923

Mother Jones,
3700 Fifth Street
Washington, D. C.
Dear Mother:
  Thank you very much for the information contained in your favor of December 9th.

Am glad indeed to hear from you. Keep me advised as to where I may be able to find you.

Wishing you continued good health, I am,

Very sincerely yours,
[E. F. Morgan]

TLC (Ephraim F. Morgan Papers)

From John H. Walker

December 13, 1923.

Mother Jones,
c/o 3700 Fifth St., N. W.,
Washington, D. C.
Dear Mother:

I went over and saw Mr. Paulen yesterday, the Deputy Collector for the Springfield District of the Internal Revenue Department of our government. He had a copy of the statement that had been filed in which it said that you had no husband and no income for the year 1921. I explained the situation as best I could but in the face of the communication from Secretary Green, which I understand they are required [to?] file under oath, that you had received $2350.00 as salary for that year, there was nothing could be done except to pay it.

For failure to pay during the period (which individuals are required under the law to pay) the penalty is from $25 to $100. He assessed the minimum penalty 25%, which made it $13.50. Then there is a fine from $5.00 to $100.00 in cases of that character, and he assessed the lowest fine possible under the circumstances which was $5.00. I paid him $72.50.

I am enclosing the copy which he made out to me in the way of a receipt.

I paid $67.50 by check. The $5.00 fine he said had to be paid in cash, to be submitted with his report to the Revenue Department at Washington. He said they had a rule against accepting that money in check, because of the fact that some checks that had reached them, had become valueless by the time they reached there.

I am very sorry that the situation developed as it did, but this was the best that could possibly be made of it.

Trusting that this finds you in [improved?] health and good spirits, with best wishes I am,

Sincerely yours,
[John H. Walker]

TLC (John H. Walker Papers)

To John H. Walker

December 14, 1923

Mr. John Hedge Walker,
626 LaFayette Street,
Springfield, Illinois.
My dear John:

I received your letter yesterday. It took several days for it to reach me. You can say to Mr. Palling that I am 94 years old, that I have lived in America 88 years and that never in all those years has the government asked me to pay any tax for I have nothing to pay tax on. I have seen most every President in the last 40 years and they never mentioned it to me in the White House, nor in the War Department nor in the Department of Justice nor in any other Department that I went to for the workers. I have been with the Miners off and on for over 30 years. I never in all those years put in a single bill for salary. I did not even when I was in the Knights of Labor put in a bill for salary. I sent in a bill for expenses it went in twice a month to the Miners. When I got my return check I cashed it and paid no attention much to the amounts I am not a commercialist nor a financier. I spend it just as fast as I make it. As to the year 1921 I was here there and everywhere that duty called me and there are some that Mr. Palling refers to it was not for salary alone but as I never kept an account of what [the?] money was for I am not able at this date to itemize. I was sick last for four months. I had to have doctors and nurses. I know nothing in the world of taxes I have nothing to pay taxes and the matter never in all my [history?] was referred to me before. I have been in the public eye for 50 years nearly I don't see why the matter was not brought up before. It seems strange, John, that Mr. Palling should be the one to bring me to time. I did not know I had to pay taxes on my clothes. I think, though, that the matter can be clearly by William Green. He can show that he hasn't from me for any services that I ever rendered to the workingclass. When I spoke in Detroit sometime ago they sent me a check for $60 I gave that to Sec. Mooney for the striking miners of Mingo. I don't know whether they ever got it or not. In fact I never gave any attention to taxes as I have no property or anything else. I think if you explain the matter to him he will readily understand it. I am staying now at the home of a man in the service of the Government for many years. I never heard anything about taxes. I never heard anything from any public official in Washington. I don't see why I should be attacked at 94 I have nothing to pay taxes on. When I was sick the Chicago Federation of Labor sent $100 to me and the Janitors organization, their National Office sent me $50. I don't whether I ought to pay taxes on that or not but I paid it over to the doctors and nurses. You explain this matter to him and I think when he gets his reply from Green he will be sort of satisfied. He might charge Rock-feller for taxes for feeding me in the Bull Pen for three months in Colorado.

Well John I will write to you soon again. I am not exploiting the workers and they and their poor wives and children are in need when I have a dollar they have 3/4 of it.

With love to all at home, John, I will write you soon again. I have been suffering severely with rheumatism since I have been here. I am awfully nervous I don't think I will ever get over that attack.

Mother Jones

TLS (John H. Walker Papers)

From John H. Walker

December 17, 1923.

Mother Jones,
3700 Fifth Street, N. W.,
Washington, D. C.
Dear Mother:

This is to acknowledge receipt of yours of the 14th. Glad to hear from you. You got my name wrong although, it is not John Hedge Walker it is John Hunter Walker, and I am not ver much for hedging. I am enclosing a copy of a letter that I got from Secretary Greene when I wrote him for information on this matter. I am almost sure it was Green that suggested that they write to you in care of me here in Springfield in the first place, and that he suggested to them that per-haps you would want me to represent you in the latter case. I am almost sure that that is the reason that the representative of the Reve-nue Department of the United States Government suggested to you that you have me act for you in this matter. I am sorry if I have made a mistake in the matter mother, but in the face of the law governing this man in his action and the information that was given to them by Secretary Green, I did not see how he could do anything other than what he did do, unless he put himself clearly in violation of the law, and liable under the law.

I don't think that he has had any option in the matter, and I believe he made it just as easy as it was possible for him to; at the same time it is possible that I made a mistake in agreeing to what was done, and if you feel that way about it, I shall try to have the action cancelled, and have it put in the shape that it was in before hand.

I agree with you that it looks mighty bad for a representative of the government to do what they did in your case; however, I know that there are a great many people in this country that would like nothing better than that kind of information in connection with yourself and I would have [gone?] a good deal out of my way to have avoided their getting any information of that kind.

I explained to him just as thoroughly as you have in your letter that in all the years you have been working you did not charge salary,—that when you got any money you usually found an excuse for giving it to some poor devil that needed it, and you did not have any left. At the same time you did not keep any account of it,—I was satisfied you could not make out a list of that kind, and when he told me that in any donations that you made before they could be deducted, that it had to be some organization organized for that purpose. I knew that you did not make any donations through that kind of an institution, so that so far as the law was concerned there could not be any deductions.

Trusting that this finds you getting better, and with best wishes I am,

Yours sincerely,

[John H. Walker]

TLC (John H. Walker Papers)

To John H. Walker

Washington D. C
Dec 18—1923

Dear John[1]

Your letters came to me. You [know] that whatever you do for [me] is allright   you know there is no power on Earth could [shake] me confidence in you   You know I do not keep account of [things]   If you [knew] how much I had to give poor devils who were [threatened] with arrest from that March   I could say nothing to anyone for it [would] get me into trouble.

I did not every before know anything of Tax for I never had anything to tax   When the Mexican Gov gave me a little money I took care of it.

You [know] the bills from the office were paid every fifteen Day   I kept no account of it   I am feeling better since I got your letter   You are one soul I would [trust] my life with.   I would give anything to see you.

Lewis-Murry were here yesterday   They and Sec Davis went to see the Pres at the White House   I think the mission was to see if there could not [*one or more pages missing*] The miners themselves have no love for *justice* or *honor* or they would [not] stand for such treatment by there officers

This [is] not the old Labor Movement   It is not What can I do [for] the poor helpless men and women—it now is how much is in it for me   John I will send a checque for what you [paid] Let the other stay where it is untill I need it   Say nothing about it   the dark hour may come—That *Hage* was a mistake of the Type writer   I said J H.   I hope that Reve fellow is satisfied

Love to all at home

Mother

ALS (John H. Walker Papers)
1. Shaky handwriting and omitted words make this letter almost unintelligible. Contrary to practices elsewhere, the bracketed words include not only questioned decipherments of the handwriting but also suggested omissions.

To John Fitzpatrick

December 20, 1923.

Mr. John Fitzpatrick, President
Central Body,
166 Chicago, Illinois.
My dear Mr. FitzPatrick:

I have not neglected that poor fellow in jail in Pittsburgh. I am working quietly on the matter here. I think after New Years I will be able to do considerable work that will be successful. We are working to find who the members of the Pardon Board are in order to be able to approach them.

I know a newspaper man here who is very close to the Governor and I think I will be able to do a little successful work, that is I hope so, anyhow.

I will go up and see the Governor after New Years. You can not do much of anything before, they are all tied up in politics. I hope to be successful, though, and get that poor helpless wretch out of jail and take him to his wife and children.

I hope you will have a happy Christmas and the coming year will bring peace and prosperity to you and the work you are so arduously engaged in.

Sincerely,
Mother Jones

TLS (John Fitzpatrick Papers)

1923

To John H. Walker

Washington, D. C.
Dec. 25.—1923.

Dear John

This is Christmas day   I felt I must send a line to you. I got a severe attack of Rheumatism   I fear I will never get over it   This climate never did agree with my health even when I was [strong?] but I have every comfort that can be given to me. I am afraid that I will have to go west

I would like to see you   There is Terrible condition of affairs in West Virgna   I would like to see you to tell you some things   All Cabin Creek is gone   The poor Devils are living in tents   They will not organize Cabin Creek a in some years   They had better let those poor Devils & quit raising money to half feed those little children this winter

There never was a such an outrages deal given to a lot of men by the [*omitted word*] they paid & trusted   Their National office has never brought those traitors to time   They did not send Van bittner the great Internat represent[ative] but he could could go to Kansas—& Nova [Scotia?] to crush honorable men in to slavery.[1] I begin to think [*remainder of letter missing*].

AL (John H. Walker Papers)
1. When the UMWA charters were canceled in Kansas and Nova Scotia, Van Bittner, a loyal supporter of John L. Lewis, helped reorganize the districts.

From John H. Walker

December 27, 1923.

Mother Jones
c/o 3700 Fifth Avenue, N. W.,
Washington, D. C.
Dear Mother:

This is to acknowledge receipt of your letter of the 18th. Glad to hear from you. Perhaps I should not have written the way I did, but sometimes it seems that everything goes wrong and the load just gets a little larger than my capacity to carry it. However, I was very much pleased to hear from you and to learn that you had not gotten my letters at all, and that you were simply writing out of your feelings before you got the copies of the letter from Green and a clear understanding of the situation.

I am glad that it is definitely disposed of however. Sorry that I could not have gotten the thing adjusted in a better way, but that seemed to be the very best that he could do at that time.

Things seem to be in a terrible shape in that West Virginia situation. I don't know what to make out of it. With the national or interstate contract expiring the first of April and the joint conference beginning now, industrial conditions as bad as they are, it makes it look not as well as one would want it. However, the presidential election being pending and as Coolege seems to be able to depend only on the national spokesmen of our organization for support from organized labor, I am rather under the impression that the interests and the people who are supporting him, will go out of their way a good deal to prevent a national strike of the coal miners of our country on the eve of their primary and election. I think too they will go out of their way to make the settlement as good as they can make it for the effect that it will have politically, so that there is a possibility that the powers that be, may adjust matters in West Virginia and work out a general settlement. I sincerely hope so, at any rate, in the interest of our organization and the men, women and children depending on it.

It may be possible that I will get to Washington within the next month or so, and if I do I shall surely take advantage of the opportunity to have a long visit with you, and at any rate it wont do a darn bit of good to worry mother.

I am glad that you seem to be getting better and I hope you will continue to improve until you get back your old time health again. Unless you have it to spare, and do not need it at all, don't send me any checks here.

With love and good wishes I am,

Sincerely
[John H. Walker]

TLC (John H. Walker Papers)

From Mrs. Peter Benner

Garrett
Somerset Co Pa
De 27 1923

Dear Mother Jones

it [has been]¹ a long time Since I saw you or could get in tuch with you I often think of [when] you and I was to gather in Portage But I Rote to Indanaplus to find out whre you was I wold like to see you agan I am left a Widow now and I am 71 yeas old I have no one to help me to get a living there is no work heir all is shut down I keep

Boarders wen there is work now I cant get Eny to keep and Mother I asked the Locals to helpe me and thy Said Wen my husband dide he took his clam a long with him   I am sure he did not take me with him he was one of the first to Join the union Wen thy first come in Wen they was Established a union he was a nigth of Labor Before and he Joined the united mine workers and was a Loyal true union man untill death clamed him he took his honer with him and Mother I am going to ask you if you will try to get me a Litel Relief thy wont give me Eny help heir They are helping som and wont do Eney thing for me so I will as[k] you [if you] will ask the miners to help me in Some Litel masure   husband and I was thrown out of our home Because we kept organizers and worked for the union and Mother if you will Pleas see what you can do for me as I shant as[k] Eny one here to do Eney thing for me I am in a Shape I need help I am 71 yers old and meny of my Relitives Belong to the union So Moth[er] if you can do Eneything for me I will Be so thankfull for What Ever it is So I will close hopeing you a happey New Year

from Mrs Petter Benner
union miners Wife

ALS (William Green Papers)
  1. This bracketed supplement and others below have been suggested to give meaning to a text which is very difficult to read.

From John H. Walker

December 29, 1923.

Mother Jones,
c/o 3700 Fifth Street, N. W.,
Washington, D. C.
Dear Mother:

  This is to acknowledge receipt of your letter of the 25th. Glad to hear from you. There is nothing new to say in the matter.

  Trusting this finds you and Mr. Powderly and the rest of the folks well, I am with best wishes,

Sincerely,
[John H. Walker]

TLC (John H. Walker Papers)

To John H. Walker

Washington, D. C.
Dec 31—1923

Dear John

I just got your letter. It made me feel the world was not so dark after all   dont ever apolize to me for anything you do   I know it was the best you could   I know what burden you have to meet. You & Ed Nockels are the men as long as I live I look to you. The W Va has no one to blame for the condition they are in but the officers   What the miners should do is to take them out & hang them for an example to other *Traitors*. John I told you long ago that those fellows would never go to jail[1]   They have plaid a shrewd game to fool the people   Now they come up to the Department of Labor to send down some of Concil-iators   That both sides were getting tired giving money to attorneys

What a Damanable game to play on the poor men   They lost time   The last time they were in Court they hired a fellow to bribe the jury foreman   The fellow is in jail but they dont to jail who commit the crime   The strange part of it is that the national don't say word against it but they could crucify those who stand for a princi[ple]

Lewis & Murray[2] were here last week   they and the Sec of Labor went to see Cooledge   I did not hear what for

I think you will hear of a compulsory arbitration bill brought at the next Congress There is something rotton   Strange that those fellows that have ruined the organization in West Va and Kentucky can go with their work of Destruction   I was in W. V. a month ago   If I could see you there is something rotten   I am not well. I am dis-courage   I look at the work of years   John, Seales is here Talking   A happy new year   Love to all at home

Loyally yours
Mother

ALS (John H. Walker Papers)

1. Of the 543 persons arrested following the march on Logan and battle of Blair Mountain, only three were convicted; William Blizzard and Frank Keeney, the principal leaders, escaped punishment.

2. Philip Murray (1886–1952), president, District 5, UMWA, 1916; vice-president, UMWA, 1926–1942; president, United Steel Workers, 1942–1952; president, CIO, 1940–1952.

To Ephraim F. Morgan

[1923?]

My Dear Gov

Just a few points   Ask that crowed if a member of their organization did not go to the White House & Strike the Table in Mr. Tumul-
tys office & ask the Federal Troops be sent Mingo at once   everyone
wondered why he was not thrown out of the White House   he went to
the D L they asked who the H—— he represented, the U. M. W.
When were you a member of the Miners   I represented Mr. Keeney—
Mooney—Give them back a little of their own medicine

AL fragment (Ephraim F. Morgan Papers)

1924

To John H. Walker

Washington D. C.
Jan 11—24

Dear friend

I am all in to day can only write a few lines It looks as if will not get well again I had the Dr. yesterday So far I have not had any relief I saw Van Bittener at the Dept. of L. yesterday Al *Hamilton* has all his tools in control of the Miners organization *Hughs* Phil M. V. B. *Zimmerman*[1] The own the West Va gang If I could see you I could tell you much more than I could write I am afraid I will have to go to Los Angeles I am all broke down That W. V. ruined my health No gun man ever made the attack on me that Mooney & Keeney did

When J L—[*one word illegible*] called at the White House two weeks ago, (The Pres) *said* I wish you gentlemen the fullest measure of success in your honest endeavor to faithfully represent your constituants

In doing this you rely upon the Justice of your cause and not on any influence that you can bring to bear from others, do not rely on Politic or Politicians Only so far as you are right can you hope to *succeed*

They would not be heard of if it were not for the work I did I saw Hoover[2] the other day I think from what he said thing will move
  Love to all at home

Loyally
Mother

ALS (John H. Walker Papers)

1. The references are probably to Philip Murray, vice-president, UMWA; John Zimmerman, former executive board member from Illinois; and Van Bittner, international organizer. Hughs's identity is uncertain.

2. Secretary of Commerce Herbert Hoover's calendar lists an appointment with Mother Jones for 2 January 1924 but does not give the subject of the meeting.

To William Green

Washington, D. C.,
January 14, 1924.

Mr. William Green,
1106 Merchants' Bank Building,
Indianapolis, Ind.
My dear Friend Mr. Green:

I hope you have not put me down as an ingrate and one that did not appreciate your kind remembrance of me at Christmas. I have not been well and one thing another has been keeping me putting it off. I concluded that you would fully know that I appreciated your kindness even though I had not put it in words.

Enclosed you will find a letter that was sent to me. I am not in a position to render the assistance to this poor creature that I would like to, but the contents of the letter will show you she is in need and I am sending it to you with the conviction that you will do your part to help the poor creature. I hope you will have a peaceful and real business like convention and that harmony will previal. I will not be able to attend it on account of my health much as I would like to attend.

I hope you will do something to stop those miners giving their money away as they have been doing to people who do harm after getting the money.

Hoping you will have a happy New Year and that peace will come to you, and I would like to see you as I have much to tell you that I cannot write. I am working hard here to get a few poor creatures out of jail.

With best wishes for your future happiness, I remain

Sincerely and truly your friend
Mother Jones

TLS (William Green Papers)

From John H. Walker

January 16, 1924.

Mother Jones,
3700 Fifth Street,
Washington, D. C.
Dear Mother:

This is to acknowledge receipt of your letter of the 11th with enclosure. Glad to hear from you. That fellow seems to talk pretty straight. I had some other information in connection with him and it almost makes me respect the man. I hope he does stand up honest, clean and straight and do the right thing. At the same time, I hope for the sake of the women and children and the most of the men too are honest poor devils, for their sake too, that an agreement may be reached in the coming joint conference.

I am very sorry to hear of your continued illness and I sincerely hope that you may get feeling better in the near future. At the same time Mother I think the milder climate will be better for you. I would like to have you with us, but Mrs. Walker is not well—she is ailing continually, although she is able to be around, and it is bad enough for me to have one cripple to take care of. I don't know what I would do with two, and particularly two like you and her. I guess I would get eat up.

Trusting this finds you in good health and better spirits I am with best wishes,

Yours,
[John H. Walker]

TLC (John H. Walker Papers)

From William Green

January 19, 1924.

Dear Mother:

I was glad to hear from you but you did not need to write me and tell me that you appreciated the little Christmas present I sent you. I know you were glad to receive it even though you did not tell me so.

I was sorry to learn you are ill. However, you are showing good judgment by deciding to stay in Washington rather than to risk your health by coming to Indianapolis while the International Convention is in session. My advice to you would be to stay where you are, conserve your strength, take care of yourself, all during the coming winter.

I hope I may arrange to help the widow who wrote you and whose letter you enclosed.[1] I wish from the bottom of my heart that we could stop the drain upon the miners' treasury and their funds for unworthy purposes.

With best wishes and kind regards, I am,

Sincerely yours,
[William Green]
Secretary-Treasurer.

TLC (William Green Papers)
1. See the letter to Mother Jones from Mrs. Peter Benner dated 27 December 1923.

To Ephraim F. Morgan

Washington, D. C.,
January 31, 1924.

Honorable Governor Morgan,
Charleston, W. Va.
My dear Governor:

I have not written to you for some time knowing the responsibility you have on your shoulders and no time to be writing unimportant letters.

I had a meeting with Gov. Pinchot[1] a few weeks ago with regard to a young fellow who is in jail in Pa. He has a wife and little children and in the course of conversation, he referred to some Pa Coal Miners who were in jail in W. Va., and I told him if he got in touch with you and there was any possibility [within?] the law of pardoning them he need not fear but that you would do it. I say that in the 24 years I have gone in W. Va. and being mixed in all the industrial battles in it, I have never found a Governor more open nor more [fair?] minded and with the high keen sense of justice of Gov. Morgan. I told him I would you to be a man of honor and a man of deep thought and before you acted you gave all matters deep thought. I also said that if I could approach all Governors as I could Gov. Morgan many things would be avoided. But that many men in your position think the whole state and all in it belongs to them. One instance that convinces me of the man's grand and human instincts was in regard to a woman who came to see me when in Charleston the last time, who with tears dropping on her breast she told me her sad story. I took her to the Governor and she told the sad story to him. He gave her $20.00 and a letter to bring her husband home. The man left the state. He wanted to come home but was afraid of getting arrested but the Governor told him to come and he would see that he was protected. Those were acts that I myself witnessed convinced me that in the history of 24 years there was a man in the executive chair that would do his duty impartially, although he has been misrepresented, I have witnessed many kind human acts of his and as long as I live I shall always appreciate the deeds he did for poor suffering wretches. I told Gov. Pinchot to apply for pardon for these men and though you would grant it at once. I also had a talk with Mr. Hoover but did not go into the matter as deep as I did with Gov. Pinchot but I convinced him that W. Va. for the first time in 24 years had a real humane Governor.

I have not been well, Governor, all winter and I think I shall go West in the course of a month to a better climate. I hope you are getting a little rest and that they are not stabbing you with their slimy pens as they were doing. I still retain for you, Governor, the same deep respect that I formed you during the conflict when I had experience with you and found out of what material you were made and I was convinced that you could be approached at any time for a just cause.

I am with deep respect

Yours sincerely.
Mother Jones

TLS (Ephraim F. Morgan Papers)
1. Gifford Pinchot (1865–1946), forester and conservationist, had just begun the first of two terms as governor of Pennsylvania.

From Ephraim F. Morgan

Charleston, West Virginia,
February 1, 1924

Mother Jones,
3700 Fifth Street N. W.,
Washington, D. C.
Dear Mother:

I acknowledge receipt of your very kind letter of January 31st, and I certainly appreciate the good things you said about me to Governor Pinchot and Secretary Hoover.

You have been a great help to me during my work and at many times a real inspiration.

There are several Pennsylvania miners in the penitentiary sent there for that terrible riot at Cliftonville about which you read some time ago. Application was made for a pardon for some of them, in fact all applied, but in going over the cases I found that they had agreed when they were sent to the pen that if their terms were made short they would not apply for pardon during the term.

It was also stated in some of the petitioner that some of them were not in good physical condition, and the confinement was injuring their health, but I had an investigation made in each case in regard to this complaint and found it incorrect, consequently, under the circumstances I felt it my duty to dismiss the applications.

I want to assure you that when I feel the facts and circumstances justify me under the law, it is always a pleasure to grant freedom to any of the poor fellows who may be imprisoned in our state institutions.

I hope that you will regain your good health again, and that you may have many more years added to your life to bring sunshine and happiness to those who need advice and comfort.

Very sincerely yours,
[Ephraim F. Morgan]

TLC (Ephraim F. Morgan Papers)

To John H. Walker

February 11, 1924.

Mr. John H. Walker,
626 Lafayette St.,
Springfield, Ill.
My dear John:

I have not heard a word from you for a long time and I suppose you were at the convention, and things did not seem to me to go off very smooth there. It is an outrage the way they treated Howat,[1] but it may react sooner or later.

I wish you would write and let me know how things are getting on and how Mrs. Walker and Esther are. I need not ask how you are for I know you are worked to death.

I had a letter from Fitzpatrick and it made me feel good. The boys in Chicago have been so good to me. I expect to go to Chicago soon and look forward to seeing you. In the meantime write me a few lines.

With love, I am

Sincerely yours,
Mother Jones

TLS (John H. Walker Papers)
1. Although fifteen resolutions in his favor were introduced at the UMWA convention in January, the members voted against reinstating his membership.

From John H. Walker

February 14, 1924.

Mother Jones,
c/o 3700 Fifth Street,
Washington, D.C.
Dear Mother:

This is to acknowledge receipt of your letter of the 11th. Glad to hear from you and to know that you are still active.

I was not at the convention. That is the first time in twenty five years that I was not a delegate to the Mine Workers International convention.

I expected just what happened in the convention with reference to

Howat. I wrote a friend of his in Kansas saying so, before the convention took place.

He seemed to be very optimistic at that time. They did not seem to think that there was any chance for that sort of thing happening. I guess perhaps they have changed their mind now. Sorry, but I am exceedingly glad that the prospects are so good for their getting an agreement signed up. I think it would be disastrous if the Mine Workers had to go into a fight, the way things are at the present time.

I may be in Washington shortly and if I am I expect to see you. If I do not get there however, will be glad to see you in Chicago and talk things over again.

Yours truly,
[John H. Walker]
President

TLC (John H. Walker Papers)

To John Fitzpatrick

Washington, D. C.,
Feb. 29, 1924.

Mr. John Fitzpatrick,
166 W. Washington St.,
Chicago, Ill.
My dear Mr. Fitzpatrick:

I am sending you this letter to let you know that I have been working every angle that I could reach with influence for that boy in jail. The matter was started going as Mr. Powderly knew the Lieutenant Governor very well and got him to use his influence. I also got in touch with the Attorney-General who will use his influence and the Department of Labor took it up with President Tighe[1] and he was up at the Department two day ago. He told them he would hire a lawyer to tend to the case and do every thing he could for the boys. So you see I have left no angle untouched to get this poor fellow home to his wife and children.

I hope that things are going smoothly with you. I expect to leave here pretty soon to go down to W. Virginia and get some poor fellows out of jail.

Then I am going West to carry on my work for Smidthy. My heart aches for him and I am not going to leave anything undone to get him out until I see him home with his Mother.

Things do not look very favorable in the West to me. I had a letter from Denver, stating that things were in bad shape and I got a letter from California. The tailors had 1,200 members in their organization when I was there. They now have only 60 and all the force that was on the weekly paper had to get off. But we must keep up courage and get more life into the men in the rank and file and some of those organizers have to be retired. I hope to hear from you soon.

Sincerely yours,
[Mother Jones]

[*Holograph postscript*] Things look bright for that boy in Pa. I have a lot to tell you

TL with holograph note (John Fitzpatrick Papers)
  1. Michael F. Tighe (1858–1940), a conservative union leader, was local officer, organizer, secretary, and president of the Amalgamated Association of Iron, Steel and Tin Workers over two generations, 1877–1936.

To Emma Powderly

Chicago,
March 31, 1924.

Mrs. T. V. Powderly,
3700 Fifth St.,
Washington, D. C.
My dear friend:

I guess you think I got lost not hearing from me before but one thing after another occurred so that I was unable to take the time. It was a lucky thing you made me wear my heavy cloak. I would have frozen to death if I had the others. It began snowing after I left Washington and is still snowing here yet. The weather is not at all agreeable, but just as soon as I possibly can I am going west. I hope Mr. Powderly is well and tell him take care of himself. And, will you please send that little fur cape to the office here so that I can have it when I need it. I am not feeling any too well. A fellow gave me some radium stuff Saturday to put in the bath and it may do me some good. I would like to have a good talk with Mr. Powderly on conditions in W. Virginia as I found them, but I cannot do it in a letter.

I hope everyone in the house is well and give them my love and don't work so hard Emma. With best wishes,

I am yours,
Mother Jones

TLS (Terence V. Powderly Papers)

To Emma Powderly

Chicago,
April 8, 1924.

Mrs. T. V. Powderly
3700 Fifth St.
Washington, D. C.
My own dear friend:

I received my fur cape and it took me all day to unwind the string that tied it and I thought it was rather heavy and so I looked around and found the pocket was sewed up. I opened it with care and found its contents. I then relieved myself of the surprise at the way it was tied.

I expect to leave here tomorrow for Los Angles and send all mail to 2759 Marengo Street, Los Angeles, Calif.

I have not improved in health since I left you, but I was a great deal of trouble to you, you gave up your own room, and that worried me to death because you needed that room after your long day's toil. I know how often you felt tired and needed to go down and lay down there and that with your great generous heart you surrendered that room to me. It is one of your great traits to give up your own comfort to make life a little brighter for others.

Give my love to Daisy and to all members under th roof and tell Mr. Powderly that a great many have been making warm inquiries about him.

With love to Aunt Alice and all the family, When you hear from me again it will be from Los Angles.

With deep love and gratitude to your kindness to me, I remain,

Sincerely yours,
Mother

How is Aunt Lizzie? Is she still grunting?

TLS (Terence V. Powderly Papers)

To William Green

2759 Marengo St.,
Los Angeles, Calif.
June 30, 1924

My dear friend Mr. Green:

I waited in Washington all during March, expecting to see you but I failed owing to the fact you were so dreadfully busy you could not attend the Council gathering, as I expected.

1924

Well, you see what I told you in the hotel in Indianapolis that evening, has come true in West Virginia. The mistake the National made, was that they did not take over that office immediately when the march was made. And there is another grave question I would like to have you know about, but I cannot write it to you, as I cannot give the information to anyone but you. The brutal action of those officials has destroyed the organization which was built up thru the suffering and sacrifices of men, women and children, in the hope that in the long years to come a ray of sunshine might be brot into their lives and make the world a better place for them to live in. I have much to tell you and would give anything to see you. The organization must be built up again in West Virginia, but it is going to take time to do it.

I have been suffering all winter and summer with rheumatism. It followed the attack of pneumonia I had. I am taking treatments for it here and am getting a little better, and I hope to be well enough to go East pretty soon.

I want to go to West Virginia to see the Governor to see what I can do to have those poor devils turned free, as they were not responsible for that march. I understand they are to be tried in Logan, which means conviction. I recieved a little information—and I feel if I can see the Governor I may be able to aid in setting them free.

I worked hard in Washington to liberate the poor fellows who were arrested during the Steel Strike, and I think I have the wires layed to accomplish it, as I reached the Governor, the Lieutenant Governor and the Attorney General.

I dont know when I will be able to see you, but I have much to confide in you for the benefit of the organization. Those beastly traitors—if I had my way I would make an example of them—hang them to the highest telephone post I could find, as an object lesson for all the other traitors.

Write to me because I get lonely when I do not hear from you. If I go to West Virginia to see the Governor, I will stop off to see you on my way there or back. I am going to try to help set those poor fellows free.

I had a letter recently from a friend about the gang who expected to "clean up the State Federation of Labor." It is their kind that corrupted the labor movement in the State of West Virginia. I had the fight to make alone against that crowd of vultures, and you were the only one that I could go to or trust. If I could have approached the head officials as I did you, there might have been a different story to tell today. However, I am in hopes that we will be able to start over again and reconstruct the whole machinery of organization. Be careful of the men you send in there to take charge of that office.

Do not worry because this letter is written on a typewriter. The party doing it is an old time friend of mine, and what I say is under cover to you.

With best wishes for your health, and assuring you of my deepest confidence in your honor and sincerity in a great cause, I am as ever,

Your friend,
Mother Jones

TLS (William Green Papers)

To John H. Walker

Los Angelos Calif
July 2—24

Dear John

You no doubt think I have forgotten you. No I have not I have been sick ever since I left you. I have been taking treatment for my Rheumatism but I have not been very successfull. Yet I have a little more strenght than I had some time ago

Well John the one faithfull friend I had for the last 45 years has passed away   Terence V. Powderly   he fought my battles for years he faced all the Slanders & boldly Deffended me   Such men are scarce. You & Nockels Fitzpatrick & Jay Brown[1] of Seattle are those I could depend on   I want to see you   There is so much you should know before I pass away from this Earth

Well they had a great time in St Paul[2]   McDonald has signed his Doom so far as the Labor Movement is concerned   after the campaign they Land a lot of those fellows in jail   Mark what I tell you. What they should have done was to [unite?]. You know most those fellows at head are nothing but Pie Counter hunters   The Socialist Movement lost it breath so they had to start something to fleece the poor Devils for a soft job—There is no Labor Movement out here.

I saw Germer the other day.   he is Sect for the oil workers.   he had an auto worth 2000 Dol a fine pair of silk stockings a pair of shoes must have cost 25 Dol. The poor devils pay the bills   John the Labor Movement is [fleeced?] more than any other Institution

Well I am getting tired   Will close untill I see you   They want me in Johnson City on Labor Day it may be the last Labor Day I will see

fondly
Mother

ALS (John H. Walker Papers)
1. Jay G. Brown was president of the International Union of Timber Workers.
2. At a convention in June of the Federated Farmer–Labor party in St. Paul, Minne-

sota, which was dominated by William Z. Foster and his Communist Workers' party, Duncan McDonald, former president of the Illinois Federation of Labor, accepted the nomination for president of the United States.

From John H. Walker

Springfield, Illinois,
July 7, 1924.

Mother Jones,
2759 Marengo St.,
Los Angeles, California.
Dear Mother:

This is to acknowledge receipt of your letter of July second. Glad to hear from you and to know that you are gathering a little strength and hope that you may be able to recover completely.

Industrial conditions are exceedingly bad here and that has kept everybody busy. I sincerely hope that the change in West Virginia may be for the better. My opinion about it is that there is a long period of industrial depression ahead of us and that the labor movement will be rather severely tried during that time. After it is over, I think the experience and knowledge that comes from it will help the movement, but I don't look for its being built up very much during that experience, and the mining industry is perhaps getting more than its share of the depression.

I was sorry to hear of Powderly's going. I knew that you would feel it keenly, as you say, he was one of the few that could be depended upon at all times to stand for the thing that was right and they are very few, these days. The folks are all well and were inquiring for you.

If you can make it to Johnston City next Labor Day, I know everybody will appreciate it very much and will be mighty glad to have you. I have agreed to go to Evansville, Indiana on that date.

I am returning Cairn's letter as requested. Nockels I think, should be out of the hospital by now, and I guess he is getting completely well and in good shape by this time. His wife has been very ill and she is not entirely better yet.

With best wishes I am,

Sincerely,
[John H. Walker]

TLC (John H. Walker Papers)

From William Green

July 18, 1924.

Mother Jones,
2759 Marengo-st.,
Los Angeles, California.
Dear Mother:

I was pleased indeed to receive your letter dated June 30th. I did not know where you were until I received it. I thought you were in Washington. I thought of you when I read an account in the newspapers of the death of our old friend Mr. T. V. Powderly. Only a short time before he died I received several communications from him which communications were sent me in response to an invitation I extended to him to attend the dedication of the Mitchell Monument at Scranton, on May 30th. I was sorry indeed when I read of the death of this old warrior in the ranks of labor.

I know of course you must be intensely interested in the developments which have taken place in West Virginia recently. The International Union has now assumed full charge of affairs in District No. 17. Brother Percy Tetlow[1] is in charge and is directing the administrative work of the organization in that field. You know he is trust-worthy and competent.

I hope I may have the pleasure of seeing you soon and that I may enjoy a long talk with you. Take good care of yourself. I am sure that the climate at Los Angeles, where you are now living, will be helpful. I am very hopeful that you will overcome the illness from which you are suffering.

Mining conditions are very bad. There is scarcely any work. Throughout the bituminous coal fields the mines are either closed down or are working very poorly. We have strikes in West Virginia, Kentucky and Canada. We are battling against unfavorable economic conditions and I express the hope that conditions in the mining fields will improve this fall at least.

With every good wish, I am,

Very truly yours,
[William Green]
Secretary-Treasurer.

TLC (William Green Papers)

1. Percy Tetlow (1875–1960), one of the charter members of the UMWA, served in the Spanish-American War and World War I and on several national advisory bodies during the New Deal and World War II. He led the UMWA in their establishment of a welfare and retirement system.

To John Fitzpatrick

2759 Marengo Street,
Los Angeles, Calif.,
July 31, 1924

Mr John Fitzpatrick, President,
Chicago Federation of Labor,
166 West Washington Street
Chicago, Illinois.

My dear Mr. Fitzpatrick

I have just received a letter from Mrs. Pinchot, wife of the Governor, notifying me that Mr. Dolla has been pardoned. I am glad to convey this news to you, if you have not already been informed from some other source. I am enclosing the letter which she sent me, so that you will be able to see for yourself what has happened.

I shall leave for Chicago next week. I am to speak at Johnston City, Illinois, on Labor Day, and I want to have a few days to visit with you and Ed.

I hope that poor Ed. is back again at his desk. It looks so lonely to go in and not find him there. I have not written to him, knowing that he has more than he is able to bear, and so long as you keep me posted about his condition, I am not going to bother him.

When you write to Jay Brown, tell him I want his address. I don't know where to locate him, consequently shall enclose letter herewith and ask you to forward it to him.

I have not been any too well, but I am going to muster up enough courage to go East.

With best of wishes to you, and devotion to the cause, I am,

Loyally yours,
Mother Jones

[*Holograph note*] Send the enclosed letter to Brown   I see the Labor herald takes the credit for Dola release   You know they could not get him out in a hundred years

TLS with holograph note (John Fitzpatrick Papers)

From Claude Erwin

Los Angeles[, Calif.]
August 16th 1924

Mother Mary Jones
166 Washington St.,
Chicago, Ill.
Dear Mother;

I am mailing you under seperate cover a set of the pictures of the San Pedro raid victims. Also some of the pictures of the Funeral of Fellow-worker Sundstedt.

I have been unable to get any of the Ku Klux pictures but will endeavor to get them later. I have been unable to get any of the sworn statements of the victims because the police refuse to give them up and it will take quite some time before I can get in touch with the ones who swore to those statements.

We have had three raids and eleven arrests in the past week in San Pedro. Each raid and arrest was made without a warrent. These raids were made by the police and they seized organization supplies and personal property.

Two of the raids were on a private residence while the family were away from home.

We are entering suit against the City of Los Angeles Monday for all the raids and property seized and destroyed.

I shrink at the thought of going into the masters court for redress but it is forced on us. If the workers of the U. S. would rise up and protest against such injustices as have been perpetrated in Calif. these injustices would soon disappear.

We have thirty-five different trials coming up in the next five weeks for violation of the Busick Injunction. Ten of these come up next week. I was sorry you couldn't remain in Calif. and take in some of these trials and see how they dish out Justice in this state of C. S. laws and injunctions.

Hoping you are in good health and had an enjoyable trip to the east I am

Fraternally Yours for Industrial Freedom
Claude Erwin, Secty.

P. S. Any time I can be of any assistance to you just let me know.

TLS (Mother Jones Papers)

To John H. Walker

John R, Walker
626 Lafayette St.,
Springfield, Illinois.
Dear friend John,

You are the last one of earth that I thought would neglect me. You have not sent me a line since I have been out here. You know a line from you always cheers me.

We have had great changes since I saw you. Sam went to sleep in Smoky Hollow and Green took his place in Washington.[1] I think, John, that Green was the best selection that they could have made. If that Matha Wall[2] or any of that machine got in there I do not know where the Labor Movement would drift, but I had great hopes for its future progress with Green. He is supplanted by Kennedy of District 7.[3] Kennedy is a good fellow but he is a part of the machine and he can be handled very nicely. I noticed that Lewis did not get to be secretary of the Department of Labor. It is a lucky thing for the department that he did not get in there. His whole machine would be in there and some of the good fellows would have to take a walk. I felt quite sure, since I was in Washington last October, that there was very little hopes of his getting the position. If he got on the cabinet I do not know what we would do.

Well there are great changes taking place anyhow. I have a good deal to talk to you about when I get to Chicago and I hope that you will make it convenient to come in and see me.

John, I have not been well ever since I have been here, and I have given up all hopes of regaining my health. I am going back to stay at Powderly's. You know in Washington I get to see some of the old timers occasionally. While that does not bring back my health, still it does away with the blues.

I see that you have had a terrible time in Herrin.[4] That fellow Young was a bad egg and it is no loss to have him out of the way. Perhaps peace may come now that he is gone. They have a hard time in Colorado. The Ku Klux control the whole state now. They are putting Lindsey[5] out of business and they will put everyone else out that does not suit them. I am afraid that they are going to create a great deal of trouble before they are done away with, not alone for the state, but for the national government as well.

I notice in the worker that you and Fitzpatrick, and Nockles are not behaving yourselves very well. If the Worker does not pursue some other tactics besides attacking the honest people in the Labor Movement I fear they will go out of business some day. They are pursuing the very same tactics that the Socialists did, Condemning everyone that does not agree with their philosophy.

Well, give my love to Mrs Walker and Esther, and I hope they are all well. With Best wishes I remain yours until I see you in Chicago. A Happy New Year to all at home.

Mother Jones

TLS (John H. Walker Papers)

1. After the death of Samuel Gompers, William Green, secretary-treasurer of the UMWA, succeeded him as president of the AFL, 19 December 1924.

2. Matthew Woll (1880–1956), president of the International Photo-Engravers Union of North America, held many offices in the AFL and served on the War Labor Board in World War I and the National War Labor Board in World War II.

3. Thomas Kennedy (1887–1963), president of District 7, UMWA, succeeded William Green as secretary-treasurer, 1925–1947; vice-president from 1947 to 1960, he assumed the presidency on the death of John L. Lewis.

4. For three years, violence in Herrin, Illinois, had brought repeated intervention by the National Guard. In the latest episode, 24 January 1925, Glenn Young, a former Department of Justice agent with a reputation as a killer, died in a clash between his Ku Klux Klan followers and deputy sheriffs.

5. Benjamin Barr Lindsey (1869–1943), a pioneer in setting up juvenile courts, constantly battled the political establishment in Colorado until his disbarment in 1927; he later practiced law and was judge of the superior court in Los Angeles.

From John H. Walker

Springfield, Illinois,
February 7, 1925.

Mother Jones,
c/o 2759 Marengo St.,
Los Angeles, Cal.
Dear Mother:

This is to acknowledge receipt of your letter of recent date. Glad to hear from you and to know that you still have enough strength to grumble a little yet. I don't think it is so very long since I wrote you, and still I suppose the time passes pretty quickly when you are busy and it hangs pretty heavy on your hands when you are not busy. Every moment of my time is taken up with the legislature, just having convened. There are so many things that need to be done and I am doing the best I can.

Yes, I think Green will make a good man in that position. I agree with you references to Kennedy except that I am hopeful that if he gets in a position where he can be independent, that he will be. Tom is a good man at heart and has a good deal of ability.

If you will let me know a little ahead of time, I will arrange to be in Chicago and see you on your way to Washington. I am hopeful that the situation in Herrin, is going to clear up. My guess about the Worker, is that that gang are on the payroll of the other side.

Yours,
[John H. Walker]
President.

TLC (John H. Walker Papers)

Assignment of Bond

31 March 1925

This argentine Bond from now on is the Property of Mrs. Ema Powderly

Mother Jones

DS (Terence V. Powderly Papers)

To John H. Walker

Washington D. C.
July 30/25

Dear friend

Owing to the Terrable condition of my Health the Dr says I have to leave this climate   I have suffered terrable agony   Will be in Chicago next Monday & Tuesday   We may never meet again   I want to see you before I go West

I have so much tell you that you should know

Love to Mrs. W. [and?] Ester

be sure t see me

Loyally,
Mother

O John I am all boke down cannot hold a pen in my fingers They are crippled

ALS (John H. Walker Papers)

To John H. Walker

2759 Marengo St.,
Los Angeles, Cal.
Feb. 15—1926.

Pres. John H. Walker,
626 LaFayette St.,
Springfield, Ill.

Dear John:

I have been on the scrap pile ever since I saw you, and I have been going to write to you time and time again but, owing to my condition I kept postponing it. I got some medicine that a Dr. in Syracuse New York, sent me for rheumatism. It did me a wonderful amount of good, but the weather for the last week or so has been damp and unfavorable to my desease, and I am again beginning to feel the old pains coming back. My Dr here sent after some more of the medicine and when I receive it, and begin to take it, I feel I will get relief.

Well John, the anthracite strike was to a great extent a fiesta. Just think of making a five year contract after what the men suffered. The Morning Examiner here (a Huret Paper) made a statement "that the miners, when putting a man at their head should look around for a man with brains or, go over to the Operators and get one."

West Virginia is on the scrap pile from information sent to me there. Its a terrible enditment against the officers. I have some letters from there that I would like you to see but I cannot send them to you by mail. I expect to go to Washington the last of next month, and on my way will stop off at Chicago. You may come up and see me and I will let you see those letters that I have. I want to have a talk with you alone, and then with Nockels and Fitzpatrick. I wan't to arrange, legally. I want you to form a committee to handle the profits from the book I wrote, and it is to go into a fund to defend the poor wretches that are placed behind the bars by the capitalists courts, and their only crime is fighting for the bread they produce, for their children. I makes no difference to me whether they are I. W.s or A. F. of Ls, I will contribute my part to their defense. I know that Mrs. Powderly will always take care of me so I am not worrying about that, but those poor fellows have no one to look out for them and their little ones crying. When I pass away the boys at Mt. Olive will see that I am laid to rest with the boys that gave up their lives some twenty seven years ago in

Verdon Illinois. I don't want those dam Isms to get a dollar of it. I will have to get a lawyer when I go to Chicago to look into that thing for I don't trust that Charles Kerr.[1] The book is not printed as I wrote it anyway, and I have never been satisfied with it.

I see that the miners of Ziglar and Farringtons henchmen are at loggerheads with each other. I sent ten dollars John, to those poor fellows to help defend them, in Ziglar. There were some mighty good boys down there. John, there seems to be some disrupting hand at work in the miners union as well as other organizations. It dos not appear on the surface but the silent work is going on just the same. In 1922 tey had two Open Shop Papers, the capitalists had, now they have three hundred and thirty six open shop papers that they are circulating. The Labor papers don't seem to give any warning to the workers with regard to that. I have a great deal to talk to you about for the good of the miners organization, when I see you. I could sit here all night and write to you but I don't feel able John, to do it. When I was coming here, I don't think I would ever have gotten here if it had not been for Fitzpatrick who came to the Hotel and took me to the train and put me in. Fortunately when I got to Los Angeles I had a good place to come and stay. Miss Flaherty has taken the best of care of me not withstanding that she is not in the best of health herself. I hope I'll get better and that I will be able to see you when I am going thru Chicago.

There is a peculiar apathy in the labor movement to day, unknown in its history before. I regret very much that Green did not give Percell,[2] the delegate from England a more cordial reception than the papers said he did. So far as I was able to read I think the delegate was perfectly right in his speech that he delivered at the convention in Atlanta. I am very much afraid that fellow Rickert[3] is going to influence Green. He was the hidden adviser of Gompers. Green is a good fellow, kind hearted and honest to the core, and well meaning but there are a lot of well meaning people in the Insain Asylum, John. Well, my love to all and write to me just as soon as you get this letter. I hope Esther is doing well and also Mrs. Walker. I will close with the old time friendship. Most sincerely yours,

Mother Jones

TLS (John H. Walker Papers)

1. The Charles H. Kerr Company of Chicago had published Mother Jones's autobiography.

2. Albert Arthur Purcell (1872–1935), British trade union leader and member of Parliament, had attended the convention of the AFL in Atlanta the preceding November; Green led the convention in rejecting his appeal for international relations with Soviet Russia.

3. Thomas A. Rickert (1876–1941), president of the United Garment Workers of America, continued during the Green regime, as in that of Gompers, to hold positions of power in the AFL.

From John H. Walker

February 22, 1926.

Mother Jones,
c/o 2759 Marengo Street,
Los Angeles, Cal.
Dear Mother:

This is to acknowledge receipt of your letter of the 15th instant. Glad to hear from you and to know that you are still living and taking an active interest in the movement.

Speaking of the anthracite strike, it is too bad that men have to suffer for any reason, but I am quite sure that if the anthracite strike had not been called, that we would have had a much worse situation in the bituminous industry than obtains there at the present time. I think that strike saved the bituminous situation for the time being. I don't know whether that justified the calling of the strike or not; but I do know that it meant saving things from going to the bad completely in the bituminous districts.

The fact that the anthracite coal operators made absolutely no effort whatever to operate their mines non-union, and then that they made this settlement under the circumstances, has caused some gossip, but I think considering the circumstances at the time of the settlement being made, that the mine workers were lucky to get the settlement they did. That at least will maintain a nucleus of a national organization. The bituminous situation is such as to make me fearful for the future. I don't see how anything can be done to prevent suffering and injury to our people, and our organization, unless industrial conditions improve a good deal, and then perhaps a national strike being called on the eve of the presidential election might be successful and get a settlement that would save the situation.

From the information I get, the organization is in bad shape in Nova Scotia, British Columbia, Washington, Utah, Colorado, Texas, Arkansas, Oklahoma, West Virginia, Old Virginia, Pennsylvania and portions of Ohio and Indiana.

Now Mother, on these other matters, I dislike very much to write you, because during all of our lifetime, we have agreed almost entirely on the different issues, but in this, I disagree with you. I think you had such feeling on the John Mitchell matter that you could not give it your usual calm, cool, impartial judgment; and I have as much feeling the other way. So that for that reason, I would not want to connect myself with that book. Then, there is the other reason. The uses to which you want to put those funds. For the average unfortunate poor devil, who, because of ignorance, is a fanatic or an extremist, foolish, I have nothing but sympathy,—but I agree with you, there are a lot of well meaning people in insane asylums. I don't want to do anything to those kind of people that will cause them to suffer unnecessarily. At the same time, I want to, if I can, protect the rest of society from them, and particularly the trade union movement, which holds within it, I believe, the only hope of humanity. My judgment about it is that the most of the active spirits in the socalled I. W. W. or Communists organizations of today, or the Workers Party, are stool pigeon detectives on the payroll of the detective agencies that are employed by the anti-union corporations, that they are being employed to prevent the unions accomplishing any progress for their membership; to do the things that will turn the sentiment of the average man against them; to create dissention and division within them; to destroy every man or woman who is honest that they cannot control, and to destroy the labor movement itself.

In this particular case that you cite at Zeigler, they tried to set aside the present agreement in our state. Every coal operator in the United States is trying to have it set aside, and when the officers of the sub-district called a meeting of the membership to talk the matter over with them, fully, frankly and out in the open, these fellows put the lights out and tried to murder Lon Fox, than whom there is no more decent, kindly or honest officer of any organization of any kind in the world—a man with a family.

This same aggregation of individuals have left nothing undone that they could do to assasinate me in every way possible and they tried to associate me with this situation with which I have had nothing to do whatever. They have destroyed a number of organizations. For a number of years their efforts have played into the hands of the enemies of the miners union, both outside and within. There is not a single thing about them that is not bad, except the intentions of the well-meaning, ignorant ones who are honest, and they are the only ones too that are known to be honest, that make it possible for the stool pigeons, the emissaries of the enemies of labor, to do their rotten work; and because of these things, I cannot convince myself that I should take a position that means either becoming a party to their work, by negation, or by giving them encouragement, through taking a position that I will try to get them out of jail, if they are sentenced to it, by the socalled capitalistic court (and there is no one knows what those courts are, from the point of view of labor, better than I do).

I say this with perhaps as much regret as I have ever said anything in my life, but that is how I feel on the matter, and because you have requested me to do these things, I am compelled to speak.

All the folks are well so far as I know. My father died recently, and mother is living in Westville. She wants to finish her days in the old home. It is rather difficult, because she is all alone and all of them depend on me to take care of the situation. I am enclosing copy of the News Letter, which contains a clipping concerning my Father's death.

Trusting that this finds you in good health and spirits, with sincere regards I am,

Yours
[John H. Walker]

TLC (John H. Walker Papers)

To John H. Walker

3700 – 5 – Street
Washington, D. C.,
June 10, 1926.

Mr. John H. Walker,
Springfield, Ill.
Dear John:

I am writing you a few lines to let you know that I am still alive but I have been very sick after you left me that night, I got a sinking spell towards morning and I longed for the train to come to take me to Washington. I am feeling better and feel better today than for a long time and Mrs. Powderly has been taking the best care of me.

I have been using electric pads and I feel sure that helps me. I was afraid John that we would not meet again because I was so sick. I longed for the train to leave Chicago but I am down in Mr. Manning's[1] office today getting a few letters written. It is a good thing that there are a few good people in the world as I do not what we would do if there was not.

I had a letter from an old friend of mine in Florida and I wish that you knew him and could meet with him. I hope that Esther and Mrs. Walker are feeling well and I do not what I would do if Miss manning was not a good friend to me and writes for me as I would not be able to write to you as I would not be able to write myself.

With love and devotion to you, I remain your friend

Mother Jones

325

TLS (John H. Walker Papers)

1. John J. Manning, of the Shirt, Waist and Laundry Workers' Union (later United Garment Workers), played an active role in the AFL Union Label Trades Department from its founding in 1909 until his death in the early thirties. Two of his sisters also worked in the department.

From John H. Walker

June 14, 1926.

Mother Jones,
3700 Fifth St., N. W.,
Washington, D. C.
Dear Mother:

I have your letter of June 10th. Glad to hear from you and to know that you are feeling a little better. Just got back from a ten days trip on the road myself. Esther is in the hospital on account on an operation on her tonsils. It was pretty severe, but she semms to be getting over it alright now. Her mother is fairly well.

Industrial conditions are exceedingly bad and the prospects for the future are not any too good, still there are a good many active and well informed men and women in the labor movement today, and I have hopes that we will be able to weather the storm ahead. The blackest spot in the whole lot, is the coal mining industry. The Miners Union is in bad condition and my judgment is that it is going to get worse before it gets better. Everything is in about as good condition in Illinois as could be expected. We are in better shape than any other state that I know of.

With warmest regards, I am,

Yours,
[John H. Walker]

TLC (John H. Walker Papers)

From Katherine [Schmidt]

June 25th [1926][1]

Dear Mother:

It was awfully decent of the Warden to give the original portion of letter to Smidie saying he might want to sent it to me. So I am making few copies for our friends.

How are you, dearest? I so wish we could be together again. I miss you so much.

Children join me in sending love.

Hastily.

Katherine

Oh, Mother, see article in Sunset Magazine—July issue, about the Warden and prison. Older sent one of his men over to get it.

TLS (Mother Jones Papers)
1. The accompanying envelope gives the year and the place of origin, San Francisco, California.

From John H. Walker

August 25, 1926.

Mother Jones,
c/o 3700 Fifth Street,
Washington, D. C.

Dear Mother:

I am sending you, under separate cover, copy of a magazine that was written by Ed Carbine, and one of the Archibalds, last winter, I think, assisted by his wife. It is in rather homely language, but it portrays conditions as they were in the early days, and as I remember them in the mining communities in norther Illinois, prior to, and during the struggle to establish the miners union, as well as in the many years of bitter struggle to extend the organization and to build progress on the foundation that had been laid. It has the merit of being real, as are its authors. I know that it will interest you. He has a statement referring to yourself on page 29.

Trusting that this finds you in good health and that you are not worrying too much, with sincere regards and love, I am,

Yours very truly,
[John H. Walker]
President.

TLC (John H. Walker Papers)

To John H. Walker

Alliance, Ohio
Sep 28/26

Dear Friend Walker

Just a line to tell you I have not forgotten you.

I have been here with an old friend[1] of Ruskin Tennessee 30 years ago. She & her Brother live together about 3 miles from town She feeds me on goats milk & fresh eggs   With the care I have got I [*one word illegible*] weak & good for nothing   I will for Washington next week   Mrs. Powderly wants me home   She is a little afraid to have me away   I spent so much for Dr. with no relief. I suffer day night from my [knees?]. John I suffer more that I can tell you. There is a Dr. here that says he can help me but cannot cure me. I have little hopes of ever getting well again

This friend & her good Brother are getting every remedy they hear of but no relief   I am getting so nervous. I leave here next Sunday for Washington. I got a back set that night before I left Chicago   My knees began to torture me   I have not got over it since nor never will   I have not got Eds book yet after I read it will write   he was one faithfull soul.   good be relied

The papers here had a lot about Pres. Farrington   he is not the only traitor the miners have   Write me 3700–5th Street Washington D. C.

Love to all at Home

> Loyally
> Mother

ALS (John H. Walker Papers)
  1. Susana DeWolfe; her brother was Samuel Steiner.

From John H. Walker

October 3rd, 1926.

Mother Jones,
c/o 3700 Fifth Street, N. W.,
Washington, D. C.
Dear Mother:

This is to acknowledge receipt of your letter of September 28th. Glad to hear from you, altho sorry to learn that you do not seem to get well—that you are suffering so much. I sincerely hope by the time this letter reaches you, that you have had a rest and that care and medicine will have improved your condition.

The miners' situation looks hopeless Mother. That combination have got complete control—are going to do what they please—I don't think it is possible to do anything with them. It is going to take time and the miners themselves to cure it if it is to be cured at all, and the near future looks rather dark.

I understand Farrington was drugged just before he left New York and that that was responsible for his signing the agreement that he did.[1] That however hearsay, but in view of what was done to Frank

328

Hayes, it seems rather likely. My information was that Farrington was going to fight the program that was agreed upon by the large interests who are attempting to consolidate the coal business and the getting it in the control of one concern, and that they were desperate in getting him out of the way. He was no angel, but he was a good deal better than a great many of them who were on there, and I do know that he has done a great many good things and made a great many good fights for the labor movement. There are a lot of things he would not do. Ther is nothing that the men who tried to get rid of him, would not do. As between them and Farrington, he was much the better.

Poor Carbine—he has only one failing. If it was not for that, he would have done a lot more good for himself than he has done.

The situation in Illinois is much about the same as when you were here last.

Trusting that this finds you better, and with love and best wishes I am always your friend,

[John H. Walker]

TLC (John H. Walker Papers)
1. In September 1926, the news became public that Frank Farrington, president of District 12, UMWA, had signed a contract dated 1 July 1926 to serve as labor adviser to an Illinois coal company. John L. Lewis seized the opportunity to oust him from the presidency.

To John H. Walker

Washington, D. C.
Nov the 13 1925[1]

Dear John
Just going to send you a line   I have not heard from you so long   I have not just saw this morning that Keeney was Editing the Ill. Miner   Why did he not stay in W. V. and do his Education perhaps John down all of history the workers have crowned their Trators cruci-fied her Saviors and he remaned in his office when I went to Mammoth [Marmet] to stop that March there would have been a different condi-tion in W. Va. today.   he was not heard of when I was faceing ma-chine guns & Bull Pens   he struck me in the face   I have not got over that schock yet   he never offered an apology   look at the condition those poor fellows are in today. When I went to that women from robbing the Miners Magazine that Al Hamilton started in Indianapolis to slander you he told me to leave her alone   John L. Lewis sent her in   you had better watch that fellow don't be so dam easily fooled   I know those fellows, John   The fellows who betrais you once will again it bennifits their Pockets—

I have so much to tell you   I am suffering with pain from [Rheuma-tism?]

fondly
Mother

I had a beautiful letter from Gov Hunt of Arizona   There has been one true friend   he stood like a stone wall to me since I first met years ago

Love to all at home

ALS (John H. Walker Papers)
  1. Another hand has written in "(6)."

From John H. Walker

November 20, 1926.

Mother Jones,
3700 Fifth St., N. W.,
Washington, D. C.
Dear Mother:

This is to acknowledge receipt of your letter of the 13th instant. Glad to hear from you and to know that you are still taking an interest in what is going on. It is not the Illinois Miner that Feeney [Keeney?] is editing. It is a paper that has been started by the communists called the "Coal Miner". My information about it is that another person here in Springfield is really editing it, one whom you and I know, is out of the organization at the present time.

The prospects for the future don't look any too bright, but I am battling away doing the best I can.

Trust this finds you well and with best wishes I am,

Yours very truly,
[John H. Walker]

TLC (John H. Walker Papers)

To John H. Walker

3700 Fifth St., N. W.
December 16, 1926.

Mr. John Walker,
Springfield, Ill.
Dear John:

I am just writing to you to wish you amd Mrs. Walker and Esther a Merry Christmas and a Happy New Year and hope that the incoming year will bring you peace and happiness.

I will have to go back to California owing to the condition of my health and if I stop off at Chicago I would like to have a talk with you. I have some mail that I got from W. Va. that might be of some service to you but I cannot send it to you through the mail. As soon as I arrive in Chicago I will call you up as I will have to stay there a couple of days.

With all the best wishes, and blessings of the season, I remain

Sincerely and loyally yours,
Mother Jones

TLS (John H. Walker Papers)

From John H. Walker

December 21, 1926.

Mother Jones,
3700 Fifth St., N. W.,
Washington, D. C.
Dear Mother:

I have your letter of the 16th instant. Glad to hear from you and to know that you are still in the land of the living and active, and contemplating coming through here.

Anticipating the pleasure of seeing and talking to you at that time, I am with every good wish,

Yours,
[John H. Walker]

TLC (John H. Walker Papers)

From Susana DeWolfe

Alliance, O. R. D. #3
March 24—27

Dearest Mother

I was made very happy to receive your good letter and sorry that you had been ill instead of enjoying a good climate.

I was beginning to think you had been washed away in the Los Angeles flood, it seems you have an affinity for rain, but I'm glad you escaped the Calif. rains, it must have been serious.

Everything here is as it was when you left, we have been having hard rains for days and we could hardly get out to the road, the grass has become green as the result of it, and spring cannot be far off, although much chilly weather will have to be endured yet, before summer comes. I hope you are getting back your strength, and will be all O.K. again. Of course Mother you can expect set backs, but as long as you keep up your fine courage and the will to live, you will get on, and have much good out of life. I hope Mrs Powderly is well again, and hope she does not overdo, as we get older we have to let many things slide easy.

[*In margin*] My friend Mr Hunter the Poet died a year ago with cancer.

Ive dropped down on the lounge in the midst of sweeping to write a few lines to you, the Parrot is watching me write, I ask him shall I say hello to Mother Jones and he answered *Yes*.

Sam is not working yet, only triming some trees for a neighbor, but he is improving he has gained 6 lbs and I consider it great economy for him to get this rest, as it will be the means of him living longer. O course it is always inconvient not to have a pay day, but we keep cheerful with high hopes for better days. We may have to do some changing, we are thinking some of moving, but are not sure yet, in order to meet our payments.

People here always ask about you. I'm glad Miss Yarnell made you a visit. Glad to know she received my letter. I feel very happy that I have had the pleasure of doing just a little for you. It will always be a happy thought in my life, and I hope circumstances will so shape themselves that I can do still more. We send our love and best wishes and write when you can

Your children
Susana & Sam

ALS (Mother Jones Papers)

To John H. Walker

My Dear friend

I will be in Chicago on Thursday the 17. If possiable come up & see me   I do not expect to come back this way   We may not meet again. Some things I wish to you about

Loyally yours
Mother

Will be at the Washington Hotel

ALS (John H. Walker Papers)

From John H. Walker

April 30, 1927

Mother Jones,
800 Elizabeth Street,
Pasadena, California.
Dear Mother:

I am very sorry I missed you while you were going through Chicago recently. I was in Chicago at the time. I did not get your letter before I left Springfield so that it was only when I got back to the office that I knew that you were going through. I sincerely hope this finds you well, and that I might be able to see you when the A. F. of L. convention meets in Los Angeles this year.

Yours sincerely,
[John H. Walker]

TLC (John H. Walker Papers)

From Susana DeWolfe

R. D. #3 Alliance O.
Sept 9 [1927?]

Dearest Mother

I have been so anxious about you, and knew you must be sick somewhere, Mrs Powderlys letter confirmed that feeling. I was so glad to receive her letter telling me about you, these long trips to Cal. are too exhausting for you and I hope you will soon regain your strength so you can be home again.

Life is going on here much as usual. I have not so many flowers yet as I had at the little cabin, but in time will have [*one line missing*] I must try to get it to you, & hope it will reach you O. K.

Sam started to work but the pace is so great I do not know if he can keep up. Overproduction, and no happiness or peace is the rule now, making wrecks of humans seems to be the great game.

I put up some curtains at my windows in the kitchen and the wind blew them against Bobbies cage and he had them punched full of holes before I noticed him, he saw I was mad and looked over his shoulder at me like a naughty kid, he is trying to take a nap now has his blanket around him and his bill tucked in.

All summer and for several days past I have canned peaches we got nearly a bushel from the trees here. We have lots of apples, I have to chop my own wood now since Sam is working he does not have time, but there is so much laying around it isnt hard to chop. I like it better than coal it goes out sooner than coal and we are having our warm weather now, everything is a month behind in growth and I hope it will continue and not have a frost too soon.

My goats are out lying under the trees so calm and peaceful, Trotsky does not seem to feel good this morning & Trixy is visiting somewhere and it seems rather quiet in the old house, but I always have plenty to do. I'm not getting many eggs   chickens are moulting.

I'm going to the garden and gather some beans for supper Labor Day   Sam when he sat down to breakfast, he said I wonder where our dear Mother Jones is. We put out the flags and had a quiet day, thinking how beautiful the day was compared to last year, but we had a great day then, didn't we Mother,[1] this year they had a banquet in Canton, and that is all Labor doesn't make enough noise   Every village & town should make a stir. I have some stupid company just come, so I must close and will write to you again & Mrs. Powderly

With Love
S. DeWolfe

ALS (Mother Jones Papers)

1. The Alliance Labor Day celebration the preceding year had featured Mother Jones as a speaker.

To John Fitzpatrick and Ed Nockles

3700 Fifth St., N. W.
Washington, D. C.
November 14, 1927.

Mr. John Fitzpatrick
and Mr. Ed Nockels,
Chicago, Ill.
My dear old time Friends:

I have been wanting to write to for some time, but I have been unable to do so. I have been quite sick and was in the Garfield Hospital hanging between life and death and I have not regained my strength since coming out.

I will be 99 the first day of next May and I want to live to be 100 and come to Chicago to celebrate the anniversary.

I hope all is well with you both and when you see Walker tell him I would like a line from him. He has grown to be the most indifferent fellow among my friends.

I have some good friends in Washington in the Label Trades Department, Mr. Manning and his sisters. I owe them a debt of gratitude which I am afraid I shall never be able to repay.

Give my best wishes to friends and enemies alike.

With deep devotion and gratitude to you both, for the old time friendship, I remain

Sincerely yours,
Mother Jones

TLS (John Fitzpatrick Papers)

From John H. Walker

November 17, 1927.

Mother Jones,
3700 Fifth Street, n. w.,
Washington, D. C.
Dear Mother:

I just received copy of a letter you wrote John Fitzpatrick and Ed Nockels in which you complain about my indifference. There is no indifference Mother, except that I am getting old I guess and am absorbed completely in the work I am trying to do. I don't see any one and I have not written any one outside of connection with the work of the office.

Glad to know that you are still with us and that you expect to celebrate your one hundredth birthday anniversary in Chicago next year, and if I am well and able to go, I expect I will be there whether you invite me or not.

> With sincere good wishes, I am
> Yours,
> [John H. Walker]

TLC (John H. Walker Papers)

From Katherine [Schmidt?]

> San Francisco
> Nov. 18. 1927

Darling Mother

Our letters have crossed each other enroute. I was so glad to hear from you today, and to know you are able to dictate letters to your friends.

This is only a brief note to greet you for Thanksgiving Brother and I are so much richer than hosts of others, because we can give thanks for having you as our most beloved friend. We cannot put in words, dear heart, what you have meant to us, and only hope it will be our privilege to have a home you can come and share with us. You have shared our sorrows, and also the sorrows of hundreds of others; so at least a small degree of pleasure should not be denied to you. You are richly entitled to the best the world has to offer.

Make sure, Mother dear, that you do not take cold. Have you plenty of warm clothing?

Wonder if I will hear from the Yarnell girls at Thanksgiving? I do hope Catherine will not forget you.

Tomorrow—Saturday—I am going over to spend the afternoon and stay all night with Anita. We are going to take care of her nephew's baby (5 months old) while the parents go to the Foot Ball Game. She always asks about you, and sends her warmest love. Her address is 3936 Harrison St. Oakland, Calif. should you want to write her.

Once more, oceans of love to you precious Mother, and do hope your Thanksgiving will be pleasant.

> Devotedly
> Katherine

ALS (Mother Jones Papers)

From Catherine Yarnell[1]

Williams Ariz
Nov 24 1927

Mother Jones.
3700 Fifth St.
Washington D C.

With good wishes for happy Thanksgiving day   Have left Los Angeles for winter   Sorry I will not be there dining your Stacy.

Catherine Arnell.

Telegram (Mother Jones Papers)
1. Catherine Yarnell (1869–1948), a Los Angeles philanthropist, may have been Mother Jones's hostess during some of her California sojourns.

To John Fitzpatrick

December 14, 1927.

Mr. John Fitzpatrick
Chicago, Ill.
My Dear Friend:

Received your letter some time ago and was more than glad to hear from you.

I understand that the Governor offered a parole to Mooney but he would not accept it. He wanted a full pardon. If he does not accept a parole I am inclined to think he will spend his time behind prison bars. It is sad to think you have such men to deal with and that one has to put forth their best efforts to get their freedom, and then not to be appreciated any more than he appreciates it. If I could get Schmiddy and J. P. MacNamara out I would not bother with Mooney until he got tired of his boarding place.

I hope to be able to carry out your good wishes on my 100th anniversary, in Chicago and I shall do all I can to retain my health and strength to meet that occasion and tell Ed this letter is for both of you.

Trusting that the coming years will bring peace to you and Ed and all the boys, I remain

Most sincerely yours,
Mother Jones

TLS (John Fitzpatrick Papers)

From Cora Meyer[1]

3003 Juneau Ave
Milwaukee Wis.
Jan. 9—1928

My dear Mother Jones

I have been wanting to write you a long time. I read your Autobiography—the *Trade Council Librarian* recommended it *and* I've surely more than appreciated your wonderful services to the Labor movement—than too I note—you practically stand alone among the big *Employed Officials*—for relief for Colorado miners, here even the Socialists refuse Colorado Miners relief

One of the big Socialist officials leaves here to protect his and other Socialist's profits, in Colorado—Butterfly Mine. he takes up the "managership" of this mine.

However, our Jewish *and* Finnish people—*and* the *new* women's organization are working for *Colorado miners* relief.

I'm sending you a copy of the "Labor Defender" which will give you an idea of the Defense movement—the International Labor Defense is organizing—I wish you many more Happy New Years. Lucy Parsons of Chicago HayMarket Fame spoke here for I. L. D. Jan 1st.

Fraternally
Cora Meyer

ALS (Mother Jones Papers)

1. Cora Meyer (1895–1966), an official of the Milwaukee Office Workers Union, was active in many civil rights cases, 1920–1960; in 1929 she left the Socialist party to join the Communist party.

To John Fitzpatrick

January 11, 1928.

Mr. John Fitzpatrick, President,
Chicago Federation of Labor,
Chicago, Ill.

My dear Friend Mr. Fitzpatrick:

I am just going to write a few lines and tell you I received your letter some time ago but as I did not feel well could not answer it.

When I was coming back from Calif. I wanted to stop off and have a talk with you and Ed but I felt weak and thought I had better not stop but go straight to Washington. I was not here three days before I had to go to the hospital where I spent 4 long weeks, but fortunately I had some good friends in Washington such as Mr. Manning and his sisters in the Union Label Trades Department who were good and kind to me and so was Pres. Green.

Poor Schmiddy got turned down when he asked for parole. I think he made a mistake when he did not let some one else make the application. They are not so apt to comply with such a request as they are if it comes from some one with influence. Poor fellow, I am afraid he will not get out in a hurry. The one I feel sorry for is his poor sister. It is not often you find such a loyal sister as she has been. However, we must make the best of the worst and not give up hope.

Hope things are getting along smoothly and that Ed is in good health. Tell Ed from me I wish I was near him so I could get a little tonic when I did not feel well. Tell him I never forget him when I have a bad spell. I hope to be able to meet you all again. You know I have not given up hope to see my 100th anniversary and I will be in Chicago to feast with you. At least I hope so.

Some day perhaps I will have a chance to talk over the radio.

With best wishes to all and tell them to be good that a new day will dawn.

Sincerely yours,
Mother Jones

TLS (John Fitzpatrick Papers)

From John H. Walker

August 29, 1928.

Mother Jones,
3700 Fifth St., N. W.,
Washington, D. C.
Dear Mother:

I am enclosing check for one ($1,000) thousand dollars to repay you for the loan you so kindly made me, to help me in finishing the payments on my home and for our girl's education. Everything is all right now and there is no good reason why I should keep this money any longer. I appreciate very much your loaning it to me and if there is anything that I can do at any time to show that appreciation in a more substantial way, all you will have to do is call on me.

With sincere regards and best wishes, I am

Yours,
[John H. Walker]

TLC (John H. Walker Papers)

To John H. Walker

September 13, 1928.

Mr. John H. Walker,
Springfield, Ill.
Dear John:

Your letter was a welcome visitor. It relieved me of a great deal of worry. I was limited to three dollars and hardly knew what to do. Whether to ask William Green to help me or to apply to the poor house but your letter completely settled the question. I had forgotten all about that John. It entirely changed my feeling and I am a different woman today than I was the day the letter came.

You know I do not like to sponge off any one or live like a pauper. I wish Jim Lord had your principle and paid me what he borrowed from me like a man not to rob an old woman like me. But I will make him pay that money yet some how.

With love to yourself and Mrs. Walker, I remain

Sincerely and loyally yours,
Mother Jones

P. S. The Miners are up against it. That fellow Lewis was a crook the day he was born and so was Murray and Fagan.[1] I am glad the miners are waking up to them.

TLS (John H. Walker Papers)
   1. Probably P. T. Fagan of Pittsburgh, president of District 5, UMWA.

From John H. Walker

September 18, 1928.

Mother Jones,
3700 Fifth St., n. w.,
Washington, D. C.
Dear Mother:

This is to acknowledge receipt of your letter of the 13th instant. I am mighty glad I was able to send that to you at the time that I did, to know that it helped. However, I am sorry that you did not write me before, because I could have gotten it for you any time, and I want you to know that whether I owe you anything as a direct personal loan or not, I feel that I owe you and all the folks that have lived like you, for everything that I have in this world that is worth having, and as long as I have a dollar you will be welcome to it.

I don't want you to want for anything that you really need; I don't want you to suffer. Please write me any time that you feel you need anything and I shall find some means of taking care of the situation and I won't consider it in the light of helping you. It will be just repaying, in a small measure, the obligations we are all under to you.

I am sorry about Jim Lord, Mother. He is not right mentally. I am afraid I can not hold him where he is now very much longer. His mind is disintegrating more and more, and soon, I am afraid, he will have to go to the asylum.

Your comment in your post-script, I think is correct. They have done the most terrible things to these men, women and children and to the whole labor movement and the cause of humanity that has been done in our generation. I have more respect for the ordinary murderer than I have for those men who conciously did what they have done.

With sincere regards and again, Mother, insisting that you will write me if you are ever in need again, I am,

Sincerely yours,
J H Walker

TLS (Terence V. Powderly Papers)

From Roger Baldwin[1]

March 5, 1929.

Mother Jones
3700 Fifth St.
Washington, D. C.
Dear Mother Jones:

Joe Davidson,[2] 12 West 69th Street, New York City, who did your bust some years ago, wants to get an autographed copy of your biography. So does E. W. Marland,[3] Ponca City, Okla., who bought a copy of the bust from Mr. Davidson. He is an oil man, but a great admirer of yours.

I am sending the books under separate cover, all wrapped up and addressed to these men, ready for posting. Will you just open them, write your name on the inside, wrap them up and mail them? If you can say a word of greeting to Mr. Davidson and Mr. Marland, I know they will appreciate it.

So I may know that this has been done, will you be good enough to sign and mail the enclosed postal card?

With warmest greetings to you, I am
Ever your friend,
Roger Baldwin

TLS (Terence V. Powderly Papers)
1. Roger Nash Baldwin (1884–1981) directed the work of the American Civil Liberties Union, 1917–1950.
2. Jo Davidson (1883–1952), sculptor of famous public figures for two generations, did a bust of Mother Jones which is now in the National Portrait Gallery.
3. Ernest Whitworth Marland (1874–1941), land speculator and oil wildcatter, served Oklahoma as governor and congressman, 1932–1936.

From the Chicago Federation of Labor

Chicago Ills
Apr 30 1929

Mother Jones
3700 Fifth St N W Washington DC
Dear Mother

On behalf of the Chicago Federation of Labor we are indeed happy that you reached the ninety-ninth milestone in your wonderful and unselfish life We wish you a pleasant journey to the century milestone when we hope to have a real jubilee and birthday party in Illinois stop When we look back into the past we begin to realize the tremendous service you have rendered to the men women and children of labor stop Through your untiring energy and self sacrificing efforts you have brought joy and hope into the lives of the oppressed and discouraged workers of America stop We join in wishing you many happy returns of the day

Chicago Federation of Labor
John Fitzpatrick President
E N Nockels Secy

Telegram (Mother Jones Papers)

To Tom Mooney

[Washington, D. C.,
March 21, 1930][1]

To the Labor Prisoners
My dear Boys,

Your most lovely box of roses arrived safe and in beautiful condition. You boys will never know the happiness it gave me to receive them, for each rose brought a message of its own of appreciation and love. At the same moment they also filled me with sorrow and longing to be with my boys in their troubles. Just as they each spoke of their appreciation of all I had done in the past, they also cried out to me to come to you at present, and also how much you and the ones coming after would need me in the future.

Well, dear boys, here on my bed I lie, with all being done for me that a loving heart and kind hands can do. I cannot help but feel that I would like to be left among you for some time yet, but just as the time comes to each of us to leave the earthly ties and go Heavenly, I know that my days are few.

God bless and protect my boys! The one last message I would send is to be true always to what you think is right. No matter the punishment, stick to your principles boys and you will always be true boys of

Mother Jones

With love. Write again,—will be glad to hear always.

TLC (Thomas J. Mooney Papers)

1. This letter was mailed from Washington, March 21, 1930, addressed to Tom Mooney (1884–1945), who with numerous IWW prisoners was serving time in the California penitentiary.

Last Will and Testament

Hyattsville, Maryland
April 28/30.

Last Will and Testament of Mary Jones

I, Mary Jones, a citizen of the United States and resident of Prince George's County, State of Maryland, being of sound mind, memory and understanding, do make my last Will and Testament, hereby revoking all former and other Wills, heretofore made, in manner and form following,

First, All debts, should I have any, or that I may hereafter contract or assume, including my funeral expenses & transportation to Springfield, Illinois.

Second, I hereby devise and bequeath all cash in the First National Bank of Hyattsville, Md., Bonds, Real, Personal and mixed property, which I now have and which I may hereafter acquire to, Edward N. Nockels and John Fitzpatrick, of Chicago, as Trustees, to dispose of as they deem best, after my death,

Third, My body to be sent to Springfield, Ill. for burial.

Fourth, I hereby appoint, Edward N. Nockels and John Fitzpatrick, Executors of my Estate, without Bond,

Mother Jones

We hereby certify that the aforegoing Will of Mary Jones was signed by her in our presence, and acknowledged it to be her last Will   In testimony of which we have at her request and in her presence, and in the presence of each other,

Subscribed our names as Witnesses

Lillian M. Burgess
Walter E. Burgess
G. Hodges Carr[1]

DS (Records of Cook County, Illinois)

1. Mother Jones spent the last fifteen months of her life in the home of Lillie May and Walter Burgess; G. Hodges Carr, a neighbor from Hyattsville, was an agent for the American Surety Company of New York.

From John H. Walker

April 29, 1930.

Mother Jones,
Washington, D. C.
Dear Mother:

Am very sorry that it is impossible to be with you in person on May first the anniversary of your one hundredth birthday. It will give you more pleasure to know that I am giving my time to the work I am doing. The men women and children of labor in Illinois and of the Reorganized United Mine Workers of America out of their hearts overflowing with gratitude for what you have done for them hope that you are well in both spirit and body and that you may have many happy returns of that occasion.

J. H. Walker, Secretary-Treasurer
United Mine Workers of America Reorganized[1]

Telegram (John H. Walker Papers)

1. John H. Walker, Adolph Germer, Alexander Howat and other opponents of John L. Lewis set up this rival organization which enjoyed a brief, limited success, largely in Illinois.

From John D. Rockefeller, Jr.

May 2, 1930

Mother Jones,
Silver Springs Maryland

Please accept my heartiest congratulations on your one hundredth birthday anniversary stop   Your loyalty to your ideals your fearless adherence to your duty as you have seen it is an inspiration to all who have known you stop   May you have continued health and happiness so long as life lasts.

John D Rockefeller Jr

Telegram (Rockefeller Papers)

To John D. Rockefeller, Jr.

Washington D C
May 3 1930

John D Rockefeller Jr.
New York, NY

Your good wishes and hopes for continued long life on my 100th birthday was a happy surprise and among those messages most appreciated by me   knowing all the responsibilities on your shoulders it was a human act to think kindly of me at this time and your message was the expression of a Christian heart—

Mother Jones.

Telegram (Rockefeller Papers)

To John Fitzpatrick

Mother Jones,
Hyattsville, Maryland.
June 20, 1930.

Mr. John Fitzpatrick, President,
Chicago Federation of Labor,
623 South Wabash Avenue,
Chicago, Illinois.
My dear Boys:

Your kind message received on May first, and I want to assure you that I was overwhelmed by the expressions of the great number of my friends who remembered me on my one-hundredth birthday.

It is a great pleasure for me to look back on the hearty cooperation I received from the loyal workers in our fight for freedom.

Yours for Justice,
Mother Jones

TLS (John Fitzpatrick Papers)

To William H. Amerland[1]

Mother Jones
Hyattsville, Maryland.
June 25, 1930.

Mr. W. H. Amerland,
Wabasha, Minnesota.
My dear Friend:

I received your letter of May first asking me to send you my autograph, with any inscription or thought I might make.

I am complying with your request and enclose it herewith.

Yours very truly,
Mother Jones

TLS (William H. Amerland Papers)
1. William H. Amerland collected eighteen volumes of autographs which are preserved at the Minnesota Historical Society.

From John H. Walker

October 18, 1930.

Mother Mary Jones
C/O Mrs. Walter Burgess,
Hyattsville, Md.
Dear Mother:

I am enclosing letter I received this morning.

I sincerely hope that this may find you in good spirits and recovering your strength again.

Matters seem to be going along about as well as could be expected in our work. The prospects seem better now of our being successful, than at any time since the adjournment of the convention. I only wish you were able to be with us to give us the benefit of your advice as well as your assistance otherwise.

  With best wishes, I remain as ever

Your sincere friend
[John H. Walker]

TLC (John H. Walker Papers)

Undated

To Finley Peter Dunne[1]

[Undated]

To our good Dooley:

All greetings and good wishes from your devoted friends and comrades.

Eugene V. Debs
Mother Jones
Robert Hunter

ALS (Finley Peter Dunne Papers)

1. Finley Peter Dunne (1867–1936), Chicago journalist, became famous as the creator of Mr. Dooley, whose Irish dialect comments on current affairs captivated readers at the turn of the century.

To John Fitzpatrick

[Undated]

Pres Fitzpatric

This is to request you to put on a respactabe front when [you go?] to feast with the high *class Thieves* once a year

Mother Jones

ALS (John Fitzpatrick Papers)

To Adolph Germer

[Undated]

Tell my dear comrades that I am sorry that you were not elected on the Board   the S P is not clear yet on the Revolution

Mother

Love to my [*illegible.*]

Postcard (Adolph Germer Papers)

To Emma Powderly

[No heading, undated]

My Dear Emma:

I have been wanting to write you a line or two, but put it off from day to day. I was all in when I came here but I am beginning to feel a

349

little better anyhow. Miss Flaherty has been doing all she can to ease my suffering, and the weather has been beautiful here since I came.

Two packages came to day, for which please accept my appreciation. When you get the time send my Paper Bag, and whatever things that are there. My winter Coat and my Fur.

I get lonesome every night when I don't see you around. Miss Flaherty looks after me. She does not have to go up and down stairs as you did.

I'm not going to write you a long letter now for I feel a little tired but when I get rested more than I am now will write you a long one. I know that you will have a little bit of rest since I came away.

My love to all in the house,
Mother

TLS (Terence V. Powderly Papers)

To Unknown

[Undated]

My Dear Old Pals:

Just a few lines before I leave Philadelphia, to let you [*torn*] how lonesome I was on the train after I parted with you. Tell Leonard I nev[*torn*] had such a good time in all my life as I had last Saturday and Sunday. There [*torn*] just enough of us together to appreciate each other and enjoy each other's comradeship. The only thing I was afraid of was that Mrs. Vaner Weyde [*holograph interlineation:* was tired], for I was fully tired Sunday night myself. I am sitting down in our friend Boland's room   he is using the Typewriter for me and we only wish we were with you or you we [*torn*] with us. Tell Leonard I want him to rest more than he has been doing. He se[*torn*] so awfully tired Saturday night. The hot weather, no doubt, had a great deal [*torn*] do with it. It has been baking here ever since I left New York. I will wri[*torn*] you a few lines from the Cola Fileds when I reah there.

I have not slept enough yet. When I reach the coal fields [*torn*] going to take a rest. Believe [*holograph interlineation:* me] lovingly and loyally yours until the shadows [*torn*] in the Far East.

[*typed signature*] Mother Jones

TL (Mother Jones Papers)

From Catherine Yarnell

Los Angeles
California
[Undated]

Dear Mother Jones—

I sincerely hope that you are feeling very well after the long trip across the continent—And I know you are very happy, to be with all your dear friends in Washington D. C. I miss you very much indeed, and wish we could take a ride today, this glorious spring day, it is always so fresh and green after our rains in Southern California—so we could then have a good talk—You are always such a joy and inspiration to me— You always do inspire our with new hope and vision— Old Los Angeles can furnish no news, of much importance—the same old thing every day, in the year—

Am very glad to send an encouraging report about Esther— She has improved so very much, in the last few weeks— I had been anxious about her for so long, it is quite a relief to see her improve— I am inclosing a check for three hundred dollars, am anxious for it to reach you on your birthday—With many sincere and loving wishes, I am as always your devoted friend,

Catherine Yarnell

ALS (Terence V. Powderly Papers)

Index

Abbott, Leonard Dalton, 112
Adams, K. C., 197, 198n
AFL, xxxviii, 18, 101, 142, 143, 158, 167, 177, 193, 231, 254, 263, 264, 318, 321, 322, 326n
Alabama, 242
Alliance, Ohio, xxxviii, 334
Amalgamated Assoc. of Iron, Steel and Tin Workers, 310n
American Civil Liberties Union, 276–77
American Railway Union, xxiv
Amerland, William H., 347
Ammons, Elias, xxxii, xxxiii, 126
Anderson, Albert Barnes, 176, 177n, 288
Anthracite field, xxv, xxvi, 246, 321
Appeal to Reason, The, 113n, 116, 126–27, 128, 130, 184, 185n
Arbuckle, W. Va., 23, 28
Arizona, xxvii, 65, 85, 146–50, 159, 220
Arkansas, xxvii
Arnot, Pa., xxv, 22
Autobiography, xxxvii, 86, 122, 264, 270, 283, 284, 322, 338
Avondale, Ala., xxvii

Baldwin, Roger Nash, 342
Baldwin-Felts Detective Agency, xxxi, xxxiv, 126, 210
Barnes, B. F., 47, 48
Barnes, John Mahlon, xxix, xlii, 66, 71–72, 75–76, 82, 85, 87, 88, 89, 90, 93, 102
Barrett, George, 268
Bates, Mrs. George A., 96
Batley, Charles, 164–66, 204
Belleville, Ill., 10
Benner, Mrs. Peter, 299–300, 305
Berger, Victor, 78, 79n, 80, 92, 102, 103, 109, 112
Billings, Warren K., 162, 164n, 172
Birmingham, Ala., xxiv
Bisbee, Ariz., xxxviii, 85
Bittner, Van, 298, 303
Blair Mountain, battle of, xxxvi
Blakeley, William, 33, 34n
Blizzard, William, 249, 250n, 253, 301

Bloomington, Ind., 176
Blossburg Coal Co., xxv
Boland, John Peter, 78, 79n
Borah, William Edgar, 107–08, 118
Boskill, Samuel, 11, 17, 18
Brandeis, Louis Dembitz, 132
Branstetter, Otto, 196, 200
Brewer, George D., 77, 78n, 82, 184, 185n
Brewer, Grace, 184, 185n
Brewery workers' union, xxvii
Brick makers' union, 231
Brooklin, W. Va., 25
Brophy, John, 229, 230n, 231
Brown, Jay G., xxxiv, 313, 316
Brown, John, 112, 132
Buffalo, N. Y., xxxiv
Burgess, Lillian M., xxiii, xxxviii, 345
Burgess, Walter E., xxiii, xxxviii, 345
Burke, Thomas, 16, 17n
Butte Mine Workers' Union, 130–31
Butte, Mont., 53, 54, 93, 130–31

Cabell, Charles A., 119, 120n
Cabin Creek, W. Va., 165, 290, 298
Cahill, Edward, 11
Cairns, Thomas Francis, 268–69, 283, 284, 286, 314
Calero, Manuel, 97–100
California, xxiv, xxxiv, xxxvii, xxxviii, 142–45, 151, 152, 157, 158, 162, 163, 164, 170–72, 185–86, 200, 201, 289, 310, 317
California Building Trades Council, 144
California Federation of Labor, 143, 144, 187n
Callery, Phillip Henry, 65
Calumet, Mich., 118
Cannon, Joseph D., 85–86, 87n, 97, 100
Capper, Arthur, 151, 152n
Carbine, Ed J., 146, 147n, 205, 207, 209n, 327, 328, 329
Carbondale, Ill., 3
Carillo Puerto, Felipe, 225, 226n
Carr, Ellis, 94, 97
Carr, G. Hodges, 345

353

Index

Carroll, J. W., 22, 23, 24n, 25, 26, 31
Cedar Grove, W. Va., 29
Central Competitive Field, xliv, 12, 24
Chandler, Harry, 289, 290n, 291
Charleston, W. Va, xxx, xxxiv, xxxvii, xxxviii, 106, 107
Chase, John, xxxii, 43, 44n, 84, 96, 126
Chicago, Ill., xxiii–vii, xxxiv, xxxvii–iii
Chicago Federation of Labor, xxxvii, 143, 144, 155, 166, 294, 342, 343
Chicago Labor Party, 198
Child labor protest, xxvi, 45–48
Chilton, William Edwin, 165, 166n
Cincinnati, Ohio, xxviii
Clancy, Eugene A., 151, 167, 169, 173
Clark, James Beauchamp, 95
Clay miners' strike, 10
Clinton, Ind., 42
Coal miners' strike (1900), xxv
Cockran, William Bourke, 162, 164n, 166
Coeburn, Va., 18
Coffeyville, Kan., 151
Collins, Justus, 23, 24n
Colorado, xxvi, xxvii, xxx, xxxi, xxxii, xxxiii, xxxix, 49, 50, 52, 62, 64, 71, 89, 90, 94, 122–39, 141, 151, 182–83, 242, 246, 249, 338
Colorado Federation of Labor, xxxii, 50, 94n, 249
Colorado Fuel and Iron Co., xxxi, 138
Communists, 229, 281, 286, 287n, 324, 330
Communist Workers' party, 314n, 324
Conroy, Catherine M., 90, 91n
Conroy, Joseph, 90, 91n, 105
Conroy, Peter Joseph, 90, 91n, 105
Consolidation Coal Co., xxv
Cooley, Phillip A., 173
Coolidge, Calvin, 299, 303
Copper miners' strike, xxvii, xxviii, xxxviii
Cork, Ireland, xxiii
Cornwell, John J., xxv, xxvi, xxxvi
Coxey's Army, xxiv
Cripple Creek strike, xxvi, 49
Crough, Edward, 149–50, 159

Darrow, Clarence, 58, 140, 159, 160, 234, 262, 264, 265, 266, 269, 270, 284
Davidson, Jo, xxxvii, 342
Davis, Benjamin, 29, 30, 31n

Debs, Eugene Victor, xxiv, xxv, xxix, 6–7, 12, 28, 52, 53, 55, 65, 117, 144, 157, 161, 163, 164, 211, 214, 349
Debs, Theodore, 96, 211
de la Huerta, Adolfo, 73n
Dempsey, John T., 10
Densmore, John B., 188
Denver, Colo., xxvii, xxxii, xxxiii, xxxvii, 90
DeWolfe, Susana, 328, 332, 334
Diaz, Porfirio, xxviii, 67–69, 70, 100, 216
Doherty, Mary, 226
Dolla, Mr. (prisoner), 316
Donahue, James Patrick, 119, 120n
Dorchy, August, 249, 250n
Dorr, Sara J., 185–86
Douglas, Ariz., xxviii
Du Bois, Pa., 79–80
Duffy, Thomas, 3, 4n, 11
Dunne, Finley Peter, 349
Dwyer, Alex, 78, 79n
Dwyer, Lawrence, xxxiv

Eastman, Max, 129n
Erwin, Claude, 317
Evans, Chris, 16, 17n, 18

Fagan, P. T., 340
Fairley, William, 51, 53
Fairmont, W. Va., xxv, 193
Fairmont field, xxv, 32, 33, 165
Farmer-Labor party, 206, 207n, 286, 313n
Farrington, Frank, 133, 245, 248, 257, 258, 261, 328, 329
Federated Shopcrafts and Brotherhoods of Texas, 255
Fetherling, Dale, xxiii
Fitzpatrick, John, xxxiv, xlii, 154–56, 179, 206, 226–28, 234, 262–63, 297, 309–10, 313, 316, 319, 321, 322, 335, 337–39, 343, 345–47, 346n, 349
Flaherty, Miss, 75, 84, 88, 102, 159, 322, 350
Flores Magón, Ricardo, xxvi, xxx, 67, 72–73, 97–101
Flying Squadron, xxxiv
Fluorspar miners' strike, 153
Foster, William Zebulon, xxxiv, 197, 198n, 206, 250, 252, 287n, 314
Fox, Lon, 324

Fraenckel, G. T., 77–78, 82
Fuel Administration policy, xxxiv

Gale, Lynn A. E., 226
Garment workers' strikes, xxvii, xxxiii, 142
Gary, Ind., xxxiv
Germer, Adolph, 81, 92, 94, 102, 133, 144, 163, 313, 346n, 349
Gildea, Charles P., 78, 79n, 80, 81
Glen Jean, W. Va., 23
Goebel, George, H., 83, 84, 92, 94, 103, 104
Golden, Christ J., 272
Gompers, Samuel, xxxv, 179, 221, 318, 319n
Gooding, Frank R., 58, 59n
Graham, Samuel, 173–74
Green, William, xxxvii, xliii, 141, 154, 155n, 172, 236–38, 241–42, 243–44, 256, 259, 265, 267, 272–73, 280, 281, 282, 286–88, 289–90, 291, 293, 294, 295, 298, 304–05, 311–13, 315, 318–19, 322, 339, 340
Greenbaum, Leon, 35
Greensburg, Pa., 82–84, 85
Greenwood, W. Va., 31
Grow, Cyrus F., 160

Haberman, Roberto, 225–26
Haddow, John, 49
Hagelstein, Henry, 166
Haggerty, Thomas T., xxv, 18, 33, 34n, 137, 139, 216
Hall, Bolton, 58, 59n
Hamilton, Alfred Reed, 198n, 202, 208, 217, 262, 264, 266, 269, 278, 303, 329
Harding, Warren Gamaliel, xxxvi
Hargrove, George, 165, 166n
Harlin, Robert, 206, 207n, 208, 209, 217
Harriman, Florence Jaffray, 133
Harriman, Job, 98, 100n
Harris, Mary, xxiii
Harris, Richard, xxiii
Hatfield, Henry Drury, xxxi, 137, 240, 292
Haverhill, Mass., xxv
Hawkins, Horace Norman, 122, 125n
Hayes, Frank J., xliv, 100, 120–21, 131, 140, 144, 163, 178, 179, 186, 189, 329
Haymarket incident, xxiv, 227
Haywood, William Dudley, 80, 81n

Hazleton, Pa., 3, 4, 32
Hazlett, Ida Crouch, 93, 94n
Hearst, William Randolph, 221
Helena, Mont., 54
Helper, Utah, xxvii, 50
Herrin, Ill., 249, 251, 264, 318, 319n
Hickey, G. C., 274
Hilquitt, Morris, 78, 79n, 84
Hoban, Michael John, 21, 22n
Hoehn, Gottlieb, 65, 66n, 69–71
Hogan, Daniel, 60
Holt, Savory, 274, 275
Homestead strike, xxiv
Hoover, Herbert, 303, 306, 307
Hoover, J. Edgar, xxxv
House, Edward Mandell, 167–68
Houston, Harold W., 265, 268
Howat, Alexander, 151, 152n, 186, 206, 207n, 208, 209, 217, 221, 229, 231, 235, 236n, 245, 246, 248, 249, 264, 269, 309, 346
Howells, William Dean, 129n
Huerfano Co., Colo., xxxii
Hunt, George W. P., xlii, 146–50, 183, 220, 223, 266, 283, 289, 330
Hunter, Robert, 58, 59n, 349
Huntington, Ark., 75
Huntington, W. Va., 17, 18, 28, 33, 231
Hyattsville, Md., xxiii, xxxviii

Idaho, 63
Illinois, xxxvii, 3, 24, 27, 29, 42, 65, 133, 142, 146, 151, 153, 156, 163, 178, 189, 192–93, 207, 217, 222, 232, 246, 247, 249, 252, 254, 266, 286, 287, 318, 324, 327
Indian Territory, xxvii
Indiana, 161, 176
Indianapolis, Ind., 29
Industrial Relations, U.S. Commission on, xxix, xxxiii, 132–33, 140, 163
International Assoc. of Bridge and Structural Ironworkers, 174n
International Workers Defense League, 142–45, 166
Iowa, 24
Ireland, John, 21, 22n
Irons, Martin, 63, 64n, 125, 258
IWW, xxvi, 94, 321, 324

Jackson, John J., xxv, 33, 34, 35, 45n
James, Benjamin, 3, 4

Index

Janitors' union, 294

Johnson, Clark, 29, 31n

Johnson, William (Chicago alderman), 44, 56

Johnson, William (mine superintendent), 56–57

Johnson City, Ill., xxxviii

Jones, George, xxiv

Jones, Jerome, 171

Jones, Mary Harris: early life, xxiii–vi; emergence as a public figure, xxiv–v; imprisonment of, xxv, xxx, xxxii, xxxiv, 33–36, 107–16, 124–26, 130, 175, 264–65; as UMWA organizer, 1900–1904, xxv–vi, 3–52; in Mexico, xxv–vi, 97–101, 216–33; and children's crusade, xxvi, 45–49; and march on Logan, xxvi, 264, 329; as Socialist activist, 1904–1911, xxvii–ix, 52–104; as UMWA organizer, 1911–1922, xxix–xxxvi, 105–267; and *Autobiography,* xxxvi, 250, 264, 270, 283, 284, 322, 338; declining years, 1923–1930, xxxvii–ix, 268–351; income tax of, 291–93; will of, 344–45

Jones, W. E., 54

Kanawha field, 24, 25

Kanawha Valley, xxv, xxx, 24, 25

Kansas, 151, 194, 212, 235, 246, 249, 251, 269, 298, 309

Kansas City, Mo., xxiv, 71–72, 87, 194, 212

Kaplan, David, 151, 158, 159, 160n

Kasten, Frank, 176, 177n, 231

Kearney, Dennis, xxiv

Keating, Edward, 120, 121n, 183, 184n

Keeney, Frank, xxxvi, 179, 180n, 232, 264, 268, 301, 302, 303, 329, 330

Keily, Joseph T., 95

Kelly's Creek, W. Va., 29

Kennedy, Duncan, 119, 120n, 275

Kennedy, Thomas, 318, 319

Kern, John Worth, xxxi, 114–15, 161, 165, 175

Kerr, Charles, 322

Kerwin, Hugh L., 272, 279

King, William Lyon Mackenzie, xxiii, xxxix, 136–38, 139

Knights of Labor, xxiv, 87, 294

Kopelin, Louis, 184, 185n

Ku Klux Klan, 290, 317, 318

LaFollette, Robert Marion, 111, 114

Laing, John, 15, 16n, 20, 25

LaMonte, Robert Rives, 77, 79n

Langdon, Emma, 249, 250n, 251, 252

Lawson, John R., 141

Leavenworth prison, 167, 168

Lee, Ivy Ledbetter, xxxix, 139, 140n

Leiter, Joseph, 192, 193n

Lens Creek, W. Va., 30, 274

Lewis, John L., xxxvii, xliv, 178, 179, 190, 197, 198n, 202n, 217–18, 236n, 257, 296, 298n, 301, 303, 318, 319n, 329, 340

Lewis, Lafayette Arthur, 158, 160n

Lewis, Lena Morrow, 84, 88, 89n, 161

Lewis, Thomas L., xlv, 4, 23, 33, 36, 198

Lindsey, Benjamin Barr, 318, 319n

Littlepage, Adam Brown, 165, 166n

Lloyd, Caroline, 106, 109–10, 115–16, 128, 129

Lloyd, Henry Demarest, xxiv, 44, 45, 110, 111, 129

Logan Co., W. Va., xxxiv, xxxvi

Lord, James Ravell, 131–33, 136–38, 139–40, 152, 153, 159, 180, 190, 191, 192n, 197, 201, 209, 221, 225, 232, 245, 253, 263, 264, 266, 340, 341

Los Angeles, Calif., xxx, xxxviii, 65

Los Angeles *Times* bombing, xxxviii

Lowe, Caroline A., 97

Ludlow, Colo., xxxiii, 183

McDonald, Duncan, 133, 250, 252, 313–14

MacDonnell, William, 217

McDowell Co., W. Va., xxxiv

McLean, Lois, xxiii

McNamara, J. P., 151, 204, 337

Madero, Francisco, xxx, 98, 99

Magón. *See* Flores Magón

Mahon, William D., 164, 170

Mahoney, Charles, 93, 94n

Mailly, Bertha Howell, xxvii

Mailly, William, 19, 43–44, 75

Mallen, Rafael, 233

Manka, Albert, 12–15, 13n

Mann, James Robert, 120, 121n

Manning, John J., 325, 326n, 335, 339

Markle, John, 3, 4n

Marland, Ernest Whitworth, 342

Marmet, W. Va., xxxvi, 329

Marquard, Louis, 171
Marshall, Joe, 289
Martial law, xxvi
Martin, Emma T., 171
Martine, James Edgar, 118, 165
Maryland, xxv
Massachusetts, xxv–vi, 60
Maurer, James, xxxiv
Maxis, Mother Teresa, xxxix
Memphis, Tenn., xxiv
Mexican revolutionists, xxvi, xxviii, 65–
    74, 76, 77, 86, 95, 97–101, 216
Mexico, xxviii, xxx, xxxvi, 67–69, 97–101,
    125, 204, 213, 215, 216, 221, 223, 225–
    33
Mexico City, D. F., xxxv
Meyer, Cora, 338
Meyer, Edward, 174
Michigan, xxx, xxxi–ii, xxxix, 118, 119
Military intelligence agents, xxxv
Mills, Walter Thomas, 72
Milwaukee, Wis., xxvii–viii
Mine, mill and smeltermen's union, 182
Mingo Co., W. Va., xxxiv, xxxvi, 221,
    230, 237, 240, 294, 302
Minneapolis Trades and Labor Assembly,
    256
Minor, Robert, 170
Missouri, xxvii
Mitchell, John, xxvi, xli, xliv, 3–56 pas-
    sim, 323
Molders' union, xxiv, 144, 166
Monroe, Mich., xxiii, xxxix
Montana, xxvii, 93, 130
Montgomery, Samuel B., 37, 38n, 292
Montgomery, W. Va., 54
Mooney, Fred, xxxv, xxxvi, 213, 216,
    222, 226, 228, 264, 268, 294, 302, 303
Mooney, Thomas Joseph, xxxiv, 142–45,
    162–64, 166, 169–70, 171–72, 185,
    188n, 226, 337, 344
Moore, Jack, 261
Morgan, Ephraim F., xxxvi, xxxvii, xlii,
    233–34, 238–40, 242–43, 255–56, 260,
    274, 275–77, 283, 284–86, 292–93, 302,
    306–08
Morgan, Thomas J., xxiv, xxix, xlii, 65–
    66, 75, 76, 77–78, 80–84, 87, 89, 91–
    93, 94, 96–97, 101–05
Morones, Luis N., 226
Morris, Elizabeth C., 9

Morrison, Frank, 137, 138n
Morrow, Dwight, xxxv
Mt. Olive, Ill., xxxix
Moyer, Charles, 94, 146, 151, 153, 249
Mulligan Brigade, 23, 28
Munsey, J. E., 173
Murphy, Starr Jocelyn, 139, 140n
Murray, John, 157–60
Murray, Philip, xxxiv, 217, 241, 296, 301,
    303, 340

National Labor party, 207n
Neely, Matthew Mansfield, 165, 166n
New Jersey, xxvi
New Mexico, 242
New River field, 17, 25, 165, 178, 180,
    278
New York, xxvii, 54–55, 127, 129
New York Call, 113n, 174, 176n
Nichols, Thomas D., 10
Ninety-nine year leases, 214–16
Nockles, Edward N., xxxvii, xliii, 120,
    121n, 150, 154–56, 176, 179, 190, 200,
    202, 206, 224, 226–28, 240, 258, 269,
    290, 301, 313, 314, 316, 319, 321, 335,
    337, 339, 343, 345
Norfolk and Western field, 32, 165
Northcutt, Jesse, 137, 138n
Nova Scotia, 298

Obregón, Alvaro, xxxv, 73n
O'Dell, Buck, 274
O'Donaghue, Denis, 235, 236n
Oil workers' union, 188
Olander, Victor A., 154–56, 188, 189, 228
Older, Cora Baggerly, 157, 160n
Older, Fremont, 186, 187n, 188n, 327
Omaha, Neb., xxvii
O'Neill, John N., 92, 93n, 94, 102
Orizaba, Mexico, 227
Ort, George, 268
Oyster Bay, N.Y., xxvi, 47, 48

Pabst Brewing Co., xxviii
Pacific Gas and Electric Co., 144
Paint Creek, W. Va., xxx, 30, 106–19
Palmer, Alexander Mitchell, 194
Palmer, Bertha Honoré, 61–62
Palmer, T. E., 194, 195n
Pan American Federation of Labor, xxxv,
    224

Index

Parker, William, 79–80
Parkersburg, W. Va., xxvi
Parsons, Lucy, 338
Partido Liberal, xxvi, xxviii, 67–69, 95
Parton, Mary Field, 140–41
Paulen, Mr. (IRS agent), 293–96
Peabody, James H., 51n
Pennsylvania, xxv, xxix, xxx, 3, 4, 8, 9, 10, 18, 22, 31, 32, 34, 38, 55, 214–16, 232, 280–82, 306, 307, 312, 321
Pennsylvania Federation of Labor, xxxiv
Penrose, Boies, 208, 209n
Philadelphia, Pa., xxvii
Pinchot, Amos, 129n
Pinchot, Cornelia Bryce, 316
Pinchot, Gifford, xxxviii, 306, 307n
Pinkerton Detective Agency, xxiv, 90, 144, 145
Pittsburgh, Pa., xxiv, xxxiv
Pocahontas field, xxxiv
Populist party, xxiv
Powderly, Emma, xxxviii, xli, 122, 203, 223, 271, 279, 284, 288–89, 311, 320, 321, 325, 328, 332, 334, 349
Powderly, Terence Vincent, xxviii, xxxvi, xxxviii, xli, 58–59, 63–64, 69, 108, 113–14, 119, 122–25, 192–93, 202–03, 213, 214–16, 223, 224–25, 235–36, 244, 246, 247, 256, 257, 258, 270, 271–72, 279–80, 288–89, 309, 310, 311, 313, 314, 315
Powerhouse men's union, 176
Pratt, W. Va., xxx, 107–15
Preparedness Day parade, xxxiv, 145n, 188n
Prevey, Marguerite, 82, 96, 157, 161–62
Price, Utah, 62
Princeton, W. Va., xxxiv, 210
Progressive International Committee, 281n
Provoker, The, 78–102 *passim*
Pullman, Ill., xxiv
Purcell, Albert Arthur, 322
Purcell, George, 12, 36, 37, 38, 39, 40

Railroad Brotherhoods, 197
Railroad strike of 1877, xxiv
Rangel, José Maria, 95
Red Special, 144, 163
Reece, John P., 38, 39n
Reed, John, 129n

Rend, W. P., 23, 24n, 28
Rice, Bernard, 33, 34n
Richards, J. A., 30, 31n, 42
Richardson, Friend William, 289, 290n
Rickert, Thomas A., 322, 323n
Rihl, Comrade (bookkeeper), 87, 88
Riley, James, 229, 230n, 231
Rivera, Librado, 67, 72–73
Roan, John M., 31
Robinson, Ira Ellsworth, 165, 166n
Rockefeller, John D., Jr., xxx, xxxii, xxxiii, xxxix, 127–28, 132, 134, 135–36, 136–38, 139, 173, 174, 346
Roosevelt, Theodore, xxvi, 45–48, 46n, 55, 56, 58, 64
Rosiclare, Ill., 153
Ruskin, Tenn., 327
Russell, George E., 180
Ruthenberg, Charles E., 287
Ryan, Albert, 151, 167
Ryan, Frank M., 173

St. Clair, James William, 36, 37, 38n, 39
St. Louis, Mo., xxiv, 10, 67
San Francisco, Calif., xxxiv, 142, 166, 185
San Francisco Building Trades Council, 143, 166
San Francisco Labor Council, 143
San Pedro, Calif., 317
San Quentin prison, xxxviii, 151, 167, 204, 289
Sarabia, Manuel, xxviii, 67
Scharrenberg, Paul, 186, 187n, 188
Schlitz Brewing Co., xxviii
Schlosser, Anthony, 4
Schmidt, Katherine L., 157–60, 202, 255, 326, 336
Schmidt, Mathew, xxxvii, xxxviii, 151, 158, 159, 160n, 204, 289, 309, 326, 337, 339
Schwab, Charles Michael, 22
Scott, Grant, 285
Searles, Ellis, 216, 217, 261
Shamokin, Pa., 24
Shoaf, George H., 117, 118n
Siam, 220
Silva, Prisciliano E., 95
Silva, Reuben, 95
Simons, Algie Martin, 80, 81n, 117
Simons, May Wood, 87, 103n, 161
Sisters, Servants of the Immaculate Heart of Mary, xxiii

Slayton, J. W., 43, 44n
Slick, Comrade (bookkeeper), 76, 87, 88
Smeltermen's union, 53, 182
Smothers Creek, W. Va., 31
Sneed, William, 153
Snyder, Frank, 224
Snyder, J. E., 194, 195n
Social Democracy, xxiv
Social Democratic party, xxiv
Socialism, xxviii–ix
Socialist Congress, 77, 81
Socialist Labor party, xxiv, 87
Socialist Party of America, xxiv, xxvi,
    xxvii, xxviii, 43–44, 60, 67–69, 75–97,
    101–05, 110, 112, 144, 157, 161–62,
    163, 174, 338
Solomon, U., 91, 92n
Spargo, John, 78, 79n, 84, 93, 94
Springer, J. A., 26
Springfield, Ill., xxxvii
Stanaford Mountain, 62
Steffens, Lincoln, 226
Steiner, Samuel, 328, 332, 334
Stephens, William Denison, 186, 187n,
    188
Stevens, Dan W., 256
Stevensville, Mont., 53
Stokes, James Graham Phelps, 77, 79n
Stokes, Walter Watson, 134–36
Streator, Ill., 27, 29
Streetcar men's union, 164, 170, 176, 177
Strickland, Frederick Guy, 104
Strikes: of transit workers, xxiii, 176–77;
    of railroad workers, xxiv, 197; of coal
    miners in Pa., xxv, xxvi, 82–85, 90,
    105, 321; of coal miners in Colo., xxv,
    xxvi, 119–40; of textile workers, xxvi,
    xxvii, 45–48, 87; of telegraphers, xxvii;
    of copper miners, xxvii, xxviii; of gar-
    ment workers, xxvii, xxxiii, 142; of coal
    miners in W. Va., xxx, 30–35, 106–19,
    233–34, 237, 240; of clay miners, 10;
    of fluorspar miners, 153
Sullivan, J. C., 50, 94
Sullivan, Jesse V., 240

Taft, William Howard, xxvii, xxviii, 69–
    70, 73–74
Tarbell, Ida M., 129n
Telegraphers' strike (1907), xxvii
Tennessee, 242

Terre Haute, Ind., 28
Tetlow, Percy, 315
Texas, xxvii, 255
Textile workers' strikes, xxvi, xxvii, 45–
    48, 87
Thomas, Mary Hannah, 137, 138n
Tighe, Michael F., 309, 310n
Tincher, Thomas, 25, 26n, 30, 31
Tippet, Tom, 251
Tobin, Daniel Joseph, xxxv, 230
Toronto, Ontario, xxiii
Towers, Alois, 191, 192n
Townsend, Tom, 268
Trade Union Educational League, 281n
Transit workers' strike, xxxiii
Trinidad, Colo., xxvi, xxxii, 48, 49, 50
Tumulty, Joseph Patrick, 169, 173, 239,
    302
Tunnel and subway workers' union, 139
Turner, John Kenneth, 126, 127n
Tveitmoe, Olaf A., 140, 141n, 158, 160n
Twining, Luella, 80, 81n
Tynan, Thomas, 183, 184n

Uhlich, Robert, 130
UMWA, xxv, xxviii, xxix, xxxiii–v, xxxvi,
    xxxix, xliv–v, 3–56 passim, 128, 130–
    31, 133, 138, 139, 140, 147, 154, 156,
    161, 163, 172, 178, 181, 186, 187, 188,
    189, 191, 197, 198, 202, 204, 206, 207,
    208, 216–18, 236–38, 241–42, 243,
    245–54, 257–69, 273, 278, 280–82,
    285, 287–88, 294, 299, 301, 302, 303,
    308, 309, 315, 322, 323, 326, 327, 328,
    329, 340
UMWA, Reorganized, 345
Union Label Trades Department, 326n
United Garment Workers, 326n
Utah, 62, 204, 242

Valentine, Mr., 179
Vandling, Ill., 3
Van Horn, W. D., 28
Victor American Coal Co., xxxi
Villa, Francisco, 125, 126, 216
Villarreal, Antonio I., xxxv, 67, 72–73,
    101, 225
Virden, Ill., 322

Wade, Martin, J., 173
Walker, Esther, xliii, 221, 224, 229, 250,

Index

252, 259, 262, 263, 302, 322, 325, 326, 330

Walker, John Hunter, xxxvii, xliii, 15, 16n, 25, 52–53, 146–47, 151–52, 153–54, 156, 176–82, 186–92, 196–211, 216–19, 221–24, 230–33, 236, 240, 244–54, 257–71, 274, 291–301, 303–05, 308–09, 313–14, 318–31, 333, 335–36, 339–41, 345–48

Walker, Maude Helena Davis, 112–13, 212

Walker, Ryan, 113, 194–95, 212–13

Wallace, Edgar, 246, 247

Walling, William English, 77, 79n

Walsenberg, Colo., xxxii, 125

Walsh, Frank P., 151, 152n, 153, 162, 169

Warner, William, 12–15, 38

Warren, Fred, 80, 81n, 117

Washington, D.C., xxviii, xxxi, xxxii, xxxvii–viii, 127

Watchorn, Robert, 277–78

Waters, H. B., 50

Watson, Clarence Wayland, 193

Wayland, Julius Augustus, 80, 81n, 117, 184, 194

Wayland, Walter, 184, 185n, 202

Webb, Frank C., 173

West, George, 140, 141n, 163, 170

West Virginia, xxv, xxvi, xxx–xxxix, 4–45, 62, 106–19, 130, 137, 139, 164–66, 178, 179, 180, 193, 201, 204, 210, 212, 221, 231, 232, 237–40, 242, 246, 248, 249, 251, 253, 265, 266, 267–69, 274–76, 278, 279, 283, 284, 285–86, 290, 291, 298–99, 301, 306, 312, 315, 321, 329

West Virginia Federation of Labor, 231

Western Federation of Miners, xxvii,

xxxviii, 48–49, 52, 54, 58, 87, 93n, 130, 139, 146, 153, 155, 253

White, Dan A., 96, 97n

White, John Phillip, xliv, 139, 140, 141, 146, 163, 167, 169, 170, 172, 178, 179, 197, 198n, 216, 217

Wilburn, J. M., 249, 250n

Wilburn, John, 249, 250n

Wilkes-Barre, Pa., 55

Wilkinson, John, 249, 250n, 251, 253

Wilshire, Henry Gaylord, 83

Wilson, Agnes, 21, 22n, 107

Wilson, D. Douglas, 59, 64

Wilson, Peter, 26

Wilson, William Bauchop, xxxix, xlii, 12–56, 107, 110, 113, 118, 132, 142, 159, 188n

Wilson, Woodrow, xxxii, xxxiii–iv, 118, 125, 132, 156, 157, 158, 160, 165, 167–69, 174, 175, 213–14, 227, 239

Wisconsin, xxviii

Woll, Matthew, 318, 319n

Women's Christian Temperance Union, 185–86

Work, John McClelland, 96, 97n

Workers Party of America, 287n

Wright, C. D., 40

Wright, Harry, 29, 31n, 37

Yarnell, Catherine, 332, 336, 337, 351

Young, Glenn, 318, 319n

Young, Michael J., 173

Yucatan, Mexico, 225, 228

Zancanelli, Louis, 136, 138n

Zeigler, Ill., 324

Zimmerman, John, 179, 303

Pittsburgh Series in Labor History

Maurine Weiner Greenwald, Editor

The Correspondence of Mother Jones
Edward M. Steel, Editor

Women and the Trades
Elizabeth Beardsley Butler

Other titles in the series

The Emergence of a UAW Local, 1936–1939: A Study in Class and Culture
Peter Friedlander

Homestead: The Households of a Mill Town
Margaret F. Byington

The Homestead Strike of 1892
Arthur G. Burgoyne

Immigration and Industrialization: Ethnicity in an American Mill Town, 1870–1940
John Bodnar

Out of This Furnace
Thomas Bell

Steelmasters and Labor Reform, 1886–1923
Gerald G. Eggert

Steve Nelson, American Radical
Steve Nelson, James R. Barrett, & Rob Ruck

Working-Class Life: The "American Standard" in Comparative Perspective, 1899–1913
Peter R. Shergold